PERSUASION
History, Theory, Practice

D1478448

PERSUASION
History, Theory, Practice

George Pullman

Hackett Publishing Company, Inc.
Indianapolis/Cambridge

16 15 14 13   1 2 3 4 5 6 7

For further information, please address
   Hackett Publishing Company, Inc.
   P.O. Box 44937
   Indianapolis, Indiana 46244-0937

   www.hackettpublishing.com

Cover design by Abigail Coyle
Interior design by Elizabeth L. Wilson
Composition by Aptara, Inc.

Library of Congress Cataloging-in-Publication Data

Pullman, George.
   Persuasion : history, theory, practice / George Pullman.
      pages cm
   Includes bibliographical references and index.
   ISBN 978-1-60384-998-2 (pbk.) — ISBN 978-1-60384-999-9 (cloth)
   1. Persuasion (Psychology) 2. Persuasion (Rhetoric) I. Title.
   BF637.P4P85 2013
   303.3'42—dc23   2013016875

For Leola

Excellence is an art won by training and habituation.

Will Durant, *The Story of Philosophy*

Contents

Note to Students   xiv

Note to Readers in General   xvi

INTRODUCTION   xvii

What Is This Book About?   xvii

Why Study Persuasion?   xxiii

    Your Turn   xxvii

CHAPTER 1: ASSESSING PERSUASIVE ACTS   1

Reading with and against the Grain   1

    Your Turn   6

Logic   8

    Deductive reasoning—think geometry   10

    Inductive reasoning—think empirical science   11

    Common errors in reasoning   13

    Your Turn   19

Toulmin's Model of Argumentation   19

    Your Turn   23

Critical Thinking   24

    Your Turn   28

    Checklist for assessing eyewitness testimony   28

    Your Turn   30

    Checklist for assessing arguments based on sources (authority)   30

    Your Turn   35

    Checklist for assessing the credibility of websites   35

    Your Turn   37

    Checklist for assessing arguments based on survey data   37

    Your Turn   40

Cognitive Biases   41
  Your Turn   48

CHAPTER 2: PRODUCING PERSUASIVE ACTS   **49**
The Persuasion Process   49
  The presentation of self   50
    Ethos   50
      Good character   51
  Your Turn   53
      Good sense   53
  Your Turn   55
      Goodwill   55
  Your Turn   56
      Ethos and writing assignments   56
  Your Turn   57
      Autobiography as self-rhetoric and the rhetoric of the self   57
  Your Turn   59
  The presentation of others   59
    Characterization   61
      Bios   61
      The traditional topics of bios   62
  Your Turn   67
      Stereotypes   67
  Your Turn   71
      Audience analysis (demographics)   71
      Personas   72
  Your Turn   75
      The creation of pseudoaudiences (astroturfing)   75
  Your Turn   76
      Why knowing your audience matters and what it means   76
      Creating a virtual audience   80
Emotion, Reason, and Persuasion   85
  The emotion/reason false dichotomy   85

The social construction of emotions 87

The influence of emotions can be monitored and mitigated
(and exploited) 89

Assessing your emotional involvement 90

Common emotional strategies 92

Positive emotions 104

Your Turn 104

Asynchronous persuasion and emotions 105

Your Turn 107

CHAPTER 3: THE FIVE CANONS OF RHETORIC 108

Invention 111

Dialectic 112

An example of Platonic dialectic 115

Notes on Gorgias *and dialectic* 117

Dialectical topics—argumentative heuristics 119

The basic rules of inference 120

Your Turn 121

Dialectical invention, the non-conversational form 123

Your Turn 126

Summary 130

A parody of dialectic from *Rosencrantz and Guildenstern Are Dead* 131

Transition from dialectic to topics 133

Topics 134

Your Turn 137

Aristotle's general topics of the preferable 138

The topics of praise and blame 140

Topics of interpretation 141

Topics of last resort 141

Summary 142

Stasis 143

What is an issue? 143

Asystasis—*non-issues* 147

Your Turn   149
    Framing   149
        Frame-breaking strategies   153
        Commonplaces   157
Your Turn   162
    Signs   163
Your Turn   166
        Proverbs, maxims, aphorisms: On the origin of sound bites   167
Your Turn   170
    Summary of invention   172
Arrangement   172
    Introduction (*exordium*)   179
        Division (*partitio*)   180
        Background (*narratio*)   180
        Confirmation (*conformatio*)   180
        Refutation (*refutatio*)   181
        Conclusion (peroration)   181
    Your Turn   181
Style   182
    Your Turn   186
    Diction   186
        God and devil terms   189
    Your Turn   190
        Positive, negative, neutral language   191
    Your Turn   191
        Figures of speech   191
    Your Turn   193
        The editing checklist   193
        What's the opposite of *plain*?   195
        Editorial strategies for producing a plain style   196
    Your Turn   197
Memory   197
    Origins of the art of memory   197

Mnemonics   198

Backgrounds and images   198

Segmented hypergraphics—image maps   200

Plato and memory and writing   201

Your Turn   203

Delivery   203

Your Turn   207

Body language   207

Common gestures and how they are commonly
interpreted in the Western world   208

Your Turn   210

Putting the Canons to Work: From Writing Process to Rhetorical
Practice   210

When someone gives you an assignment   217

Revising   218

Before you turn in an assignment   221

Presentations: Putting the show in show and tell   221

Slides and the persuasion process   222

Practice (rehearsal)   224

Be prepared   224

Anxiety—stage fright   225

Strategies for dealing with stage fright   226

Your Turn   227

CHAPTER 4: EVIDENCE-CENTERED FORMS OF PERSUASION   228

Academic Argumentation   228

The blueprint for academic arguments   229

Assertion   229

Proof   230

Evidence   230

Modality   231

How much proof do you need?   232

Common argumentative errors   233

Putting it together   235

    Introduction   235

    Don't bury the lead   236

    Interior paragraphs   236

    Conclusion   237

Plagiarism   237

Cross-examination   240

  Interrogation   240

  Body language and deception—tells   240

  Two approaches: Ingratiation and intimidation   241

  Examination versus cross-examination   242

    Irving Younger's 10 Commandments   245

    Alternatives to cross-examination   247

Your Turn   248

Decision making: Deliberation, justification, and intuition   249

  Deliberation   249

Your Turn   252

  Justification   252

  Intuition—pattern recognition   253

Steps for generalized decision making   256

  Basic deliberative pattern: Problem–solution   256

    Problem   257

    Solution   258

  The setting matters   258

  The role of luck   260

  The sources of bad decisions   261

  Learned helplessness   262

  Probabilities   264

  Negotiation and sales   269

    Negotiation   269

    Research is crucial   269

    Price and cost   269

    You are always negotiating with yourself   270

Contents

Negotiation basics   271

Ready, set, negotiate   272

The rhetoric of retail   273

Psychological math—shell games with numbers   274

Common sales techniques   276

Forms of indirect marketing   280

Narrative   282

Elements of a persuasive story   284

Humor   285

Your Turn   290

The dark side   291

Power and persuasion   291

Ingratiation   296

Allegory   299

Clairvoyance: The art of cold reading   301

Your Turn   305

Machiavellian rhetoric   306

Your Turn   317

CHAPTER 5: CONCLUSION   **318**

Character Traits of the *Rhetor*   318

Glossary   321

Appendix: Selections on Rhetoric and Writing from Plato and Aristotle   335

Suggested Reading   386

Works Cited   391

Index   399

Note to Students

My hope for this book is that you will keep it after the final is over, even after graduation. The advice in it is invaluable and universally applicable. If you want to be a lawyer or a doctor or a clergy person, a banker, an engineer, a scientist, an accountant, an editor, a graphic artist, a consultant in any field, an entrepreneur, or a teacher—if you want to make a living in any profession that requires persuasion (they all do)—this book will increase your capacity for effective writing and speaking and refine your ability to think critically. Even if you're not sure where you are going, this book will help you get there because it will teach you how to avoid the traps set by advertisers and fast-talking sales people and unscrupulous dealers of all kinds. It will even teach you how to avoid talking yourself into things you'll regret later in life. Well, it might.

The information, the strategies, the techniques, and the advice in this book will not stale date. Much of what I'm going to show you educated people have known for several thousand years, and some of it has been intuitively understood by the most successful people in all walks of life from the beginning of human communication. **Life doesn't come with a manual, but if it did this would be it.**

Having said that, however, perhaps I should warn you that this book isn't of the top ten things you need to know about persuasion variety. This is no quick fix. The road to successful persuasion is steep, slippery, frequently dark, littered with fascinating distractions, and seldom clearly marked. Hard work and dedication are more important than any advice anyone will ever give you. These are techniques, not tricks. You have to practice them, assess the results, fine-tune your thinking about how they work, and test again. Once you have a technique down you need to practice it until it becomes automatic, intuitive. In case I just depressed you, I will add that the value of natural talent is often overrated when assessing persuasive capacity. Great writers, speakers, and thinkers, like great athletes and great musicians, may be born with talent, but hard work and perseverance as well as inspired and timely coaching made them great. If you work hard and listen carefully to criticism, both positive and negative, you will get better no matter where you start from, and if you decide to be persuasive, given enough time and effort, you will become more skilled at perceiving and articulating the world around you. I'll come back to each of these ideas at different times throughout the book.

One last note: This book is *not* user friendly. It will make you think. It's written in a somewhat lumpy way, with unfamiliar words and interrogative interruptions in the text, to make you stop reading and start asking questions, to ponder, to doubt. If you want to become more persuasive, you have to get in the habit of asking questions. To help you get there, I'm going to stop you from time to time, break your stride, knit your brows, by asking you to doubt if what I just asserted was true because that, in a nutshell, is the kind of thinking you will need if you are to become persuasive. If the average textbook is a sleekly intuitive interface, this book is a command prompt. I'm not going to teach you anything. I'm going to challenge you to learn for yourself.

Note to Readers in General

I have addressed this book to college students primarily, but that doesn't mean you can't learn from it if you've already graduated or found an alternative path. The information and ideas in this book are applicable far beyond college. If you encounter a college reference that doesn't apply, recast the phrasing to fit your current context. When I talk about audience, for example, instead of thinking professor, think boss or director or board of directors or PTA or city hall or significant other. The content of the examples is similarly optional, and recontextualizing the advice for your own circumstances is the best way to learn from the material.

Introduction

What Is This Book About?

Each of us is born with an innate capacity for persuasion; else we would never have been able to get our caregivers to understand our needs. But once we progressed past the point where cries and gurgles prompted fulfillment, we struggled with how best to talk others into meeting the needs we couldn't meet for ourselves. Mercifully most of us can't remember throwing ourselves on the grocery store floor and screaming for whatever it was we thought we couldn't live without, and yet most of us eventually learned that tantrums, while sometimes effective, are less effective than less pathetic strategies. And thus we set about trying to find other ways to persuade. This book will greatly increase your repertoire of persuasive techniques by showing you how persuasion works and by providing you with specific, detailed strategies. The technologies of persuasion change constantly, but the basic ideas haven't changed fundamentally since they were first recorded in the fourth century before the common era (BCE). This book synthesizes those foundational ideas and updates them for current contexts, including how the concepts play out online.

The subject of persuasion is wide ranging and complex, incorporating information and practices that are too often taught in isolation from each other. Most universities departmentalize the many subjects required to become persuasive. We are taught to speak in Communication, think in Philosophy, read in English, and write in First-Year Composition. The textbooks used in each of these departments are inevitably too narrow as well. Critical-thinking books focus on logic, fallacious and syllogistic. Speech communication books focus on overcoming self-consciousness and the basic structures of informal (non-syllogistic) arguments. Composition books focus on writing, frequently reduced to usage, punctuation, and style, privileging correctness over creativity and rarely emphasizing invention, the prevailing thought being that what one should say comes from the content areas, often literature in particular. Yet a persuasive person has to bring all of these disciplines together, adding psychology, sociology, anthropology, art, design, statistics, and nowadays even usability and user experience studies as well. When we isolate these subjects, we construct a fragmentary understanding of communication in general and persuasion in particular. Persuasion is an interdisciplinary practice.

This book synthesizes and distills the advice, observations, and warnings of a vast array of people who devoted themselves to teaching others how to become effective and useful members of their communities (how to be persuasive, in other words), not specialists in any isolated discipline but quick-witted generalists who can *make sense of complex material quickly for different audiences,* skills that enable adaptive learning and interdisciplinary communication skills. Think of this book as a contemporary travel guide to a vast and venerable modern metropolis built among the still partially visible ruins of an ancient city. It's a portable map full of glosses and back-stories on the technologies of persuasion. It will tell you where you need to go, but you have to go there if you want to fully understand.

The first information technology

You may be wondering why the word *technologies* appeared in the sentence before last. We tend to think of technologies as things we plug in: electronic devices. The word *technology,* however, is directly related to persuasion. Consider the etymology of *technology. Techne* means "art" and *ology* means "study of." One of the first people to analyze persuasion, Aristotle, defined the subject you are about to learn as a *techne.* As you will see, much of that art has to do with how to locate, organize, remember, and implement words and thoughts for maximum effect. In a sense, what you are about to learn— *persuasion* from the rhetorical perspective—is the original information technology.

To the Greeks, from whom we get the early forms of many of our ideas about education, there were three kinds of intellectual endeavors: *techne, empiria,* and *episteme.*

An *episteme* is any rule-governed intellectual domain that can generate predictable results. Physics is an *episteme* in the sense that objects in the physical universe are subject to rules, and thus we can predict outcomes with certainty (at least to the extent we know the rules and can control the conditions)—how gravity works, for example. Today we might call an *episteme* a theoretical science, the key being necessarily predictable results. An *empiria,* on the other hand, is an intellectual domain that one refines through experimentation and the accumulation of vast experience, a kind of wisdom handed down from generation to generation but essentially practiced anew by each new practitioner, an activity that cannot predict success or failure with certainty because there are too many variables outside the practitioner's control. Doctoring is an example of an *empiria.* Whereas chemistry and biology are sciences, putting them together in the form of patient care moves the medical practitioner beyond the realm of scientific certainty into the less certain realm of human experience. As a person trained in science, a doctor knows with certainty that a patient with blood pressure in a specific range will have healthier outcomes than if his or her blood pressure exceeds that range. But the target is a range, not a number, and getting any given person into the right range might require different approaches. Were doctoring a pure science, one could hook a person up to a sphygmomanometer, and the machine would prescribe an effective dose of medication, but different medicines behave differently in different bodies, and so observation and monitoring of each patient is necessary. Were medicine solely an *empiria*, as it was before modern chemistry and biology, then we wouldn't know how blood pressure affects health outcomes or have blood pressure medications. By combining *episteme* and *empiria*, modern medicine becomes an empirical science.

While recent advances in neurophysiology suggest the possibility that a theoretical underpinning for persuasion might one day be possible, enabling the kind of scientific certainty afforded by physics and chemistry, persuasion in its current state is neither an *empiria* nor an *episteme*. Its results are unpredictable but not therefore random.

The third option, *techne*, in contrast to *episteme* and *empiria*, governs a universe that lacks the regularity that enables predictability. Instead of rules, a *techne* has guidelines, or, to use the Greek word, *heuristics*. These *heuristics* are context invariant to a point, but they are not universally applicable, and therefore they cannot be called laws. Every instance of persuasion is sufficiently different from every other instance that one has always to be coming up with new approaches and modifying previously successful approaches for current situations without being able to predict let alone calculate what the outcome will be. As a result, understanding how persuasion works will not make you persuasive in the way that understanding the laws of physics will enable you to calculate a falling body's terminal velocity. Nevertheless studying and practicing the guidelines can save you considerable time and frustration by reducing the amount of time you have to spend learning from trial and error. Persuasion is more like an *emperia* than an *episteme*. And yet it differs from an *emperia* because it has a much wider range of application than a practice like doctoring or lawyering. The guidelines of persuasion work across all disciplines, in any sphere of human interaction requiring communication.

The Greek word *techne* is often translated as "art," but it is also sometimes translated as "craft." The word *art* suggests high aesthetics and might therefore be a bit misleading because some kinds of persuasion are low. And yet *craft* suggests guilds and shops and processes and procedures that require specific materials and methods, like making pots or posters. The kinds of materials a persuasive effort might take are endless, from words to machines to buildings. So neither *art* nor *craft* entirely provide what we are looking for, which is why I follow Aristotle in locating the domain of persuasion among the *techne*.

So we understand that of the three kinds of thought-based ways of living, persuasion is neither a theoretical science like physics nor an empirical science like medicine but rather a *techne*, a recurrent but constantly changing activity that one learns by following guidelines and best practices until they become almost habitual or reflexive. Thus persuasion belongs to the realm of *techne*, but what is persuasion itself?

What is persuasion, and how does it relate to the more common words argumentation and exposition?

Persuasion is any process that creates a new belief or changes your level of commitment to an existing one. The persuasive process may or may not include evidence; it may or may not be rational. The belief generated (or changed) may or may not be durable. It may or may not be true. Emotions are relevant to many forms of persuasion. Intimidation is a form of persuasion; seduction is a form of persuasion; so are mathematical proofs; so are sermons. For the purposes of this book, *any act that generates or modifies a belief is a form of persuasion.*

Argumentation is a subset of persuasion, the process of getting someone to believe something by giving them evidence and reasons. (The reasons explain and support the relevance and power of the evidence.) While aware of emotional states, argumentation doesn't typically use emotional appeals, although it might seek to calm people down before proceeding. The goal is a permanent or at least durable belief (conviction) that is as strongly held as the evidence warrants. Academic writing is a form of argumentation. Law court trials are a form of argumentation. Whenever the evidence is center stage, and the people and the situation are backstage, the discourse is argumentative.[1]

Exposition is a form of writing or speaking that consists almost entirely of declarative sentences with no proof to support their truth (like the sentence you just read). The audience is simply supposed to believe the statements are true or take them for what they seem to be worth. Textbooks are expository. They are meant to teach, not persuade, but if one learns something one is changed and thus persuaded in a sense. This book is partially expository because I want to explain to you how persuasion works and partially argumentative because I want to convince you of something as well.

Rhetoric is the study of how people come to believe anything they believe, and as such it covers the widest imaginable range of disciplines and practices. Rhetoric is about persuasion and argumentation and exposition; it's

---

1. If you have the image of people shouting at each other in mind when you hear the word *argumentative*, then the definition I just gave you will seem strange. Shouting isn't arguing.

about history and critical thinking and logic and psychology and sociology and anthropology and poetry and aesthetics and statistics; it's about the bright and the dark side of human interaction. Rhetoric informs and supports all forms of communication.

And yet the word *rhetoric* doesn't appear in the title of this book—*Persuasion: History, Theory, Practice*—even though this book is ultimately about rhetoric. So why isn't the word *rhetoric* in the title? The vast majority of people associate the word *rhetoric* with political speeches, as in the expression "That's mere rhetoric," the kind of lies politicians tell to get people to believe in them while they intend to do something other than what they say. Thus, in common usage, rhetoric means political lies. People who have been to college in the United States also sometimes equate rhetoric with First-Year, the kinds of rules and guidelines that a student would encounter in an introduction to academic writing class. In this case *rhetoric* means the basics of argumentation. This book goes far beyond the basics because a stable foundation upon which to build persuasive acts requires far more than a typical First-Year Composition book provides. And finally there is the broadest common definition of *rhetoric*: well-crafted lies. This book is not about deceit, although you will learn about deceptive practices and how to avoid unintentionally engaging in or being duped by them. It might make you a better manipulator of words and people as well, but that's on you. If you want to learn about intentional deception, read the section on clairvoyance and the one on Machiavellian rhetoric. If you want to learn how to avoid unintentional deceptions, work closely with the sections on critical thinking and cognitive biases.

This book has designs on you

I want to persuade you that you are a *rhetor*. Let me explain. The Greek word *rhetor* meant one who speaks in public, and as such it didn't mean much in the culture from which our understanding of persuasion descends because any male citizen of Athens with an income affording him enough time to attend to civic matters could address the political assembly and bring cases to court. During the fifth century BCE, however, the word *rhetor* came to mean "one who speaks at public assemblies," a nascent class of professional politicians and lawyers. Until the fifth century BCE, these roles were purely amateur. The idea of making money from them was repugnant to the aristocratic landowners who held power, and thus the idea of teaching people how to make money from influencing public opinion was similarly repugnant to those whose power might be undermined by an educated class of upstarts. The noun form of *rhetor*, "rhetoric," did not exist, apparently, until Plato created it for his dialogue *Gorgias*. He created the term *rhetoric* to promote by contrast another word he made up, *philosophy*. Philosophy (the Greek *philos* meaning "love" and *sophia* meaning "wisdom") was how he characterized the goal of the intellectual technique that he taught. He called that technique *dialectic*, and we will work with it closely in a few pages. Rhetoric, by contrast, as the art of teaching people how to bend an ignorant public to the will of an equally ignorant speaker, is a straw dog, a fake alternative, a piece of salesmanship, created to be destroyed in order to promote philosophy and to denigrate political instruction, literary instruction, and word craft. A *rhetorician*, also a made-up word (we can call it a neologism if we want to dignify it some), was one who taught others how to make public speeches and thus a person who made *rhetors*. Prior to Plato, no one used the words "rhetoric" or "rhetorician," as far as we can tell, although there were certainly people teaching others various word crafts. Prior to Plato, nobody resisted the idea of being a *rhetor*, a public speaker, because the opposite of one who spoke in public was a private citizen: in Greek, an *idiotes*.

If this is true,[2] then rhetoric was created in order to promote philosophy. And thus it was a derogatory appellation from the start. Plato's representation of philosophy helped broaden the general distrust of public speaking and the people who might try to influence public decision making by participating in it. It also justified a life of quiet contemplation away from the dust and noise of the marketplace, laying the foundation for what would become academic ivory towers. Plato was so rhetorically effective that to this day most people feel insulted if they are accused of using rhetoric. Anyone who knows the subject of rhetoric well, however, knows that Plato was among the most effective *rhetors* of all time. The greatest stunt Plato ever pulled was to convince the world that his philosophy provided access to the truth while everyone else's educational practices spread lies and deceptions and mere rhetoric. Plato, in other words, was such a slick rhetorician that he managed to convince people he wasn't one at all.

It's noteworthy that Plato's student Aristotle legitimated the word *rhetoric* by providing what he considered a sound (dialectical) foundation for rhetorical practices. From Aristotle's views on rhetoric to the present day is a long and complex journey we don't have time to take in this book,[3] but, as we progress through the relevant concepts and practices that have come down to us from the past, we will stop from time to time to look at some of the monuments still standing, emphasizing the early Greek and Roman ones but recognizing that other cultures contributed to our current understandings.

As I said in the paragraph before that brief historical digression on the word *rhetoric*, I want to convince you to see yourself as a *rhetor*, a *person who consciously designs all of his or her messages for maximum influence*

---

2. Edward Schiappa, "Did Plato Coin *Rhetorike*?" *American Journal of Philology* 111 (1990): 457–70.

3. See George A. Kennedy, Brian Vickers, and Thomas Connolly for more historically focused introductions to the history of rhetoric.

and can see how others have designed their messages and why. Whether you are aware of it or not, you are already a *rhetor*; you have a constituency—the people whom you know face to face and those you know online. Moreover there are people who know you online who you don't know know you, although when you go for your first big job interview you will discover who some of them are. You have a public, and you need to keep that uppermost in mind whatever your intended or current profession. Regardless of your professional aspirations, if you want to be successful you have to be persuasive, and if you want to be persuasive then you have to understand and be able to use rhetoric effectively.

So I used the word "persuasion" instead of the word "rhetoric" in the title because rhetoric might have misled you. *Sometimes what you don't say is more important than what you do say.*

Why Study Persuasion?

People who have studied persuasion over the years have always been a bit defensive about the subject because the idea of persuading someone seems slightly dishonest, manipulative at best, nefarious at worst. The facts should speak for themselves. But facts don't speak, people do.

Self-promotion and self-defense

Everybody has opinions, and most of us want to believe our own opinions are not only worth sharing but worth accepting. Thus we argue for what we believe and try to persuade others that we are right, often actually trying to reassure ourselves in the process that we are in fact right. And they return the favor. We are constantly presenting and being presented with opinions with varying degrees of value, and we have to assess the value of these opinions so that we can speak and write with conviction and thus get our needs met. As Aristotle said, if it is okay to defend yourself physically it must be okay to defend yourself verbally.

Moreover, because we live in a world of ubiquitous corporate sales messages and because even ideas are sometimes managed like products for sale, unless you know how to see through persuasive techniques, you will buy things you don't want. Worse yet, you may think you need to live in ways that your income can't support and so chase an empty aspiration down a tunnel of endless debt. Thus, the argument goes, you should learn how advertisers and talk show hosts and smooth-talking sales people persuade, so you will be less susceptible to their wiles. But it's not just the corporate interests that have designs on what you think and how you act.

Self-awareness

Every book you read, every lecture you attend, every hour you spend listening to talk radio or reading editorials or watching television or admiring the way other people live or checking out your friends' status updates on Facebook (and whatever will soon replace Facebook the way it replaced Myspace in public consciousness), every waking hour, is an hour you've spent exposing yourself to the opinions and beliefs of other people. Unless you understand the rhetorical processes that led you to believe what you believe now (and to have rejected the beliefs you rejected) and realize that your beliefs will change over time as changing circumstances expose you to different rhetorical processes, you don't really understand how you think. If you don't understand how you think, you may find yourself arguing vehemently for things you don't really understand or judging others' beliefs incorrectly. *If you don't examine the rhetorical processes that led you to form the opinions you hold, you can neither defend your opinions successfully nor promote them intelligently.*

While it may be true that in free societies all people are equally entitled to their opinions, not all opinions are equally credible. To differentiate among them you have to understand how opinions are created and promoted and how you interact with the ones you encounter. You also have to realize that believing something doesn't mean it's true, just as liking something doesn't make it good. For more about taste and values, read the section on critical thinking.

Self-improvement

One of the earliest teachers of persuasion in the Western world was a Greek named Isocrates (436–338 BCE), a contemporary of Plato (427–347 BCE), who asserted that conceiving a desire to become persuasive could improve a person's character. He put it something like this:

> The man who wishes to persuade people will not be negligent as to the matter of character; no, on the contrary, he will apply himself above all to establish a most honorable name among his fellow-citizens; for who does not know that words carry greater conviction when spoken by men of good repute than when spoken by men who live under a cloud, and that the argument which is made by a man's life is of more weight than that which is furnished by words? Therefore, the stronger a man's desire to persuade his hearers, the more zealously will he strive to be honorable and to have the esteem of his fellow-citizens. (Isocrates, *Antidossis*)

Because people are most often persuaded by people they trust, to be persuasive you have to appear trustworthy, and appearing trustworthy is much easier if you actually are trustworthy. Thus you should make a constant practice of getting good and useful things done on time and on budget so that, when on occasion you can't persuade people because the available evidence isn't as powerful as they would like, they will be inclined to trust your judgment because you've never let them down.

In other words, by learning how persuasion works you will become more conscious of how reputation influences credibility, and this will lead you to pursue a more credible life, which ultimately will make you a better, happier, and more helpful person.

Success at work

You may have heard that employers value communication skills above all others:

> Reports from the Department of Labor's Secretary's Commission on Achieving the Necessary Skills show that employers rate communication skills as a top priority for both securing and retaining employment (North & Worth, 1996, 1998). Strong indicators continue to come from employers that oral and written skills are in high demand. Another analysis of Department of Labor data regarding future workplace skills determined that communication skills are essential workplace tools for the 21st century (Locker & Kaczmarek, 2001) and have been correlated with career success and increased financial rewards (Fisher, 1999). (Stevens)

Here's another testimonial on the value of learning how to communicate effectively. It's from Warren Buffet, a famous investor and one of the world's wealthiest businessmen:

> The ability to communicate both in writing and orally is enormously important. Most schools won't teach it because they consider it too simple. . . . However, if you can communicate well, it's a big advantage. (Ancowitz)

Buffet's assertion that schools don't teach communication might strike you as odd. After all, here you are taking a course in communication. I think he was probably thinking of MBA programs like the Wharton School when he said "schools." Regardless, I think he's certainly right about the "big advantage." According to an article from 2004 in the *Globe and Mail*, your success during and after college will depend less on what you know and more on your ability to communicate what you have learned:

> "We recognized that our biggest problem is not in evaluating the cognitive domain—it's not about knowledge," Dr. Rosenfeld says. "It's the interpersonal domain: the way of dealing with people. It's about ethics and it's about judgment." (Silverman)

Wait a minute, you might object. A person has to know something in order to communicate it, right? Doesn't knowledge precede communication? Actually, they go together. Look at it this way: Most of the technical knowledge you acquire in college will be obsolete five years after you graduate. And the chances are excellent that whatever you do in life will require learning new things constantly, things you didn't study in college, even things no one knew about when you were in college. The acquisition of ideas and techniques is an endless process. If you don't keep learning your brain will atrophy the way your muscles will if you stop moving. So knowledge and learning are necessary requirements for living well. But unless you can do something with what you know, and more often than not this requires talking and writing affectively about what you've learned so that others can benefit from your efforts (persuading), you have a head full of useless information.

A richer personal experience

Persuasion is one of the seven traditional liberal arts,[4] and one of the justifications for studying any of them is that knowledge of the liberal arts enriches your life by helping you understand the world and the people who share it with you, making it easier for you to appreciate a wider range of experiences. By understanding how someone is trying to make you believe something, you can appreciate his or her effort on a higher plane. You can question more than just, "Do I accept or reject this opinion?" but also, "Do I understand and appreciate the way the opinion is being presented?" Just as painters and writers and musicians have special insights into the artistic performances

---

4. The seven liberal arts were grammar, rhetoric, dialectic, arithmetic, geometry, music, and astronomy. The word *liberal* is for many people today a loaded term, one carrying a powerfully negative connotation. *Liberal* was once a synonym for "free," as in indebted to no one. The liberal arts were the training ground for the ruling classes and the clergy. They were the opposite of vocational training, an education designed to prepare the student for membership in a guild or trade. In this context, *liberal* is not the opposite of *conservative*. In this context, *liberal* is the opposite of *indebted* or *obligated*.

of their fellows, so someone who understands how persuasion works can appreciate the world of messages and meanings at a higher level.

No better alternative

One final reason to study persuasion: There will be moments in your life when evidence is unavailable because it doesn't exist or there isn't time to get it—like when the outcome of the activity will determine the value of the decision, but there's no way to predict the outcome with certainty. If you chose to attend college A over college B, for example, you will never know if you made the right decision because you will never know what life at B would have been like. All you can do is play up the great experiences at A and down-play the bad and forget about B entirely. The same is true of all life-altering decisions. Other times there may be evidence, but it is inconclusive. When the evidence is underwhelming, you will have to persuade yourself and others, and when that happens the techniques explained in this book will help you make the best of what evidence there is. Persuasion may also serve you well when you have to come to terms with a decision that has been made or an event that can't be undone, and your only option is to learn to live with it, perhaps even learn to embrace it; "making lemonade" is a rhetorical act. Other times, while there may be scientific evidence pointing toward the best course of action, the people you have to convince may not be able to understand the evidence. At those times, also, the techniques discussed in this book will be invaluable.

══════ Your Turn

Make a list of all of the surprising places you see advertisements. Can you think of any place where you can escape corporate messages entirely?

Who is the most persuasive non-family member in your life and why?
Did you find Warren Buffet's testimonial persuasive? If so, why? If not, why not? Now find someone who took the opinion opposite your own and talk it out. When you've finished talking it over, write a brief (like ten sentences) paragraph explaining why you did or didn't change your mind.

chapter 1
ASSESSING PERSUASIVE ACTS

Reading with and against the Grain

Most successful people have a strategy or two when it comes to reading large quantities of information, figuring out what's important and how it works, and remembering who said what. If we are reading from a book we own, we underline key passages, write summaries in the margins, make a list of key words (counting the number of entries for a word in a book's index can help you figure out what the key words are) at the top or the bottom of the page so that when we flip back through the book later we'll jog our memories about what's talked about where. We also keep a web browser open to look up unfamiliar words and ideas. If we are reading digitally, using something like the Kindle or the Nook or the iBook app, we do more or less the same things, only using the interface provided by the app to highlight and annotate information so we can find it later.

When we are reading to understand and remember, we are *reading with the grain*. We are assuming that the author knows what she is talking about, and our only goal is to make sure we get it. If we have questions, they are about words we don't recognize or references to events we are hazy about or ideas we need to look up. Or our questions are motivated by the desire to find answers that will help us ace a test or slam-dunk a project.

Textbooks invite you to read with the grain. Expository or textbook prose is designed to be swallowed whole and returned intact. An indirect effect of years of experience reading with the grain is that you may have become a passive learner. You just accept the authority of the text because it is a textbook. Reading with the grain is essential for understanding and remembering new information, but it can be counterproductive when it comes to developing your skills of persuasion because you have to actively engage with ideas and people if you want to change minds and come to understand your own better. *Active learning means, basically, doing something with what you are learning as you are learning it.* You have to try it out. Try it on. You don't have to buy it, but you have to be able to use it well enough to get a clear sense of what it is and how it fits in with what you already know. Aristotle, one of the rhetoricians you'll be hearing from frequently in this book, said, "It is the mark of an educated mind to be able to entertain a thought without accepting it" (*Metaphysics*).

This character trait is significant for persuasion especially because to be persuasive you have to be able to argue all sides of a case—at least as you work out what side you need to take, assuming you have the opportunity to choose.

Because asking questions of assertions is central to all forms of persuasion, and anticipating questions or objections is what makes a person an effective *rhetor*, it is important to learn how to read critically, to *read against the grain*, which is not to say you have to reject everything you read but rather question what every author would have you passively accept. Only through a careful process of testing and questioning can you come to understand something and so judge it correctly. Here is a more concrete explanation.

In a famous old (1966) American book on style, *Tough, Sweet, Stuffy*, in the chapter called "Hearing Voices," Walker Gibson quotes verbatim a passage from a magazine, and then he requotes it with snide comments square bracketed at the end of each sentence, like this:

> The title of this essay may strike you as a typographical error. *[Why no, as a matter of fact, that never occurred to me.]* You may be saying to yourself that the writer really means required reading. *[Don't be silly. I would be more surprised to see a title so trite. In fact your title embodies just the sort of cute phrase I have learned to expect from this middlebrow magazine.]* (Gibson 22)

Gibson's point is that *every text invites a person to become a certain sort of reader*—in this case a cheerful, agreeable reader—and Gibson would have us resist the invitation. He is not advocating we should always read like a jerk. In fact, he advises us not to: "This mean trick can be worked by anybody against almost anything," he says, and he hopes we won't play it on him. Were Gibson still with us, I would like to ask him why I should accord him a deference he denied the author he was just interrupting in the quote above. But of course Gibson isn't here.

We need to learn how to read against the grain because the author isn't with us to answer our questions or address our specific concerns. The absence of the author, by the way, is one of the reasons Plato said in *Phaedrus* that we should resist learning how to read and write in the first place, insisting that we ought to limit our education to face-to-face interactions with informed and skeptical intellectual adversaries. Anything you read, he asserted, gives you the illusion of learning rather than actual knowledge. The problem with reading is that if you don't understand what you just read you can't ask it to explain itself; and, if you don't agree, you can't argue with it. A text is nonresponsive. It always says the same thing,[1] and thus you can't learn from it,

---

1. Even if you understand it differently at different times in your life. What you bring to a text influences how you understand it, but "it" always says the same thing because the words don't change.

or so Plato said. In order to learn, you need to ask questions and seek clarification. You need, in other words, another human being. The practice of questioning the assertions that another person has made is what Plato called *dialectic* (we will get there), but right now I want to show you how to create a written facsimile of dialectic by reading against the grain.

Here is a very compact example of reading against the grain. Take the following sentence from *The New Digital Shoreline*:

> The site tracks the popularity of various textbooks and brings attention to the best free classroom material. (McHaney 129)

Read against the grain, the sentence looks like this:

> The site tracks the popularity of various textbooks and *[Is this "and" in the sense of "therefore" or in the sense of "equals to"? Are you suggesting that popular = best?]* brings attention to the best free classroom material.

In this quote, McHaney is referring to a website that uses reader voting to identify popularity, and then he seems to equate what is popular with what is best. If the readers who are voting know how to evaluate textbooks based on some objective criterion, or at least on their expert opinion, then "the popular" might mean something similar to "the best." If the readers are evaluating textbooks in a purely subjective way, then "popular" suggests convergence of taste rather than an identification of actual superiority. The expression "the best," in other words, can mean several things; therefore the author's embedded assertion that "most popular = best" needs to be questioned. Were the author able to answer our questions, he might be able to clarify what he meant by "and," and then again he might change his mind based on our question and in the next edition of the book offer a more fully elaborated explanation of the popular = best assumption. Regardless, because we are reading rather than talking with him, we need to ask questions for ourselves to make sure we aren't nodding our heads mindlessly to something not worth agreeing with, to make sure we understand, to assess our level of agreement, and to express as clearly as possible what we don't agree with.

By way of an extended example of reading against the grain, here is an excerpt from a book by Anne Coulter. I'm going to present it without questions first as a way of reminding us that we should listen before we speak.

> Of all single mothers in America, only 6.5 percent of them are widows, 37.8 percent are divorced, and 41.3 percent gave birth out of wedlock. The 6.5 percent of single mothers whose husbands have died shouldn't be called "single mothers" at all. We already

have a word for them: "widows." Their children do just fine compared with the children of married parents. (35)

By 1996, 70 percent of inmates in state juvenile detention centers serving long-term sentences were raised by single mothers.
Seventy-two percent of juvenile murderers and 60 percent of rapists come from single-mother homes. Seventy percent of teenage
births, dropouts, suicides, runaways, juvenile delinquents, and
child murderers involve children raised by single mothers. Girls
raised without fathers are more sexually promiscuous and more
likely to end up divorced. A 1990 study by the Progressive Policy
Institute showed that after controlling for single motherhood, the
difference between black and white crime rates disappeared. (37)

And now I will reproduce her words with my questions (square bracketed in
italics) throughout. Here is my "against the grain" version.

Of all single mothers in America, *[Where did these statistics
come from?]* only *[What are you implying by saying "only"?]*
6.5 percent of them are widows, 37.8 percent are divorced, and
41.3 percent gave birth out of wedlock. The 6.5 percent of single
mothers whose husbands have died shouldn't be called "single
mothers" at all. We already have a word for them: "widows." *[Does
this 6.5 percent refer to women whose husbands died while
the children were still young? How young? Why do orphans
have different criminal statistics from other children of
single mothers? If the woman remarries, do the kids cease
to be delinquent?]* Their children do just fine *[What does "do
just fine" mean? Regardless of what it means, it seems to
suggest that how a woman becomes a single parent is more
important than the fact that she is a single parent. What
is the causation here?]* compared with the children of married
parents.

By 1996, *[That was a long time ago. What's the current
statistic, and where did this one come from? And actually,
George, when did Coulter publish this book? Since you don't
know you can't fairly ask her that last question.]* 70 percent
of inmates in state juvenile detention centers serving long-term
sentences were raised by single mothers. Seventy-two percent of
juvenile murderers and 60 percent of rapists come from single-
mother homes. *[Aren't these people included in the category
"long-term sentences"? If so, why call them out specifically?
Are you suggesting that if I don't agree with you a child
will rape and then murder me?]* Seventy percent of teenage
births, dropouts, suicides, runaways, juvenile delinquents, and

child murderers involve children raised by single mothers. *[And therefore 30 percent of such events were caused by father/ mother couples.]* Girls raised without fathers are more sexually promiscuous *[How many partners over how much time identifies a person as promiscuous?]* and more likely *[What do you mean by "more likely"? What are the actual statistics?]* to end up divorced. *[Evidence?]* A 1990 study by the Progressive Policy Institute *[Who are these people? Who funds their research?]* showed that after controlling for single motherhood, the difference between black and white crime rates disappeared. *[What are the stats like for the children of rich single mothers? How do you know that poverty and neglect aren't more important than marital status (to say nothing of race) when looking into this matter? What about the successful children of single parents?]*

The Coulter piece sounds like an argument because it offers evidence to support its assertions, "a 1990 study," for example, and "Seventy percent of teenage births." But it doesn't offer any proof that the evidence should be accepted as valid, with the result that, unless we believe her to begin with, we are no less likely to believe her in the end. And if we disagree with her by default, her lack of concern for our beliefs will be irritating or even inflammatory.

Assuming that Coulter believes we will agree with her, what kind of political opinions does she assume we share with her? And if we disagree with her, what posture or attitude does she seem to be assuming we will take? My sense is that she is talking to political conservatives and that while she seems to be arguing, because she offers evidence, she is really "preaching to the choir"[2] and not arguing at all; she doesn't back up her claim with support that someone who doesn't agree with her would have to concede is true. Thus her writing seems to assume that either we agree with her or we are liberals who can be ignored, a kind of indifference to disagreement. It's my way or the highway, as the saying goes.

The problem here is that the terms *conservative* and *liberal* are simplistic labels. Writing in such a way that one must accept one term or fall by default into the other is rhetoric at its worst. Coulter's writing is designed to stir up controversy and sell books for the sake of making money, disregarding any possibility for the advancement of public discourse. That kind of rhetoric

---

2. The expression "preaching to the choir" is a metaphor for a form of discourse that might sound or look like argumentation but isn't because the audience already agrees with the speaker. No minds will be changed in the process, and therefore it is not argumentative. The choir might increase its commitment to the beliefs it already holds, which means the discourse was persuasive, but that doesn't make it argumentative.

muddies our thinking and exploits our prejudices for profit. So by allowing my interjections to get increasingly strident, I was being rhetorically naive. Gibson warned me not to adopt the posture I was being offered, but that was easy for me with Coulter because I've never agreed with her about anything. The real danger, in this case, for me, was assuming the opposite posture, the knee-jerk liberal. I let Coulter troll me. *Don't get carried away by the sound of your own objections. Reading against the grain isn't about hollering at trolls.*

If we are going to learn anything from pseudo-argumentative writing that masquerades as exposition (editorial prose, in other words), we have to be careful not to either get sucked in *or* spit out. We don't want to assume the attitudes of a stereotypical conservative or fall into the opposite stereo-type of liberal. Rather than shouting at Coulter's text, I should realize that, because she isn't around to define her terms and back up her assertions with the kind of evidence I'm looking for, the best I can do is learn from my objections to what she said. And what I learned from my objections is that I use words every day that I have never defined but really need to if I am going to develop a reasonable opinion regarding the question of what effect an increase in single motherhood has on a culture where single motherhood isn't the norm.

What is *motherhood*? Are all mothers the same? Are there different kinds of mothering? If there are, does a mothering style necessarily lead to a child becoming a certain kind of adult? Would every child respond to the same kind of mothering in the same way? And what does *fatherhood* mean? And is *parenthood* necessarily motherhood + fatherhood? And now that I'm ask-ing some real questions, what does it mean to be a *child*? If the experiences of each of these ideas is unique to each of us, then do the categories signified by the general expressions *family, motherhood, fatherhood,* and *childhood* mean anything at all?

Such, at any rate, is the practice of reading against the grain. Question everything. To help you become accustomed to reading against the grain, throughout the rest of this book, I will from time to time read what I've writ-ten against the grain for you. Every once in a while I will also try to trip you up, to see if you were paying attention and actively engaged or just passing words in one eye and out the other.

━━━━━ Your Turn

Because it is easier to disagree with someone who rubs you the wrong way, start by hunting for trolls. If you think you lean left politically (realizing the label doesn't really mean much), then read through some right-leaning journals: the *National Review* or the *American Spectator* or the *American Conservative*. If you think maybe you lean the other way, try the *Nation* or *Harpers* or *New Left Review*. Once you have some practice reigning in your impulse to shout at someone you view as an opponent, look for something that leans a little more your way, and see if you can read *it* against the grain. Eventually you should be able to read against the grain pieces you completely agree with. *Your ultimate goal is to read your own writing against the grain.* When you can do that, when you can critique your own writing, others will have a harder time doing it, and you will therefore be more persuasive.

You need to practice reading against the grain every day, until it becomes second nature, until you can't help it. Look for spoken opportunities as well. You want to get to the point where if someone says x, you will ask, what about –x or capital X or Y? Or try to reframe what the person said. If they called a situation a loss, think what would happen if you called it the cost of doing business. (See the section "Framing" in Chapter 3 for more on how to do this.) I'm not encouraging you to become a jerk or an argumentative pain in the X (or –X). You don't have to voice your questions and counterstatements; just make thinking them habitual. Sales pitches are a good opportunity for practicing reading against the grain. There's nothing inherently unethical about sales. Everyone has to make a living. But sales pitches tend to be one sided, so they offer a good place to practice reading against the grain. Next time you see a commercial for a glistening hamburger, think one hundred grams of fat and two-days worth of salt instead of salivating like Pavlov's dog. (*If you don't know who Pavlov was and why people refer to his dogs all the time, Google him.*)

Here are some concepts and ready-made questions to help you learn how to read against the grain:

> **clarification:** Are you talking about Z or F?
>
> **elaboration:** Say more about X. What kind of X is X?
>
> **exceptions:** Ok, but what about . . . ? Except that. . . .
>
> **definition:** What do *you* mean by X?
>
> **evidence:** What evidence is there to support this position?
>
> **verification:** Is the evidence you are offering here relevant and accurate?
>
> **example:** Can you give me an example? Is this example representative or overrepresentative?
>
> **level of commitment:** How sure are you about . . . ?
>
> **context:** Is this always true? Is there something special about the situation?
>
> **sources:** Where did this information come from?

assumptions: Are you assuming . . . ?

objections: You are oversimplifying. You are overgeneralizing. You are placing more weight on this evidence than it can support. You are speaking outside your expertise.

faulty arguments: Overstatement, false cause, corrupt data, incomplete data, unwarranted assertion (opinions presented as facts), etc.

Here are some useful questions for reading your own writing against the grain:

- Who am I talking to?
- Who am I not talking to (or ignoring)?
- Why did I just write that?
- Is this sentence in the right place in this paragraph?
- How might someone who disagreed with me read this sentence?
- Could this word be interpreted in more than one way?
- Does this word have a connotation I'm not intending?
- How might someone misunderstand what I just wrote?
- Why might someone disagree with what I just wrote?
- Is there another definition of this word that will conflict with what I actually mean?
- What assumption is this assertion resting on?
- How would my assertion sound to someone who doesn't agree with me?
- What experience would make this assertion questionable?

As with all of the lists in this book, you need to adapt and extend this one for your own use.

Logic

One could easily devote a semester (or a lifetime) to studying logic. But we are not going to because logic has a relatively narrow range of application as far as persuasion goes; it only works in situations where all of the relevant words have singular, unambiguous, and shared meanings, where experiences and perspectives and emotions and characters are irrelevant. These sorts of occasions rarely arise outside of carefully controlled environments. While it might be possible to take a real problem and control the discourse this carefully, your partners in the argument would have to be as patient as you are, and they would have to be partners, not adversaries or enemies. Plato's dialogue *Gorgias* has three examples of what trying to use even informal logic in an uncontrolled setting might look like—it degenerates into tedium, frustration, and even temper tantrums. (See the selection from *Gorgias* in the Appendix.)

When most people hear the word *logic* they think of the syllogism and often the paradigmatic example: All men are mortal; Socrates is a man; therefore, Socrates is mortal. A reasonable question to ask of this form of reasoning is how useful is it? Can we learn anything from practicing it? We certainly don't learn anything from the paradigmatic example. Socrates has been dead for two thousand years. Utility doesn't really bother logicians. They are primarily interested in form and providing elegant solutions to interesting problems. *Rhetors* are interested in getting work done in far less pristine conditions.

Despite logic's limited range of application, it is important to understand how logic works because it can be extremely powerful, and people often use bogus forms of it to win disputes unfairly. The most common form of logic abuse is to call an argument "fallacious" and then to harrumph, "Thus I refute thee." This tactic is known as *name calling*, and it isn't by logical standards a counterargument or a refutation even if the argument in question is fallacious. Using negative epithets is a bully's tactic. (*I just did it too. Did you notice?*) Someone who really knows logic would know better than to call an opposing argument a name. He or she would point out the logical error and then offer a better argument. A really effective persuader would first offer an improved argument in the service of his or her "opponent" and then provide a counterargument to that. Instruction, if it doesn't come across as condescending, is much more persuasive than a direct refutation. Proving people wrong just hurts their feelings. Letting them persist in their errors may do even greater harm, however, and so you need to learn how to improve a person's opinions without hurting feelings. A strict logician couldn't be bothered with emotions because logical arguments are completely impersonal, like the ones and zeros of a computer program. It's good to a have a tough skin, but it's not good to assume everyone else has one too.

So what I'm offering in this section is no substitute for an entire class in logical reasoning. It is at best a quick summary of what one might find in an introduction to philosophy class. If you never took one, you probably should.

Logic in its most basic sense means rule-based reasoning, where you accurately infer something from something else. There are two forms of logical reasoning: deductive (top down) and inductive (bottom up).

Deductive reasoning—think geometry

Sound deductive reasoning is the process of correctly drawing a conclusion from a set of true statements (a.k.a. premises):

A = B;
B = C;
therefore, A = C.

In logic, *valid* means the inference was correctly drawn from the premises. This means that a valid syllogism may have nothing to do with reality. So,

All pugs are pigs; my dog is a pug; therefore, my dog is a pig

is a valid syllogism.

When a conclusion of a syllogism is validly inferred and says something true, it is said to be both valid and sound. That is, the premises from which the conclusion is drawn are true statements, and the conclusion was correctly inferred from them:

All men are mortal; Socrates is a man; therefore, Socrates is mortal.

Unsound deductive syllogisms take three forms:

- invalid conclusion from sound premises (bad inference)
- valid conclusion from unsound premises (bogus thinking)
- invalid conclusions from unsound premises (nonsense)

Invalid conclusion from sound premises (bad inference).

All men are mortal; Socrates is mortal; therefore, Socrates is a man. (*All living things are mortal so Socrates could be a man, but he could be a cat. All we know for sure is that he is a living thing.*)

Here is another way to draw an invalid conclusion from sound premises:

All canines are dogs; Jake is a dog; therefore, Jake is a canine.

If Jake is actually a man who has doglike qualities, in other words if "dog" is being used metaphorically, we have a valid but unsound deductive proof. If, on the other hand, Jake is literally a dog, then we have a valid and sound deductive proof. The problem with the example is that "dog" is ambiguous,

having both literal and figurative meanings, while the modifier "Jake" does nothing to help because both men and dogs can be named Jake.
   Valid conclusion from unsound premises (bogus thinking).

> All cats are reptiles; Bugs Bunny is a cat; therefore, Bugs Bunny is a crocodile.

Unsound premises are untrue or misleading statements on which we rest an argument. Stereotypes and other forms of unexamined opinions often provide unsound premises. Sometimes we select an unsound premise simply because we have incomplete information. Sometimes we will select an unsound premise because it rings true, and we don't want to examine it because to do so would be to question our ideological commitments or even our sense of identity. We also occasionally create unsound premises as a consequence of a previous unsound or invalid conclusion, so that one error bleeds into another one, and before long we are dizzy. And sometimes people create unsound premises because they want to trick or deceive people, and they figure they can better get away with it if what they say sounds logical.

The third case of syllogistic errors, *invalid inferences from unsound premises,* is just nonsense masquerading as reason. These kinds of "arguments" sound right but are in no way right. Advertisers use them endlessly. Often these days they use them openly, assuming that if they show you the error in thinking as they make it you will feel like you've been let in on the joke and will thus be disarmed by their "honesty," even as they continue to make their case on the back of weak reasons.

Inductive reasoning—think empirical science

The other form of logical thinking is induction, where you draw a conclusion from an example or series of examples. The validity of such arguments rests almost entirely on the example, and usually you need a bunch of examples all clearly exhibiting the same unambiguous characteristic to provide a valid induction. Much of the time, however, one really vivid example might be enough to win an argument, even if it doesn't strictly prove the point. (For example, I found a bright red mushroom in a meadow and took a bite of it. It tasted awful, and within minutes I was so sick I thought I was going to die. Mushrooms that look like that one must be poisonous.) Most of the time, however, you need more than a single example: I was bitten by a dog; all dogs are dangerous. That's an example of really bad reasoning, an over-generalization. But most people "reason" like that all the time. One really vivid example is often enough to make us draw a conclusion. We might call it the once-bitten error. In rhetoric an argument induced from a single albeit powerful case is called a *paradigm*; and, while according to strict logic one ought not infer from a single case, if you've ever gotten food poisoning at a restaurant and from then on felt wretched even seeing an ad for the place, you know the power of a paradigm.

There's a con game that goes something like this: You get a hundred email addresses, and you pick a stock from the NASDAQ. You tell 50 percent of the people that the stock will rise during the coming week, and you tell the other half of the people that it will fall. At the end of the week you have two groups who now have an example of you telling them the truth about the future. You pick another stock the next week, and you do the same thing again. Half you tell rise, half you tell fall. Each time you do this your "clients" are getting what they think is infallible proof of your ability to predict the stock market. After a few weeks you've got a group of people who will sell when you say sell and another group of people who will buy when you say buy. Now you pick a new stock, and you tell the sell group sell. Once they do, the price goes down, and you buy up as much as you can afford. Then you tell the buy group buy. Right after they put all their money in, you pull yours out and skip town. By doing this you create the illusion of useful information; and, by means of a valid form of reasoning, inference from repeated examples, you duped people out of their money. You, of course, would never do this, and now hopefully you won't fall for it either.[3] Evidence without counterevidence to balance and test it is a straight line to delusional thinking and frequently to disaster.

The problem with inductive proof is that there are lots of ways to fake the data, cherry picking the examples being one of the most common. So always scrutinize the example. Ask for more examples. Ask yourself, Is this example relevant, Is it representative, Is it sufficient on its own if they can't produce more? Is there anything about the context that invalidates it as an example or that raises questions? Can you find something identical? If you can, is it identical or just very similar? And most importantly, what is the counterevidence?

There is another problem with inductive reasoning that doesn't require thieves and liars to wreck your day. This is called the infinite regress. How do you know when you have identified every possible specimen and therefore can be certain you know what they all have in common, the essence of the specimen? The problem is you can't be sure you have. The famous example is the black swan. It was once thought that *All swans are white* was a completely sound premise because, up until then, no one had ever seen anything but white swans. And then one day someone found a black swan in Australia. The ornithological community was dumfounded. What they had known as absolutely, indisputably true prior to the black swan observation was just wrong after the observation.

---

3. If you find con games interesting, you might want to read David W. Maurer's *The Big Con: The Story of the Confidence Man.*

Unless you have a finite set of specimens, you cannot infer an essential quality. But the set of specimens is almost never finite. Ultimately we just don't know for certain anything that we know by induction. How do you know the sun will come up tomorrow? Because it always has. Sure, but we don't know it will tomorrow. It's ultimately about perspective. If you are a chicken and every day the nice woman with the pail comes and gives you something to eat, you come to think, "Nice lady with pail equals food," until one day you come running and she grabs you by the head and shoulders and wrings your neck, at which point "nice lady with pail" becomes "chicken strangler," but by then you're dinner. The one deviation that mattered was invisible to you because your data was incomplete. The problem with life is that our data is almost always incomplete, and our perspectives are always changing.[4]

Below is a partial list of some of the more common errors in reasoning. It's worth going over the list and then looking for real-life examples of as many as you can find.

Common errors in reasoning

The most important thing to remember is that calling an argument a "fallacy" is little better than insulting the person who used the fallacy. If the label pops into your head, don't just blurt it out. Use it as a mnemonic device for a specific disproof. The point of persuasion is to improve the thinking of a group or community, not to seize an advantage by triumphantly pointing out an error. Rarely will logic alone talk anybody into or out of anything.

Below is a list of the fallacies you are most likely to come across. You should make an effort to remember these and then look for examples in everyday life, on TV, on the web, when you're arguing with friends in a café, whenever.

> **Authority:** Asserting that something must be true because someone who ought to know says it is true. Without something to back up the assertion of authority, the argument is weak at best. You need to show the authority knows what she is talking about. In some fields, of course, arguments from authority constitute sufficient proof. If the question is over the meaning of a text and the person who wrote the text explains what she meant, then that should be pretty solid proof. If you are seeking medical advice, you might well accept a doctor's authoritative opinion with nothing more than a second opinion. In most spheres of persuasion authority is marginally useful. In some fields, like logic, authority is worthless. Arguments from authority ought to be worthless in science too, although you will often see some opinion supported with nothing more than, "As Nobel Prize winner X says, . . ."

---

4. See Kenneth Burke, *Permanence and Change*, pages 5–6.

Begging the question: Assuming the truth of an assertion you need to prove true. Begging in this sense does not mean asking for it. I know you hear that on TV constantly, and so if rules of use are determined by common practice, then, yes; but, if you want the educated people among your audience to see you as educated, don't preface a question by saying, "That begs the question . . . " More importantly, don't assume the truth of a proposition your audience won't accept without evidence.

Bias: Assuming something is true or false without necessary evidence. While biased thinking is basically unacceptable as far as it goes, see the list of cognitive biases and the section "Stereotypes" in Chapter 2 to see why bias is more complicated than often first thought.

Blind eye: Ignoring significant objections, flaws, facts, or counter-arguments. Again, while nothing to encourage, it's not easy to avoid beyond superficial levels in many instances. We just don't see things as clearly as we should, and we have a hard time taking a broad perspective on issues we feel strongly about. Remember the poor guy whose stock advisor was correct 100 percent of the time right up until she left town.

Celebrity: Saying that something must be true because a celebrated person says it is or has simply associated herself or himself with it. A great deal of advertising works this way, of course. Celebrity endorsements are everywhere. A person needn't be a bona fide celebrity to lead people's tastes. Most groups have one or two people whose opinions seem to carry greater weight. Advertisers sometimes call these people the tastemakers. You probably have one or two in your circle of friends and acquaintances. Whenever you see something endorsed where the strongest argument in its favor is that it is being endorsed, knit your brows.

Common practice: Saying something is the right thing to do because it is the thing most commonly done. Not just currently popular but a long-standing practice. To say "But this is how we've always done it" is a very weak argument. Often people will think that, if they need to do something, they should emulate what others have done. Why reinvent the wheel, they might ask. But that's not always a strong way to think. Context matters. Even though nearly all wheels are round, that doesn't mean that all wheels are the same, nor do all wheels function equally well in all terrains. Just because there's a common way doesn't mean you should necessarily follow it, especially if your only reason is because it's commonly done. So whenever anyone tries to convince you that you shouldn't reinvent the wheel, ask them why not.

Double standard: Evaluating two identical things using different criteria. As is often the case with the fallacies, we don't tend to apply double standards intentionally. We simply fail to treat two instances of something as identical because to us they didn't seem identical. If we think that men and women are fundamentally different, for example, then we might decide they should be treated differently, but in doing that we would be applying a double standard to the extent that all human beings are human beings regardless of gender.

Definition: Using incorrect or misleading definitions to defend an assertion.

Dilemma: Asserting that there are only two options when there are in fact more than two. If someone says you can have this or that, consider whether perhaps in fact you can have both. Or maybe you should embrace neither.

Distraction: Taking people's attention away from what matters or appearing to be working in one direction while actually working in another. Also sometimes called a red herring. When people know they can't win an argument or suspect that even in letting it play out their cause will suffer, they might bring up something else, typically something irresistible but irrelevant. A contemporary variation of this is the Internet meme "I have no idea what you are talking about so here is a picture of a cat." People sometimes introduce irrelevant material out of ignorance of the subject or confusion about its nature. Not all red herrings are red.

Epithet: Asserting that something is bad by calling it a bad name (or good by using nothing more than an honorific term). No evidence or reasons, just words designed to obtain a reaction. For example, pointing at an advisory who has just called your integrity into question and saying, "That's an ad hominem attack." Better to bolster your *ethos* by providing even stronger evidence and ignoring the childish outburst.

Exaggeration: Overstating the case. Basically this is making a wider claim for the power of a proof than the evidence warrants. While illogical, exaggeration can be persuasive, especially in its more humorous forms. If you call attention to the fact that you are exaggerating, you might entertain or otherwise disarm your audience, and thus you might make a point you don't have solid evidence to make otherwise. You should, however, think carefully about using such a technique before you do.

Fear: Saying that something must be true because the opposite would be too frightening to contemplate, using fear to make people believe or back down. Sometimes people will invoke this fallacy with the epithet "slippery slope," meaning that if you do something apparently benign, disaster will inevitably follow. As with many of these bad forms of argument, there may be appropriate uses for fear when it comes to persuasion. If you are trying to talk yourself or someone else out of smoking, for example, pictures of diseased tissue and heart bypass scars might work. Such images wouldn't be logical arguments, but because there is certainly a causal connection between smoking and disease, and quitting is a very healthy alternative, fear might be a legitimate tactic, especially when all addicts are adept at ignoring direct evidence of their bad choices.

Generalization: Saying that all members of a group exhibit the characteristics of many or even of only some. We all generalize from experience, from a limited set of data (see the section "Stereotypes" in Chapter 2). That's how we make sense of the world and how we remember things. But if we over-generalize, that is, assert that something that is true of a limited sample is true of all members of the class, then we are making a logical error and potentially a significant mistake. Before you generalize you need to know your sample is representative of the population in question and valid.

Ignorance: Saying that something must be true because it hasn't been proven false is not an effective way to back up an assertion. Saying that the Lock Ness Monster must exist because you can't prove it doesn't is not convincing because you are evading the burden of proof, which is to show that something does exist if you say it does when most other people think it doesn't. A heap of inconclusive evidence is not a form of proof, no matter how big the heap.

Incomplete: Leaving out important information or including only the information you want people to see, also known as cherry picking the evidence.

Misleading: Unfairly describing or explaining something, ignoring significant objections, saying things that lead people to make unwarranted assumptions or adopt unwarranted beliefs. The vitamins found in green leafy vegetables are known as antioxidants, and antioxidants slow the aging process, therefore you should take vitamin supplements if you want to slow the aging process. (*Wait a minute. Even if you can prove eating green leafy vegetables helps prolong life because of their antioxidant properties, that doesn't prove that you can synthesize the vitamins and get the same result.*)

Nature: Arguing that something is good because it is natural. Inferring values from facts only. Marijuana must be better than crack because crack is all chemicals, man, and pot grows naturally. (*Uh, no.*)

Non sequitur: Literally, that does not follow: drawing an unwarranted and usually irrelevant conclusion. There's an advertisement for DirecTV that riffs on the idea of a series of non sequiturs as adding up to a proof. (Google "Don't attend your own funeral" for an example.) A more common use is to offer an opinion when a measurement or an objective evaluation is required. If someone asks you if something is good and you list all the reasons you like it, strictly speaking you've offered a non sequitur.

Novelty: Anything new is good or better than anything older. Beware the word "innovation." Not everything said to be innovative is new, and not everything new is necessarily good (*or necessarily bad, right?*).

Order: Asserting that B must have been caused by A because A happened first. The Latin expression *post hoc ergo propter hoc* means "after this, therefore because of this."

Origin: Attacking the origin of a belief rather than the logic of the belief itself or thinking that something must be true because it came from the horse's mouth. By the way, do you know where that expression comes from? Do you think it might be related to looking a gift horse in the mouth? Anyway, lawyers refer to the origin fallacy and the poisoned well, where you imply that evidence is tainted because the source is tainted. Even a thieving rascal can tell the truth. And experts make mistakes.

Personal: Ad hominem, attacking the person. Asserting that an argument must be false because the person making it can't be trusted, because they are biased or immoral or from another country or from the city or from the country or whatever. The only legitimate use of this argument would be if you could prove that what was said was said by someone who was a pathological confabulist (or a pathological liar), someone who because of some kind of brain damage was incapable of telling the truth.

Pity: Using pity as an alternative to logic. Can I have an extension? My grandmother died. Concluding that your community needs to do something about mental illness after spending several hours serving soup in a homeless shelter.

Popularity: Something must be true because it is widely believed to be true. How would you relate the concept of popular opinion to this fallacy? And what about a constitutional amendment? Well, a constitutional amendment wouldn't make it true, but it would make it law. Remember that logic has a narrow range of application.

Poverty: Something is true because a poor person asserts it—the honest poor, arguments from the salt of the earth. The opposite of poverty is wealth, and we also sometimes encounter arguments from wealth, that is that something must be good because someone rich thinks it is or got rich doing it. Can you imagine us electing a middle- or working-class person to the office of president?

Ridicule: Asserting that something must be true because only idiots and children think otherwise. You can do this by accident by using expressions like "plainly" or "obviously" or "as anyone can see." As with all of these fallacies, just because people use ridicule doesn't mean what they said isn't true. It only means they haven't offered logical evidence to support their assertion. If you Google "The Wire, The King stay [*sic*][5] the King," you will find a great example of an argument from ridicule that is asserting an ultimate truth although by invalid means.

Simultaneity: Asserting two things are related because they happened at the same time. The world is full of coincidences, far more than most of us are happy accepting as such because accepting events as coincidental amounts to embracing the random nature of events, and that conflicts with the narratives of coherence and meaning that we rely on for our sense of well-being and control.

Slippery slope: Argument against taking a specific action on the grounds that it will lead to disaster when in fact there's no proof that it will start a chain reaction. The idea of a gateway drug is an example. The domino effect of communism is a very old example.

Straw dog: Asserting that you must be right because the opposition is wrong, when you in fact constructed the opposing point of view in a very weak form. I had the audacity to accuse Plato of this in his dialogue *Gorgias*, in the introduction to this book. When you manufacture or imagine an opposition, do it thoroughly. Don't put words that no one ever said in a mouth that never drew breath.

---

5. In case nobody ever told you, the expression *sic* is an abbreviation for "sic erat scriptum" or "thus was it written." When you use that expression, you are signaling to a reader that you know what you quoted is wrong in some way, typically, as in the case above, grammatically incorrect. Grammatically, the above expression should be "the King stays the King." But that's not the way it was written.

Tautology: A circular argument. Asserting that something is true because something synonymous is true. Basically, saying something that amounts to X is X. We sometimes use the tautology "It is what it is" as a kind of proof, a maxim that supports a decision to let something happen because it seems inevitable. You want to avoid unintentional tautologies and use the devise sparingly.

Tradition: Saying that something must be true because it has always been assumed true is not an effective way to back up an assertion, unless of course you are dealing with traditional people, in which case tradition takes precedence over nearly anything.

Wealth: Something is true or good because rich people say it is or believe it or act on it. If the richest woman in the world is investing in gold, you should be to, eh?

Wishful thinking: Asserting that something must be true (or false) because you want it to be true or false, and that's your only reason. We do this all the time, in lots of different ways. Some people call it optimism.

Your Turn

Spend a week hunting examples of fallacious thinking, and put them in an electronic notebook using the name of the fallacy as a key word. Look for both obviously bad and paradoxically good uses of fallacious thinking.

Do an Internet search for "fallacies," and see if any interesting and therefore memorable examples surface.

An interesting collaborative project might be to create a test bank, where you offer a series of examples and ask, "Which fallacy is this?" Another option along the same lines might be to create a deck of electronic flash cards, or just plain old-fashioned flash cards if that's still your thing. I'm not suggesting flash cards because memorizing the names of fallacies is useful, but rather the facility with recognizing examples is.

Toulmin's Model of Argumentation

In addition to reading against the grain and hunting for logical fallacies, you can come to a deeper understanding of the value of an argument by identifying and labeling its parts. This is known as a markup procedure. To mark up a text you need a document object model—a list of all the parts that can go into the kind of text you are analyzing. By marking up or labeling each element in a given text you can see if any of the parts are missing or if it fails to conform to the model. There is no document object model for persuasion because persuasive acts are rarely purely textual, and they can be made out of too many different parts to conform to a single model. Arguments, on the other hand, do have models; and, because arguments are an important subset of persuasive acts, we're going to spend some time learning how to mark them up. But first we need to look at two models, one simple and one complex.

An argument is a debatable assertion followed by a reason to believe the assertion is true. For example, "You should get a university degree because a person with a university degree will earn a million dollars more on average over a lifetime." The first part of that sentence, "You should get a university degree," is the assertion. Everything after "because" is reason to believe the assertion is true. This basic model of argument (assertion + reason to believe the assertion) is known as an *enthymeme*. If you read the above enthymeme with the grain, you might have just nodded approval. Yes, a university degree is a good idea. But by agreeing, did you actually accept the argument or just the assertion? In other words, were you already nodding by the time you finished reading "degree," or did you remain skeptical until you read "a million dollars?" If you waited for the million dollars before you agreed, you bought the argument. If you agreed before the reason to agree was offered, you were being too passive.

Now if you go back and read the enthymeme against the grain, you will stop at the end of the assertion, "You should get a university degree," and start asking questions. "You [*Me? Me in particular or everyone in general?*] should get [*buy?*] a university degree [**Any degree from any university?**]." Then once you get to the reason-to-believe part of the enthymeme, the part after "because," you will have more questions—so many, in fact, I'm not going to put them in square brackets but rather just write them out. What does "on average" mean? How big was the sample from which they generated this average? How representative of the entire educated population was the sample? And why "should" I want to make a million dollars more over my lifetime? Will making a million dollars more over my lifetime make me a happier person? I guess I can't argue with the assertion that a million dollars more means I will be a richer person. If I live to be seventy and I graduate at twenty-two, that's about $21,000 a year more, and that's a pretty significant annual difference, but what does "richer" mean? Will twenty-one grand a year make me happier? And come to think of it, if I have to spend $10,000 a year to pay off my college loans, $21,000 will be only $11,000 for a while into the future. And then, too, were opportunity costs factored into the original equation?

Once you start asking questions of an enthymeme, the simple assertion + reason structure breaks down. The virtue of an enthymeme is that it is very efficient. It makes an assertion, often one that isn't likely to cause much controversy, and then quickly offers a reason to believe the assertion, also often just a statement that the author assumes the audience won't reject. If the audience is passive, reading with the grain, or if the assertion isn't very controversial or the evidence is compelling, then the argument's work is done in a single sentence. However, if the audience is skeptical or the assertion is controversial enough that even passive readers are startled into looking closely at the reason, then the enthymeme presents a potential problem because the reason rests on a number of unspoken assumptions. If the audience stops to question those assumptions, the enthymeme loses its argumentative power. And if the audience actually objects to the assumptions, then the enthymeme generated a controversy, which is the opposite of what an argument is supposed to do. Arguments are supposed to settle a dispute or end a disagreement, not generate a controversy.

Skeptical people, people who read against the grain, *rhetors*, in other words, need the assumptions spelled out and supported with evidence before they will agree. Skeptics want more highly elaborated arguments than enthymemes. They want assertions followed by reasons followed by reasons to accept the reasons that support the assertions.

For hundreds of years in the Western tradition of education, educated people preferred syllogisms to enthymemes as the building blocks of arguments on the grounds (*notice the metaphor?*) that a syllogism spells everything out. There's a major premise, a minor premise, and a conclusion. The argument may or may not be true, and it may or may not be formally accurate, but at least it's all there. The classic example, as I pointed out in the section on logic, is

> Socrates is a man.
> All men are mortal.
> Socrates is mortal.

The enthymemic version of that syllogism would be "Socrates is mortal because he's a man." You would just assume the "all men are mortal" part. Who could argue with the mortality of a living thing? But as that example shows, you could just make the assertion Socrates is mortal and leave it at that because no audience member who knows what living and dying mean would doubt that if Socrates is alive he will die. The assertion is enough. We don't need any evidence to support it. The problem with syllogisms is that they more often than not prove the obvious. Once we get away from the white board and out into the world, we need a more flexible but no less thorough form of argument to work with.

Back in 1958, Stephen Toulmin provided a model of argumentation that has become a standard tool for analyzing and creating arguments.

If you've ever heard someone ask, "What warrants that claim?" you've heard someone using Toulmin's model of argumentation. The model looks like this:

Argument = Claim + Data + Warrant + Backing + Rebuttal + Modal

To flesh that out a bit,

1. **Claim**: assertion to be proven

2. **Data**: evidence to support the validity of the claim (also sometimes called *grounds*)

3. **Warrant**: reason to believe the evidence warrants (justifies or at least endorses) belief in the claim

4. *Backing*: support for relevance, accuracy, cogency of the warrant; sometimes answers a plausible next question; thus links the warrant to the data.

5. *Rebuttal*: handling anticipated objections or counterarguments

6. **Modal**: level of commitment you think the argument should elicit— certainty, probability, plausibility, a grudging nod, derisive laughter

You will see why I used the coding in a minute.

Any given argument may contain some or all of these pieces. The pieces do not need to go in a specific order. The claim might come first, in which case you have something that looks like a deductive argument. Or it might come last, in which case it might look like an inductive argument, especially if you had lots of examples for the data section. The warrant might precede the data, and you might choose to deal with the rebuttals first, especially if you are going to argue for something you know your audience is likely to struggle against. The order, as I said, does not affect the validity of your argument, but it might affect the intelligibility or the cogency of it. If you put the warrant before the data, the details might distract a general audience, for example. Experts, on the other hand, that is, people who like to generate data, are primarily interested in the details of how the data were generated and how they can be replicated or at least verified. Everyone else is interested in the bottom line, or the takeaway, that is in the implications of the data. This is the most significant differ- ence between writing to experts and writing to a general audience, by the way. If you are communicating with experts, focus on the data. If you are communicating with a general audience, focus on the implications of the data.

Below are a couple of examples of Toulmin-like arguments that are marked up, or labeled, using the coding scheme from earlier so that you can see each part in isolation while still seeing the argument as a whole. This example is adapted from Toulmin's *The Uses of Argument,* Chapter 3:

> **Harry is a British subject**. **Harry was born in Bermuda**. Since a man born in Bermuda will generally be a British subject, presumably Harry is a British subject. *He might have become a citizen of another country,* or *his parents might have been aliens, which would mean he never was a British subject.*

Another example:

> **You should move to San Diego**. **San Diego has three hundred sunny days a year, nearly no humidity, and it's never more than eighty-five degrees for very long.** You have seasonal affective disorder. You hate gloomy, rainy days. And you hate heat and humidity. Seriously, you should go. *Well, okay, so I made up the sunny days statistic, and I don't have an almanac or anything,* but really you should go there and see for yourself.

And another:

> **University students should be allowed to carry guns**. **Universities are dangerous places: Charles Whitman (University of Texas, Austin, 1966), Gang Lu (University of Iowa, 1991), Frederick Martin Davidson (San Diego State University, 1996), Cho Seung-Hui (Virginia Tech University, 2007), Kshitij Shrotri (Georgia Tech University, 2010).** In each of these cases the assailant had time to do maximum damage because it took time for police and tactical teams to arrive. *Help would arrive immediately if every student were armed*: Definitely, handguns for all university students.

━━━━━ Your Turn

Okay, so now take the enthymeme, "You should get a university degree because a person with a university degree earns a million dollars more on average over a lifetime," and see if you can expand it to fit Toulmin's model. Supply the data, the warrant(s), the backing, and the modal, making sure to address potential objections (the rebuttal) along the way. Just invent the missing parts using your imagination. Or, if you want to be rigorous, get better data by researching income as it relates to education. Once you're finished with the education = money argument, go find some argumentative articles and mark up a few of their paragraphs.

The best way to benefit from the analytical power of Toulmin's model is to use it every day until it becomes a habitual way of reading. Spend an hour every day reading and marking up editorials and essays in magazines (short pieces of text with an argumentative bent). Use colored markers or pens and highlight or underline the parts of each argument (not in a library book, of course). Or get an electronic copy and use your word processor's highlight function or an app like iAnnotate to mark up the text.

You will notice very quickly that really thorough arguments, ones that have all of the parts, are quite rare outside of university settings. The vast majority of editorials that I've read lack data and are really nothing more than a string of assertions that the writer assumes any reasonable person would have to accept as true, like the Anne Coulter piece. (*Not sure you agree with me? Excellent. Mark up this last paragraph.*)

While Toulmin's model is a powerful analytical tool that allows you to find holes in other people's arguments, it also has a great deal of generative power, helping you develop your own arguments. After you've spent some time marking up other people's articles, you should spend half an hour just working up arguments at random to develop your skills to the point where creating strong arguments becomes natural or automatic. Start with a claim (an assertion); turn it into an enthymeme by providing a reason to believe the assertion; and then insert the appropriate data, back up that data, and say why that data is accurate and relevant. Next, anticipate and deal with potential objections, and then finally decide how much commitment you now have to your original claim. You will have moved from a single sentence to a complete paragraph. And you will have a more thorough argument.

Once you have generated a few of these fully developed paragraphs, take the markups out and share them with someone else to see how persuasive he or she thinks they are.

Critical Thinking

Because this book is about persuasion, it is also a book about critical thinking. To be persuasive you need to know both how to produce and how to consume persuasive communications. *Writing is about production; critical thinking (and reading against the grain) is about consumption.* It's important to keep in mind, however, that you are also a consumer of your own persuasive efforts. You need to think critically about them as well.

People sometimes have a hard time getting started thinking about critical thinking because they misunderstand the expression. In everyday speech, the word *critical* means something like "finding fault" or "refusing to appreciate" or "judging harshly." Thus when people hear the expression "critical thinking," they think *criticizing*, like a scolding parent, and they automatically think it's a bad thing. It isn't. The word *critical* also carries with it the idea of immediate danger, as in the expression "critical care unit" or "The patient is critical," and, as a result, sometimes when people hear the expression "critical thinking" they think urgency or the need for a quick decision. Critical thinking actually takes time. Alternatively, if we say something is *critical* we mean "very important." This third connotation comes from the fact that "critical" and "crisis" are etymologically related. A *crisis* is actually a turning point, a decisive moment, a fork in the road. And this connotation is a useful one. *Critical thinking is about making good decisions about what to think and what to say and what to do and developing justifications for those decisions.*

A secondary impediment to improved critical thinking is the idea that we are born as intelligent as we will ever be, that practice and technique can't improve a person's critical thinking skills. Similar arguments are sometimes made about writing and about speaking and about sports and music as well. "Geniuses are born, not made," as the saying goes. If you believe this, quit now. Schooling of any kind is useless if talent is innate. I didn't learn to read until I was in the fourth grade. And I never learned to spell. I'm dyslexic. And I'm an English professor. I don't think talent is innate. I think some people are born with advantages, greater symmetry and balance and strength when it comes to sports, a better ear when it comes to music, a quicker wit when it comes to thinking and speaking, but gifts are wasted without constant training and deliberate practice; and critical thinking, like any other skillful activity, can be improved.[6]

When we think (as opposed to when we think critically), we start with a belief and look for evidence to confirm it. Psychologists call this failure of thinking *confirmation bias*. If we are really focused on an idea, we may fail to see anything else. Psychologists refer to this as *attentional blindness*, and there's a famous study called "The Invisible Gorilla" that dramatizes the point that you can miss something important because you are focused on looking for something different. Google "Invisible Gorilla Video" and watch the students playing basketball.

Trusting your initial impressions, your gut, isn't always bad, especially if a decision is urgent. The conclusion to "Jump back!" based on a snarling sound coming from rustling bushes is perfectly good thinking, maybe even life-saving thinking. Thinking critically at such a moment might be dangerously counterproductive: analysis paralysis. But what if the sign you take for a disturbing indicator of danger does not signify anything dangerous at all? What if the snarling beast in the bushes is just a terrier with a rat in its mouth?

---

6. See *The Road to Excellence: The Acquisition of Expert Performance in the Arts and Sciences, Sports and Games*, by K. Anders Ericsson. If you don't have time for that, read Daniel Coyle's *The Talent Code*.

The difference between what you imagine exists and what actually exists can be discovered by critical thinking as long as you are willing to engage in it. Impatience and overconfidence are two of the greatest impediments to critical thinking. Fear is probably the greatest. For more on thinking with your gut, read the section in Chapter 4, "Intuition—pattern recognition."

While many of us are happy to find the holes in other people's reasoning, we are less eager to find holes in our own. If we do, we have to change our minds and admit we were wrong, and most of us hate that, so much so that we often revise our past thoughts to conform to our present thinking. It's called hindsight bias. In a few pages, in the section called "Cognitive Biases," I'll give you detailed description of how our thought processes sometimes hamper critical thinking.

Another form of uncritical thinking exploits the fact that as humans we prefer coherence to confusion, and so we are quite willing to accept an inaccurate or even false explanation of something merely because it makes sense to us. We tend to prefer a plausible lie to a difficult truth, as Aristotle said. The problem here is sometimes compounded by that fact that we sometimes make good decisions based on coherent but false understandings. Analogical thinking draws a conclusion about one thing based on a conclusion you have drawn about something similar to but not identical to that thing. So, for example, if it's true that training a dog to be obedient requires that the dog has consistent boundaries, you might think that providing children with consistent boundaries will make them good also. And you might be right. But of course dogs are not children, and obedience and goodness are not identical, so the analogy is a problematic one. The biggest problem, however, is that the analogy made sense. We make relatively successful decisions all day long based on problematic analogies and don't have to stop to wonder until something goes wrong because we didn't notice the analogy was only an analogy. (The two things were similar, not identical.)

Another example of a failed analogy has to do with writing and commas. When people are first learning to write they often assume that commas are placed where one would pause to breathe while speaking. But this isn't so. There are ten rules for using commas, and none of them have to do with pausing to breathe. After all, reading isn't speaking out loud—unless you've never learned to read silently.

Whenever something seems to make sense instantly, we are less likely to question it, and thus we may make inaccurate inferences. Psychologists refer to this effect as the *illusion of coherence*, and it's an important idea to keep in mind. Have you ever tried to explain something to yourself, say something someone did or something that happened, and come up with what you thought was a perfect explanation only to be proved wrong by a later development or a further insight? A common example might be that because you did well in high school you will do well in college. High school and college are both learning environments, of course, so you might be right. But they are not identical learning environments, and so you might be wrong. You might need to change the way you think in order to succeed in college. You will definitely have to become more independent and more self-motivating.

Critical thinker*s ask useful questions and test the validity of competing answers before making a decision, rendering a judgment, or expressing a belief.* Critical thinkers are not necessarily argumentative. They may keep their skepticism to themselves, but they don't take anything at face value, and they resist the urge to believe something just because they want to or disbelieve something because they want to. *If you are thinking critically, you are looking for and evaluating evidence before you decide what to do or think or say.*

So if you want to develop a reputation for being a critical thinker (if you want people to think you are smart and have opinions worth listening to), *insist on evidence, and learn how to assess its value.* You will make increasingly better decisions and learn to see the world more clearly. As you work to develop your capacity to think critically, keep in mind that what counts as valid evidence differs from discipline to discipline. What counts in computer science might be useless in biology. The same is true of writing, by the way. English scholars don't write the way chemists or even historians do. Once you get out of your core classes, you may need to retool, but there are some cross-disciplinary heuristics when it comes to generalized critical thinking.

The fastest way to become a more critical thinker is to get in the habit of asking two questions: What is the evidence, and how persuasive is it? Once you've discovered the evidence (both for and against), you need to test that evidence before deciding whether it is enough to warrant a decision or an action or a new belief. By testing the evidence I mean asking a series of questions based on the kind of evidence you find. I will give you several specific examples, but basically you want to know

1. Is the evidence relevant?

2. Is the evidence reliable?

Beyond that, the circumstances, the audience, and the subject matter determine what further inquiry is required. If a decision has to be made quickly, never an ideal situation but common in many realms of life (ER, air traffic control, etc.) signs or symptoms might be enough to go on without the further testing that would verify the evidence. If time and resources permit, one might choose to go with a much greater level of scrutiny in order to get a higher level of commitment. If an audience is knowledgeable, additional and perhaps more complex evidence can be provided. But if they are not, you might need to offer less evidence or even an analogical representation of the evidence—a chart or a picture that simplifies the evidence in order to enable a more dramatic inference.

While the two primary questions (Is the evidence relevant, and is it reliable?) will get you started, different kinds of evidence require different lines of inquiry. Below are several checklists to help you assess the validity of certain kinds of evidence. Think through each of them carefully as you read; decide how each one works and what is missing.

━━━━━ Your Turn

But before we move on, think back to the moment when you decided to attend the college you attended. How did you make that decision, and to what extent do you think it qualifies as an act of critical thinking?

Think up as many false analogies as you can, and then compare your list to someone else's. If you are having trouble coming up with examples, explain the assertion "The elderly are childlike," which contains a potentially disastrous false analogy.

Checklist for assessing eyewitness testimony

Is the witness credible?

Was he or she there? This might seem obvious. How can anybody be a witness if they weren't there? Strangely enough, however, because our memories are fallible (see the section "Memory" in Chapter 3 for details), we are capable of thinking we saw things we didn't. Have you ever heard someone say they saw what you know to be an urban legend? Like maybe a black lion? Or maybe you've had someone tell you they read a story about how Starbucks refused to give coffee to the U.S. Marines. These are verifiably urban legends. There are dozens of things people think they saw but couldn't have seen. So you can't just ask, "What did you see?" You have to determine that they were there, and you need evidence that they were there at the right time on the right day.

How can you be sure they saw and heard what they say they saw and heard? Could their view have been obstructed?

How far away were they?

Could noise or other distractions have distorted what they heard?

Do the witnesses have any biases that might distort their perceptions? There are a great many wrongly imprisoned people who are incarcerated as a result of eyewitness testimony, simply because we have greater confidence in what we think we see than what our capacity to really see warrants. Distortions are caused by expectations and stereotypes and stress. Once you've read the section on cognitive biases you will see that controlling for bias is far more complicated than is often realized.

What motivates the testimony? Although strictly speaking irrelevant, knowing why people say they saw something might give you reason to doubt or believe them. If the person who claims to be a witness is clearly harming their self-interest by witnessing, either perhaps by admitting to being somewhere they shouldn't have been or involving themselves in something unpleasant or unfortunate, then you might have more reason to believe their testimony. But of course sometimes people will suffer a considerable harm to help someone they love or to fulfill some strange personal need that the average person can't readily imagine. So motivation isn't enough, but it can be helpful for determining the validity of a witness's testimony or at least the weight you will want to place on it. Also keep in mind that people do the wrong thing for the right reasons sometimes, too. Sometimes people just want to be helpful so they say what they think people want to hear. Ask yourself, Does she have reason to lie? Does she have reason to tell the truth?

How long ago did it happen? Memories change over time. We fill in gaps to make the stories we tell more coherent, and we may even unwittingly add details that are logical consequences of what we remember in general but not actual details of the event. While a time lapse doesn't necessarily increase these distortions, it is a very good idea to get the witnesses to explain why they know they saw what they say they saw and not accept a firm "Because that's what I saw!" as an answer.

Are there additional witnesses? While it might seem obvious that if ten people saw something you have better reason to believe it than if just one did, you need to keep groupthink and collective delusions in mind. If the witnesses were questioned separately, so that what one person said couldn't possibly have affected what another person said, and you know for certain they never discussed the event, then you've got more reliable testimony than if there's a chance they normed their stories based on conversation. People have a tendency to go with what others are doing, and a particularly eloquent or insistent speaker can inadvertently alter other people's memories.

Can the witnesses' testimony be corroborated by other evidence? Arguably this is the most important question. You cannot rely on the vividness of the details the witness provides. Confidence is no measure of truth either. A person can bear false witness without lying.

▬▬▬ Your Turn

The power of distortion when it comes to memory and witnessing is worth spending some time researching. There are a number of famous cases of wrongful conviction on the basis of eyewitness testimony where the witness was completely believable and completely sincere and completely wrong. Perhaps the most famous case is Jennifer Thompson. Google "false memories by William Cromie," and then write a response to it. Then using Google scholar, search for "false memories" and see what kind of academic sources you can find that discuss the concept. You will need that list for the assignment following the next section.

Checklist for assessing arguments based on sources (authority)

Expert testimony can be very helpful in a number of different situations. If you don't know a subject well yourself or if you need to find a short path through a complicated and detailed collection of information, authorities can be helpful, but you need to know if the authority is trustworthy and credible. (*What's the difference by the way?*) There are a number of questions, the answers to which can help you decide.

> ***Does this author have the correct credentials?*** Authority can come from many places, from age and experience in some cultures. But for us, authority comes primarily from education, and credentials attest to education. So if a person claims to be an authority on a subject, you need to know where they studied and what degree they received, and even when they received it might be helpful because retraining and recertification is important in fields where new information is constantly being discovered. Credentials are a good starting place, but they are never enough, and there's a tendency to misunderstand their actual value. Some people think, for example, that a person who received a degree from a prestigious university is a more reliable source of information than a person with the same degree from a less prestigious place, like a Cambridge BA is better than a Washington State BA, and therefore the Cambridge graduate must be smarter than the Washington State graduate. This is not critical thinking because it's confusing a brand with an actual quality and human beings with manufactured products. A person with no formal training at all might have a much better understanding than others who do have formal

training. The point about credentials is that they are a legitimate form of weak evidence regarding a person's credibility regarding the subject they are credentialed in. Credentials are evidence not proof of credibility.

Has the author published frequently in the field before? While it's at best a weak proof of value for any given article, if the author has had frequent success getting published in the past, you can reasonably expect a recent offering is reasonably high quality. But be careful here, too. Some people are so well known in their field that they can publish anything they put their name on, even stuff that's not very good. And yet, while frequency of publication increases the likelihood that a given author's work is credible, there are academic equivalents of one-hit wonders. Even if a person only has one article, that article might be really good or really helpful even if it isn't all that good because no one else has done anything in the area yet.

Is the source peer reviewed? Academics fervently believe in the value of having peers in a field review, assess, and accept or reject work submitted for publication without the reviewers knowing who the author is or, frequently, the author knowing who the reviewers are. The blind part of the process seems to ensure against favoritism and star power. So one question to ask of a source is, Was it blind peer reviewed or not? If you are really serious, look up the publication's rejection rate. If a journal rejects 90 percent of what it receives, it's probably more prestigious and, presumably, publishes better work than one that accepts 90 percent of what it receives. (*Did you notice the modal "presumably"?*)

Does the source of the work appear aimed at a popular or an expert audience? Again, this is a weak test at best but one worth considering. An article about the economy that's published in *USA Today* is probably not as credible as one appearing in the *Economist* and much less credible than something that appeared in, say, *Econometrica* or *American Economic Review*. The assumption here is that the article aimed at the general audience has to merely please or entertain or raise a ruckus with a wide range of relatively shallow and imperfectly informed opinions about the subject, whereas whatever appears in the more specialized venues has to impress experts in the field. The higher up you go on the ladder of rarified research articles, however, the more dependent you are becoming on the opinions of other experts, and the less you can rely on your own ability to evaluate the work on its merits, unless of course you are yourself an expert in the field. It is good to read above your head because that makes you

think, but it's ill advised to quote extensively from an article or book
you know you don't fully understand.

*Is the author talking about something they know about, or are
they lending their authority to something outside their realm
of expertise?* Believe it or not, people who have worked hard and
have been successful in school sometimes have a tendency to think
they know a lot about things outside their area of expertise, and
because they know how to write and speak with authority and confidence it's easy for us to believe that they are experts in things they
are not experts in. So the next time you see me making references to
economics, knit your brows.

*Do others in the field frequently cite the author you are
thinking of citing?* One way to cross-check an authority's authority is to look for citations of that person's work by other people in
the field. If other members of the discipline find the work valuable,
there's a better chance it is valuable. But here, too, you have to be
careful. Sometimes something is referred to often because everyone wants to refute it or use it as a negative example. Such "villain"
pieces have huge citation indexes but are not highly valued, just
highly useful.

Does the author reference credible sources? Look through the
works cited section to see on what previous work the author is
relying. Are there well-known sources there? Are they current and
from credible journals and organizations and presses? Does the list
seem comprehensive? Obviously this kind of assessment takes some
familiarity with the field, and you can't expect to know right away
whether an author's sources are any good, but if you make a point of
looking at works cited while you are doing research you will begin to
notice patterns that will become more and more useful.

*Is the author affiliated with known boards or academic
groups?* If a person is a member of a recognized professional board,
especially a national or an international one, that may be good evidence they are an authority on the subjects relevant to that board.
But you need to be careful. It is possible to be a member in good
standing just by paying your dues and never having been convicted
of a serious breach of conduct. Moreover, an academic group may
oversee a wider range of activities than any of its executive com-
mittees could oversee, and thus merely belonging might prove very
little about a member's authority.

Has the work won any significant awards? Typically prizes are
only awarded to work really worth something to a field, and thus

anyone who has won a prestigious prize can be safely considered an authority in that field. However, here too you have to be careful. Antonio Egas Moniz, the doctor who developed the lobotomy, was awarded the Nobel Prize for Medicine in 1949 for that procedure, but subsequent medical experience and research have proven that the procedure caused devastating and permanent psychological damage to the recipients; and, while calls for the prize to be revoked have been rejected by the Nobel Committee, the work itself is universally discredited and Dr. Moniz thoroughly disgraced.

Who paid for the research? While producing work that benefits the corporation or organization that paid for it doesn't necessarily discredit the source, any more than releasing damning evidence against the sponsoring agent proves the source credible (some whistle-blowers really are disgruntled former employees), you have to wonder if drug trials, for example, paid for by a company that will market the drug if it gets Food and Drug Administration approval, might have stacked the evidence in their favor. The tobacco companies spent millions of dollars on research into the effects of tobacco and used the results of that research and the fact that they were spending money on it to stall efforts to regulate tobacco. Even after the medical community had universally condemned the use of tobacco, the tobacco companies continued to sponsor research that found its way into scientific journals. So knowing who paid for the research can be instructive, but you also have to ask, Does who paid for it really matter?

What motivated the research? Even if the funding source is unquestionable, you may still wonder whether the research was undertaken to prove a point for ideological or commercial purposes. As with the financial question, motivation doesn't disprove the validity of a research finding, but you should be especially guarded when an organization publishes a finding that is particularly convenient for it.

Is the authority presenting their own research or summarizing someone else's? It is possible for people to work in areas outside their expertise, and so you have to check to make sure they haven't used past success to broaden their horizons or move beyond what they really know about. Again, while it is possible to do legitimate work outside one's area of expertise, you cannot safely accept that work on the basis that an authority performed it.

What is the date of publication? Some fields change more rapidly than others. An article in neuroscience that is ten years old is probably outdated, advances in magnetic resonance imaging (MRI) having made past work obsolete. Other fields, however, such as history, might not see a significant change for years. So a better check of the value of a source isn't so much its date but the frequency with which it is cited. If everything written in the last three years refers to a paper ten years old, that paper still matters. On the other hand, if a paper came out last month but everything cited in it is ten years old, you have to wonder how current the information is. But remember to ask yourself, Does currency really matter?

Does the author's language betray a bias? If the author uses language that a reasonable person would reject, then you have to wonder how reliable the author's evidence is.

Does the author construct straw dogs or attribute opinions to an imaginary opposition that no reasonable person would actually hold? Again, you have to wonder about someone who seems to be stacking the deck in his favor. You can make a position seem more reasonable by disproving objections to it, but if the objections are weak or irrelevant, you're not really defending the position and you run the risk of offending people who have better reasons to reject the position than the ones you just demolished.

Does the author ignore reasonable objections or reject evidence that should be dealt with? This weakness is essentially the same as the one above, only instead of demolishing a weak argument, one ignores a damaging piece of evidence or legitimate counterargument. People who fail or refuse to take the opposition seriously and to show they do by correctly voicing the opposition's objections, infuriate those who disagree with them and confuse or mislead those as yet undecided. Generally speaking, whenever you encounter an argument that is defended against weak or irrelevant opposing arguments, be suspicious.

Does the author follow something like Toulmin's model? If an article or book contains mostly assertions and offers little in the way of data or warrants for supporting the data it does provide then you need to wonder if the source is credible. Similarly, if there are assertions that a reasonable person might find doubtful and the author fails to acknowledge this or dismisses without proof the value of such doubts, you should doubt the credibility of the source because it suggests either the author doesn't have the data to support their position or they don't understand the material well enough to explain it fully. And yet, just because you require evidence in places where the author doesn't offer any does not necessarily invalidate the work. You have to wonder if the author left that evidence out because they don't have it or because they didn't imagine someone in their audience would need it.

━━━━━━━ # Your Turn

If you did the previous assignment, you should have a handful of articles about "false memories" written by scholars. Do a background search on the authors of these papers to see whether or not you can establish that they are authorities in the field.

━━━━━━━━━━

Checklist for assessing the credibility of websites

There is nothing necessarily wrong with information you find online. Some people think that information found in books and in libraries must be superior because someone selected that information, purchased it (often at considerable expense), and so must have been an expert; therefore whatever is in a library is authoritative. On the other hand, anyone for very little money can post anything online, and thus the ratio of noise to information on the web must be higher. Such thinking isn't very critical in that it assumes that cost validates authority, and together they guarantee quality. Regardless of where you find the information you are thinking about trusting, you need to ask the questions of authority outlined above. In addition, if you found the information online, you need to ask some website-specific questions because it is true that anyone can post anything online.

> *Is the website domain a .org, a .com, or a .net?* The domain may tell you something, like whether or not the organization is a for-profit organization (.com) or a not-for-profit organization (.org), but anyone can buy any kind of domain name (.edu and .gov are the exceptions), so the extension is a weak test at best.

> *How professional does the site look?* There was a time ten years ago when a slick and sleek interface suggested that whoever put up the website had the money to hire a web design team, and that would suggest they were a legitimate source of information. That was less than critical thinking then, but it is even less critical thinking now because you can buy a fine looking template for nearly nothing. Yes, appearances are deceptive. Assess the information rather than the presentation of it.

> *How much similar information is on the site?* If a website is entirely devoted to one subject and has a great deal of information about that one thing and perhaps a few closely related things, then it would seem that the authors are dedicated to that work. They may still be clueless, but they are more likely to be clueless if they are writing outside what they usually write about.

Is the information original to this site, or have they leached it from somewhere else? This is a weak test of credibility, but, if you find information that's been reposted from somewhere else, try to find the original post and assess its credibility. Go to the origin of the information. *Always remember that the best test of credibility is the value of the evidence itself, not the source of the evidence.*

Is the website linked to by other sites you already have good reason to trust? Credibility can be inherited. If you have reason to trust a website, you may be able to transfer your trust to the sites it cites. However, third-party testimony is very indirect evidence, and as such you need to discount it a bit. "Like father like son" may be true, but if you were wrong about the father you will be wrong about the son.

Is the individual or organization that runs the site identifiable? If not, that's a bad sign. If so, who are they, and what evidence can you find that they know what they are doing? Read the "About" screen and the small print at the bottom of every website you are thinking about getting information from. And follow the URL to the index page of the site, to make sure that you haven't found some dark corner the site's owners don't know anything about.

Is the website a single-authored blog? Blogging software, the software that makes it easy for anyone to publish their opinions to the web, is free and easy to use, with the result that there are hundreds of thousands of blogs on the Internet. You are bound to find a few while searching for evidence to support your arguments. As always, question the evidence first. But if the evidence seems plausible (and not just because you agree with it), find out more about the author. Look at how long the blog's been around and how often it's updated. Check what subjects it specializes in. Look at the quality of the comments, and see who else has linked to the blog.

Can you find corroborating evidence elsewhere? This is the cardinal question of all evaluation processes. While it is possible for errors to become embedded in a culture, the more often something is cited, the more credible it might be. Having said that, however, I want to take it back. Culturally embedded errors are much more frequent than you might imagine. There's a commonly held belief, for example, that if a right-handed person looks up to the right just before they answer a question, they are invoking the left hemisphere of their brain and therefore fabricating the answer. That is to say, they are lying. Lot's of people will tell you this is true. They are all mistaken. At best the up-to-the-right idea is a vast oversimplification. Corroboration is handy, but it's not foolproof.

▬▬▬ Your Turn

Wikipedia information isn't any more or less reliable than what you find in a bound encyclopedia. But if you are thinking about quoting it directly, consider your audience first. Some people are suspicious of online resources, *Wikipedia* especially. Professors tend to look down on it because it is possible for anyone (non-experts) to edit an entry. So look for corroboration in an authorized source, and quote that instead, just to be safe.

But because we are on the topic of critical thinking, and because we are getting used to the practice of reading against the grain, let's stop to think about this opinion that a source like *Wikipedia* must be inferior to a source like, say, *Britannica*.[7] The hide-bound encyclopedia (*Is the epithet "hide-bound" an example of loaded language?*) was compiled by a team of editors who asked experts in each field to write the entries. Once printed, the information can't be updated without a new printing, which is expensive and time consuming, so the editors needed to get it right from the start. Once the book is printed, a person can write in the margins or pull out a whole page, but he or she can't alter the printed entry itself. In an open-source and crowd-sourced document like *Wikipedia*, on the other hand, one needn't be an expert to edit or even create an entry. Anybody can say anything. The information isn't just of dubious authority; it isn't even stable because anybody can edit it at any time for any reason. People deface entries all the time. What's there can change overnight.

Okay, we just covered a weak defense of the standard professor's position on *Wikipedia*. Now write the counterargument. Then see if you can write a stronger version of the professor's argument I gave you. In case you're still uncertain about how to proceed, here's a leading question: Can a thousand amateurs be better (*Don't forget to read against the grain. What does "better" mean in this case? Smarter? More informed?*) than one expert?

▬▬▬▬▬▬

Checklist for assessing arguments based on survey data

While arguments from authority are common, perhaps the most common arguments you will find are arguments based on survey data. If you watch the news or read popular media, you are bound to hear opinion poles quoted constantly. How can you tell if the data from a given survey is reliable?

---

7. When I wrote this sentence two years ago, *Britannica* was still being printed. It now (April 2013) lives exclusively online, although I am certain it isn't and never will be crowd-sourced.

How large was the sample? If you asked two people what the best movie of 2012 was and one person said *Midnight in Paris*, you could say in all honestly 50 percent of people surveyed thought *Midnight in Paris* was the best movie of 2012. Try it now. Ask the person next to you what the best film of this year is. Now survey the whole class. Where did your first respondent's choice rank in the larger set of the whole class's answers? What would the result be if you asked the whole school? Would the top three movies of your class remain the top three?

How was the sample acquired? Survey firms buy mailing lists from companies that keep tabs on their customers. But customers from one particular company might be a self-selected sample. The people who shop at Walmart are said to be politically different from people who shop at Target. If you wanted to sell PCs, would you be happy with an Apple mailing list? What limitations might data gathered from Twitter have?

Is the survey sample probabilistic,[8] or is it inadvertently selected in some way? For the evidence provided by a survey to be reliable, the people interviewed have to be a legitimate representation of the population in question. If you want to know what people think about an upcoming election and you conduct phone interviews using the phone book to find out, even if you get a huge number of respondents you don't have a probabilistic sample because all of your respondents answered a landline. The relevant people who have given up their landlines in favor of a cell-phone-only existence were inadvertently excluded from your sample. So even though you might reach a broad cross-section of the population by phone, it would still only be a broad cross-section of the people who still have a landline—which isn't a truly random sample.

To what extent can the sample be called "representative"? Can you be sure that a true cross-section of the relevant population can be found among all of the people who have Netflix accounts or are on Facebook or went to a Toyota website and inquired about a Prius?

How were the survey questions phrased? Not only do you have to scrutinize the construction of the population surveyed, you have to look closely at the questions asked and the phrasing used. What appear to be small, merely semantic differences in language can lead to hugely different results. It is quite possible, for example, for a person to say he or she disapproves of "homosexuality" but has no problem with someone being "gay" or "lesbian." Knowing that the connotation

---

8. You should look *probabilistic* up in a dictionary. It doesn't mean problematic or flawed.

of synonyms can vary, unscrupulous pollsters could generate the numbers they were looking for just by altering the language they used.

Did the questions contain catchphrases? Some phrases seem like labels, ways of simply naming something, when in fact they carry an implicit argument. Think about the phrase "the war on drugs" or the phrase "the obesity epidemic." Another common example, are you opposed to a "death tax" but in favor of an "inheritance tax?"

Were there any hot-button words? Words like "liberal" and "conservative" are often empty when carefully examined, but most people respond more favorably to one than the other.

Does the survey use leading or biased language? Calling the accused a "felon" or people living in America without documentation "illegal immigrants" instantly influences people's perceptions of the person or people in question and thus could skew a data set in an invalid direction. You have to look closely at the way the questions were worded.

Is the order of the questions significant? Did they seem strategically planned? It is possible to skew the results of a survey by asking questions in a specific order because, when it comes to thinking, for most of us, one thought leads to another. There's an interesting psychology experiment explained in the book *Thinking, Fast and Slow* where students were asked to evaluate their happiness. One group was asked simply, "How happy are you?" But another group was first asked, "How many dates did you go on last week?" When the researchers cross-checked the answers, the students who said they had been on several dates the week before reported a greater level of happiness than the group who hadn't gone on a date recently. Interestingly, the happy-date group also recorded higher levels of happiness than those who weren't asked about their dating lives at all. Presumably the "How's your love life?" question put some people in a better mood, and they mistook mood (which is temporary and the result of immediate impressions) for well-being (which is long-standing and not as situational) and so concluded, "Yes, I'm 4 out of 5 happy these days." This experiment suggests that it is quite possible to skew results simply by asking questions in an order designed to influence the outcome. A truly random survey should either ask all of its questions in a random order or ensure that the answer to one question can't influence the answer to a subsequent question.

Was there an "I don't know" option? Strangely enough, if you ask someone a question, they may feel compelled to answer it even if they have no clue. These are also known as *pseudo-opinions*, and their existence has been demonstrated by experiments where people are asked their opinions about non-existent issues and offered a choice of several opinions but not given an "I don't know" option. When this happens, some people will choose from the available options rather than leave the question unanswered. People manufacture pseudo-opinions on the fly because they feel like the answer must be in there somewhere, and they don't want to look dumb or noncompliant. If you give people an "I don't know" option, however, you can have more faith in your data.

What was the context in which the questions were answered? Were the respondents in a hurry? Were they paid? Were they doing something else at the time? Did they understand what they were being asked? If you wanted to know what people's attitudes toward health insurance were, would asking people in an emergency room give you reliable data? What about asking young people on the campus of a university about student loan rates as opposed to people in a retirement community? Where people are can quite literally influence the data they provide. So you have to find out where a survey was administered in order to truly understand the data.

What was the response rate? Consider this scenario: You asked ten thousand people a question. Only one hundred people answered, but out of those one hundred people, ninety people answered positively. Saying that 90 percent of people agreed with you would likely be misleading. Selecting only the most convenient data is called *cherry picking.*

Can the survey data be corroborated by other evidence? Generally speaking, the more kinds of evidence you have to corroborate a statement, the more persuasive that statement will be. So whenever possible, don't rely on a single form of evidence.

━━━━━ Your Turn

Head over to Gallup.com and look for a Gallup poll that you find interesting. Look into how the data was collected, and see if you can find any flaws in the methodology. The methods section is usually presented at the bottom of the report.

Find an article that uses survey data to make a point, and then determine which of the above advice might most usefully guide a critique of the evidence.

Note that these four checklists by no means exhaust the questions you need to ask of evidence, whether your own or someone else's. They are merely a concrete way to get started thinking critically about evidence.

In order to answer the "Should I be persuaded by the evidence?" question, you need to think about how the evidence is being presented, who is providing it, and the timing of the presentation. You also need to consider what you know about your values, their values, the emotions involved in the situation, and the prior beliefs that may or may not contribute to what is being thought and written and said—along with a whole host of things that make up the rest of this book. Without evidence you can't make a thoughtful decision, but evidence alone isn't enough. You need to be sure the evidence warrants your belief.

Cognitive Biases

Persuasive communication requires critical thinking, and critical thinking requires that you question the validity of a statement based on the available evidence before you accept or reject it and that you provide conditional acceptance at a rate consistent with the validity of the evidence. Sometimes the appropriate questions will just occur to you when you read or hear a statement; often if you apply Toulmin's model and also mark up the fallacies you can get a sense of how reliable the work you are thinking about citing is. But sometimes the right questions won't occur to you because of how your brain thinks, or rather how our brains systematically *fail* to think critically unless we stop them periodically to inspect the quality of their output. Below is a set of common cognitive biases, tendencies toward distortion that all people are prone to. While it is impossible to disable them—and in some cases you wouldn't want to even if you could on grounds of efficiency—you can be on the lookout for them in your own and in other people's thinking. If you notice one of these biases at work in a persuasive situation, then you have a place to stop and consider counterarguments. But keep in mind that just because a bias in thinking exists, the thought may not be wrong. It is possible to do the right thing for an imperfect reason—like choosing to have the hotel staff wash your towels every *other* day because the little cardboard sign in the bathroom says many guests are opting to conserve energy and water by having the laundry done every other day, and you feel shamed into going along (Goldstein 12).

As you read through the following list of cognitive biases, think of your own examples, and question mine. You might also want to revisit the "Common errors in reasoning" section, as there are some interesting overlaps. Social proof, for example, reappears here as the bandwagon,

> **Arguments from availability:** Believing something is true because we can readily think of examples that support it and cannot immediately think of counterexamples or any reason to question the examples that came so quickly to mind. In other words, we often mistake Mr. or Ms. Right Now for Mr. or Ms. Right.

Anchoring: Fixing quickly or even unconsciously on a single interpretation or explanation or expectation. Anchoring will expedite decision making, but a quick decision isn't always the best decision. At its
worst anchoring can lead to tunnel vision, where you can't see beyond
your expectations. The manufacturer's suggested retail price is the
most common form of anchoring. Nobody pays retail. When negotiating, sometimes it's a good idea to start with an outrageously grand
requirement so that what you really need will be more attractive by
comparison. Anchor high to get more; anchor low to get less. Your
expectations for yourself are anchors also. Think about that.

Assimilation bias: Interpreting all evidence presented as proof for
a single interpretation and disproof of its opposite. For a hammer, all
the world's a nail, as the saying goes. While most people recognize
some boundaries for their ideas, enthusiasts sometimes find evidence
for their preoccupation in everything they see. Consider the case of
people who think the end of the world is coming. You would think
that, when the appointed date has come and gone, they would decide
that their prediction was wrong and perhaps abandon their beliefs.
But often they simply recast their prediction to accommodate the evidence to the contrary. This is an extreme case. But many people who
are profoundly committed to an idea will find evidence to support it
everywhere. We call these people dogmatists. If we want to spin the
idea positively, we could say assimilation bias makes it easier for a
person to stay on message.

Bandwagon effect (a.k.a. social proof, or the herding instinct):
In the absence of a clear way to behave, most people will do whatever
they think those around them are doing. If you are interested in a
truly odd example, Google "the Abilene Paradox." We conform by
default, which is why it's hard to root for the away team and why cults
isolate their initiates. A recent study observed that "obesity is contagious" (Blue). The headline is, as most headlines are, dramatic and
therefore misleading. It's not that one can *catch* obesity but rather
that weight is a function of diet and exercise habits, and, if you hang
around with folks who eat well and exercise, you will too. But if you
hang around with people who like to drink beer and scarf pizza while
watching TV, you'll be getting fat together.

Following the crowd isn't necessarily a bad idea, of course. If you
are trying to get out of a sports arena at the end of an event and you
don't know where the exits are, follow the crowd. If you are trying
to find a good restaurant in a strange place, look for a lineup outside
a restaurant. If everyone you know has a particular mobile device,
getting the one they have means you'll be able to learn from their
experiences with it. While many of us learned to avoid following the

crowd with rhetorical questions about jumping off a bridge, the fact is all people are hardwired to conform to social norms, no matter how disparaging the words we use to describe the phenomenon.[9]

Coherence: As the "obesity is contagious" assertion should have made you realize (if you were reading against the grain), context is important when trying to determine the validity of a statement. When no context is given, people may supply one. People feel compelled to make sense of things, especially things that don't really make any sense. A plausible fiction is much more compelling than an implausible truth. If you can explain something to yourself in a way that is consistent with your understanding of the world, you will accept that explanation no matter how wrong it may be. Just because something makes sense doesn't mean it's true. In fact, the more sensible something seems, the more you should step back for a second and take another look.

Confirmation bias: Looking for proof instead of disproof. Google "the Wason selection task" for a specific example of how this failure of critical thinking works. And then explain it to someone else.

Composition (a.k.a. the gambler's fallacy): If a coin lands heads up three times in a row, what are the chances that it will land heads up on the fourth? 50/50. With only two options, heads or tails, any time a regular coin is tossed it has a 50/50 chance of landing on heads, no matter what happened before. The past has no statistical relevance to the future. A corollary of this is that there are no hot streaks in sports (Gilovich).

Endowment effect: People tend to overvalue their own possessions and undervalue other people's. That is, they want to sell for $10 an item they wouldn't buy for $5. The comedian George Carlin summed this up with the following observation: "Other people's stuff is shit. Your shit is stuff."[10]

Exposure effect: People tend to like the familiar and dislike the unfamiliar. People who are afraid of dogs haven't spent enough time with the common house-pet variety, or they have spent too much time with the ones trained for fighting or for guarding warehouses. One way to help people overcome a phobia is to expose them slowly,

---

9. For an interestingly positive application of social proof, have a look at Richard Thaler and Cass Sunstein's *Nudge: Improving Health, Wealth, and Happiness*.

10. As I recall this quotation is from a 1981 routine called "A Place for My Stuff." I'm not sure. You should fact-check me on it.

in a controlled environment, to the thing they fear until eventually
the thing no longer frightens them because it has become familiar. I
recently overheard a woman in a supermarket say she didn't want to
use a newly installed self-scanning checkout station because "those
things never work." The attendant kindly guided her through the
process. And it worked! The process of exposure is sometimes called
familiarization. Its opposite, de-familiarization—to make the normal
strange—is a common artistic technique.

False dilemma: Offering only one or two options when at least
one other is possible, and often there are more. Keep in mind that
if someone offers you one or two alternatives, neither of the two is
almost always an option, and sometimes *both* might be an option.

Fundamental attribution error: What a person does is thought
to be necessarily the result of their character rather than their situation. If a person does a bad thing, you assume it's because they are a
bad person. We don't consider that perhaps the situation they found
themselves in led them to do it. Same for assuming that only good
people do good things. Sometimes the situation drives behavior, and
character may have nothing to do with it. Perhaps a person's character is just the sum of their habits and routines. Interestingly, when it
comes to self-assessments, most of us will attribute our good deeds to
our characters and excuse our bad deeds as having been caused by the
situation we found ourselves in. And yet we will cut other people no
such slack.

   I was reminded of this effect recently when I saw a news clip about
some parents who got into a brawl over high school graduation rega-
lia. Apparently someone didn't order enough caps to go with the
gowns, and the result was bruises and bloodshed—caught on a camera phone, of course, else it wouldn't have made the news. Anyway,
my first thought was, what horrible people are these! And I was about
to go on a rant (in my head) about declining moral standards when I
thought, fundamental attribution error. A better response would have
been, What was happening that prompted these people to behave so
badly? There had to be more to the story than just the absence of caps
or gowns that would put people into such a competitive frenzy.

Halo effect: Being so dazzled by a person's beauty that you think
they can do no wrong. While the halo effect is typically associated
with physical attractiveness, the fundamental error is letting an early
positive perception influence a subsequent interpretation. In a sense,
the halo effect is why you never get a second chance to make a first
impression. More positively, however, the halo effect can come in

handy if your second effort is mediocre. You might get a pass based on the strength of your first. On the other hand, if your first effort was really successful, people might be disappointed by the second simply by contrast. Have you ever heard of the *sophomore effort effect*? By the way, dialectically speaking, if there is a halo effect, do you suppose there's a pitchfork one as well?

Hindsight bias: Once a decision is made, people often come to think it was inevitable or predictable. Often, too, once something has happened or has been decided, people choose to believe it was for the best or always meant to be. The best way to understand this is to re-watch a movie you liked. Once you know how a movie ends, you see differently everything that leads up to that end. Things that were in no way obvious seem so obvious after they happen that you might actually convince yourself you saw them coming, even if you never did.

Naive realism: The sense that *you* know the truth, and others are just delusional or dysfunctional or evil. The quickest short circuit for critical thinking is refusing to believe it's necessary. Common sense isn't always your friend.

Recency effect: People tend to remember the last item in a list more readily than the ones that preceded it. When it comes to uncritical thinking, people have a tendency to use the last apparently relevant example they can think of as evidence for or against believing something. Most people live in the present, which isn't necessarily a bad thing, but thinking that the world is a horrible place because something horrible just happened isn't thinking critically. If you just watched the local news, for example, you might be more inclined to think the world is a dangerous place filled with murders and car accidents and fires than if you just spent thirty minutes watching a pleasant nature show. The recency effect cuts both ways of course. Just because the most recent example is a positive one doesn't mean all instances are going to be positive. As you may recall from the section on induction, the nice lady with the chicken feed is also a chicken strangler. Imagine that you are the public spokesperson for an oil refinery that has a ten-year-long unblemished safety streak, but this morning one of your tanks blew up, and now you're standing in front of a dozen TV cameras with fire burning out of control as a backdrop. What do you say?

Reduction: Oversimplifying a circumstance or description or observation. We tend to abstract and generalize from our interactions with the world, probably as a way of helping us remember and certainly as a way of helping us deal with the overwhelming amount of detail bombarding our minds and senses. If we take reduction too far, however, we end up with incomplete perceptions and misunderstandings.

Stereotypes, in the common use of the term, are a concrete example of reduction: An entire group is reduced to a small set of characteristics that may or may not actually belong to every member of the group, and then all members of that group are seen to possess those characteristics. *Our experiences confirm our prejudices because our prejudices tend to inform our perceptions and inferences.* It's not that the world is the way we think it is, or that we make of it what we will, but rather that we are too easily pleased by our habits of mind. Whenever something just seems right to you, take a second look, staying alert to the possibility that you might be more eager than accurate.

Representativeness heuristic: Assuming a skewed sample is representative of a general population. Kevin Dutton offers a great example in *Split-Second Persuasion* (79–80). Given a man over six feet five inches tall, is he more likely a basketball player or a banker? A lot of people would figure basketball player. But there are way more bankers than basketball players, so the chances are better he's a banker. Make sure your sample is truly representative.

Search satisfaction: Accepting as valid proof the first evidence you find that supports your hypothesis or prejudice or assumption. Here's an example: If a baseball bat and ball cost $110.00 and a bat is $100.00 more than a ball, how much is a ball? If you said $10.00 you got the same answer I got, and like me you got it wrong. The answer is $5.00. The first time I saw the answer I couldn't believe it. What is $110 – $100? $10, obviously. But, What is $110 – 10? is the wrong question. The right question is, How much is X if $100 + X = 110 – X$? That question, if you did the math correctly, gives you the right answer (Kahneman 44). To be perfectly honest, to this day I don't quite see how this works. I've memorized the answer and so if you gave me a problem resembling it, I might get it right; but if you gave me a slightly disguised version of the same question, I'd likely get it wrong again. At any rate, the lesson here is unambiguous: If you are sure your answer is right, make sure you asked the right question.

Simultaneity and causation: When two things happen in rapid succession, it's often tempting to think the first caused the second, but this isn't necessarily the case. In fact, causation is often extremely hard to prove, unless we are talking about dominoes. If you want to prove A causes B, you would have to prove that no Bs exists without A, and then you would have to produce an A where there wasn't already a

B and show that B then happened—all the while carefully controlling for other factors so that you could be sure it was A and A only that caused B.

Here's a less algebraic example: People have noticed that neighborhoods with highly educated populations tend to have lower crime rates. Some people hear this and think, well, education must lower crime rates. So, increase education and reduce crime. That would work if education caused law-abiding behavior in the way a catalytic converter causes a reduction in carbon emissions from a combustion engine. But you can't bolt an education onto a person. *Education* isn't a simple, concrete entity. It's an abstract concept that means different things to different people, and each different kind of education will affect each individual person differently. Not to mention differences in people's genetics and physiology and perhaps even biology. Education doesn't *cause* law-abiding behavior even if it correlates. At best, education is a contributing factor to law-abiding behavior.

Specificity: Specific threats are more frightening than vague or abstract ones, even if statistically less likely by comparison. People are more afraid of terrorism than heart disease, for example, even though the odds of death by the one are nothing compared to the odds of death by the other. Why is the weaker threat more frightening? When you read (or hear) the word *terrorist* what do you see? When you hear (or read) the phrase *arterial sclerosis* what do you see?

Here's an even more vivid example: Deer are more dangerous than sharks. In a stats fight, Bambi totally eats Jaws. You are way more likely to get killed hitting a deer while driving than you are likely to get bitten by a shark while swimming, because you drive more than you swim, and there are more deer on roads than sharks in swimmable parts of the ocean. But the word *deer* conjures the image of a petting zoo animal, whereas *shark* conjures three rows of razor sharp teeth ringing a mouth big and forceful enough to bite a deer in half. The more vivid the story, the more convincing it is, no matter how out of touch with reality the story may be. And the opposite is also true. An abstract truth that is hard to visualize will have a hard time finding an audience no matter how true it is. *Be concrete and specific, and you will be more persuasive.*

Sunk-cost bias: Persisting in a hopeless direction because you've invested too much time and energy to have the heart to give it up. Only future costs should be considered when making decisions, but most people can't help thinking the past must contribute something to the future. This is why slot machines can be so addictive. If you ever hear yourself saying, "I've worked so hard on this, I can't give up now," you might want to make sure you're looking forward not backward.

Taste/value confusion: Often people think that what they like is good and what they dislike is bad. Was the movie good? I loved it. Strictly speaking, that answer is a non sequitur. Whenever you evaluate something, think past your personal preferences.

Your Turn

Of these cognitive biases, which one strikes you as the one you most often encounter? Which ones are entirely new to you?

In the explanation about simultaneity and causation I wrote, "Education doesn't *cause* law-abiding behavior even if it correlates. At best, education is a contributing factor to law-abiding behavior." If you think I might be wrong about that, good for you. Give me a counterargument. I can think of a couple of ways you could make a case for the assertion that education causes law-abiding behavior. (*I could help you write the counterargument, but it's your turn.*) Every argument hinges on the definitions. Define the key terms carefully.

As far as persuasion goes, naive realism is the worst mistake you can make. Given everything I've said in this section on critical thinking, can you explain why I made that assertion? Do you think I'm right? Now, can you come up with an argument in support of naive realism? (Hint: You might want to change the name, maybe to something like "common sense.")

chapter 2
PRODUCING PERSUASIVE ACTS

The Persuasion Process

While it is obviously important to learn how to become an astute recipient and not just a passive or even appreciative consumer of persuasive acts, it's even more important to develop your capacity for producing persuasive communications. There's no better way to learn how to appreciate something than to try it yourself. More importantly, in the process of developing your skills as a persuasive communicator, you will begin to understand both what you believe and how you come to believe; you will become more familiar with how you make up your mind and how your mind works, which in turn will help you understand how to change your mind as well as how to change other people's minds.

The persuasion process is a long-term endeavor. It's a way of seeing and being in the world, not something you bring out and dust off occasionally. You have to live the persuasion process—habitually ask questions, seek evidence, remain skeptical but open minded—if you are going to become truly persuasive.

The next several sections contain the primary persuasion concepts and thorough explanations of how each concept works, along with exercises to help you understand each one by practicing and thinking about it. Realize, however, that becoming a persuasive person is not like learning to ride a bicycle in the sense that you can't, through repetition and trial and error, simply learn a technique and from then on perform it at an unconscious level. Some of these persuasive practices will become second nature or automatic, like riding a bike, but others will always require conscious thought and reflection in action. Even when some of the processes become second nature, you still need to remain mindful at some level because, just as mindless consumption of food is bad for the waistline, mindless production of persuasive acts is bad for the reputation.[1] Listen first. Then think about how you would persuade. Then decide if you should.

---

1. Did you buy that analogy?

The presentation of self

Ethos

> Since rhetoric exists to affect the giving of decisions—the hear-
> ers decide between one political speaker and another, and a legal
> verdict is a decision—the orator must not only try to make the
> argument of his speech demonstrative and worthy of belief; he
> must also *make his own character look right* [emphasis added]
> and put his hearers, who are to decide, into the right frame of
> mind. Particularly in political oratory, but also in lawsuits, it adds
> much to an orator's influence that his own character should look
> right and that he should be thought to entertain the right feel-
> ings towards his hearers. . . . There are three things which inspire
> confidence in the orator's own character—the three, namely, that
> induce us to believe a thing apart from any proof of it: *good sense,
> good moral character, and goodwill* [emphasis added]. (Aristotle,
> *On Rhetoric*, 2.1)

Ethos is a Greek word for "character." In rhetoric, *ethos* refers to the techniques a speaker or writer uses to appear smart, credible, and sympathetic.
People believe people they like, and they like people who seem like them or
even slightly better than them, but not in an arrogant or condescending
way. To establish a positive *ethos* you need to positively reflect the audience's attitudes, values, and beliefs about themselves. Some people think
this means telling the audience what they want to hear, flattering them, as
Plato's Socrates asserts in *Gorgias*. Flattery (let's call it *praise*—that word is
so much nicer) is significant, but it's only one technique for creating a positive *ethos*, and you have to be very subtle about it.

If someone knows you are praising them, and they also know you are
trying to get something significant from them, then they may become suspicious and therefore more difficult to persuade. Rather than saying nice
things about a person, admire what they admire and disapprove of the things
they disapprove of. If they are dressed well, talk clothes. If they have a cool
phone, talk technology. If they are wearing some kind of fan insignia, talk
sports or music or whatever the insignia represents. If you know what they
do for a living, praise the job or the industry. If it's an audience you are talking to, praise the forum that brings them together, or even the place where
the meeting is being held. In general, you want to get them to trust you not
by saying "Trust me" but by saying and doing things that make them feel
good about themselves, which will in turn make them feel good about you.
As with all things persuasive, *show, don't tell*. Demonstrate reliability (good
character) and aptitude (good sense) and caring (goodwill), and you will
create a positive *ethos*.

While Aristotle restricted *ethos* to the representation of credibility in a particular speech or text, your reputation may precede you, so consider the impact and the consequences of your words and actions even when you are not directly engaged in being persuasive. Everything you say and do should be geared toward leaving a positive and lasting impression.

Good character

People tend to attribute actions to character. If you do good things, that is, things people like or can at least appreciate,[2] then you will be considered a good person and vice versa. Psychologists call this tendency to equate behavior with character the *fundamental attribution error*, suggesting that what each of us does is not a function of our character but rather a cluster of effects, habits, contexts, opportunities, genetic predispositions, and so on. Despite what modern psychology tells us, most people still think that you are at some level what you do and that if you do good things you have a good character, which in turn means you are trustworthy.

Most of the character traits listed are obvious if you stop to think about them. The thing is, a lot of people don't think about them. Some people hit on them naturally, by instinct almost. These people are natural *rhetors*. The rest of us have to learn them and practice them until they become second nature.

- Be respectful but not obsequious or condescending. Know your place, but don't be content to stay there forever.

- Be considerate. Consider the context before you invoke a rule or make an assumption.

- Be punctual. You'd be surprised how much you can learn by getting there ahead of everyone else and how much unnecessary resistance you can generate just by making someone wait.

- Be prepared. Even insignificant details can influence a decision: do your homework.

- Be consistent. Erratic or unpredictable behavior generates suspicion or confusion; although, if you are important to the group, on occasion it might create mystery or intrigue. If you are going for this rhetorical affect, think whimsical rather than erratic.

- Be conscientious. Do what you say you will on time and on budget.

- Be pleasant. Don't complain; don't find fault; don't make people guess what you are thinking or otherwise make life harder for people.

2. If you have to do something unpopular, explain why you are doing it. That won't make people like it, but if your reasoning is sound, they won't hate you for it.

- Own your mistakes. Don't blame others; don't make excuses.

- Be open minded. Listen before arguing; entertain ideas you don't warm to immediately.

- Don't disagree just because you can.

- Be generously humorous. Learn how to tell a joke at no one's expense and how to take one.

- Gracefully accept both criticism and praise.

- Know your job, and don't tell others how to do theirs.

- Listen actively. Repeat what people say to yourself and once in a while out loud. ("If I'm hearing you correctly, . . . ")

- Don't be thinking ahead to what you are going to say next and thus miss what the other person is saying.

- Don't speak just for the pleasure of hearing yourself speak.

- Don't bring up irrelevant topics or otherwise sidetrack the discussion.

- Don't offer unwanted advice, unless you absolutely have to.

- Pay attention. Make eye contact, lean in, and tilt your head like you're listening intently. (See Chapter 3, "Common gestures and how they are commonly interpreted.")

- Mirror movements and posture of the person you are speaking with. Don't overdo this; as with all rhetorical advice, subtlety is everything.

- Remember names, and use them, but don't overdo it. You'll seem overly earnest if you keep using someone's name during a conversation.

- Dress the part, not too far up or too far down.

- Don't gossip maliciously. That piece of advice may surprise you. Gossip is generally considered ill mannered, but talking about other people in a group is a bonding experience, and it can also help people save face. Anyone who has ever gotten divorced or suffered some unpleasant personal event that they'd rather not talk about can tell you that the grapevine saves a great deal of misery. Malicious gossip, on the other hand, tears groups up and isolates individuals.

- Don't flirt overtly. There's a big difference between making someone feel good and leading them on or making them uncomfortable.

- Don't flatter overtly. Same reason as above.

- Don't revel in your vices. Nearly everyone has some kind of black leather jacket in the closet, but it's not a good idea to wear it to every event.

- Don't flaunt your virtues. Self-righteousness is very unappealing.

- Show, don't tell. Evidence, evidence, evidence. Don't just smile and say you're a great person. Do great things.

Your Turn

Believe it or not, these behaviors are how people judge character. If my collection seems grotesquely superficial to you, that's good. What is on *your* list when you are appraising other people? What about when you are appraising yourself? What's the significance of the difference between your list and mine, assuming there is one?

Just before I started the list of good character traits I said some people know these things instinctively, and the rest of us have to learn them, but when I said that I was leaving at least one class of people out. There are some people who simply don't care what anyone thinks about them. They just do what they do, and others can learn to live with it or go away. This intentional indifference (they know better, they just don't care) to other people's impressions can have a number of consequences, both positive and negative. The positive consequences tend to cluster around the impression that the person is very honest or brutally honest or that they are independent minded, authentic, genuine. The negative impression is that they are selfish or self-righteous or narcissistic. Regardless, unless you are significantly superior to everyone else at whatever it is you do, you won't get as far in the world by being indifferent to other people's impressions. People will attribute your actions and your expressions to your character, so think about how you will be perceived before you say or do something in a public setting.

Good sense

If you want people to listen to you, you have to say things worth hearing, and this obviously means knowing what you are talking about, but it's not simply a matter of displaying your knowledge. You don't want to sound like a know-it-all or come off in any way pretentious or pedantic or smarter than thou. You have to strike a balance between sounding informed and knowledgeable and yet being open to input and willing to listen. People don't like being

talked down to or feeling like they've just been schooled. If you make either
of these mistakes, people won't be inclined to listen to you no matter how
good your advice or how knowledgeable you are. So listen carefully before
you offer advice, and, if possible, help the people you are dealing with see
what needs to be done; leave them with the impression it was their idea all
along or that they were instrumental in the decision. Even if a person agrees
to something, they may be unhappy with the results if they only just agreed.
You need them to really embrace the advice, own it. Below is a blueprint
for creating a favorable impression. Read each item carefully (slowly while
thinking about how to incorporate it into your everyday life).

1. Do your homework. Make sure you know everything there is to know
    about the people, the situation, and the problem before you get there
    so that you don't have to ask hundreds of questions. You want to ask
    whatever questions you couldn't answer in advance, and, if there
    aren't any of those, ask a few pertinent ones just to show you are
    responsive to people's needs. Know the past; know the present; and,
    to the extent possible, know the future. No one can predict the future,
    of course, but not everyone is traveling the same road or at the same
    speed, and so while it may be someone's future it may be your past
    already. But don't give people the been-there-done-that vibe.

2. Make sure the people in the audience know they have a problem[3] and
    acknowledge that it is their problem and not somebody else's.

3. Demonstrate that you can solve that problem for them:
    Provide examples of previous solutions.

    Demonstrate that you have the skills and resources to solve the
        problem. (Resources include knowledge, people, time, material,
        insurance, and a reasonable plan B.)

4. Before you offer a solution, make sure it is commensurate with the
    problem:
    Don't offer long-term solutions to short-term problems.

    Don't offer expensive solutions to unimportant problems.

    Don't offer elaborate solutions to simple problems.

    Don't offer solutions that will create new problems.

    Don't make promises you can't keep.

    Build delays, cost overages, and unexpected problems into the
        estimate.

---

3. Is "problem" too strong a word? What are some synonyms that suggest a milder
connotation?

If you underestimate, eat the difference.

Do whatever it takes to get it done on time and on budget.

5. Show, don't tell. If people infer that you can do it based on the evidence you offer, they will feel like the decision was entirely their own. You didn't "sell" them; they "bought" you.

━━━━━━━ ## Your Turn

Who is the most sensible person you know, and what do they do that gives you that impression? Have you ever met someone whose judgment you didn't trust at all? What was it about them that made you doubt their judgment?

Goodwill

Everybody thinks they know what is in their own best interests, and thus they trust themselves first, then others with similar interests, and then authorities. Trust is based on the belief that the other person wants for you what you want for yourself, or wants something compatible with what you want. If you both want the same thing but only one of you can have it, then you are competitors not allies, and competitors don't have goodwill. Not that they will necessarily behave badly, but they are not out to serve your interests because that will defeat their interests. On the other hand, if you can both want the same thing, and working together increases the chances of you both getting it, then you will trust each other. This situation is often referred to as a *win-win*.

Generally speaking, trust is based on an assessment of the compatibility of interests and competences (see the section "Good sense" earlier in this chapter). If you can convince your audience that you can benefit only if they too benefit, they will listen to you more readily because they have reason to believe you mean to do them a good turn.

When it comes to trust in authorities, we assume that professionals offer only good advice because if they offer bad advice they will ruin their reputation and thus their livelihood. Because we are not experts in their field, we can't verify their advice, apart from getting a second professional opinion. So we will tend to assess the professional's demeanor and surroundings instead. Basically, do they dress the part and have offices consistent with what we think such offices should look like? There have been studies done on malpractice suits that indicate that a doctor with a lousy bedside manner is more likely to get sued than one who appears empathetic and takes time with a patient. In other words, if a professional demonstrates goodwill but proves incompetent, he or she is less likely to get sued over it. Goodwill can trump good sense. *Show them that your interests are the same as or compatible with theirs.*

Your Turn

So how do you show someone that your interests are compatible? How can you unpack the commonplace "You scratch my back, and I'll scratch yours"? If you are both engaged in a common enterprise, then sharing credit and information, and when necessary blame, will go a long way toward proving to your co-workers that you have goodwill. Helping people get what they want or at least not getting in the way or making a big deal of getting out of the way might do the same thing. What other techniques can you think of? If you're struggling to come up with some, create a scenario, and walk through it in your head. Imagine you're a recently hired director in an organization that has ten members, all of whom have different roles to play, and you need all of them to follow your lead, but you can't just tell them what to do. And let's say you are a lot younger than they are, and so they are suspicious of you. What would you do to make them feel like you have goodwill toward them?

Ethos and writing assignments

I'm going to tell you a secret I will deny if we ever meet in public. Professors make judgments about your character based on the work you turn in, and those judgments affect your grade. Bosses, too. (Those judgments affect your pay.) They can't help it. It's what people do—the fundamental attribution error. Error though it is, most of us make character assessments based on others' actions and communications, and others judge us based on our actions and communications, too. For the first three years of my undergraduate education my professors thought I was lazy because every paper I turned in had spelling mistakes in it. I'm not lazy. Okay, I could have worked harder, sure, but I'm not lazy. I'm dyslexic. I transpose letters. It takes me way longer to proofread than it does most people. I had to read everything I wrote backward from the last word to the first and stare closely at every word. If I put all my cognitive energy into doing that, I'd never write anything. And that was in the day of the typewriter, when cutting and pasting literally meant scissors and glue. Word processing software and specifically spell-checker software got me into graduate school not because it made me smarter but because it kept profs form (from—*did you catch that?*) thinking I was a slacker.

To maximize your grade potential, do everything you can to convey a positive *ethos* to your professors. Make your writing conscientious and considerate. Don't put the work off so long that you have to cut corners to get it done. Get the small stuff right (no matter how long and tedious the task). Imperfect grammar, punctuation, and citation details slow down your readers, and the more time they have to spend on stuff they think is trivial but prerequisite the worse their impression of your *ethos* will be.

But this cuts both ways. If you get the superficial stuff right, you might get a better grade than the work really warrants, so relieved the prof might be to get something at least polished. Not every A is a good A. Your professors are offering a professional judgment, but you need to develop your own judgment by comparing what they say to what you expected to hear. So before you turn something in, write a note to yourself about what you think you should get and why. Then compare the note with the professor's advice. Don't just look at the grade. Look closely at the comments, and think them through. If there is a significant disconnect, then you need to rethink your original assessment of what the assignment called for. If by then you are still hazy on what you need to do differently, go talk to the prof. You need to make sure you understand what is expected and that you are prepared to do a better job the next time out. (Going to see your prof and asking relevant questions will do spectacular things for your *ethos* with him or her, by the way.)

━━━ Your Turn

While we are on the subject of a positive ethos, if you miss a class, don't ask the prof, Did I miss anything? or, even worse, Did I miss anything important? Explain why these two questions are lethal in terms of the three characteristics of a positive *ethos*.

Here's a triumvirate of bonus questions: Why did I share my dyslexia story with you a moment ago? How does self-disclosure support the creation of a positive *ethos*? When might self-disclosure fail as an *ethos* technique?

Autobiography as self-rhetoric and the rhetoric of the self

To become a successful *rhetor* you need to talk and write about yourself effectively. Some people love to talk about themselves. Some people would rather die. Some people don't understand themselves very well, and others dislike themselves intensely. It's tricky, too, to talk about yourself without sounding narcissistic or self-promoting or just boring. One of the standard techniques for self-praise without blame is to have someone else praise you. People are often persuaded by third-person descriptions. This is why we have letters of recommendation, introductions at keynote speeches, celebrities promoting products, friends of friends on Facebook or LinkedIn, and so on.

While we tend to think that only celebrities and important people and rich, vain people write autobiographies or memoirs, the representation of self is rhetorically important for all people. It's tied to the idea of *ethos*, where you choose your words, your examples, and even the structure of what you say with an eye toward establishing that you have goodwill toward your audience, good sense in general, and the ability to get the right thing done on time and on budget (a loose translation of the Greek word *arete* or "excellence"). But there's more to self-rhetoric than *ethos*.

While reputation isn't strictly speaking part of *ethos*, and you can't present an autobiography every time someone asks, How do you do? what people think of you over time will definitely play a part in how they interpret your messages and your actions, and thus you have to think about how you represent yourself, how you talk about yourself, how you answer the question, So what's your story? You also have to think about how you talk to yourself about yourself.

How you represent yourself (both to yourself and to others) plays a key role in both self-fulfillment and self-destruction. If you represent yourself positively, show up on time, well groomed and well rested, your prose carefully edited, your slides in order, and so on, people will be inclined to think well of you and so provide opportunities for you. If you represent yourself negatively, if you come across as distracted or slack or sloppy or self-centered or immature or whatever, people won't think of you when they need a job done, and you might lose out on an opportunity. If you represent yourself inaccurately, suggesting you can do things you can't, you may inadvertently set yourself up to fail by having someone give you an opportunity to do something you can't accomplish, denting your reputation and undermining your self-confidence in the process. On the other hand, if you represent yourself to yourself negatively, if you dwell on the negative or speak to yourself in ways that undermine your self-esteem, or if you otherwise incline toward self-defeating behaviors, you will get in your own way, failing even to seek opportunities for advancement or success while making others who might be inclined in your favor to rethink giving you a chance. *Self-talk is destiny.*

One last complexity to consider when it comes to representing yourself: just because you can do something doesn't mean it would be rhetorically wise to let people know you can. If you are adept with computers, for example, and the word gets out that you can troubleshoot software glitches and remove viruses and set up wireless connections, you may become your co-workers' go-to person for things unrelated to your actual job description— and so sidetrack yourself. Learn everything you can, but show your skills selectively and with forethought. Never be too useful, especially to powerful people.

When it comes to autobiography, you need to be constantly mindful of inadvertently documenting yourself online. Your Facebook profile, your comments on blogs, your own blog, each of the trails that you leave online whether you are aware of them or not create an online presence for you, and any time anyone Googles you—as prospective employers and even dates will—a kind of biography will emerge. Thus you need to start thinking today about how to best represent yourself online. What pictures should you upload to Flickr? What should you pin to your Pinterest board? What random thoughts should you tweet? If you want to use effective communication as a tool for your success, you need to write often, and keeping a blog is an excellent way to both practice your writing and develop an audience for yourself. But if you do, be as careful about what you write as how you write it.

Your Turn

To get a vivid sense of the power inadvertent autobiography can have, Google "Are social media making the resume obsolete," an article published on CNN by Doug Gross. Then spend a few minutes Googling yourself and reviewing what kind of digital impression you are leaving. If you want to, you might ask someone in your class who you don't know very well to review your Facebook page and tell you what impression you made.

Practicing the part of self-rhetoric where you are talking to yourself is a bit more difficult. You need to make notes during the day for a few weeks to get some data about how you talk to yourself about yourself. Whenever you find yourself talking to yourself, saying anything from "You go!" to "You dork," stop and make a note of whether the self-talk was positive or negative and what triggered it. If the balance is negative, you have to wonder, Would you ever let anyone else talk to you like that? On the other hand, if the balance is overwhelmingly positive, you have to wonder if maybe you should raise your expectations.

If you are up for a serious writing challenge, here is a prompt: Thought is a form of behavior. Discuss.

The presentation of others

Persuasive people, *rhetors*, often have to describe other people, whether it's providing a character reference for a job candidate or for a client, giving an introduction for an invited speaker, introducing a new member of a team, saying an official good-bye to someone, or just figuring out how to introduce two friends who haven't yet met. The list of opportunities to talk about people is fairly endless, and the more public your roles in life become the more often you will need to characterize the people you know.

While it may be some time before you will be called upon to give an extended introduction to a person or compose a biography, you will need to assess people and figure out where they are coming from and therefore who they are, how they think, what they value, and what they don't, because you will need to be able to predict how they will respond to messages and social interactions. Reading people is a significant life skill, and one way to develop that skill is to write about people. Characterization is the kind of writing (or thinking or speaking) where you describe a person or type of person such that you explain what they are likely to think or say. Characterization will help you develop *the two most important elements of persuasion, theories of mind and a sense of audience.*

A theory of mind is how we describe the human capacity to infer from people's behavior and statements and actions what they are thinking and feeling. To be able to get along with people requires that you "get them," as we say colloquially, and that means feeling like you have a sense of what's happening in their heads. Strictly speaking, of course, we don't really know what's going on in another person's head. If they are present we can ask them, but even that may not tell us what we need to know because not everyone is all that self-aware, and not everyone wants to share everything. Moreover, our inferences about who a person is are more important to us than who the person really is in themselves. I don't mean that we don't care who other people are; it's just that who they are to us means more to us than who they might be to themselves because we interact with our representation of them only. We don't have direct access to their stream of consciousness or their experiences. We can only infer who they are and how they think by what they say and do.

So in a way, the people we know, even the ones we spend a lot of time with, are rhetorical constructions. They exist independently of our thinking. I'm not saying we hallucinate each other. I'm only saying that we construct a rhetorical understanding of groups and individuals based on cultural expectations, inferences and assumptions, and past experiences. When we write these rhetorical constructs down and flesh them out with details, we can begin to develop a self-conscious understanding of how we think we know people. If we just do it in our heads, without writing it down, we remain less aware of the processes that persuade us to see a given individual one way rather than another.

As a *rhetor* you have to make a habit of characterizing people, specific individuals you know and casual acquaintances and even strangers. Characterization, the process of constructing a detailed understanding of a person, is an important step toward being able to persuade because *rhetors* have to tailor their messages for the people who will receive them; and, without knowing or at least having a vivid sense of who is receiving a message, you are throwing your words around at random.

Characterization is also important because people are often willing to accept other people's representations of them, and thus as you construct a character in a sense you offer the other person a role they may accept. If they are rhetorically astute like you are becoming, they may read that offer against the grain or negotiate with you about it. But if they aren't rhetorically astute, they may just let you make them over in the image you offered. If I just scared you, good. There's a big responsibility in characterization. Our first attempts are going to be playful fictions so you can get a comfortable sense of how characterization is done. But while we are creating fictions now, in time you will come to understand that it is by these means that you develop your understanding of people.

Characterization

Bios

The Greek word *bios* means "life" in English. The rhetorical forms related to *bios* are

encomium: formal commendation of a person

panegyric: elaborate compliment

apologia: justification for an individual's actions

psogos, **or vituperation:** formal condemnation of a person

eulogy: praise of a person, typically of the dead but not necessarily

epitaphios: funeral speech

A *bios* might contain passages that perform these more narrow functions, but it is a more general form, talking about a person's life in detail, creating a complete profile.

In the following section there is a list of the topics out of which characters are frequently created. Obviously how many and which of the topics related to a person's life should be covered when creating an extended *bios* are determined by the age of the person being talked about, as well as the kind of life he or she leads and the circumstances for the composition or speech. Unless you are writing a book, you can't cover *everything*. You could center the entire piece on just one topic if it was particularly indicative of who the person is or was. Your goal is always to tell a story about a person that reveals something of their character. You may be trying to help the person (get them a job, introduce them to someone important) or hurt them (get them convicted, fired, passed over), or you might be trying to accomplish something for yourself by talking about others (basking in the reflected glory of some famous person you know or borrowing some authority by vicarious association). Your purpose for characterizing someone should determine the details you select and shape the way you present those details. For now, however, we just want a list of as many possible topics as we can think of.

Because characterization is a form of description, as always you want to be as specific and concrete as possible. Details, details, details. Involve all five senses. Leave your audience with the impression that they were there.

The traditional topics of *bios*

Birthplace: Geographical location. Because cities have personalities in a sense, you can convey quite a bit about people just by saying where they were born and grew up. If the city itself isn't well known you can characterize the location—small town, rural, sea coast, north, south, high plains, badlands, bush country, and so on.

Family: Ancestors and siblings. What a person's parents did for a living and who they were might be instructive because we infer things about people based on their occupations and assume that such a way of life would have some influence on their children. Whether a person is an only child can say something, as can the order of birth if someone has siblings. The youngest is always said to be different from the eldest, the middle child different again, and so on. Whether you believe birth order or single child status have an actual impact on character is an interesting opinion to ponder, but it's not entirely relevant for our purposes here.

Education: How much or how little, where people went to school, influential teachers, classmates (famous people who also went to that school), events that occurred while they were at school, the effect education had (or didn't) on them, the extent to which they are proud or ashamed of their education. All of these details say something about a person's character because these are all formative experiences. So if a person were a successful high school athlete, you have a different sense of them than if they were a slacker on a skateboard or drama club stand-out or editor of the yearbook or a ghost no one remembers.

Occupation: How people get their jobs, what their trajectories are (or were), what part occupation played in their identity—assuming it does. If their occupation doesn't play into their identity, this might be an even more valuable source of ideas for a *bios*. Some people would rather be fishing, as the bumper sticker says. By the way, one way to get a fix on characters is to imagine what their bumper sticker would be, assuming they have one. Or are they the kind of person who has a hundred stickers? Or would they rather lose a finger than paste something on their car?

Wealth: How much people have, how they spend it, attitudes toward money (their own and other people's). If they had money, did they show it off, and if so how? How visible was their wealth? If they were broke, did they economize well, or were they living off other people? Did they share what they had with others, or were they stingy?

Character traits: Sense of humor, how hard someone works, temper, passions, preoccupations. Psychologists today sometimes talk of the five factors of character: openness, conscientiousness, extraversion, agreeableness, and neuroticism. The acronym for this is OCEAN. Google it. Then think about how you might arrange these traits to provide insight into the person you are writing about.

Foibles and eccentricities: These superficial but interesting attributes add texture and immediacy, even a sense of intimacy; they make your audience really feel and see the person you are talking about, and that makes them feel like they know him or her. Sometimes people will use an attribute of a person as a nickname or shorthand way of referring to them. This *handle* can be kind or cruel or just evocative. Just as an aside, what handle would you give yourself based on a vivid but superficial attribute? Was it positive or negative?

Health: How someone dealt with physical adversity as a sign of character. If a person were sickly as a child, we would make some inferences about their childhood and thus who they became. If people suffer as adults with a chronic condition, we might assume that says something about who they are. If they are cancer survivors or diabetics or have weight issues and so on, we can make something of that. Maybe they've never been sick a day in their life and yet somehow don't seem robust. Maybe they walk with a limp proudly. And then again, maybe they are very careful about their diet and spend a lot of time in the gym. Maybe they are superbly healthy. What can you make of that? Maybe they are worried about getting sick. How would that detail help explain who they are?

Physical appearance: Height, weight, skin tone, hair, eyes, physical fitness. All of these attributes provide a sense of who people might be or what they might be like. When you meet people you are taking these traits in and associating them with others you've met like them whether you are aware of it or not. When you describe someone you need to account for this fact.

Manner of dress: We tend to think that the clothes make the person, that people dress the way they do as a way of communicating who they are, and many of us interpret what people wear as saying something about them. Advertisers play on this tendency, of course, telling you that if you are a certain kind of person you will want to wear their clothes (logos and labels, as well as types of clothes and accessories). And since nearly all of us buy advertising, you may actually be able to tell something about people by their preferences for a label, or at least what kind of label they want to be associated with. This is a risky form of thinking because people don't always buy the clothes they wear, and not everyone has the money to indulge their brand identity. And, of course, some people are very subtle about how their clothes signify their identity. Clothes, in other words, are far more accidental than health is. Anybody can wear anything; it's just that most of us don't, given an option.

Manner of life: Hobbies, clubs, organizations, modes of transportation (did they ride their bike everywhere, insist on public transportation, drive a gas guzzler, a minivan, a scooter?), vacation spots (destinations, dwellings, itineraries).

Struggles: Achievements, failures, family events. Depending on what you are trying to do, what people overcome in life and how they deal with adversity can say a great deal about them. And of course if they never struggled for anything but were content with nothing or born with everything they needed or born with nothing, those situations can be used as evidence with which to build a characterization.

Habits: What people have become so accustomed to doing that they would have a hard time stopping. Sometimes people are conscious of their habits, but often they are not because they have done them so much they have become automatic. If you interfere with what someone habitually does, you can expect resistance; whereas, if you can attach what you need to something someone is in the habit of doing anyway, they will likely comply. Some habits are significant and have an impact on a person's life, like smoking or exercising or using a bike or a car to get around. Others are just things people always do that don't amount to much over time. Regardless, habits can be telling. If someone is always playing with their hair or picking at their clothes you might infer that they are self-conscious or uncomfortable. If they are tapping their feet or rubbing their hands all the time, is that nervous energy? Maybe it meant something once, but now it's only a habit.

Affectations: Some people want to be something they aren't or aren't yet, maybe to seem more educated than they are or more experienced or better at something than they are. And sometimes people just want to fake it until they make it. What people *want* to be seen as can be a good indicator of how they think. Although at this point we are only listing the topics one might use to describe someone, it might be worth noting that affectations suggest a place where you can be maximally persuasive because what people want but don't feel they have are sources of anxiety. So if you tell someone who wants to be funny that they just told a very funny story, they will be much more pleased than someone who already thinks they are funny. If you see somebody pretending to be something they aren't, you've learned something important about how they think.

Attitudes: Optimistic, pessimistic, cynical, trusting, fun loving, serious, gregarious, introverted, competitive, laid back, energetic, neurotic, and so on. (*You need to add to this list.*) Attitudes are best illustrated with anecdotes rather than simply said. The best application is when you can just tell the story and know your audience will draw the inference about what the person is like from the story itself. Reciprocally, you can learn a lot about a person you've not met by stories told about them.

Spiritual beliefs: Some cultures place a great deal of significance on a person's religious beliefs and will make all kinds of assumptions about people based on those beliefs or even the appearance of those beliefs. If the person you are speaking of spiritually matches who you are speaking to, then you have a set of opportunities that you wouldn't have if they didn't match. And of course, if they don't match, you have another set of opportunities.

Favorite sayings: A catchphrase, something a person always said, either a quotation they were fond of or a maxim they created.

There is a parallel rhetorical exercise here known as the *chreia*, where you tell a brief anecdote that sets a scene, and then you quote what the person said on that occasion. This is a very common rhetorical form among sports fans: great things famous athletes have said and when and why they said them. The same goes for politicians, famous writers, and actors, as well as military and business and professional people—pretty much any endeavor that has enough enthusiasts to have generated some famous members will have *chreia*. Often the folklore of an enterprise is handed down by means of these very short anecdotes.[4]

---

4. One of my favorite sources of *chreia* is the Cynic Diogenes of Synope. The word *cynic* is derived from the Greek word for "dog," and the cynics were a sect of ascetic (not aesthetic, big difference) philosophers who disparaged all social niceties and insisted that as human beings were animals we ought to live as beasts do—drinking nothing but water and eating raw food and sleeping on the ground under the stars. I suppose today we would call them the homeless by choice. Anyway, Diogenes lived in the streets and was proud of it. Once, when Socrates invited him home, he stamped

Favorite books, movies, music, games: Again as evidence of character. If a person is a gamer, what's their favorite game and what might that say about who they are? If people have a favorite book or movie, the plot or setting of that movie might provide insight into their character or details with which to make a case for one characterization or another. It might not, too, of course. When the person read the book or saw the movie might have been more significant than the object itself.

Favorite possessions: Some people are all about their things, the cars they drive, the latest fashion accessories. Did they buy it, rent or lease it, inherit it, borrow it from a friend?

Friends: Concrete or abstract, likes. Because what a person likes suggests something about choices, you can learn a lot about how a person thinks by contemplating their tastes, assuming they acquired them intentionally. Some people just fall in with those they meet, and in such cases you can't learn much from who they know. Although you learned a lot from the fact they don't much care who they associate with.

Enemies: Concrete or abstract, dislikes. Again, choice can be seen as an indication of character.

Heroes: Influences. If you know something about the person whom your character most admires, then you know what your character aspires to or appreciates. That, too, gives you a sense of how people think because it gives you a sense of their values. If they like a larger-than-life character they are a very different person than if they like the one who never said much but played an important role in the events.

Abode: The type of building someone lives in and their neighborhood.

That's the standard list of topics for a *bios*. What did I leave out? To use the list, you need to go through each item and decide if you have any relevant information for it and then if there's anything useful to be made of what you know for that topic. One way to decide about what would be useful is to figure out your goal. What are you trying to accomplish, and how does that help you select and shape the information you've gathered.

---

his dusty feet on the sage's carpets and said, "Thus I tread on your vanity." Once he went so far as to say, "The only place to spit in a rich man's home is in his face." If you find Diogenes the Cynic interesting, Google "the sayings of Diogenes of Synope." If you are interested in *chreia*, have a look at Hock and O'Neil, *Chreia in Ancient Rhetoric*.

If your goal is *encomium* and the person you are praising was prone to bad behavior, you will need to choose very narrowly. If your goal is *vituperation* and the person actually did good things, you would question their motivation or show how what they did wasn't truly good, or how it had unfortunate or unforeseen consequences, or how they really did it against their will or against their natural inclinations. If you need to either praise or blame and the person wasn't particularly good or bad, you could talk about the momentous times in which they lived, or the great friends (or enemies) they had, or, worse comes to worst, the great people they admired (or hated). Whatever your goals and purposes always focus on providing concrete details, bring the person to life before your audience's eyes.

Often when we praise someone we are really praising the milieu in which they live. Such *bios* are really a celebration of a group effort and to some extent a group identity, and it just happens to be that person's special turn. When you praise someone in public, however, you need to be mindful of the fact that many people hear praise of another as implicit condemnation of themselves, and, rather than feel a swelling pride in group identity or admiration for another's accomplishments, such people will feel resentment or hostility or worse. Every "Attagirl!" is a potential finger in someone else's eye.

━━━━━ Your Turn

All right, we've walked through the process so now it's your turn to characterize someone. You can either pick someone you know personally or a historical figure. The first time you do this, don't worry about the purpose of the details. Just get the details down. After you've got some data, think about how you would shape the details to make a point. Imagine, for example, that you are a lawyer and you've got a client who is innocent of what they are accused of, but there is some strong evidence against them. Which of the elements would you use to get this person acquitted? What if they are found guilty, and now your only goal is to lighten the sentence?

Stereotypes

Whenever you describe someone you don't know very well or analyze a person you've just met, you will make some assumptions about them based on how they look and sound, their stature, their complexion, their hair, their clothing, their accent, their vocabulary, and so on. When you describe those characteristics in detail, you get a relatively vivid but superficial sense of who they are, as we just did in the section on characterization. Strictly speaking such attributes are accidental in the sense that they just happen to be; they don't necessarily have any affect on a person such that you could necessarily draw accurate inferences from them. Whenever we generalize from weak or irrelevant data we are *stereotyping*, an almost universally rejected form of prejudicial thinking. The etymology and the history of the word, however, reveals something interesting about the difference between thinking and critical thinking.

The word *stereotype* is a combination of the Greek word *stereos* meaning "firm" or "solid" and *typos* meaning "impression," as in a mold. A cookie cutter is a kind of stereotype. The word *stereotype* was first used in 1798 by a French printer named Firmin Didot to describe a process for creating metal plate copies of typeset texts. In those days, a printer assembled (it was called composing) each letter of a word and each word of a sentence and every sentence of a text into a form that held the collection of letters in place. He then covered that plate with ink and then pressed a piece of paper onto the ink-covered letters, producing a paper and ink copy of the metal text. Over time, as multiple impressions would wear out the metal type, the prints would become less crisp, and the type would have to be replaced, which took time and cost money. Moreover, because there was just the one original metal copy, only one paper copy could be printed at a time.

The stereotype process made an inexpensive metal copy of the expensive and time-consuming original. Because the metal plates could be produced cheaply, the printer could produce multiple copies of them and then use the multiples to produce many more paper copies of a text at once. The resulting increase in speed and efficiently of printing eventually drove the price of books down and made them readily available to a much wider audience. Middle-class people could now own their own libraries. The stereotype process enabled the first information revolution.

The word *stereotype* took on a new meaning in 1919, when an American writer named Walter Lippmann published *Public Opinion*. In that book Lippmann explained that the human mind made sense of experience by creating useful generalizations from sensations. The amount of data we receive through our senses is so great that it would overwhelm us if we didn't filter it in some way. Lippmann named the filtration process *stereotyping*, and he described the process as a kind of fiction writing:

> By fictions I do not mean lies. I mean a representation of the environment which is in lesser or greater degree made by man himself. The range of fiction extends all the way from complete hallucination to the scientists' perfectly self-conscious use of a schematic model, or his decision that for his particular problem accuracy beyond a certain number of decimal places is not important. A work of fiction may have almost any degree of fidelity, and, so long as the degree of fidelity can be taken into account, fiction is not misleading. In fact, human culture is very largely the selection, the rearrangement, the tracing of patterns upon, and

the stylizing of what William James called "the random irradiations and resettlements of our ideas."[5] The alternative to the use of fictions is direct exposure to the ebb and flow of sensation. That is not a real alternative, for however refreshing it is to see at times with a perfectly innocent eye, innocence itself is not wisdom, though a source and corrective of wisdom. For the real environment is altogether too big, too complex, and too fleeting for direct acquaintance. We are not equipped to deal with so much subtlety, so much variety, so many permutations and combinations. And although we have to act in that environment, we have to reconstruct it on a simpler model before we can manage with it. To traverse the world men must have maps of the world. (3)

Lippmann's point is that we don't encounter reality directly. Rather we create a mental model, a representation of reality, and we interact with the model. Any given representation may be less or more accurate, from hallucination to scientific representation, but representations are all we have to go on. Our understanding of the world and everything in it is a human construct. That's not to say that there's no real world out there, just that we know it only indirectly. What we know of it are generalizations. Lippmann's ideas about representation and reality were adopted by a great many thinkers over the last hundred years and developed into the theory of the social construction of knowledge. If you've ever read Plato's "Allegory of the Cave" in *The Republic* (VII, 514a–20a), this is the absolute opposite of that. The doctrine expressed in *The Republic* is known as realism, the foundational assumption of which is the world is directly knowable given the correct methodologies. Lippmann's position, one far more generally accepted today than realism, is that our understandings of the world are psychological (rhetorical if conscious) constructs.

From the standpoint of persuasion, what Walter Lippmann had to say about stereotyping is interesting because it explains how the thinking that preceded us—commitments made in our absence, as it were—influences the way we encounter the world. *We all have a whole set of unexamined beliefs that affect the outcome of our persuasive processes and, to a greater and lesser extent, guide us to certain conclusions.* If you think it is possible to think past these unexamined beliefs, by identifying or examining them, that's fine. If you don't think it's possible, from my perspective that's fine too. Regardless, you need to think about the relationship between the world and how you know it because that understanding is a form of rhetoric; it shapes and filters your ways of engaging with people and ideas. If you are inclined to think, as Plato seems to in *The Republic*, that it is possible to apprehend the world directly, that is, without any rhetorical intervention, well you and

---

5. James, *Principles of Psychology*, vol. ii, p. 638.

I are never going to agree about that. And yet I'll grant you that whenever you have the leisure to think before you decide, it's always better to create your representations based on data. Look at the evidence closely. Search for counterevidence. Question your assumptions. Question other people's assumptions. *Think about how you think before you see what you always see and say what you always say.*

Inspecting your tacit beliefs, your habits of thought, your assumptions about how things work and how people are is just generally useful because it switches off your autopilot and invokes your critical thinking skills. But when it comes to characterization, it is especially important to question your patterns of thought about people because most of us go from day to day imagining what people are like based solely on what they do for a living or how they dress or what kind of car they drive, superficial, largely accidental attributes rather than actual evidence. While prior assumptions may be available resources when it comes to characterizing people in order to make a point, when it comes to really understanding what people need and how best to serve them, you have to be more analytical. You can't just fix on one of the topics of a *bios* and make it all up from there. You have to look at all of the available evidence.

If two people are accused of beating a third but only one of them did it, and one of the suspects is a six-foot-three, throat-tattooed, gang-affiliated male, and the other suspect is a five-foot-one, Chanel-suit-wearing mother of two young children, who do you suspect is guilty? What if you learned that the victim was married to the Chanel-suit woman and sleeping with the babysitter? What if the tattooed man was the babysitter's boyfriend? What if the babysitter . . . ? If you drew a conclusion after each of those questions, you were thinking stereotypically (*and you weren't reading against the grain*). Appearances are deceptive because they are shaped by assumptions and expectations, fictional constructs, as Lippmann explained. Nevertheless, if the assumptions are good and the information is accurate, your conclusion might be useful even if the thinking was flawed.

The more aware you are of these patterns or habits of thought, the more objective you are. The prevailing opinion these days is that purely objective thinking is impossible because you can never think completely outside the patterns. Even if Lippmann was right, that's no excuse for accepting vague and unexamined or too frequently used patterns as legitimate premises upon which to build arguments about the world. When people are under pressure, frightened, or in a hurry, they will often use rapid cognition, with mixed results. But people often also think rapidly because they are too timid or complacent or self-righteous to question their patterns and habits of thought. Most people are all too eager to have their prior beliefs affirmed and are so threatened by counterevidence that they refuse to believe it when they see it. Beware the common cognitive biases.

━━━━━ Your Turn

I'll admit my example of the gang member and the Chanel suit is lame. See how many descriptive scenarios you can come up with that might lead a person to make a stereotypical judgment, and then share your best example with others to see how they respond.

━━━━━━━━━━━━━━

Audience analysis (demographics)

I took you on that meandering tour of characterization and stereotyping to set up the following advice about what is arguably *the most important part of learning how to be persuasive: audience analysis.*

To persuade people you have to understand them, who they are, how they think, what they need, and what they think they need. If you start with yourself then you won't be successful unless you are exactly like them. And if you start with the product or the idea you are selling, then your success will depend on the existence of a preexisting connection between them and what you are talking about. On the other hand, if you begin the persuasion process with a clear understanding of to whom you are talking, you have a much better chance of tailoring your message to them. Madison Avenue spends billions of dollars a year on demographics (*What does the etymology of* demographics tell *you?*), on trying to figure out who their market is, where (geographically, socially, economically) their market is, and thus how to move them. Large-scale retailers keep data warehouses full of information from which they hope to glean a better understanding of their market. Walmart, apparently, has discovered that demand for strawberry Pop-Tarts in Florida increases whenever a hurricane has been forecast (Hays). Google uses your searches to select the advertising that shows up in the browser sidebar when you log into Gmail. Facebook mines your every *like* for data that may predict what you are going to buy next. Target may know you are pregnant before your family finds out (Hill).[6] For many of us, data acquisition based on our habits and attitudes is just a fact of digital life; for others it's an apocalyptic threat to privacy. At any rate, the big players in the retail world have warehouses full of data out of which they can generalize market segments, audiences in other words. While you may one day have access to that kind of data (and you should be aware now that your data is being warehoused), you can start constructing a systematic impression of an audience without that data.

---

6. For a bit more context on this last provocation, have a look at p. 212 in *The Power of Habit*, by Charles Duhigg.

Because a full characterization of actual audience members is rarely possible, a general profile may be a workable substitute, as long as the description is thick enough that you are fairly certain you are making warranted generalizations. These general profiles are known as *personas* among marketers and technical writers. Personas are generalizations; they are not people, and they are not individual characters.

Personas

A persona is a fictional representation of a person composed out of generalized information about real audience members. A persona differs from the characterizations we were playing with earlier in that the former are descriptions of unique individuals whereas personas are specific examples of generalized types out of which an audience may be composed. A character is a single individual; a persona is a type among many relevant types. This type is given a name, specific personality traits, attitudes, possessions, and activities. He or she is not an archetype or a stereotype; she or he is neither an idealized form nor a collection of assumptions and prejudices but rather a faithful representation of an audience segment that is then used as one of many guiding principles when shaping messages.

The practice of creating personas is both straightforward and complex. You come up with a series of questions the answers to which will give you a clear and specific image of a segment of your audience. You imagine the answers. You get a picture that reflects the persona, and you create a document that includes the image, the questions, and the answers. This document then becomes a "member" of your audience. In businesses where communication is the central focus—public relations firms and technical writing businesses, for example—these documents are often turned into posters and pinned to corkboards or taped to walls. They are concrete reminders of an abstract idea. They remind you that *you are communicating with real people with real needs and real lives.*

While demographics is a discipline unto itself, there are stock questions you can ask to get a sense of who you might be dealing with. Following is a list of such questions. But first, the primary questions are, What's in it for each segment of your audience? Why do they care, or why should they care if they don't yet? These questions are the foundation of your persuasive efforts. If you don't have a clear answer to these questions, you have a serious rhetorical problem.

Beyond this we can group the remaining questions into seven categories, with subquestions under each. This is a pretty detailed list, but it's not complete. It's just to get you started thinking about who you are dealing with so that you can start to think about how to tailor your messages.

Values

1.   What do they value? Money, time, respect, prestige, equality, autonomy, community, friendships, institutional associations?

2. Who (and what) do they admire?

3. Who do they pretend to admire? Keep in mind that public and private values are not always identical or even compatible in some cases.

4. What do they long for? More time, more money, help with a difficult task, affirmation of their value as a person, prestige, the past, a bright shiny future?

5. What do they fear? Unfamiliar things, obstacles, illness, financial problems, losing respect, being alone?

6. What do they regret? Are there relevant past decisions that might influence this one?

7. What do they hope for?

Knowledge

1. What do they know? You don't want to tell people things they already know unless you are trying to show them that you know those things, too (like on a test or when writing an essay for a prof).

2. What do they need to know? You need to know what relevant information they are missing.

3. What mistaken beliefs, prejudices, or preoccupations do you need to correct? There will always be some mistakes or confusions that might impede the reception of an idea. When I introduced the idea of critical thinking, as you may remember, I started out by saying that *critical* doesn't mean "negative" or "really important," two common interpretations of the word that would get in the way of you thinking critically about critical thinking. I assumed you might have those ideas about *critical* in your head because they are the most common uses, and so I spent some words trying to change your prior knowledge of the word *critical*.

4. What habits of mind and behavior have they got that you might be able to use?

5. What habits of mind and behavior have they got that you might need to correct or overcome?

Way of life

1. What do they do for a living?

2. Who are they when they are at home?

3. Is their job their identity, or is it just a job?

4. What institutions and practices and people do they identify (or aspire to identify) with?

5. What is their marital status?

6. What is their religious affiliation?

7. What kind of income do they have? And what do they imagine is their income potential?

8. Where do they live (country, state, city, neighborhood)?

9. What kind of dwelling do they live in (apartment, house, room, condo, townhome)?

10. Where have they lived and traveled?

11. What kind of education do they have?

12. What leisure activities do they pursue?

13. What are their favorite movies, books, and TV shows?

Consumer information
1. How do they dress?

2. Where do they shop?

3. What do they drive?

4. What kind of vacations have they gone on? How often do they get away?

Media interfaces
1. Who are their Facebook friends?

2. Who do they follow on Twitter?

3. Or do they ignore social media and online life in general?

4. What are their cable preferences?

Work life
1. What is their role in the place where the decision has to be made (actor, reactor, leader, follower, decision maker, early adopter, pioneer, visionary, reluctant participant, recalcitrant resister, naysayer, person who needs to feel important, one who wants to be left alone)? What other roles can you think of?

2. What role do they wish they had or wish others saw them as having?

3. What is at stake for them? What is their interest in the matter?

4. What conventional beliefs and unconventional beliefs do they hold?

Contextual considerations
1. Where and how will the message be received?
2. When will the message be received (time of year and time of day)?
3. How do their moods change over time (seasonally and daily)?
4. Might they have any immediately pressing needs (hunger, sleep, etc.)?

When generating personas it is important to avoid over-generalizing. Be as concrete, detailed, and specific as possible. But keep in mind that you are creating a type, a representative of an audience segment, not a character or a person.

Your Turn

There are many ways to practice creating personas. I will give you a pragmatic application shortly, but before we move on spend some time creating a couple of detailed examples for yourself. Go to a crowded place on your campus, and watch the people as they hang out and pass by. How many types of student can you see? Once you have your types, using details from as many examples of each type as you can, create a persona that could stand in for all members of that type—the verbal equivalent of a cardboard cutout. Your goal is to create four or five (or however many) personas that would reasonably represent the students on your campus. If you take a photograph of a person as a way to jog your memory as you create a person, don't make that image public. Don't post it online anywhere or even send it as an email unless you have that person's written permission.

The creation of pseudoaudiences (astroturfing)
The expression *grassroots movement* denotes an advocacy movement or collective desire to change something on a grand scale that grows organically, spreading contagiously, one person or small group at a time. The idea is that opinions and activities are more authentic or honest or trustworthy when they come from the bottom up, when they are created by small groups of people who have no grand ambitions or power or money but want to make a positive difference. When enough people with a similar idea or opinion find each other—sometimes called the *tipping point*—more people are sure to be attracted to the cause, and thus the idea snowballs into a movement that can have significant impact. Social networking software has increased the rate at which like-minded people can find each other, and as a result today it's easier than ever to create a community out of isolated individuals who share ideas

but not geographical or economic circumstances. And these social networks can accelerate change.

Marketers and salespeople and shadowy organizations have noticed that it is possible to fake a grassroots movement, thus the expression *astroturfing*. Businesses and organizations give their personas cyberidentities by creating Facebook accounts, Twitter accounts, and Flickr accounts for them. They even leave comments on popular and relevant news sites or blogs under artificial email accounts. This digital trail suggests that an actual person with a personal opinion is propagating an idea, whereas in fact a paid employee is performing a job duty by appearing in disguise everywhere online, promoting an idea: pseudopeople creating pseudopopular opinion.

━━━━ Your Turn

Doubtful? Good. Do a Google search for the California corporation Centcom, or have a look at "Revealed: US Spy Operation That Manipulates Social Media," by Nick Fielding and Ian Cobain, from March 17, 2011, of the *Guardian*. How many other ways can you imagine public opinion being manipulated?

Why knowing your audience matters and what it means

It is a cardinal rule of rhetoric that you know your audience.[7] One of the reasons you need to understand who you are talking to is that who people are affects how they hear and see the world, and as a persuasive person you have

---

7. Are you reading against the grain? You might want to push back here. While rules aren't made to be broken, you can't truly follow a rule if you don't understand it. You need to carefully examine all rules, even the "cardinal" ones. So let's push back on "know your audience" for a moment. Must you always know your audience, and what does it mean to know an audience? You might like to read, "The Author's Audience Is Always a Fiction," by Walter Ong. When being a member of an audience means basically doing a job, then the person isn't a full person so much as the embodiment of a set of conventions (rules) and expectations and wisdom of the job. In such cases you don't need to know your audience, just what their conventions and expectations are. Every partner/opponent is different, but the rules of the game are the same.

Then, too, if you are a musician or a poet or an artist of any kind, you might prefer to be your own audience, to follow the dictates of your own aesthetic as it evolves, indifferent to whether or not you ever have any commercial success. And then again, if you are in a setting where you have only to execute orders, audience doesn't matter so much as commander's intent. Google the concept of commander's intent if you've not heard it before. If you have, Google it anyway just to make sure you know what it means.

to take these unspoken rhetorical affects into account, even though as you now know they are in a real sense rhetorical constructs. Even when your audience consists of actual people, your understanding of them is a construct.

Our practices of interpretation perform rhetorical work; they filter and refract. They alter what messages come through. This is why people can understand the same sentence differently. For one person it will be a fact, a statement requiring no evidence or arguments; while for another it will be a lie, a statement that no further evidence or arguments could justify; while for a third it might be accepted as a premise but will require more evidence if he is to grant it the status of a fact. Consider the assertion in the middle of the following table in the light potentially cast by the stereotypical (and simpleminded) divide between political liberals and conservatives.

Conservative	*Assertion*	*Liberal*
Experience		Experience
Nationality		Nationality
Ethnicity		Ethnicity
Gender		Gender
Age	Anything the	Age
Politics	government runs,	Politics
Faith	private business can	Faith
Occupation	run better.	Occupation
Income		Income
Parenting		Parenting
Education		Education
Emotional state		Emotional state

If you were going to replace the general categories on either side of the assertion—experience, nationality, gender, and so on—how would you do it? Which categories would you delete as irrelevant? If they all seem irrelevant to you, then what categories would be the relevant ones?

Given who you are, what is your estimation of the truth-value of the statement, "Anything the government runs, private business can run better"? Who might you have to be (or become) to give it a different truth-value? If you were going to rewrite that sentence, how would you rewrite it to reflect your own belief system? If you're not really sure, read it against the grain, and then compare your against-the-grain with someone else's in your class. Do you think you will have the same opinion twenty years from now?

There are no pure meanings in human interaction in the way there are elements in nature because every input has to be interpreted, and interpretation alters meaning: Meaning is always a function of expectations, assumptions, knowledge, personal experiences, cultural experiences, emotional states, social settings, and biases. Even age, gender, and class play a part in how each of us interprets what we hear and see. Every meaning is influenced by previous interpretive acts whether the interpreter is aware of the influences or not. If we really want to believe something, we won't require any evidence at all. If we really want to reject something, no evidence in the world will change our minds. Worse yet, the same evidence may support an assertion at one time and undermine the same assertion at another time. If you've ever fallen out of love and wondered what you ever saw in that person, you know what I mean. The traits you loved become the ones you hate. You just interpret them differently.

Let me try to offer you a concrete example of how interpretive practices perform rhetorical work. The next few paragraphs are a quick trip through the way my mind sometimes works, my inner interpretive rhetoric followed by immediate reflection on those interpretive practices. I'm not offering it to you as some kind of ideal way to think, far from it. It's a deeply flawed series of intellectual experiences that flashed through my head in the space of about two minutes while I was doing an hour on a cross-trainer at a gym. If I hadn't written it down right after I got back from the gym, I would have forgotten it completely. I have these sorts of insights into how I think all the time. I encourage you to track your own and think about them too.

CNN regularly asks its viewers to email opinions, some of which it airs as an audience participation moment (the contemporary, Internet-enabled, instantaneous equivalent of the old fashioned op-ed section of a newspaper). They do this, presumably, to make people feel involved and to spark watercooler controversy. In my experience, the occasion rarely leads to carefully crafted opinions. But it often leads to useful examples for classes on persuasion.

On January 5, 2010, Jack Cafferty, one of CNN's presenters, posed the question, "Should police be held accountable for using Tasers?" One woman from Georgia wrote something like, "The police should be able to do what they need to do. They are here to protect us." That is a rather nifty enthymeme. A statement followed by a kind of maxim which if accepted would give us a reason to accept the statement as true. But what kind of person would simply accept this enthymeme? What would you have to believe, and who would you have to be, to assert that because the police are here to protect us they should be able to Taser us at will? (*Did you notice I rearranged the enthymeme? Was what I offered a fair substitute, or did I make a substantial change?*) At any rate, stuck as I was on a cross-trainer and unable to escape CNN, I wondered, What kind of person thinks the police can do what they want because they are here to protect us?

And so I started thinking: I guess that someone living in an affluent suburb would be more likely to say such an enthymeme or agree with it than someone living in a poorer part of the city. In both cases experiences and assumptions and incomes and politics would lead people to hear the statement very differently, as a simple truth or a dangerous lie. Someone else might find it amusingly naive, or irritatingly self-righteous, or just optimistic, or. . . . Well, how do *you* hear it?

When I heard, "The police should be able to do what they need to do. They are here to protect us," my first thought was a derisive, Yeah, right! Upon maybe thirty seconds of reflection I was able to explain to myself why I disagreed with the woman from Georgia: The police are here to enforce the law. To the extent I am protected by a law, their efforts may protect me. In contrast, however, to the extent that a law threatens me, their efforts to enforce the law will have an unpleasant effect on me. (*Try a Toulmin markup on that*.) But it took me even longer to realize why what she said so irritated me.

I unknowingly built my affluent suburb assertion on the unexamined belief that faith in the police is a function of wealth. The more you feel you have in a given world the more you trust the goodness of that world and therefore the trustworthiness of its authorities. The more deprived you feel, the less you trust authority. I don't have any data to back that warrant. I just think that every organization is designed to protect itself, and therefore if you are in you are safe, and if you are out you are in danger. And yet I inhabit a fairly privileged place in society; I'm white, male, heterosexual, middle class, gainfully employed, married, and so on.

So why didn't I just nod in agreement with the woman who said the police are here to protect us? Do I identify, somewhat absurdly, with an underclass? So maybe I wasn't actually irritated by her assertion that "the police are here to protect us" so much as I was irritated by what I unconsciously assumed a person would have to believe in order to say it. But that assumption was mine, not hers. Suddenly I realized what I was thinking had nothing to do with her. I was making assumptions about who would believe what that person said and then attributing those beliefs to her even though she never expressed them. I had, in a sense, made her up and then took issue with her.

The minute I realized that I was imagining I could read her mind, that I was attributing a belief she might or might not have based on my interpretation of what she said, I realized I was being self-righteous and a bit simpleminded. I still think that "the police are here to protect us" is a questionable assertion rather than a maxim upon which to base an enthymeme because I can think of several instances in American history when the "us" wasn't "all of us." But in retrospect I realized that the rhetorical analysis I performed at the gym had nothing to do with the person who ignited it. My audience at that moment was me, and I wasn't even all that self-aware just then. I had ten minutes left on that infernal machine, and maybe I was using hostility to burn the last few minutes hot.

If that CNN respondent had been actually present and I'd followed my slightly mindless inclinations, she and I might have found ourselves in a Jerry Springer situation, a pseudodrama caused by uncritical assertions designed to sell advertising on cable TV, a bad facsimile of real rhetoric, a shouting match instead of an exchange where it's possible to learn from people you don't (and likely won't ever) really agree with.

As someone studying persuasion your first response to an assertion shouldn't be a gut reaction, a derisive "Yeah, right," or a self-righteous "Right on," or even a reasoned counterstatement, "I disagree with your premise. . . ." Your first response should be a series of questions:

- What assumptions enable/disable the enthymeme that person just made?

- Where is this person coming from? (The "where" is a metaphor for a sum total of life experiences, a person's constructed identity.)

But then you have to flip the questions, turn them on yourself:

- Where am I coming from?

- What unsaid and until now unexamined beliefs informed how I heard the enthymeme?

That's a very complex thought process. How can a person possibly participate effectively in public discourse if so much thinking has to precede a response to something someone just said? Well, it takes practice and careful examination of your own beliefs prior to participation. Effective presence of mind takes years of preparation, provided by constantly focused daily practice and regular feedback from other people. You're just getting started. Keep going, but don't expect an overnight transformation. If you ask those types of questions enough, over time you will refine your answers, and eventually the answers will automatically replace the questions, which will speed up your process. When this finally happens, don't forget to ask yourself the questions occasionally anyway, just to check the answers. A well-informed autopilot is an excellent tool, but given the right conditions (or wrong conditions, rather) it can fly you into a mountain.

Creating a virtual audience

What we just went through is a representation of how one might tend to turn thinking into critical thinking. You don't just accept the first thing that comes to mind as what you believe but rather try to figure out why you thought it and whether or not you really believe it. Your thoughts, in other words, are evidence of your thinking processes, and, if a thought is defective, you know you need to revisit the process.

In the case of CNN, I had to scrutinize the assumption I made about the other person's assumptions. I wasn't always this reflective a thinker. I got more reflective and less reflexive through lots of interactions with other people, by running my ideas before an audience so often that eventually I was able to anticipate objections and confusions better, with the result that my writing created fewer objections and confusions. That process took a long time, and maybe it always has to, but I have an idea about how you might be able to accomplish the same thing in maybe a little less time: construct a virtual audience on which to try out your ideas before you present them to an actual audience.

Because the word *audience* is extremely abstract and therefore basically meaningless on the surface, because most of us don't have much experience literally standing in front of a crowd of people, creating a virtual[8] analogy for an audience will increase your capacity for persuasion. Here is how to create a virtual audience.

Go to iStockphoto or Google Images or CreativeCommons.org or anywhere else that has lots of photographs, and type in "thumbs up" and "thumbs down" or "approval" and "disapproval" or any other pair of positive and negative adjectives you can think of, and contemplate the images that come up. Find at least one positive and one negative image you can make an emotional connection with. You're looking for images a bit more memorable than the emoticons of a smiley and a frowny face, but that's the basic idea.

From there, see if you can refine the sensations of approval and disapproval these images inspire in you. Let me work out a hypothetical example for you. The level of detail here is far more important than the images chosen or even the character traits used. Your virtual audience needs to be your own. I'll explain why in a minute.

> **The white-gloved perfectionist** The details person is preoccupied
> with punctuation, spelling, subject-verb agree-
> ment, proper citations, well-formed sentences,
> well-chosen words, and so on. This is the person
> who picks lint off my jacket and runs a white
> glove over the place I just dusted. I'm not exactly
> sure why I chose the image of an upper-class
> (pearls, starched collar) scowling white woman
> to represent the details of this persona. Maybe
> because the picture reminds me of my maternal
> grandmother who somehow managed to sound
> disapproving even when she laughed. At any rate, I need a white-
> gloved perfectionist because I'm not naturally all that detail oriented.
> I need to remind myself to pick up after myself, and I have to be kind
> of stern with myself about it because I'm inclined to run on ahead.

---

8. What's the difference between *virtual* and *fake*? What about *virtual* and *artificial*? And *virtual* and *real*?

The conditioning coach or music teacher
The person who constantly demands more, more, more. Do it again. Do it faster. Do it better. I chose the coach for this figure because that persona represents for me the ideal of a teacher. Someone whose own success depends on mine and whose ability I admire so much that I really want to impress them. The internalization of this persona is why I can spend an hour a day on a cross-trainer scrutinizing random enthymemes.

The skeptic In addition to the images that keep me focused on surface details and training and practice, I need an image that will also encourage me to take my thinking from reflexive to reflective. This image is some variation on the skeptic, the hard-nosed, piercing-gazed, brow knitter. The persona who doesn't care about surface details but who needs evidence, data, numbers, proof. The one who's always saying, "Show me the evidence; where's the proof? That assertion is unwarranted. What are you assuming? Have you considered this? What about that? Is this really the best you can do?" For me, the image of comedian George Carlin is perfect for this because of his humorous way of calling out a liar.

The enthusiast is the last member of my virtual audience. While the is-that-the-best-you-can-do types motivate me to try harder, to keep working even after I'm sick of it, if they were the only people in my audience I would be less productive than I need to be. The

problem with constant criticism, even constant constructive criticism, is that over time it can engender self-doubt. Suddenly it's not my performance that is being critiqued but my character, and then my self-esteem is at risk. This is unhealthy. I need a counterbalancing influence, an eyes-on-the-prize persona, someone who is positive about me always and basically enthusiastic about the promise of whatever I'm working on. Some people use their pets for this purpose, as an external representation of a constantly positive attitude, hence the picture of my pug Jake (the dog who taught you logic a few pages back). Other people find an idol or historical figure of note as a good way to stay motivated when the going gets tough. What would Aristotle say?

Do I really have these images taped to my wall? No. Well, I do have a picture of Carlin in my screen saver rotation, and Jake sleeps on a chair in my home office. I have internalized my audience, and it is composed of a much wider array of personas than just these four examples. Some are actual people who I know or have known, family members, my wife, professors, students, colleagues, friends, but by now my audience is pretty much internalized to the point that it's abstracted; I don't necessarily see this audience as individuals. I use this internalized idea of what is likely to persuade and what isn't to develop something that's nearly ready for public consumption, and then I share it with actual friends and colleagues to get their feedback. I don't always like what comes back, and I don't always act on it. Even if I like the criticism that comes back, sometimes I discount it and keep refining the work anyway. But I always seek feedback, and I always listen.

I don't expect my personas will work for you. Each of us uses our own experiences and our own reactions to these experiences out of which we need to develop a set of standards and expectations for our own performances. We can learn from each other certainly, but we also need to learn how to teach ourselves.

As an alternative to a Google search for "approve" and "disapprove," think up as many synonyms as you can for both of these words, and then see if *you* can make the faces you associate with each word. Do it in front of a camera, and create a gallery of your own expressions of approval and disapproval. If you are any good at this, you may discover that just making the expression can influence your attitude. While smiling is a sign of happiness, a genuine attempt at a heartfelt smile can actually cheer you up. Sitting straight with your chin up can actually improve your confidence.

At any rate, whether you use your own face or images of other people, your virtual audience should be composed of as many personas as you need to focus on constantly improving your efforts on as many different levels as required to turn your spontaneous thoughts into ideas worth sharing.

But before you start pasting pictures on the wall, take a careful look at yourself:

- What is the best way to motivate you?

- Are you a details or a big-picture person?

- Are you focused or scattered?

- Do you take criticism personally and become temporarily disabled by it, or do you use it as inspiration to improve and fix the problem?

- When things aren't going well, do you blame yourself or others?

- How do you deal with the anxiety of potential failure?

- Do you plan more carefully and put in more hours, or do you procrastinate in order to protect your ego in case you do fail? How do you respond to praise?

- Do you get all "Gee shucks, I hardly even tried," or do you look for ways to do it even better next time?

- Do you try to identify and correct weaknesses or always play to your strengths?

- Are you inclined to take everything personally, or can you see past the personal to the work at hand?

- Are you motivated by intrinsic or extrinsic rewards?

- Do you care how you are doing in relation to those around you, or are you focused only on your own performance?

- Can you delay gratification easily, or does resistance to temptation exhaust you?

Compose your imaginary audience with the mix of taskmasters and enthusiasts that suits your personality type and learning style. Ban any of the miserable figures from your past who make you doubt your potential, but don't just fill the wall with enthusiasts. Create a virtual audience that will help you identify and correct weaknesses while allowing you to benefit also from your strengths. Make sure there's at least one persona there who will help you see past yourself, who can help you focus on the work and minimize thoughts of how the work reflects your identity or your future plans. One A on a chemistry test won't make you a rocket surgeon. One F on a history test doesn't mean you're doomed to repeat the past. *You are looking for trends, not events.*

Whenever you are finished working on a piece for a while, read it out loud while facing the images of your virtual audience in turn, and imagine how each persona would respond to your words. Try imagining them reading over your shoulder as you write. Sound weird? Well, it is kind of weird, but it's helpful. Pretty quickly you'll be able to just glance at a picture on your wall and know what you need to do next.

As you encounter more and more readers and actual audience members, add nuances to the types on your audience wall. Internalize the practices that appeal to each type until you no longer need to see the sticklers and the enthusiasts because you reflexively know what needs to be done before you give your work to someone else to read. You are imagining your audience, approximating a reality that will stand in for an audience until what you've done is ready for real people to assess and work with. Each of your teachers along the way may contribute an image or a piece of an image to that concept, but *you want to be thinking beyond your teachers and mentors.* You want to become your own best audience, the one who is quick with an appreciative smile or a triumphant fist pump when you get it right but doesn't let you slack off or settle for good enough when you know there's better out there. At the same time, however, there are times when good enough is indeed good enough. Don't let perfection be the enemy of the good. Your goal is to become the person who can ask you the right questions at the right moments, the one who can help you generate heaps of ideas and then separate the crap from the gold.

Once your virtual audience approves a given effort, give that piece to a few trusted, thoughtful friends, and listen carefully to what they say. Don't just lap up the praise or fend off the criticism. And don't take either personally. Someone once said, "You're never as good or as bad as anyone ever says you are." I can't remember the reference exactly, but it's great advice no matter who said it. Here's another, if a bit melodramatic, way of thinking about criticism: What your friends consider your virtues, your enemies will consider vices.

Emotion, Reason, and Persuasion

The emotion/reason false dichotomy

For many years, books on argumentation and critical thinking have equated emotional appeals with logical fallacies—*argument ad baculum* (intimidation, fear), *argument ad misericordiam* (pity or shame), *argument ad populum* (bandwagon, social proof)—and thus have left readers with the false impression that emotions are illogical, irrational, and therefore counterproductive of critical thinking and rational argumentation. Recent research in neurophysiology and psychology, however, has effectively proven that the reason-emotion binary is a false assumption. Because we don't have time to go into the evidence deeply, let me save a little time (*Notice the rhetorical move there?*) by making two arguments from authority in defense of the idea that emotion and reason are not discrete faculties.

According to Jonah Lehrer,[9] in his book *How We Decide*, "feelings are what let us understand all the information that we can't directly comprehend. Reason without emotion is impotent" (26). If you can't feel, you can't think effectively because you can't decide. You can ruminate endlessly and list arguments and observe evidence, but you can't evaluate any of it with sufficient conviction to make a decision if you try to reason without feeling. All the logic and evidence in the world won't change a person's mind if he or she isn't motivated to change. And motivation comes from emotion—motion, movement. So disengaging the head from the heart, to use a very old-fashioned metaphor, is like disconnecting the wheels from the ground.

A psychologist from Harvard named J. J. Ratey has gone so far as to assert that it would be "ridiculous" to continue treating reason and emotion as separate domains (223).[10] If feelings are key to understanding and thus key to thinking, then you need to understand how emotions influence decision-making processes, perceptions, and beliefs if you want to be persuasive. If you find this line of inquiry interesting, Google for information and articles on "the somatic-marker hypothesis" or "the Iowa Gambling Task."

If arguments from authority leave you cold (*metaphor alert*), an argument from tradition (which is also a fallacy) isn't likely to persuade you either. Nevertheless, the rhetorical tradition has never separated emotion and reason in practice because since Aristotle it has been understood that:

> Emotions are those things through which, by undergoing change, people come to differ in their judgments (*On Rhetoric*, 1378a 19–22).

---

9. A few months before this book went to press, Jonah Lehrer was involved in a scandal that resulted in his being fired from *The New Yorker* and *Wired Magazine*. The outrage was such that *How We Decide* and his later work *Imagine* were pulled from the shelves. Apparently Lehrer republished his own work as if it had never been printed before, what amounts to essentially padding a resume and a significant breach of authorial ethics. Worse, he was revealed to have fabricated the content of several interviews, an unpardonable breach of journalistic ethics. Given his current circumstances, I thought to remove the quotation above but upon further reflection, I'm leaving the reference in as a cautionary tale. Having published three books before the age of 30, Lehrer showed great promise and he may yet return to prominence. But he did himself and his community a significant disservice by failing to adhere to clearly defined rules.

10. Given what you know about assessing arguments from authority (one of the logical fallacies), how would you question (read against the grain) the two pieces of evidence I just offered? By the way, did you notice the argument from ridicule in Ratey's calling the opposing argument "ridiculous"?

If the primary purpose of persuasive efforts is to help a group of people render a judgment, and emotions affect judgments, then a *rhetor* has to understand how emotions affect judgments.

Because we aren't actually talking with each other, I have no idea whether you agree with me or not about the emotion-reason split being an erroneous assumption, but, regardless of your position on that point, I need to move on. So if you continue to believe in an emotion-reason dichotomy, suspend your disbelief for what follows.

The social construction of emotions

It seems safe to assert that most people perceive their emotions as internal, spontaneous events. We may externalize feelings involuntarily, by laughing or crying or turning red or breathing quicker, and we might on occasion choose to display our feelings for a rhetorical purpose, like expressing joy when a loved one arrives and we want them to know how happy we are to see them or when we cheer with our friends when our team scores and we want them to know that we are on their side and a part of the group. But for the most part we tend to think emotions flow from the inside out and that, while we can sometimes control how we express them, we can't control the feelings themselves. Emotions just happen.

I'd like to propose an alternative perspective on how the emotions function and the purpose they serve in persuasion processes. From a rhetorical perspective, emotions are both indispensable and unavoidable, but they are not completely spontaneous; we can actually control what we feel and not just how we express those feelings. Our emotions are the rhetorical result of how we represent to ourselves what others are doing or saying or appearing to experience. Thus we can control what we are feeling by changing how we represent what we are perceiving, and we can influence what others feel as well by the same means. Not only can we do this, we all do it; we just don't notice most of the time.

Have you ever watched a toddler fall down and look around to see if anyone is watching before deciding to cry? If he has an audience, he will begin to wail. If no one seems to notice or show much concern, he won't. Have you noticed this? To me this suggests that rhetorical performance of emotion is innate. That is, without an audience to validate a sensation, the feeling isn't exactly the same. Of course, if a child cuts himself or bruises his head on falling, the actual shock and damage to his body will force him to cry out whether there's an audience or not. Still, we seem to have an innate sense that whoever is watching and how they relate to us matters.

If you haven't seen a toddler searching for an audience perhaps we share this experience: If I'm at a ball game and everybody's cheering, I find it very difficult not to cheer when something important happens even if I'm indifferent to the outcome. If I'm rooting for the away team and they score, I'll cheer but a bit self-consciously. Such is the power of the crowd. If I'm alone, watching the game on a small TV out of the corner of my eye, I'm not likely to jump out of my seat. Even if I'm wearing a team shirt and sitting alone in front of the big flat-screen, I'm not going to jump up and down and cheer if we score or weep if we lose, because I don't have anyone to mirror those emotions for me or share them with me. Emotions may be internal sensations, but they are often displayed for the benefit of the group; they often serve, in other words, the rhetorical purpose of affirming our identity and affiliation. If we were with different people we would have different feelings, and we would feel some of the same feelings differently: Emotions are rhetorical constructs. You don't have to agree with me here. I just want you to ponder the implications of this perspective.

So from the perspective of persuasion, it is a given that to be an effective *rhetor* you need emotional intelligence.

1. You need to understand how emotions influence both your own and other people's decisions.

2. You need to be able to infer emotional states in others by correctly interpreting non-verbal cues such as facial expressions and posture.

3. You need to be able to anticipate emotional responses based on context and culture and basic human psychology, especially when you can't see your audience.

4. You need to understand your own emotional states and how they influence what you believe and what you think and what you say.

5. You also need to be able to control not only how you express your emotions but also to some extent what you actually feel. This last requirement is obviously the one that takes the most practice and conscious effort and is arguably beyond the capacity of most people. Most of us mirror what others are feeling and so can't quite step out or up. A really great *rhetor* can.

Emotional intelligence is not merely sympathy, or the ability to feel what others are feeling as they are feeling it, because if you allow yourself to get caught up in the moment you may get confused or distracted or find you are unable to respond effectively. On the other hand, if you go too far in the opposite direction, remaining entirely aloof from what others are feeling, you may make significant rhetorical mistakes. You might, for example, fail to interpret their facial expressions correctly or fail to anticipate the imposition on their time that the email or text you are sending them is about to create and therefore incorrectly think that your people are perfectly content with what you've asked them to do, when in fact they are seething with anger and resentment and will sabotage your efforts at the first opportunity.

Here is a concrete example of a systematic emotional failure. While it often happens that people respond to emotions symmetrically—you move up, they move up; you move down, they move down in a proportional fashion—there are some interactions that are asymmetrical—you move in, they back off. The classic example is *asymmetrical schismogenesis* where a rift between people escalates because what one person does to produce a specific emotional response actually produces the opposite response, which they then misinterpret. Rather than realizing they did the opposite of what they needed to do, they just think it didn't work, and so they try it again, which makes the situation worse because the other person backs off even further.

Deborah Tannen has an excellent example of a sadly common married-couple interaction pathology known as *nag-withdraw* in *You Just Don't Understand: Women and Men in Conversation*. I hope you've never had the misfortune of being in a relationship where one person thinks the other is ignoring them and so makes frequent demands to be acknowledged while the other partner interprets those demands as unfair or demeaning or controlling and so tries to deal with their unwillingness to participate in that way by simply ignoring the person or emotionally hiding from them. Nag-withdraw is the result of a failure to understand how emotions influence decisions. The nagger and the withdrawer have each represented to themselves what the other person is doing and feeling in such a way that they have trapped each other in a downward cycle of increasingly intense misery. What they are feeling is unnecessary and, as long as the resentment isn't left simmering too long, relatively easy to fix. Just do the opposite of what you always do. You don't have to be a rhetorical genius to extricate yourself from unhappy interactions.

The influence of emotions can be monitored and mitigated (and exploited)

While the reason-emotion split is untenable—modern cognitive psychology having proven it non-existent—the split offered us some comfort when making decisions because we all know how volatile and inconsistent emotions can be. We can perhaps guard against the most intense emotional appeals, for example, by realizing that arguments and relationships are neither games nor wars and thus something won and lost, by recognizing metaphors for what they are and so mitigating their impact. We might also recognize that we are feeling something intensely and thus choose to wait before responding—count to ten before speaking, or walk around the block before hitting reply. Waiting to see how temporary an emotion is or how fleeting its intensity might be is a good idea because we tend to overstate or overreact when feeling strongly, and nearly all feelings fade with time.

The word *emotion* is related to *movement*, and movement implies *change*. "Nothing dries quicker than tears," as Cicero warned (*De Invention*, 1.69). If you want to test the effectiveness of this advice, the next time you feel like doing or buying something on impulse, promise yourself you'll do it or buy it tomorrow, and then walk away. If you still want it badly enough to go back for it, go for it. This procedure can protect you from buyer's remorse. Stepping away for a moment, whether literally or figuratively, is a good rule of thumb in nearly any context that will allow it. Whatever you are saying to yourself prior to speaking or acting may or may not be the direct cause of what you are about to say or do because persuasion isn't purely logical or even entirely rational.

Assessing your emotional involvement

You need to know what attracts and what repulses you and why so that you can *avoid making lasting decisions based on fleeting impressions*. To monitor your emotions you need to pay attention to your pulse, your breathing, your sweat glands, your posture, even changes in the way your skin feels. Don't just listen to the words in your head; listen to the beat and the rhythm. Try to understand how what you are feeling is influencing your current perceptions and so helping you form your current opinions. There's nothing wrong with letting your inner voice run wild from time to time; just don't mistake intensity for clarity or accuracy.

To begin the process of discovering your own rhetorical buttons, you can work with four ideas about what causes changes in emotional states:

Identity: who you think you are or aspire to be

Affiliation: the groups you identify with or want to be identified with

Status: your place within your groups

Autonomy: independence

Identity is about being who you think you are (or should be) or who you aspire to become. Thus any belief, activity, or behavior that is consistent with that self-concept will make you feel happy, while anything that contradicts it will make you feel unhappy. If you think of yourself as the sort of person who likes to work hard, for example, and you get sick or hurt and have to lay up for a while, you will suffer more intensely from sitting around watching TV or reading or whatever than someone who actually enjoys (or has become habituated to) lying about, watching TV and reading.

Let's have a look at a more dramatic example of how identity can influence belief. Consider the death penalty. If you identify with the victims of crime or you feel as though each of us is always personally responsible for our actions and must therefore be held accountable, you will more likely approve of execution as a form of punishment than not. You may, on the other hand, identify with the condemned no matter how distantly. Perhaps you feel as though you were falsely accused in the past (of something trivial by comparison, of course), or you've gotten away with something and never did it again and so feel like everyone deserves a second chance. Or perhaps you feel that responsibility for our actions is to some extent determined by factors outside our own control, or you suspect that authorities have made mistakes in the past. In these cases, you might be less likely to approve of the death penalty. I'm not talking about reasoned arguments here. I'm just explaining how your gut works. Our opinions about the big issues in life are determined to some extent by who we think we are or who we think we are supposed to be. Or—and this is more disturbing—who others make us think we are supposed to be.

Let's take a non-dramatic subject for a further example. Why would you pay $100 for a pair of non-prescription sunglasses rather than say $10 for sunglasses of the same quality? For the brand. Because wearing that brand makes you feel more like the person you want to feel you are. You are paying for their advertising with your identity. Now let's go the other way. How would you talk yourself into the $10 sunglasses even when you have $100 in your pocket? Would you use the concept of thrift? Or would you talk to yourself about vanity to create disdain for worldly goods? Is the antidote to vanity disdain? Or is disdain for trends just a different flavor of vanity?[11]

In addition to identity, most people's emotions are influenced by affiliations with communities, both those to which we belong and those to which we would like to belong. Being included is a powerful feeling, as powerful as its opposite, exclusion. Thus adopting or accepting the label a group goes by can have a profoundly emotional effect on your beliefs and perceptions. This is why we have uniforms and team insignias and pep rallies and rituals and marriage ceremonies and rites of passage. Belonging to a group to some extent absolves you of the task of answering some of life's more difficult questions, because you can simply adopt the attitudes and beliefs and behaviors of the group.

How that group treats you and thus your perception of your place within it directly affects your emotional states. In rigid hierarchical organizations, like the military, individual status and how people can and cannot relate to each other is obvious: It's stitched on their clothing. There are some fairly rigid cultures (like prisons and schools where uniforms are required) where status is much less obvious and apparent only to insiders. In less rigidly

---

11. For an interesting example of how people can be persuaded to adopt a brand using a rhetoric of nonconformity, have a look at Rob Walker's explanation of the resurgence of Pabst Blue Ribbon beer in *Buying In: The Secret Dialogue Between What We Buy and Who We Are.*

hierarchical organizations, merit determines status, and thus one's status rises and falls as one's skills and accomplishments rise and fall. There are also horizontal organizations, where everyone is granted equal status. Knowing how status is granted is important for deciding how to deal with different people. In nearly any setting, of course, kindness and attention are primarily important regardless of rank or status.

For most people, status varies throughout the day as we move from one group to another. We're up in some places and down in others and equal in yet other places. These changes in status mean that we may feel some things more keenly in one place than in another, which means that while some persuasive efforts will work on us at one place and time the same approach won't work if circumstances change.

Autonomy is a sense of independence, individuality, and self-sufficiency. Most people need to have some sense of autonomy to feel good about themselves, but some people lean more towards group identity than individuality. The most effective way to make people feel good about themselves is to make them feel unique, in control of their own destiny, and valued as an independent being. But if you take any of that too far you may make them feel lonely or isolated, under too much personal responsibility, and alone in the world. Most people need balance between affiliation and autonomy.

Common emotional strategies

In essence there are two emotional strategies, elevation and denigration: pulling people up and putting them down. Oddly enough you can almost always accomplish the same goal using either strategy. Keep your friends close and your enemies closer, as the saying goes. Regardless of the strategy, when it comes to emotional thinking you need to understand whether you are doing what you are doing in order to affect your own emotional state (to make yourself feel something) or whether you are trying to accomplish something else by influencing someone else's emotional state. You can do a lot of damage to yourself and others if you don't understand the difference.

This is where the colloquial idea of being in (or out of) someone's league is very useful. If you outrank someone, for whatever reason, you need to calibrate your approach accordingly. If you are very attractive and you flirt with someone who is less attractive but doesn't know they are, you are being cruel, unless you are somehow going to do something nice for them in the end, which almost never works. Same goes for size and wealth and status and skill and knowledge and every attribute valued by people. Pick on people your own size. Don't slum. Don't climb. Don't toy with people's feelings.

Don't mess with your own or anyone else's feelings just for the sensation of it. Given the rock and the hard place of those two options, you might decide to retreat into a *purely rational* form of discourse. But unless you are creating a mathematical proof, purely rational discourse is a delusional option. If you ignore your own emotional state you won't fully understand how you are motivated to think what you are thinking or say what you are saying. And if you fail to account for the state you find your audience in, your actions can have all manner of unintended consequences, from unwanted resistance or unwanted admiration.

What follows is a list of important emotional states with some elaboration of how they work persuasively. While this list will help you start thinking about feeling, you need to develop your own understandings of emotions over time based on personal experience and further reading. If you found the preceding discussion bewildering, entertain this one idea: your emotions, like your beliefs, are optional. You can choose what to feel and what to think.

How we talk to ourselves affects our beliefs and commitments just as much as how we talk to others can influence theirs.

> **Anger.** Anger is caused by the perception that your status is being devalued. So if a person disses you, the appropriate, reasonable emotional response would be anger, and anger would be expressed as an urgent desire to regain your status. To deny this understanding of anger is actually to replace one kind of rhetoric with another. *Turn the other cheek* is the maxim of a very different kind of rhetoric. (Through humility comes power.) At any rate, the easiest way to anger somebody, if you accept the definition I offered, is to denigrate (disrespect) him or his people or country or his things or ideas—anything, in other words, he values. On the other hand, if you realize someone is angry or you notice that something important has just been denigrated, you can diffuse the situation by apologizing (because this suggests you regard the other as an equal or a better) or by approving of something else that the person values.
>
> If you want to visualize this, imagine a school (or prison) yard confrontation where one person gets in another's face and tries to use his height in an intimidating fashion (pressing his forehead down on the other's). If that second person then backed down or stepped back, he would be addressing the imbalance of his previous act. If the intimidator won, the intimidated would acknowledge his inferiority, and the imbalance would go away. The situation would be diffused. Of course, if he doesn't back down, the contest for superiority will be decided by other, more confrontational, means. In a less overtly violent rhetorical environment, say an office building, superiority is still often indicated by height: taller, more imposing chairs or offices that are located on higher floors in the office tower demonstrate superiority. Even seating arrangements at a table can signify hierarchy and thus have an emotional effect on everyone in the room.

In addition to relative size, proximity to the center can indicate status. The closer someone sits to the person in authority or the place of honor, the more "in" he or she is. Thus you can calm people down by bringing them in and anger them by pushing them away.

Knowing when to express anger is an important social skill. You cannot successfully display anger to someone who can hold you in contempt of court or write you up for insubordination or otherwise punish you for it (unless your actual goal is to provoke them to punish you). On the other hand, while you can express anger to someone you have the power or authority to punish, will that fix the behavior that set you off in the first place, or will it simply satisfy your anger? And then again, if the conflict is with your equal, you may need to express your anger or else lose status. If someone takes advantage of your generosity and you just let it happen, you may have just subordinated yourself to her. So, for example, if someone asks you to cover for her at work or help her finish a project she will get credit for, when will it be in your best interest to help, and when would you be better off with a curt "Sorry. I'm busy"?

Some people care deeply about their place in the hierarchy; others don't care at all. You need to know where you fit in and how you feel about it. You need to know this about everyone else you deal with as well. Of course, generally speaking, it's best to accord everyone equal deference. You never know whom you will meet on your way down, as the saying goes. And often people choose a leader based on how a candidate treats social inferiors. At the same time, you don't want to appear too solicitous or people will think you have low self-esteem or that you lack autonomy and can find happiness only by pleasing others; some will try to take advantage of you, and others will think you're weak or flippy-floppy, while some others will think you are easy going. You have to learn how to strike a balance between autonomy and affiliation.

Making people angry. By belittling or ridiculing something someone values, you will make them angry by threatening their sense of status; they will need to address the threat or lower their estimation of their status in their own or in other people's eyes. Some people use anger to distract or humiliate others. This can work, for example, if you are more powerful than the other person and they don't know it. So you set them off, and then you put them out. A common example is trash-talking in sports. The way to combat trash-talking, of course, is to remain calm. Don't let them get to you; throw the trash back. Because trash-talking is so common it is a generally accepted sporting behavior. There's almost something ritualistic about it. But putting someone down is incredibly hostile behavior, and belittling people in any setting other than a sports arena will inspire animosity, which is almost always counterproductive to persuasion.

People sometimes engender anger in order to make others act impulsively. They may also make a person angry at a third person in order to get closer to the one they've angered or to get revenge on someone they themselves wouldn't be able to reach. And then there are people who just get angry easily and for little apparent reason, either because they feel the world underestimates their value while overestimating lesser people or because of physical damage to the prefrontal lobes from an accident or some devastating emotional trauma that has left them raging. *The more pervasive the emotion, the more character-trait-like and the less emotion-like the behavior becomes.* There are also people who are easily aroused to anger but won't display the emotion openly, and these people can be very dangerous since they will take their time seeking revenge. Still others will find a substitute target for their anger either from lack of self-knowledge or because they can't repair their status by attacking whatever it was that attacked them.

Unintentional belittling. While a certain amount of self-promotion is necessary in most settings, even a self-preserving self-promotional "Hey look what I made!" can be received as an invitation to competition rather than as a request for simple confirmation of skill. Especially competitive people can't help but reciprocate with an even louder "Hey look what *I* made!" and this can quickly escalate if you aren't paying attention or lack emotional control. In other words, some people feel belittled by any statement or action that supports or promotes anyone else. That sounds awful, but it's probably more common than we realize because most people recognize the impulse to outdo others as childish and therefore something to suppress. Well-adjusted people don't do it, but they still recognize when they feel it.

Fear. Fear, according to Aristotle at any rate, is caused by the real or imagined sensation of immediate personal suffering. Fear is a favorite emotion of advertisers and politicians because one of its effects is to make us want to hurry up and do something about whatever is frightening us, or to give over some of our autonomy to someone else so they can protect us from whatever is scaring us. If we give over some of our autonomy, the advertisers (and politicians and bosses) have us, and, if we hurry up, we disengage our critical thinking facilities, and they have us even quicker. Because most of what people fear never comes to pass, we waste a lot of energy worrying, and that's to a great many industries' persuasive advantage. If you find yourself fretting about something, one way to deal with it is to imagine the threat less vividly or talk to yourself about the resources you have for overcoming the result if the worst happens. See the upcoming "Confidence" section. If for some reason you need to frighten people, because they are unconcerned about some impending disaster or indifferent to something because they don't take it personally, then dramatize the disaster, and describe the devastation in detail. Show pictures of others who have suffered the consequences, and point out how difficult it will be to repair the damage once the damage is done. Be careful to leave the impression that hope remains. If you make your audience despair, they will lose interest and fail to act.

Pity. The inverse of fear is pity. If it's someone else's suffering you are cringing at, according to Aristotle, that's pity, not fear. Pity is a weaker motivating force than fear because it's less personal. Even though pity doesn't appeal directly to our self-interest, it can be very powerful all the same, especially when combined with guilt or a sense of responsibility for the sufferer's condition or for analogous conditions elsewhere. Pity evokes a desire to help our fellow people and thus appeals to our altruistic side as well as our desire for distinction through heroism or at least for pitching in and thus feeling like a member of a caring community.

The expression *but for the grace of God* is a rhetorical effort to ward off evil and thus is a rhetorical effort to lessen fear by expressing pity as sympathy (and borrowing confidence from a higher power, for some people). It's a superstitious rhetorical act that many of us perform reflexively. It has rhetorical power for us because we imagine that disasters are not random but visited on people for their sins or transgressions, and thus we encourage ourselves that we are not like those people who suffer. It's a rhetorical act in the sense that it encourages us; it displaces fear with thoughts that we are right with our god or with the world. (One needn't be religious to be rhetorically moved in this way.)

Confidence. If the suffering is far away rather than immediate, then the fear is less intense. If the suffering can be endured or reduced, then the fear is reduced because the temporary is less distressing than the permanent when it comes to imaginary dangers. If the imagined danger becomes real, that is, permanent, the emotional space changes. At any rate, if people are under-confident you point out that there are resources and remedies available (money, guns, and lawyers) and that lesser people have endured greater suffering. In other words, you encourage them to feel like they will survive, or at least that the suffering is a long way off, and maybe by then there will be a cure, or that they are the sort of people who don't cower in the face of such threats (identity). Minimize the impact of the threat, and fear abates.

An alternative method for combating (note the metaphor) fear is to rouse anger. If you can make people feel superior to the threat, believe they can overcome it or successfully deal with the consequences of it, they will feel encouraged; and then, if you make them feel like fear in the face of it threatens their status, they will become angry (if they think they can beat whatever is threatening them), which will make them eager for a fight. Thus, as they replace the image of disaster with the image of victory, they are no longer afraid. In other words, give them hope, and make them take the threat personally. This is the rhetorical reasoning behind talking about cancer as something one can *fight*, because thinking you can *fight* a disease and therefore *win* encourages you to undergo the treatments that are often very distressing and is why people continue treatment even after the defeat is inevitable, because the rhetoric of the medical industry presents itself as a war and calls those who fight courageous.

Frustration. People are frustrated whenever their needs or desires aren't being met, and people who are frustrated tend to be impatient with whatever is impeding them. If you want to speed up a decision-making process, you might try to set up the meeting just before lunch or right as people are trying to get out of the office or at any time when you can imagine they will be feeling frustrated or hungry or tired or otherwise distracted and impatient. If you want to be really devious, stop them while they are on their way to the bathroom. On the other hand, if you want to make sure a decision is carefully arrived at, make sure there's plenty of time and the room is warm, bright, and comfortable and no one is hungry or thirsty.[12] You can also try to create artificial impatience by saying that time is running out or that a deal like this is once in a lifetime (the principle of rarity). See Chapter 4, "Common sales techniques" for more of this.

Sympathy. We reach more generous decisions if we feel sympathetic or imagine ourselves in the places of the people we have to judge or if the people are friends of ours, as long as whatever they did they didn't do to us. If they did it to us, we would feel betrayed and not just wronged. If they did it to someone we dislike, we might take secret pleasure in it. I say "secret" because, while it's not unnatural to feel some pleasure at the misfortunes of people we dislike, expressing that

---

12. Don't believe me? Good. Have a look at "Extraneous Factors in Judicial Decisions," by Shai Danziger, Jonathan Levav, and Liora Avnaim-Pesso.

feeling is just wrong. You might be thinking, hey, it's wrong to even have that feeling (schadenfreude), but I would suggest that refusing to feel what you feel is a form of delusional thinking, an emotional fallacy, if you will. Just as we have to be able to entertain an idea without accepting it, we need to be able to feel things without necessarily acting on them.

Shame. Shame is the sensation you feel whenever you imagine others thinking less of you for doing what you are doing. Ever heard a parent tell a little boy to "walk it off" or "man up"? That's the rhetoric of shame.[13] This is why our friends and older family relations and our mentors are so important to us, because we take their estimation of what we've done as the measure of how we should feel about what we've done.

The way to relieve shame is to normalize the behavior, recall someone famous having done it or that many others do it, perhaps by a different name, or that you were compelled to do it; or talk yourself into believing that you won't get caught or that if you do the misery of being found out won't be worse than the joy of what you are feeling now or the value of the outcome when whatever shameful thing you are doing is successfully over. In a nutshell, all normalizing arguments are of the "everybody else is doing it" variety.

Envy. Envy is an example of asymmetrical sympathy, where someone accomplishes or acquires something and, rather than feeling pleased for them or even a competitive desire to accomplish or acquire in the same way (zeal), you feel negatively toward them or even maybe toward yourself. Another person's win is somehow your loss, even when you're not playing the same game or competing for limited resources. If you know somebody is inclined toward envy, then you have to think twice about demonstrating success in front of them, unless of course you want to upset them. The primary rhetorical complication for some people here is that they want to feel their own pride and so tend to launch into a list of their recent accomplishments without caring or anticipating how the other person will react. Not everyone who is quick with an "I'm so pleased for you" really feels what they just said. Think about how, when, and where you celebrate what and for whom.

Ever watch kids playing and one kid takes another's toy, to the tearful consternation of the one who has been robbed, and then the mom or dad offers another toy to calm the one crying, and suddenly

---

13. By the way, what does it say about the rhetoric of gender that you are less likely to hear a parent tell a little girl to "walk it off"? Why don't we say "woman up"?

the other kid loses interest in the toy he just grabbed? It's not the toy, of course, that the more aggressive (or is it assertive?) kid wants. It's possession. If someone has something, we want it too, and if someone we admire has it we want it more. If someone who we think is inferior to us has it, we will either decide it's not really for people like us, or we will be indignant that they have it and we don't. Objects that have this contextualized value are known as positional goods.

Decision paralysis. While desire motivates us to reach for some things, we can become hesitant if we have too many options. Given a choice among ten alternatives we suddenly can't outweigh the similarities and the differences, and so we freeze. Even if eventually we do decide, we don't quite know how to value our choice because the now abandoned options are too numerous to help us see what we chose as clearly preferable. This is why we might instinctively narrow our options, just as we instinctively focus on one object at a time when seeing the world around us. If you give people no options, they may resent the offer and decline. If you give them too many options. you won't get a decision, or you will get a weakly appreciated decision. After a decision has been made, people often feel differently about their choice. Sometimes we will look back fondly on the alternative not chosen and thus feel a little less content with what we did choose. If we had to struggle to acquire whatever it is we chose and triumphed in the end, then we value the object even more. This is why you don't want anything you have to offer to be too easily acquired, too common or too simple. But you don't want to go too far in the other direction either, since that will scare people off. Whatever it is it has to be rare enough to seem special but not so rare as to be unattainable or so distinct as to be incomprehensible.

So people enjoy being able to choose, but only to a point. Too many options lead to indecision. And then again, when you give people options they may not choose what you want them to choose. This is why people sometimes offer false choices (comparing apples to oranges). This way you create the illusion of choice, and yet you can control the outcome. You will read more about emotions and choices in Chapter 4, "Common sales techniques." For now keep in mind that motivation is connected to the perception of the possible.

Special pleading. Special pleading is claiming that some generally accepted rule ought not to apply to you because of your unique or at least rare circumstances. If you special plead with yourself you are feeling sorry for yourself, and that is likely to be very counterproductive. If you are always excusing your own failings by blaming external circumstances or other people, you can develop what's known as

learned helplessness, where you have basically thought and talked
(persuaded) yourself into remaining in a miserable place. You have so
damaged your self-esteem that you can't help yourself anymore. You
can do this to someone else by constantly doing things for them and
always absolving them of all responsibility. If you've read *Phaedrus*,
you've come across this idea in the analysis of the Lysias speech. Relying on others for too much or for too long makes you dependent on
them, and that can weaken you. And of course like nearly everything
persuasive, this cuts both ways. If you try to make someone else
dependent on you, you can become dependent on them for your sense
of identity and thus bring yourself down with them.

Befriending. Because of the power and nature of *ethos* when it
comes to decision making, the friendlier you are the more persuasive
you are, to a point. The basic strategy is to like what the other person likes, to show enthusiasm and support for whatever interests the
other person. If you come on too strong, of course, the strategy will
backfire. It's also possible to invert this strategy and appear aloof or
superior. People who need to be liked might find this distance attractive. People with high self-esteem, of course, won't notice you're there.
Not everyone has the same idea about what a friend is. For some people a friend is someone who is somehow useful to them. For others, a
friend is one who shares a similar situation or circumstance. For others a friend is whomever they happen to have known for some time.
And of course there are some people for whom having many friends is
an important condition for happiness and others for whom one or two
is plenty. There are different levels of friendship from acquaintances
and colleagues to companions and intimates. From a persuasion
perspective, the network of people you know is more important than
any one individual might be because a network links you to the world
beyond your direct contacts.

Gifting. You can create a positive feeling in others by giving them
things, obviously, but the magnitude of the gift matters: too much
and it's no good; too little and it's insulting. Everything depends on
the relationship between the giver and the receiver, and relationships
are dynamic; they change over time and from setting to setting sometimes even. People in need are grateful for even a small gift. People
who need nothing will prefer immaterial offerings. In nearly all cases
the more the gift seems to signify that you were actually thinking
about the person when you chose it will make the gift more powerful,
unless of course the relationship is a business one, in which case it
might make the gift creepy.

Some people view all gifts with suspicion, as an effort to ensnare.
This is because of what's called the *rule of reciprocity*. People

generally believe they should do for others what others do for them, and thus giving somebody something is perceived as asking for something in return, whether that's what you intended or not. Immaterial gifts in the form of insights and recommendations (movies, a cool website, recipes, places to stay when traveling, a new technology, a way to explain why somebody did what they did, a way to cheer someone up or see the bright side of something distressing) are therefore often the best gifts because they please with little obligation beyond mild gratitude. Many people are competitive when it comes to giving. If you give them too much, they will go past gratitude toward resentment or envy. They may even come to think they are better than you, that what you offer as a gift they see as tribute, something you are obliged to give them.

As with everything, taken to an extreme gift giving can have destructive consequences. Look up the concept of a "potlatch ceremony" for an example of institutionalized gifting.

Taking. Benjamin Franklin tells a story in his autobiography about how he used gifting in reverse to befriend someone predisposed to dislike him. By asking to borrow a book (a rare and therefore prized possession in those days) from the man, Franklin softened his adversary's attitude toward him. Franklin voluntarily indebted himself to the other man and thus humbled himself, in a very indirect and light-handed way, of course. Franklin could have gone the traditional route and offered the man gifts, but, because the other man felt superior to Franklin, the gifts would have seemed like tribute. Thus the opposite approach was rhetorically astute. Sometimes receiving a gift is more persuasive than giving one.

Self-disclosure (sharing). Talking about yourself, your family, your life goals, your struggles, and your achievements can draw people closer to you by showing that you are willing to be vulnerable with them, the essence of a personal friendship. But of course if you disclose too quickly or too much, an incommensurate amount compared to what they've given, then you put them off. If you disclose too little, you seem aloof or uninterested or even sneaky somehow, and that might be bad or good depending on whom you are dealing with. Some people interpret aloofness as a challenge. Some people interpret it as sophisticated and therefore attractive. Some people interpret it as a sign of coldness or insensitivity. As with all exchanges, and communication always comes down to exchange, you give what you get, and you should almost always consider reciprocating in kind. However, you should also always be conscious of the fact that what looks like one thing to you may not be how the other person sees it. What seems cold to you might be formal to another person and therefore

appropriate as far as they are concerned. A person you take for aloof
might just be introverted. A gregarious person might be suffering
from low self-esteem, or they might just be extraverted. Emotions
require critical thinking and even reading against the grain.

Flattery. Flattery is an act of giving someone a compliment in order
to get something in return, although often just for the sake of engen-
dering good feeling. Flattery works best if people don't know you are
flattering them,[14] or if they do but don't suspect you have any real
designs on them, or if they are the sort of people who want to be
flattered (nearly everybody enjoys a little flattery). Flattery typically
works best on the vain, the young, and the insecure. It also works
best if the people doing the flattering have the status or experience
to know what they are praising. If you praise someone for doing
something they perceive trivial, they may perceive you as sucking
up or think you're simple minded or ignorant. If you praise them for
something they think difficult, especially if they aren't totally sure of
their skill at it, they may really appreciate your efforts. The simplest
form of flattery is to *like what the other person likes,* or to show an
interest in what they have to say (which won't work if the intended
isn't interested in the flatterer's opinion).

　　If you are going to use praise, praise them for something they
suspect they lack: Don't tell a conventionally beautiful person you
think they are beautiful; tell them you think they are smart. Young
people want to be mature; old people want to be youthful or well
preserved. If someone doesn't have a lot of money, admire their
thrift and their spiritual indifference to possessions. If a person is
rich, admire their social conscience. If a person is highly educated,
admire their knowledge of pop culture. If you want to be subtle,
look for the thing they seem to be reaching for and admire that
with them.

Bullying. Bullies make themselves feel good by frightening and
humiliating or otherwise putting others down. We associate this
behavior with the schoolyard. It's all over the news these days, but
it happens in all walks of life and at all ages. There are bullies in
nursing homes and boardrooms. Whenever anyone tries to increase
their own self-esteem or their group's status at another's expense,
they are bullying. Any aggressive display of superiority can be a
bullying tactic, whether it's the roar of an engine, the size of a ring,

---

14. If you have your doubts that flattery has to go mostly unnoticed to be successful,
good for you for reading against the grain. Have a look at Piercarlo Valdesolo's
"Flattery Will Get You Far."

a display of learning, or calling someone's beliefs childish. What seems to some people like a friendly invitation to compete might be perceived by someone else as aggressive and therefore bullying. Even being too helpful can be a kind of bullying. *The Simpsons'* Nelson is a bully, but so is *Peanuts'* Lucy van Pelt.

Emotional blackmail. Emotional blackmail is obtaining compliance by threatening to withhold affection or deny access to something the other person wants, increasing community by weakening autonomy. At the risk of appearing judgmental, of all of the negative emotions discussed here this one strikes me as the most dysfunctional. This is partially because most of the people who use it don't realize they are withholding, and the people who feel the effect aren't always responding to actual behavior on the other person's part. They just think they are. The whole relationship is illusory. Sometimes the person you think you are dealing with is more a construction of your imagination than an actual person, and thus inevitably they may not give you what you want, which would be your fault rather than theirs.

Disparaging. Being negative, or *negging*,[15] is belittling. It is used not to create anger but rather a sense of inferiority. This is basically what happens when an aggressor denigrates a pleaser, a person whose self-worth requires others like them. When the same technique is applied to a person who feels superior, anger is the result. This is why you might decide to stand up to bullies, whether physical or emotional, even if you have to take a beating. If you do that, you will either obtain equal footing in the eyes of the bully or assert your superiority. Better yet, just walk away and move on.

Distraction. Sometimes people use emotions to distract others. The most common example is trash-talking in sports, where you say reprehensible things to your opponent to get them off their game, to get inside their head. But the techniques are everywhere. I've heard salespeople make slightly disparaging comments to younger customers, suggesting they maybe don't have the money for such-and-such an item, which invokes the buyer's pride and makes them want to buy it all the more. Some people might argue that all emotions are distractions because they disable reasoning. This is an arhetorical position; one I reject.

---

15. If you've not heard that expression, look it up in the Urban Dictionary. I'd tell you I'd wait for you to come back, but I know some of you won't be coming back for quite a while.

Positive emotions

So far I have been concentrating on negative emotions, but you need to remember that, because rhetoric is about proving opposites, you can always invert the techniques discussed so far to provide positive emotions. Interestingly enough, there is some research in psychology that suggests that our ideas about emotion tend to exclude the positive.[16]

People tend to remember negative experiences more keenly than positive ones. It's not exactly clear why this is so, but it may have to do with the fact that negative emotions make us focus; they have what is sometimes called a narrowing effect (Heath and Heath 121). We tense up, we clench our fists, and we zoom in on whatever might be threatening us. If the threat isn't a physical threat, we do more or less the same things all the same. We tighten our jaws and pinch our brows together. Oddly enough, this physical performance of anxiety actually invokes our critical thinking capacities, according to Daniel Kahneman, who goes so far as to suggest that if you want to jump-start your critical thinking processes put a pencil in your mouth, with the point on one side and the eraser on the other. This will force you to make a concentration face, and that will make you concentrate, apparently (Kahneman 54).

If it is true that we tend to focus on the negative, then over time we would likely build up a store of negative memories that would likely have an impact on our general outlook toward life. Aristotle said old people love as though they will soon hate and hate as though they will soon love. Their emotions are sharp and weak (brittle). Young people, on the other hand, have intense and vivid feelings because they have very little experience, and therefore imagine that what they happen to be feeling now they will feel forever.

━━━━━ Your Turn

Do you think Aristotle might have been right about age and emotion? Can you elaborate on his idea that age (hint: age = experience) influences emotion would lead to his characterization of youth and old age? Having done that, what do you think his attitude toward people in their prime of life might be and why?

There's an African American game of verbal sparring called *the dozens* or *jonesing* or *signifying*. You may know it by *yo momma*. The idea is to insult your adversary in such a way that you actually get a rise out of him. If you can wreck his composure, you can steal the ball, literally or metaphorically. Ritual insults are a form of combat training, and while the practice is competitive, the goal may actually be cooperative in the sense that the stronger

---

16. Have a look at Barbara L. Fredrickson's "What Good Are Positive Emotions" if you find that idea intriguing.

your companions the safer your group. See how many insults you can come up with during the next ten minutes. Then find someone to shadowbox verbally with.

During the beginning of the end of the Second World War, the British prime minister Winston Churchill made a speech that resonates to this day. London was in ruins from Germany's bombing raids, and Churchill got on the radio and said,

> We shall fight on the beaches, we shall fight on the landing grounds, we shall fight in the fields and in the streets, we shall fight in the hills; we shall never surrender, and if, which I do not for a moment believe, this island or a large part of it were subjugated and starving, then our Empire beyond the seas, armed and guarded by the British Fleet, would carry on the struggle, until, in God's good time, the new world, with all its power and might, steps forth to the rescue and the liberation of the old.

Based on the ideas about how courage is inspired, how does this passage encourage? For whom might it fail?

Asynchronous persuasion and emotions

What if you can't observe your audience?

When a person is reading something, his or her emotional involvement is completely different from when communicating face to face. You can't see them, they can't see you, and each person's reaction can't resonate with those around them so there's no groupthink possible. As a writer, your feelings are only indirectly available to the people reading your words. What you feel will likely be very different from what they feel, and by the time they read it your feelings may have changed.

Not all writing serves the same purposes, and thus the level of emotional involvement varies. Writing intended to convey information should have minimal authorial presence (minimal *ethos*) and therefore little emotional impact since we typically have emotions as a response to other people.[17]

As you write, if you find yourself getting carried away by your own prose, the chances are increasing that you are leaving your audience or some

---

17. Some people have abnormal emotional responses to inanimate things, *paraphilia* it's called. It used to be called *fetishism*. For most people, however, feelings are a response to other people or memories of other people, and when something inanimate stirs a feeling it's by association with someone, not something.

segment of it behind. This happens because you can feel the implications of everything you are not saying as well as everything you are saying, and if you don't say it your readers are very unlikely to get it.

Writing happens over time, and so what you are feeling during one session may not be what you feel when your return to the task. The words you left when you were last at it might remind you of what you were feeling, and if you are an emotional writer the words may rekindle whatever set you writing in the first place, but then again maybe not. So you need to think not so much about how what you are writing makes you feel as try to imagine what it will make someone else feel, mindful of the fact that they are not you.

Here's a concrete example: Email isn't as common as it was fifteen years ago. We're all moving toward texting and tweeting, but when email was first becoming the standard form of business communication people inadvertently set fires by missing an important rhetorical difference embedded in the rhetorical situation of email. Email is close to synchronous and therefore much more like face-to-face communication than traditional writing had been. If someone is standing in front of you and says something that irritates you, you probably don't react right away. Social decorum requires you take a breath. But when an irritating piece of email arrives out of the blue, and you're sitting there alone at your computer, no person to socialize your reaction, you might just fire off an ill-considered response.

Even if there wasn't any emotional content in the original message, because email enabled a quick response, people often didn't think through what they would say, with confusion resulting. Additionally, people were emailing when in the past they would have used the phone and so had voice cues to infer from or walked down the hall and talked, thus having voice and body cues to work with. The result of the absence of these cues was often inadvertent clumsiness. And sometimes people went the other way, confusing email with mail and so insisting on using the "Dear" salutation and having a paragraph of pleasantries, newsy like, when email was really more of a work solution than a form of social interaction or gift exchange the way letters were.

Emoticons were a way to try to solve this rhetorical problem, using an icon to speed up the process of putting the correct kind of emphasis in what you wrote, reducing the time it would take to use words alone. A smiley face is way faster than providing detailed approval. And it doesn't leave an actionable electronic trail because, while it communicates, it doesn't really mean much once the context is gone.

A more recent version of the same rhetorical failure happens when people respond to trolls in the threaded discussions on blogs and electronic magazines. Trolling, as I'm sure you know, is making a habit of saying controversial, inflammatory things to get a rise out of unsuspecting people. It's a weak form of trying to assert control or develop authority or otherwise hijack someone else's space. Responding angrily to a troll encourages the troll to respond back in escalating fashion. Hence the standard rhetorical advice, don't feed the trolls. Ignore them, and they will lumber off to peddle their misery elsewhere.

Today we also have a slightly more sophisticated version of trolling in news websites and back-channel sites for television programs. CNN's *Cafferty File* is a good example. These apparently news-related sites are designed to stir controversy and thus increase hits which in turn provide a warrant for increasing the fees charged for advertising. User-generated content is a slick way to get money for nothing. The Internet may enable us to freely communicate, but some people have figured out how to monetize our freedom.

Your Turn

Think back to the last time you felt something really intensely, and write about the situation. What were you feeling and why? Now pull back a bit, and think about the circumstances. Who was there, what time of day was it, what else was going on? Do you remember any similar experiences from the past, and if you do can you find the thread that binds them? You needn't share this diarist bit of writing with anyone if you don't want to. But imagine that you were going to turn a diary page into a page in your autobiography. How would you change it for public consumption?

The most efficient way to deal with any emotion is to distance yourself from the scene that is enabling it. Focus on the future. Remember that nothing is permanent, and remind yourself also that successes and failures have far less impact on a person's happiness than it is easy to realize on the cusp of some big change. If you aren't sure you believe me, good. Look up "lottery winning and happiness."

chapter 3
THE FIVE CANONS OF RHETORIC

Anyone who would be persuasive needs to be able to design and deliver a message effectively and efficiently, whether on paper, over the web, or in person, given time for reflection or spontaneously. As with developing any form of expertise, becoming a more effective *rhetor* requires you break rhetorical performance down into practicable pieces and then create a routine that you can rehearse regularly, adding levels of challenge as your skills increase, until a performance becomes almost automatic. This practice of breaking an activity into a series of practicable actions is known as deliberate practice, a phrase coined by Anders Ericsson in 1996.

Deliberate practice, rather than mere repetition, is what leads to improved performance. Every time you have an assignment, you want to think of it as another opportunity for improving each of the following skill sets. And as with *ethos* and the emotions, you want to be thinking long-term improvement over time and not just a one-off application. What you don't want to do is the same thing over and over again, even if what you did last time succeeded. If at first you succeed, up your expectations. Regardless of the outcome, reflect and refine each time.

Traditionally, rhetorical performance has been divided into disciplines known as the offices or, more commonly, the canons. Here is Cicero on what he calls simply the divisions:

> Since all activity and ability of an orator [Latin for *rhetor*] falls into five divisions, . . . he must first hit upon what to say; then manage and marshal his discoveries, not merely in orderly fashion, but with a discriminating eye for the exact weight as it were of each argument; next go on to array them in the adornments of style; after that keep them guarded in his memory; and in the end deliver them with effect and charm. (Cicero, *On The Orator,* Book 1, Section 31, 40, 41)

The five divisions are as follows:

English	Latin	Greek
Invention	Inventio	Heuresis
Arrangement	Dispositio	Taxis
Style	Elocutio	Lexis
Memory	Memoria	Mneme
Delivery	Actio	Hypocrisis

You can learn a great deal about a rhetoric[1] by looking at which of these offices is emphasized when people are being taught how to be persuasive. Literate cultures have tended to ignore memory. You don't have to remember something if you can read it again later (not to mention being able to look up anything you want on the device in your pocket). Literate cultures have also given little thought to delivery. After all you don't have to worry about how it is going to sound or how you are going to stand and what kinds of gestures you are going to make if other people are going to read your ideas in your absence. But memorizing and memory are not the same concepts. Even with ubiquitous connections to the Internet, memory matters. Understanding how your memory works and working to make it more effective are both key to becoming a more persuasive person and a better consumer of other people's persuasive efforts.

Delivery also matters in a literate world for several subtle reasons. Many people read in their heads; they sound out the words and "hear" them. Thus even though you won't deliver something you've written, it matters how it sounds. And in fact a great way to know if something you are writing is coherent is to read it out loud or have your computer read it to you. Ask yourself, does it sound convincing? What kind of a person do you sound like? Does it sound like you? Does it sound like the best possible you? Or does it sound like someone else entirely? Delivery in another sense of the word also matters. Will the thing you are writing be delivered on a screen or on paper? If your words are intended for a screen, then you have a great many options to consider: layout, font, color, images, sounds, video, hyperlinks, pop-ups.

The list of options goes on and changes every few years. If your message is going to be received as a text message or any other short-form factor (like a Twitter feed), it needs to be shaped differently than if it will be read as an email on a big screen. If a text message, you may have a character restriction,

---

1. The phrase "a rhetoric" suggests that there are multiple rhetorics and that any given one is a kind of algorithm. Given certain statements in, certain beliefs come out. A rhetoric is a nexus of principles and attitudes and significations that produces related beliefs and actions. While a rhetoric might have a material basis, like a physical condition or an economic or social circumstance, there are verbal and discursive manifestations of it that both signify the existence of the rhetoric and produce somewhat predictable results. A concrete example might be the rhetoric of tobacco addiction. The condition is the body wants nicotine. The rhetoric is all of those reasons a smoker has for smoking and how she talks herself into smoking even when she's trying to quit, to the point where a no-smoking sign will make a smoker want to light up. Tobacco is a negative example. A religion can be a positive one. A rhetoric in this sense is a way of talking and writing and thinking that controls what can be thought and said and, therefore, to some extent, even done. If you change your rhetoric, you change your mind in a profound way. The world no longer looks the way it did. Such changes tend to be gradual and go unobserved to the point where looking back you think you always thought that way, absent evidence to the contrary.

and the person getting the message may be driving or otherwise occupied when it arrives. It will likely arrive immediately (unless they are on a plane or have their phone off for some reason), so the exchange might be almost synchronous. You need to take that into account when crafting the message. If you are sending an email, you don't have to worry as much about character count, although few people read emails carefully, and the longer an email is the less closely it will be read. Generally speaking, if you can't say it in five sentences or fewer, maybe you need to think about it some more.

An email exchange may or may not be synchronous, depending on whether the recipient receives the email via their phone or is at a computer when it arrives. Just five years ago the text or email decision wasn't necessary. Five years from now it might be irrelevant. How will delivery be different five years from now, do you suppose? I read recently that "phones" may soon come with data packages that exclude voice because people prefer text. I've also heard that the desktop computer is dead and that soon laptops, too, will be obsolete. Each of these changes has rhetorical effects, and as a *rhetor* you need always to be thinking of the context of production and the context of consumption.

The relative importance of invention has varied over time as well. Aristotle, the person whose work is everywhere in the pages you are reading, thought invention was the most significant part of the rhetorical process. He thought that while some subjects afforded more precise and reliable forms of persuasion, what today we would call scientific realms, where basically indisputable assertions allow for certain conclusions, there were many realms of human decision making where the facts were unknowable to the extent that we would have to rely on rhetoric to make a decision, and thus invention was critical in those settings because it was synonymous with thinking.

On the other hand, during the Enlightenment, when the promise of scientific method gripped human imaginations, public thinkers developed an almost transcendental commitment to the idea of natural facts and objective truths and so believed that rhetoric's domain covered nothing but style, restricted to the plain style, no emotion, no poetry, just the facts. Today invention has returned to the center of the rhetorical process. I'll let you decide for yourself how important you think invention is and to what realms of human experience and understanding you think it can and should be applied. At the same time as I'm giving you license to decide for yourself how important invention is, you should notice that I devote far more time and space to it than the other four canons, so you may want to factor that in as you decide.

The canons provide a pattern for deliberate practice, a critical thinking and reading and writing process that will help you both produce more effective communications and also develop the disciplines that will make you a generally more persuasive person over time. The process is most apparent if you order the canons in a particular way: first you come up with what to say (invention); then you put the arguments in the order the audience needs to receive them in (arrangement); then you choose the words, metaphors, illustrations, and sounds that best match the subject matter and the audience's expectations (style); then you memorize it (memory); and finally you utter it flawlessly, using gestures, text, graphics, and video to reinforce and dramatize your meaning (delivery). The rhetorical process, however, is rarely this linear, especially when the final delivery will be in writing.

Each performance is influenced by your previous ones as well as by ones you've watched in the meantime. You are always learning how persuasion works, choosing among alternatives, discovering preferences, coming to understand other people's preferences, and developing theories about why they did what they did and why you do what you do. You may not be entirely aware that this is what you are doing, but it almost certainly (*Notice the hedge "almost certainly"?*) is, and, if you want to become a more persuasive person, you can come a long way by making a conscious effort to understand these processes and make notes to yourself about them. Try them out, and assess the possible relationships between the outcome and the efforts you made.[2] You learn how to be persuasive by watching how it's done on others and on you and by practicing what you observe.

Throughout the next five sections we will look at each of these canons separately and in some detail. Our goals will be to give you several rhetorical heuristics for creating potentially useful ideas, a way to judge the merit of a given idea, a plan for organizing your persuasive efforts, and a vivid sense of what it means to be a *rhetor*. Perhaps most importantly of all, you will get a sense of what and how to practice deliberately.

Invention

If you have ever stared at a blank screen and wondered what to say or ever found yourself at a moment when you had to choose between competing alternatives and you couldn't think your way to a decision (or having decided, come up with a justification), then you have encountered the fundamental rhetorical question, what to think. Not what to say—that's the second rhetorical question. The primary question is what to think, and here we have the technologies of invention as methods for generating potentially useful ideas.

---

2.   In this context *process* is really a metaphor, unlike when we talk about a manufacturing process like an assembly line. With an assembly line, what goes in determines directly what comes out. With the rhetorical process, the results aren't always perceivably tied to the efforts. There's always a certain amount of random in real life. Sometimes we get lucky, and sometimes we get unlucky. Also, there are so many variables that go into a real-life situation that it's impossible to know them all, let alone control them. Approximate understanding is most often the best hope.

Invention is a process of asking the right questions in the right order (dialectic and stasis theory) and searching the collective wisdom of the community (history, literature, proverbs, maxims, topics, commonplaces) for ways to explain, promote, and demote ideas, attitudes, beliefs, decisions, and actions.

The process of invention is generative. You are trying to come up with as many ideas as the situation and topic will allow. So turn your judgment down to zero while inventing. Keep an open mind. Every thought possible is worth recording. You can assess, select, reject, and prioritize everything you come up with later. It's easier to prune a tree than grow one, as Quintilian said.

Dialectic

Dialectic (a.k.a. the Socratic method) is a more or less friendly form of cross-examination where one person helps another test the validity and consistency of his or her opinions by asking a series of questions designed to provide accurate and precise definitions of the key terms and determine the correct relationship of each term to the others—what is, what is good, and their opposites essentially. Ultimately the goal is to answer one question: What is the best way to live? (And thus, necessarily, what ways of life must one avoid?) *Dialectic is about testing beliefs in order to correct values and opinions.*[3]

Not all dialectical practices lead to a satisfying conclusion. If you take the process of asking questions far enough, it becomes apparent that most if not all of our beliefs are indefensible assumptions. We believe some things just because we believe them. Technically, such beliefs are said to rest on tautological arguments. When you come to realize that you believe something only because you believe it, you've arrived at what is known as an *aporetic* moment. (You'll see why when you read about stasis theory.) A dialectic that leads to the realization that we don't have good reason to believe something we nevertheless believe is called *elenchus*, and Plato offers several examples among his dialogues. These arguments that come to nothing can be extremely frustrating. And it is worth remembering that Plato's mentor and model, Socrates, was condemned on a charge of corrupting the youth and for basically being a prime irritant to society. He was offered exile as an alternative, but he chose to kill himself instead to insist on his innocence as emphatically as possible. Thus with an ironic flourish, I'm sure he relished, vindicating himself while also proving his detractors right, irritatingly defiant to the end.

---

3. The Greek word for a correct opinion is *orthodoxos*. *Ortho* means "correct," as in orthodontist, and *doxa* means "opinion." What does the word *orthodox* make you think of? What does that tell you about how you interpret the word?

I mention *elenchus* not because that is what I'm going to show you but as a warning that even *non-elenchic* dialectic can be tedious and frustrating, and people often become impatient with it. From our perspective, exasperation is an expression of a lack of mental discipline, not a reasonable conclusion. If you want to think effectively you have to stick it out, even when you would rather do almost anything else, and there is always the risk that you will have weaker beliefs rather than stronger ones when a dialectical session ends. Dialectic is a mental discipline.

While all of Plato's dialogues are fascinating and in various ways instructive about dialectical methods and purposes (not all of them *elenchic*), *Gorgias* can be read as a handbook on dialectic in general, and so I will use it as the basis of this section on dialectic as a method of invention. If you haven't yet read it, you might want to read it now, especially since it is also the origin of the word *rhetoric*.

Gorgias is a series of three conversations about the purpose and nature of education, where what Plato calls *rhetoric* is pitted against what he calls *philosophy* (words he invented) and shown to be hideously lacking because, whereas rhetoric would teach people to speak mindlessly, philosophy would teach people to think. The champions of rhetoric, Gorgias and his students Polus and Callicles, believe that if a group of people have to make a decision that affects the community then the most eloquent person will prevail over the subject-matter expert. If rhetoric prevails, ignorant people will be led by powerful and equally ignorant people, while the learned will be ignored, and everyone will suffer. Therefore, Plato seems to assert that philosophy must triumph over rhetoric.

One of the strangest consequences of the success of this argument (and it has been spectacularly successful, especially among people who subsequently called themselves philosophers, not surprisingly) is that to this day we imagine subject-matter experts are *less* articulate than people with superficial knowledge of the subject, that engineers and doctors and similar professionals don't need to become highly effective communicators; they can simply hire technical writers and speechwriters and ghostwriters—people who don't know what they are talking about and therefore can talk about it well. A corollary of this weird consequence is that subject-matter experts are often unwilling to cultivate eloquence and feel a bit nasty whenever they feel compelled to communicate with a general audience. They feel like they've had to dumb down what they know or that they are merely popularizers. Their colleagues may take a similarly harsh view of them, also, especially if the popularizer gets rich doing it.

Here's a concrete example: I know a professor of nutrition. He is a research scientist, but he is also a nutritionist for several of the U.S. Olympic teams. When I asked him about his job with the athletes he said he was a walking placebo affect. And then he explained: Sports nutrition is a science that designs an optimal nutrition regimen for each athlete based on his or her metabolism, sport, physique, blood chemistry, and so on. The effects of the regimen take months to happen. Unless an individual meal gives an athlete food poisoning, what he or she eats just before an event has no impact. And yet, he told me, just prior to an event he would sometimes get a frantic phone call late at night, and the conversation would go something like this:

> Olympic Athlete: Doc, I was out with a bunch of the other athletes, and I wasn't thinking, and I ate a plate of nachos and drank a beer. All those carbs. I screwed up. What am I going to do?
>
> Doctor: I'm glad you called. This is important. Are you nauseated?
>
> Olympic Athlete: No.
>
> Doctor: Do you have cramps or diarrhea?
>
> Olympic Athlete: No.
>
> Doctor: Ok, here's what you do. You know that packet of dehydrated electrolyte sports drink you got in your kit?
>
> Olympic Athlete: Yeah.
>
> Doctor: Mix a tablespoon of that with water, sit on the edge of your bed, and drink the mixture slowly. Then lie down. You're going to be fine. You're not the first athlete to make a dietary error. Just before she won the gold last year, a gymnast you know did what you did and followed my advice. Everything's going to be fine. Drink the sports drink and go to bed.
>
> Olympic Athlete: Thanks, Doc. I feel much better already.

My nutritionist friend confided in me that everything after "Do you have diarrhea?" was placebo. We'd call it rhetoric. The science of nutrition is too complicated to explain quickly over the phone to a panicking athlete. And the knowledge that one meal makes no difference unless you get food poisoning from it wasn't going to help him or her sleep because when people are scared they want to do something they think will help, hence the firm and reassuring tone and the advice to mix up and drink a sports drink and go to bed. The sports drink had no medicinal effect, even though the act of mixing a powder with water probably relieved the athlete's anxiety and thus helped him or her fall asleep. The actual prescription was calm down, go to bed, and get some sleep. Under the circumstances, telling the athlete to calm down and go to sleep would have been sound science but lousy medical advice. If you don't take the psychological state of the recipient into account, the message is useless, no matter how true it is, a point Plato grudgingly concedes only many years after he wrote *Gorgias* (in *Phaedrus*).

We might call this the spoonful-of-Gatorade technique. You mix knowledge with a clear understanding of your audience's emotional state, and that prescribes a positive course of action. I wish my nutritionist friend were around when Plato was "proving" Gorgias wrong about the relationship between knowledge and persuasion and medicine and rhetoric.

On the other hand, it's possible that the people who have held that Plato truly believed in a rigid distinction between rhetoric and philosophy, persuasion and knowledge, were reading him too rigidly.

Plato is famously ironic in the sense that it is very hard to figure out if he means one thing or another, and if you read him repeatedly his meanings seem to change the way light plays on water. The performance is dazzling and hypnotic, but the shimmering is also blinding after a while, and eventually you get frustrated by how the ever-changing surface makes perceiving the depths impossible. (Surface *and* depth *are metaphors, not realities. Don't be rhetorically naive.*) He says repeatedly, for example, that he is a friend who wishes the others well, but then he repeatedly finds fault with their arguments and mocks them openly on some occasions and covertly, it seems, on others, until they are all either bored or fuming silently, and Socrates is making a long-winded speech of the kind he started out by denying Gorgias the right to make. Socrates *seems* to be enacting the idea that your best friend is an honest adversary who will alternately infuriate, bore, and frustrate you, unless you are up to the challenge, which his current "friends" are not. At the same time he also *seems* to be doing his best to beat his opponents in a game of verbal dexterity, using all the tricks and techniques he says one should never use.

Because it isn't clear what Plato was trying to *tell* us, perhaps it's reasonable to conclude he wasn't trying to tell us anything at all. Maybe he was trying to *show* us something, specifically how to have (and not have) dialectical conversations. If he were actually telling us what to think (philosophy is better than rhetoric), then we wouldn't need to think anymore. Ironic, I know. By being ironic, by refusing to tell us what to think, he was encouraging us to become skeptical, to question the obvious, to read against the grain, to think for ourselves.

At any rate, I am asserting here that *Gorgias* is first and foremost a manual on dialectic. Don't take my word for it. Go read it for yourself. See the *Gorgias* selection in the Appendix.

An example of Platonic dialectic

Following is a truncated version of the exchange between Socrates and the successful businessman Callicles. I'm offering it here as an example of how dialectic works. You really should read the entire dialogue because the same intellectual habits are discussed repeatedly in different ways, and repetition is often helpful for learning. The forms of correction being applied in each

instance vary depending on the personality of the character Socrates is trying to educate (correct).

Callicles believes that all pleasures are good (the good = the pleasant).
Socrates will prove that there are two kinds of pleasure, good and bad, and
therefore not all pleasures are good (and not all pains are bad). The argument proceeds according to a basic rule of dialectic, which is that words that
are absolute opposites (p and –p) function in such a way that anything that
is true of one is necessarily false of its opposite. (Your enemy's enemy is your
friend.) Thus, if p exists, its opposite, –p, cannot exist—not at the same time
at least. They are antithetical. Another dialectical rule to keep in mind is that
a noun and its adjectival form have the same truth-value. If gold is valuable,
then anything golden is similarly valuable.

> Socrates: Is the opposite of fortunate unfortunate?
>
> Callicles: Yes.
>
> Socrates: Then a person cannot be both fortunate and unfor-
> tunate at once. (According to the rule of non-contradiction, a
> thing cannot both be and not be simultaneously; x cannot equal
> both p and –p at once.)
>
> Callicles: Yes.
>
> Socrates: Now, with the opposites health and sickness, can one
> be both healthy and sick at once?
>
> Callicles: No.
>
> Socrates: So one becomes healthy at the moment one ceases to
> be sick?
>
> Callicles: Yes.
>
> Socrates: Now, consider good and happiness and their opposites,
> evil and misery. Are these not also absolute opposites such that
> the moment one becomes one, one ceases to be the other?
>
> Callicles: Yes.
>
> Socrates: You cannot be both at once?
>
> Callicles: No.
>
> Socrates: Now then, if we find that any pair of things can be
> possessed together, then they cannot be good and evil. Do you
> agree? Think carefully before you answer.
>
> Callicles: I agree.
>
> Socrates: All right. Is thirst painful?
>
> Callicles: Yes.

Socrates: Then if one is thirsty, one is in pain?

Callicles: Yes.

Socrates: And when one drinks, does the pain go away all at once or gradually?

Callicles: Gradually.

Socrates: So there is a time when one is still drinking but yet not entirely free of pain?

Callicles: Yes.

Socrates: So for a time at least one is both drinking and still thirsty. That is experiencing pleasure and yet still in pain?

Callicles: Yes.

Socrates: Thus, some good things are unpleasant, and therefore good does not equal pleasant. (495a–499d)

Dialectic is a bit like applying the rules of geometry to the construction of opinions. Your first encounters with these kinds of dialogue may make your head hurt; you may find them frustrating because it's hard to keep track of the argument as it unfolds and because you're only eavesdropping on the conversation—you can't jump in and redirect the discussion when you think it's gone wrong. You're inability to redirect the conversation will likely irritate you. You see an opinion you agree with getting railroaded, and you'll want to tag the loser and get in Socrates' face. Or your weak champion will answer in a way you know will lose the debate, and you'll want to tug his sleeve and hiss, "No! No! Say this instead."

My reading of Plato is that the "No! No! Say this instead" effect was exactly the response he was going for. Plato wanted to engender in us a desire to debate our moral precepts and question our cherished beliefs. He wanted to show us how to think; and dialectic, for Plato, is how you should think. I should really emphasize this: He's showing you how to think not telling you what to think.

Notes on *Gorgias* and dialectic

And now that you've read *Gorgias*, let me extract the primary principles for you.

Principles

- Dialectic is not about winning (453b–c); it's about learning. Socrates says, "You must think of me now as eager to serve your interests" (455c).

- The questions are designed to clarify confused or confusing ideas and eliminate contradictory opinions.

- The goal is to develop disciplined habits of mind.

Personal characteristics or attitudes required for dialectic

- Be docile (teachable): Be prepared to change your mind, willing to be schooled (458a), but not passive on the one hand or utterly relativistic on the other.

- Be patient: Don't jump to conclusions, anticipate, or assume.

- Be candid: Don't strategize or dissemble; you're not trying to win. You are trying to learn.

- Be shameless: Don't worry about your own or other's feelings or vanity (*Is vanity a feeling? What kind of feeling is it? What feelings is it similar to, and what feelings is it different from?*)

- Be calm (or detached): People who are unaccustomed to critical thinking associate their beliefs with their identity and so take any challenge to their beliefs as a personal threat. You can't learn to think carefully if you can't entertain ideas you don't like or get defensive when what you believe is questioned.

- Be selfless (without ego): The disposition of one who doesn't take arguments personally is selfless, or without ego involvement. It is hard to remain calm if you think you are being personally attacked just because someone is questioning an opinion you hold dearly.

- Be brave: Willingly accept the consequences of your beliefs, or be prepared to abandon them if they are disproven or to weaken your commitment if your defense proves less compelling than you thought.

Practices

- Question every assertion, especially the obvious the commonplace and anything that sounds like received wisdom or common sense. Reinvent the wheel.

- Assume nothing. Every word must be defined, every relationship among words scrutinized, and every connotation inspected before being accepted.

- Use plain, direct, unambiguous language.

- Define each word using induction to identify its essential characteristic before placing it in a statement.

- Identify what is currently at issue. (See "What is an *issue*?" in the "Stasis" section of this chapter, for the definition of *issue*.)

- Secure agreement on a statement before drawing an inference. (Agreed-to statements are sometimes called *premises* or *common ground*.)

- Ask simple rather than compound questions. A simple question is one that can be answered with a *yes* or a *no* without thus affirming or denying more than one statement.

- Don't ask complex questions, those that require an *it depends* or a *yes and no* (466c–d).

- Evaluate statements only after agreeing on the meanings of the words (463c).

- Summarize and secure agreement at each phase before moving to the next level.

- Conversation ends or shifts when a contradiction occurs. Gorgias says if a person does wrong, it's not the teacher's fault; but later he says he can make anyone persuasive, which implies even bad people and suggests he is to blame if one of his students does something unethical (457ff).

- Keep the conversation flowing toward its inevitable destination even if it's going badly. In that case, let it wreck completely, and then start again in a different direction; don't try to avoid an unpleasant conclusion or skip ahead to the place you want to be.

- Accept the conclusion once it becomes apparent, even if it's not what you thought it would be or what you wanted. Gorgias exhibits the proper behavior—Polus' sullen silence and Callicles' dancing about, the improper behavior.

Dialectical topics—argumentative heuristics

Analogies: Shoes are to shoemakers as *rhetors* are to rhetoricians.

Essential characteristic of the word in question: What attribute identifies it and only it? Not what it is like or unlike but what it is. For example, man is a featherless biped. There are other bipeds and other featherless creatures, but only man is both, and thus featherless biped can be offered as an essential definition of *man*.

Collection: Find commonalities among apparently dissimilar things.

Division: Find distinctions among apparently similar things: appearance/reality, conviction/knowledge, convention/nature.

Definition: Use the essential definitions when constructing statements for subsequent testing. For example, "since oratory is one of those crafts which mostly uses speech, and since there are also others of that sort, try to say what it is that oratory . . . is about" (451a–b).

Hierarchies of value: If A is greater than B, and B is greater than C, then A is greater than B.

Arguments from examples (induction): Shoemakers make shoes, and painters make pictures, and doctors make people healthy, and lawyers justify clients, then rhetoricians must make *rhetors*.

Arguments from opposites: If all pleasure is good, all pain is bad; some pain is good, therefore pleasure is not the opposite of pain, and perhaps not all pleasure is good.

Arguments from grammatical forms: What's the relationship between trust and trustworthy? Is one better than the other? What kind of person prefers the packaging to the package? What's the difference between grace and graceful?

Arguments from the converse: Shift focus from means to ends, to ends to means.

Inference from premises: You have to know what you are talking about; so to talk about justice you have to know justice, and if you know justice you are just.

The basic rules of inference

- If two things are the same, then what is true of one is true of the other (properties), and what can be said of one (attributes) can be said of the other. If you find something that can be said of one that can't be said of the other, then you've discovered that they are not the same thing. At best then you have an analogy rather than an identity.

- If two things are different, then properties and attributes of one are not properties or attributes of the other. If you find that anything you can say of one you can also say of the other, then you've discovered the two things are not different. Keep in mind that a difference has to make a difference to be a difference. People find careful distinctions tedious if they can see them but can't see that they matter. You will be accused of splitting hairs or counting angels dancing on the head of a pin if you shave your words too closely.

- If two things are similar but different, attributes and properties of one will be equivalently similar to the attributes and properties of the other—what is best among the better people is better than what is best among the lesser people. (*Did you just insist I define "better people"? Good.*)

- If two things are opposite, what is true of one is false of the other.

- If two things are inverse, as properties or attributes of one change, properties or attributes of the other change in the other direction.

- If two things are correlated, then when one changes, the other does but not in a causally related way.

Your Turn

Forms of argument to avoid (rhetorical tricks)

If you've read the dialogue, find the places where Socrates tells Polus and Callicles not to use the following forms of argument.

- witnesses:

- testimonials:

- quotations:

- unique events (or people presented as paradigmatic examples):

- threats:

- bullying:

- ridicule:

- ad populum:

- ad hominem:

- "rhetoric" (speeches designed to cajole or threaten, or any long discourse that requires the audience to hear and read with the grain rather than providing opportunities for questions and careful examination of disagreements):

- ingratiation, admonition, appeals to emotions, ego, and so on:

- ambiguous definitions:

- evasive expressions:

- dancing around the question:

- confusing the issue:

- distracting your opponent:

- playing to the crowd:

- avoiding the issue or delaying the conclusion (filibustering):

Given that dialectic is difficult and that the first example I've offered is from classical Greece, you may be thinking that dialectic is an archaic form of discourse. Who applies geometry to opinions anymore? Well, smart people everywhere.

Dialectic is an important intellectual practice because throughout life you will find yourself being presented arguments, formally and informally, where you may feel the need to push back, and dialectic gives you a set of practices and techniques for pushing back. *Dialectic is the conversational form of reading against the grain.*

You need to be careful with dialectical practices because people don't like to have their opinions corrected, and they will be hostile toward you for doing it, unless you are truly protecting them from a dangerous error, and even then they may resent you for it. If you are a teacher or an older colleague or someone whose experience or rank puts you in some position of authority, you can more easily get away with using dialectical practices overtly. If you are not in such a position but feel compelled to question, limit your questions to those with maximum impact (help the person define their terms more carefully), and leave the other person to draw the inferences for him- or herself. Don't play "gotcha," and don't come off sounding like you knew the answer all along. (Rarely are there answers: Dialectic teaches us that opinions are onions, layer upon layer upon nothing.) If people come to hate you they won't take your advice no matter how good it is. They won't deliberate with you either. If you come across someone who holds their opinions lightly, if they are willing to try out ideas and see where they lead, or if they can separate who they are from the things they say, then you've found someone you can practice dialectic with. An alternative is to pick a subject neither of you cares anything about. That way ego and prior commitment won't get in the way of the thought processes.

If rather than correcting an ill-considered or simplistic opinion your goal is mutual deliberation, then you may find dialectic easier to employ, since everyone involved realizes the decision will affect each person equally, and no one has yet made up their mind, and no one is trying to dominate the conversation or engineer a decision. If suspicion and ego can be suspended, dialectic can clarify a situation for all involved. Notice that I said "can," not "will." Dialectic is potentially useful because it can help you clarify your opinions, but it can also render doubtful opinions you had thought were sound.

Dialectic exists only in live conversation. Plato's dialogues are facsimiles, representations, not an actual dialectic. If you want to practice, you can use your phone to text with a partner, or use a chat script that the class can watch and participate in. You can also get a sense of how dialectic works (and realize that it is a real form of persuasion) by locating examples in literature and film.

Dialectical invention, the non-conversational form

While dialectic is best performed with a partner, it is possible to practice it on your own, either in your head or at a computer (or with pencil and Post-it notes if you'd rather). There's a rhetorical limit to the value of logic set by the fact that many words have multiple meanings and therefore cannot be treated like abstract symbols or ones and zeros. But that does not mean that we cannot reason about complex ideas and thus come to a better understanding. Let's take the word *love* as an example. What is love? Chances are you either responded with a Hallmark commonplace (see the upcoming section "Commonplaces"), or you dismissed the question with a joke, or you just squinted at the page in disbelief—who doesn't know what love is? Well, if we know what love is, shouldn't we be able to define it? (*Before you move on, stop and think for a minute. Are there not in fact some things you know you can't define? There's something called tacit knowledge. Google it. Not all knowing is the same kind of knowing.*)

One way to define *love* is to begin by making a list of all of the people you've ever loved. (Plato calls this process *collection* in *Phaedrus*.) Now separate the list into loves that were sexual and loves that were not. (Plato called this process *division*.) Having realized that there must be at least two kinds of love, sexual and non-sexual, you might begin to suspect that there are perhaps even more ways to divide up love, especially if you have ever loved someone from afar, as the saying goes. Because there are many similar but different feelings, ideas, and relationships that might be called (or mistaken for) love, it would be helpful if we had more than one word to think with. Here is a partial list of the kinds of love:

> *Epithumia:* sexual desire, overwhelming, fleeting
>
> *Eros:* romance, sexual desire plus companionship plus possible future
>
> *Ludus:* "playa" love, temporary, narcissistic (friends with benefits?)
>
> *Storge:* (happy) marriage, comfortable companionship
>
> *Agape:* unconditional (sexual typically but not necessarily), spiritual
>
> *Phileo:* friendship, various intensities, non-sexual but intimate at some level
>
> *Pragma:* mutual benefit, political love (politics makes strange bed fellows), convenience
>
> **Unrequited:** one sided
>
> **Infatuation:** mostly in your head, a crush, intense but transitory

Parental: wanting what's best for the beloved without concern for reciprocity (not entirely unconditional—tough love)

Sibling: shared formative experiences, possible element of rivalry

Self-love: self-esteem, but also narcissism and onanism

Puppy love: childlike, undeveloped or misplaced, possibly smothering

All manners of distortions (mania) and confusions (boundary transgressions): when one participant can't quite remain in a single category, or one person fits in one category, but the other is closer to a different category

Presenting these definitions of love as a list might suggest a hierarchy. (I didn't put them in an order even though I put them in a list. See if you can put them into a numbered list where the "best one" is number one and the "worst" is number fourteen. (*By the way, is the list complete?*)

LOVE

sexual		non-sexual
epithumia		phileo
ludus	s	puppy
agape	e	pragma
eros	x	infatuation
self		unrequited
storge		parental
		sibling

If you wanted to talk about each of these kinds of love to discover what you can think about love, you might decide to represent the division in a potentially less hierarchical way. Maybe a two-column table would work.

Representing the ideas in this way, however, highlights the boundary between sexual and non-sexual and so suggests transgressions and misalignments. (Draw a line from a word on one side to a word on the other, and think about what that relationship entails.) The way we represent the division carries with it an implicit argument about the nature (*metaphor alert!*) of love. This is an important rhetorical insight: How you display words, even to yourself, affects how you and others understand them, whether you are aware of it or not.

Most of these words for love refer to continuums rather than discreet categories. That is, they blend and morph, and over time one can become another. The traditional example is how *eros* becomes *storge*, the difference between being happily married at twenty-five and then *still* happily married at forty-five. They are also dynamic in that they change depending on the people and circumstances involved. (Most ideas do, not just love.) When we say a person has fallen out of love, usually what we mean is that their idea of love no longer fits the person they attached it to, either because that person has changed or because the idea of love has changed or circumstances have changed. When one person's idea of love starts out as *eros* and stays there while the other person's idea starts out as *eros* but becomes *storge*, trouble is inevitable. Another example of unfortunate love is when one person mistakes *epithumia* for *eros* and unintentionally misleads the other until the fire goes out.

Another way to learn more about how you might answer the question, What is love? is to put the list in different orders. Imagine that a person's understanding of love has developmental stages. What order would you put the list in? (You can omit some stages if you think they aren't relevant.) This intellectual move—to take a word, find multiple types, and then consider them on a continuum—is to make an event a process, and it's an example of a frame-breaking technique.

Another way to think about love is to imagine the consequences of different pairings: What kind of relationship will *epithumia* have with *phileo*? What happens when *agape* meets *ludus*? Or *epithumia* meets sibling?

Having recognized that love is multivalent, it might make sense to think now about emotions and relationships that are similar to love but not love exactly. Some people would prefer to believe that there is one *true* love, some blend of the best from the list above, and to reclassify the other loves as perversions or mistakes. To accomplish this argument, you would have to make a list of pseudoloves and then show how they are not love, that is that true love has one quality that all of the pseudoloves don't have.

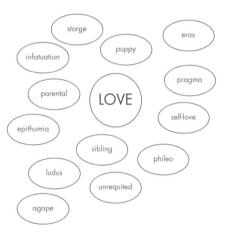

Careful thinking requires analysis of complex words into elements, wholes into parts. Distinctions are at the heart of dialectical (critical) thinking. If you can arrive at distinctions that all participants in an argument can accept, then it might be possible to have a reasonable conversation about remarkably unreasonable things, like love.

If you like to visualize thought, go to bubbl.us (or download a concept map app), and practice making concept maps. If you prefer trees to maps, try gliffy.com. If you are really into visual thinking, you might want to invest in OmniGraffle or SmartDraw.[4]

I spent as much time on the concept of love as I did partially because being able to distinguish which type of love you are feeling and which one

4. These are two feature-rich computer programs that might be worth the money if you are inclined toward visual thinking.

the other person is (and isn't) feeling is an important life skill. You might think that creating lists based on division is way too cerebral for an idea like love, and perhaps you are right, but the exercise can produce interesting insights. I also chose love for this demonstration of dialectic for reasons of tradition. Plato's *Phaedrus* is about rhetoric and dialectic but uses discourses about love (see the *Phaedrus* selection in the Appendix) as a kind of lure to attract the attention of people who might find some other subject less compelling. If you have time you really should read it.

But I also chose love because it has, not all that surprisingly, captured so many people's imaginations that we have many many words for it, suggesting that the experience of love is multifaceted, making it an easy example. If you want to practice dialectic, chose a word that might have multiple meanings. If you want to be dramatic about it, chose a word that is commonly thought to have only one meaning (like *taxation* or *winner* or *homeless*) and find (*invent?*) several for it.

Your Turn

So dialectic is a kind of thinking where you collect different examples of something. Locate the essential characteristic they all share, and then identify each one's unique difference. You might leave it there, or you might then try to assign a relative value to each example. If, on the other hand, you've discovered during the division process that you actually have apples and oranges, you may decide that each deserves it's own evaluation criteria, that is there is no basis of direct comparison, and therefore it's time to move on. To get good at this kind of thinking takes a lot of practice. And it's helpful to practice deliberately, so begin by locating words that are general terms for different but similar phenomenon, and see how many kinds you can list.

I'll start you off with a few gray-line examples, slowly fading out so you can step in. Then after a couple of those I'll leave you to work out examples entirely on your own. Try dividing the concept of *criminal*:

> **Types:** motivated by opportunity, greed, lust, anger, mistaken think-ing, identity as outcast, addiction (there's a difference between thieves and fiends, to paraphrase the aging punk band Green Day); habitual; transgressive (casual pot smoker, maybe?). What can we add to the list? Can we divide the list into an initial binary in order to start think-ing about it more deeply? Well, what about habitual versus one-timer?
>
> How about *laughter*? How many kinds of laughter can you think of?
>
> **Types:** good-natured laughter among companions, derisive (mock-ing) laughter, conspiratorial laughter, embarrassed laughter, insolent

laughter, grim or gallows laughter, dismissive laughter. What else? Would getting a handle on the types of laughter be helped by listing the kinds of laugh—chuckle, guffaw, and so on—or does the idea of intensity muddy the water?

How many kinds of *friend* can you think of?

Keep a running list of big category terms like *friend*, and whenever you have time create the subcategories. You can do this kind of thinking instead of doing sudoku or crosswords on the bus. You don't have to invest hours at a time, but you should do it regularly. Whenever you hear or read a noun that might have more than one meaning, ask yourself, what kind of X is this X? Another excellent dialectical technique is to ask, what is –X? If the opposite of X doesn't line up exactly, if everything you can say of X you can't say of –X, then –X is not the absolute opposite of X, and then again maybe you didn't define X correctly to begin with. What's the opposite of dull? Sharp? Exciting? Smart? Shiny? You need to be certain that you've got the correct definition, that what you say of X is true of X and only X and that the opposite is true and only true of –X.

The next step in the process is evaluation. Once you've collected examples and separated the similar and the different and thus found the essential definition, then you can evaluate the quality of the idea in question. Here you are trying to determine an order of preference or objective superiority. One kind of friendship is better than another, for example. Presumably from there you could decide about specific friends, that is the people you know, but dialectic is more theoretical than that. It's more interested in the concepts than any particular embodiment of a concept. At any rate, here's an example of dialectical thinking applied to a common kind of assertion.

I came across the following assertion this morning (June 17, 2012) while reading random news articles online (something you should be doing): "There is a very strong argument to be made that Fiona Apple, thirty-four years old, is the greatest popular musician of her generation" (Dan P. Lee). This assertion kind of startled me because I think of her as a one-hit wonder and hadn't thought about her at all since her big hit. An uncritical response would have been "No Way!" or "Huh?" What would a dialectical approach have looked like? Well, if you're ready to strike out on your own now, go for it. If not, I'll run another example for you:

> **Collection:** Who are the other "popular musicians" of her generation? Division: Do we need to account for all kinds of "popular" and all kinds of "musicians"? In other words, is the class of "popular musicians" sufficiently cohesive and undifferentiatable such that we can assess them all on the same greatness scale? Does it make sense, for example, to compare 50 Cent to Fiona Apple? If it does, fine. If it doesn't, fine. We just need to make sure that the items in our category are all of the same kind. Once we have narrowed our category

sufficiently, then we need an evaluative criterion, a set of characteristics that we can measure in each example and a way to add up the
measurements. In this case what are the parts of "greatest"?

How do we define "greatest"?

Awards?

Sales?

Number of positive critical reviews?

Personal preference? (Subjective criteria modifies the idea of greatest
to mean my favorite.)

Airplay?

Number of downloads?

Do we need to pick one of these or exclude one or more of them and then put
them into a weighted hierarchy? A weighted hierarchy would be something like
sales and awards, in that order, but where ten Grammys is equal to one million
sales. So if an artist got two Grammys and one million sales and another got no
Grammys but four million sales, the second artist would be the greatest.

Finally we need to decide whether or not our criteria of evaluation warrant
a strong approval or a weak one. In other words, can we reasonably expect
any music buff to agree with our analysis and determination, or could some
people reasonably object? Try to imagine who the people are who might reject
our arguments. What beliefs and experiences might they have that would
keep them from agreeing with us? If our only criterion for greatness was personal opinion, then we can't say more than, "I think Fiona Apple is the greatest singer-songwriter of her generation, and here's why: . . ." But if we have
more objective criteria, we can make a more objective kind of argument.

Given all of this forethought, now we are ready to back up or reject the
assertion that Fiona Apple is the greatest singer-songwriter of her generation.

You should make a habit of inventing simple general assertions, like the
ones below, and then picking one or two a day and working through them. If
you come up with one that is too general, plug some names of people into the
sentence, and see if that gives you something to go on. Examples are always a
great place to start. Just keep in mind that your goal here is ultimately evaluation, not biography.

1. It's better to be rich than famous.

2. It's better to be lucky and good than just good alone.

3. Being really good at one thing is more useful than being good at many
    things.

4. Beauty beats brains.

One last piece of advice about how to increase your skill with dialectical thinking: The distinguishing characteristic of a critical thinker is the ability to make fine distinctions, to carefully separate similar things, to find differences where most people only see similarities. To get good at this you have to make a habit of playing with words, that is, thinking about synonyms and near synonyms and figuring out how (and when) they differ. This isn't quite the same as taking big words like *courage* or *charisma* and enumerating each of the types like we were doing a couple of pages ago. It's taking two similar words and figuring out how they differ. Below is a pretty long list of possibilities. This should keep you going for a while. Before you begin, put them in order from easiest (for you) to hardest, and then work your way down. Also consider if they are in the same grammatical form and whether or not that makes a difference.

alone :: lonely

reason :: cause

sign :: symptom

ambiguous :: incoherent

complexity :: confusion

simplify :: reduce

strategy :: tactic

zero :: nothing

objective :: goal

need :: want

knowledge :: truth

knowledge :: information

knowledge :: wisdom

wisdom :: judgment

degree :: education

conspicuous :: obvious

avocation :: vocation

peace :: silence

sound :: noise

leisure :: idle

stupid :: foolish

art :: practice

science :: art

disinterested :: uninterested

benign :: indifferent

immoral :: amoral

selfish :: self-centered

lie :: mistake

inept :: clumsy

brave :: stupid

opinion :: belief

friend :: accomplice

frequent :: regular

subject :: discipline

childlike :: childish

stingy :: frugal

progress :: improvement

challenge :: threat

helpful :: useful

opportunity :: crisis

accurate :: precise

If you don't like these examples, or you've worked through all of them, get out a thesaurus, and find some new ones. Once you feel relatively comfortable distinguishing similar ideas, up the intensity of the workout. Pick one pair, and write a story about how one word becomes the other or how the perception of one is revealed to be the other in reality.

Summary

Dialectic is an important intellectual practice because throughout life you will find yourself presented with arguments, formally and informally, where you may feel the need to push back, and dialectic gives you a set of practices and techniques for pushing back. At the same time, you will also encounter moments in life where you feel no inclination to push back, and at such moments dialectic is even more important. Question the obvious. *Dialectic is the conversational equivalent of reading against the grain.* When done silently in your head or on the computer screen as you think through concepts, dialectic is the intellectual equivalent of musical scales or calisthenics. It teaches you to define your terms carefully and think the implications through, to make good connections and sever bad ones. Do it until it becomes habitual. Be careful, however, to never take it too far. Extremity distorts everything. There may be some beliefs you believe just because you believe them, and sometimes you might want to be okay with that. At such times, however, you shouldn't try to convince other people your faith is one they must share.

A parody of dialectic from Rosencrantz and Guildenstern Are Dead

Tom Stoppard is a contemporary British playwright who has written some spectacularly good comedies of the intellectual slapstick variety. One of his early pieces is *Rosencrantz and Guildenstern Are Dead*, in which he dramatizes what happens to the two bit-part players in Shakespeare's *Hamlet* when they are off the stage of *Hamlet*. It's a kind of behind-the-scenes reimagining. And it's very funny, if you like parody and intellectual games. It's funnier watched than read. You may be able to find a scene on YouTube. The two bit players, who will eventually be sent to a neighboring king with their own death warrants, are killing time between acts of *Hamlet* by playing Elizabethan tennis and having a pseudodialectical conversation, the back and forth of tennis dramatizing dialectic's give and take.

In case you were wondering, the following bit is a parody of dialectic because, instead of asking questions of statements, the characters answer a question with another question. The circularity of what results underscores the way in which dialectic can descend into mere competition, the desire to win overtaking the will to learn. The existential angst that permeates the scene is also appropriate for dialectic because it's a practice that would try to rationalize existence, something one might argue is ultimately impossible. And then again, perhaps the angst I sense comes from the fact I know where these two souls are headed.

ROS: Do you want to play questions?

GUILD: How do you play that?

ROS: You have to ask a question.

GUILD: Statement. One–Love.

ROS: Cheating.

GUILD: How?

ROS: I haven't started yet.

GUILD: Statement. Two–Love.

ROS: Are you counting that?

GUILD: What?

ROS: Are you counting that?

GUILD: Foul. No repetition. Three–Love, and game.

ROS: I'm not going to play if you're going to be like that.

GUILD: Whose serve?

ROS: Uh . . .

GUILD: Hesitation. Love–One.

ROS: Whose go?

GUILD: Why?

ROS: Why not?

GUILD: What for?

ROS: Ha. No synonyms. One all.

GUILD: What in God's name is going on?

ROS: Foul. No rhetoric. Two–One.

GUILD: What does it all add up to?

ROS: Can't you guess?

GUILD: Are you addressing me?

ROS: Is there anyone else?

GUILD: Who?

ROS: How would I know?

GUILD: Why do you ask?

ROS: Are you serious?

GUILD: Was that rhetoric?

ROS: No.

GUILD: Statement. Two all. Game point.

ROS: What's the matter with you today?

GUILD: When?

ROS: What?

GUILD: Are you deaf?

ROS: Am I dead?

GUILD: Yes or no?

ROS: Is there a choice?

GUILD: Is there a God?

ROS: Foul. No non sequiturs. Three–Two. One game all.

GUILD: What's your name?

ROS: What's yours?

GUILD: You first.

ROS: Statement. One–Love.

GUILD: What's your name when you're at home?

ROS: What's yours?

GUILD: When I'm at home?

ROS: Is it different at home?

GUILD: What home?

ROS: Haven't you got one?

GUILD: Why do you ask?

ROS: What are you driving at?

GUILD: What's your name?

ROS: Repetition. Two–Love. Match point.

GUILD: Who do you think you are?

GUILD: ROS: Rhetoric. Game and match!

Transition from dialectic to topics

Plato chose to teach us dialectic by dramatizing the activity, offering many different examples of dialectical conversations from which, with patience and perception, we could infer the rules. He never came right out and said, "This is how it's done." He just did it over and over again in different ways, with slightly different outcomes. Reading his dialogues as a way of learning dialectic is a bit like trying to learn how to play chess (or persuasion) without anyone ever explicitly telling you what the rules are. It's very lifelike in that sense. That's why I spent so much time spelling out the rules and procedures for you.

Plato's successor Aristotle took a different approach to teaching and had a different idea about rhetoric. He saw rhetoric as a form of human communication that could be analyzed though classification like biologists study plants. Unlike Plato, Aristotle believed the ethics of persuasion was a secondary concern because he was merely observing a phenomenon, not teaching people what to do or how to live. His is an instrumental rhetoric in the same sense as the character Gorgias seems to have understood rhetoric, a tool that can be used for good and ill but which is amoral in and of itself.

Aristotle's *Rhetoric* is, however, dialectical in the sense that he begins each section with a careful set of definitions, and then he divides the pieces into parts and then uses the parts to generate a series of enthymemes out of which one could construct new arguments for different purposes in different situations. (See the selection from *Rhetoric* in the Appendix.)

Topics

First, an important distinction you might miss: In *Rhetoric* the word *topic* is not synonymous with "subject." The word *subject* refers to an area of inquiry, like songbirds of South America. *Topic*, on the other hand, means a "pattern of thought."

In response to the problem of what to think, early teachers of persuasion (those who preceded both Aristotle and Plato) collected conventional wisdom in the form of proverbs, maxims, and aphorisms, organized by occasion. They then offered example speeches where an assertion was supported using these conventional expressions as a kind of evidence. To understand the differences among the three rhetorical forms, read the section "Proverbs, maxims, aphorisms: On the origin of sound bites" in this chapter. What the three have in common is that they are ways to express received wisdom, common sense, and orthodox thinking: things people say when they can't or can't be bothered to think critically before they speak or write. There isn't anything inherently wrong with saying what everyone always says. In fact, on emotionally intense occasions, a few platitudes might save everyone a great deal of pain. What, for example, do you say to someone whose dad or mom just died? "I'm sorry for you loss" is more than enough most of the time. A smile or a hug and something else to talk about might be much more rhetorically astute.

On less intense occasions, however, a lack of originality might suggest the *rhetor*'s grasp of what's happening is superficial or merely conventional. Additionally, learning how to communicate effectively by using common expressions doesn't help you develop abstract thought. If you are stuck building your texts out of the common stock of opinions and expressions, you can get some things done, but you might also become a prisoner of convention, unable to achieve insight or create new ideas.

Aristotle claimed his method of invention was superior. His method was to keep a list of abstract patterns of thought from which one could invent entirely new arguments. In *On Sophistical Refutations* (in the concluding paragraph) he explained that, whereas his predecessors gave their students speeches to memorize and practice and thus did the equivalent of giving people who needed shoes lots of shoes to choose from, he taught his students how to make shoes for themselves, and thus his students could tailor (*cobble—don't mix your metaphors*) shoes fitting their unique circumstances and needs. As with arguments, so with shoes, one size does not fit all. (*Notice the proverb—or is that a cliché—there?*)

The topics in Aristotle's sense are patterns of thought that come in two forms, the general and the specific. Specific topics relate to specific fields of inquiry, while general topics are applicable in any kind of discourse. The concept of intention (what a person had in mind when they did or said something), for example, is a special topic of interpretation employed (most usefully at least) in law courts (where what Aristotle called *forensic rhetoric* takes place). The value of the American dollar relative to foreign currencies is a special topic of economics (in America), although it might also be used in (American) politics. On the other hand, the topic that more of a good thing is better than less of the same thing is a general topic because it can be used almost anywhere.[5] Aristotle's *Rhetoric* is basically a long list of topics organized by the kind of speech each one was best suited to: a set of patterns or molds (or lasts if you like the shoe metaphor) that you can select from in order to build an argument. If you need to build something in a hurry, prefabrication saves time.

Here is Aristotle on the topics specific to political-policy decision making (a.k.a. deliberation):

> [When deciding what to do, all people choose what they think will make them happy.] We may define happiness as prosperity combined with virtue; or as independence of life; or as the secure enjoyment of the maximum of pleasure; or as a good condition of property and body, together with the power of guarding one's property and body and making use of them. That happiness is one or more of these things, pretty well everybody agrees.

---

5. Remember to read against the grain. What's the opposing opinion for more of a better thing is better than less? Supersizing when it comes to food is dangerous. Economies of scale—the more you can make, the cheaper each unit is (a special topic of economics)—when applied to the food industry leads to an epidemic of obesity. Less of a good thing might actually be better. And less of a good thing might make that thing itself better.

Notice how he begins with an unarguable assertion that all people seek happiness. It's not that one couldn't argue this point; in a post-Freudian world perhaps we would feel compelled to argue it, but rather that as a basic premise it is a pretty solid foundation because most people would just accept it as true, uncontroversial at least. Following the given premise, he defines the key word, offering in this case several variations to choose from so that you can tailor your argument to better fit your audience. Having defined happiness, he enumerates the parts:

> If happiness is something of this sort, it is necessary for its "parts" to be: good birth, numerous friendships, worthy friendships, wealth, good children, numerous children, a good old age, as well as the virtues of the body (such as health, beauty, strength, physical stature, athletic prowess), reputation, honor, good luck [*eutykhia*], virtue. (1.5.4)

Before we move on, have a careful look at that list. Could you place the list in order from greatest to least? Has he left anything out? Should any of his items be excluded in our world? The dialectical test for exclusion would be that a given word does not in fact produce or at least encourage happiness. Notice, however, that Aristotle isn't debating the presence of these words on his list of the divisions of happiness. He's just putting them out there on the grounds that this is what most people believe. His rhetoric is a dialectical rhetoric in the sense that his pattern is assertion, definition, division, examples. But it is a practical rhetoric in the sense that it shows you how to use popular patterns of thought to facilitate public decisions. He's not interested in using dialectical rhetoric to discover the truth. He's interested in getting socially significant work done.

So if you ever had to promote a course of action, you would consider which of the above components were relevant to the subject and the audience and the occasion (organized perhaps by most relevant to least) and then think through the scenarios the action might create. If we do X, these good things will happen. If we don't, these bad things will happen. If someone else is advancing a course of action, you can analyze the arguments by reversing the process. What topics did they include, which ones did they leave out, and how compelling are the augments they came up with? She said if we do X, Y will follow; how strong is "follow"? Is it causal, correlative, possible, imaginary?

Let's look at all of this more slowly, and let's look at what is likely to strike you as the weirdest element first: good birth. How could you use "good birth" to convince someone to do (or not do) something? Everything hinges on the definition, right? For the Greeks, "good birth" (*eugenese*) meant being born in a city to parents whose parents were also born in that city. As a thought pattern, *eugenese* refers to something like, you can trust (or not) the child because you could trust (or not) the parents (and grand-parents). We encounter the same pattern expressed as conventional wisdom in expressions like, *The apple doesn't fall far from the tree; from a bad egg, a rotten crow; like father (mother) like son (daughter).* While the proverbs are rhetorically serviceable, you have a great deal more rhetorical dexterity if you can abstract the pattern of thought from which the common sense expressions are derived: the abstract principle of inheritance, like begets like. You would be even more convincing if you selected the pattern of inheritance with the audience and occasion in mind. Young parents, for example, are probably keen to hear that concept. Teenagers? Maybe not so much.

If you are talking about prenatal care, "good birth" means something different (healthy child, easy delivery) than if you are talking about family planning (healthy child, parents emotionally and economically prepared). And then again, if you are talking to people who believe all children come from God, then "good birth" is non-differential because all births are good because they are all gifts from God.

The more abstract you get, the less special the topic becomes, and thus the more portable, more generally useful, it is. So for example, you might urge a course of action on the grounds that it comes from (is descended, was parented by) something everybody already recognizes as good and thus will readily infer that what descends from it must similarly be good.

══════ Your Turn

Before you leave Aristotle's political topics, see if you can work out an example or two for yourself. Given *environmentalism*, create a public policy argument. It would make sense to choose "prosperity combined with virtue" as a primary definition of happiness. You could use *virtue* alone, but that would appeal to only the idealistic people in your audience. Adding prosperity might draw in those who tend to equate environmentalism with antibusiness interests. Okay, so which of the elements of happiness can you use? Seems like the idea of inheritance and legacy are going to play a part. How would environmentalism produce "friends" and (*or?*) "numerous friends"? What can you do with the remaining parts? Do you need to add to the list of elements of happiness before you move on? We are, after all, many generations and cultures removed from the Greeks. Maybe the elements of happiness need to be updated.

Aesop's Fables offer a great opportunity to practice abstraction. Pick any.

Aristotle's general topics of the preferable

Aristotle observed that when it comes to decision making, often we have to choose from among multiple options, and thus a set of tools for comparing and contrasting options would be useful. What follows is a very loose adaptation of the general topics of the preferable (*On Rhetoric*, 1.7).[6] Any one of these topics might be more or less useful for any given subject or circumstance. And any of them might be utterly ridiculous in a given situation. You will also notice that in nearly all cases the same topic could be used both for and against the same assertion. In *On Rhetoric*, Aristotle was concerned with describing how convictions are obtained and laws passed. He was not interested in strict logic. He had the *Prior Analytics* and the *Posterior Analytics* for that. *When selecting topics for an argument, you have to use your judgment based on your understanding of what you are trying to do, for whom, and when.*

The purpose of any inventional strategy is to generate ideas. Once you've come up with everything that's possible, then you select the most effective and appropriate among them. Don't be afraid of generating nonsense during an inventional phase. Relax your mind, and play with the ideas. As you read through these topics, think of an example and a counterexample for each one.

- What is scarcer is preferable to what is more abundant if value is the issue.

- What is abundant is preferable to what is scarce if the thing in question needs to be useful.

- What is more difficult is preferable to what is easier once it has been accomplished.

- What is easier is preferable to what is more difficult at the outset.

- The original is preferable to a copy.

- Whatever comes directly from the source is preferable to anything that comes from further downstream.

- The elemental is preferable to the amalgamated.

- The ornate to the plain.

- The simple to the complex.

---

6. Note that we are talking about a set of intellectual techniques, not a pattern for a particular kind of essay, although you could create a comparison-contrast essay using some of these techniques.

- The end is preferable to the means if it can be had by itself.

- The autonomous is preferable to the dependent.

- Something the opposite of which or the loss of which is a greater misfortune is preferable.

- Those things are greater whose effects are greater.

- A preference for fine things is better than a preference for common or cheap things.

- What the wise desire and what the better people want is preferable to what the common folk desire and worse sorts of people want.

- The pleasant is preferable to the unpleasant.

- The durable is preferable to the disposable.

- What is praised is preferable to what is ignored or merely tolerated.

- People prefer to do things that they want to do over those things they have to do.

- People prefer newer things to older things.

- People prefer ancient things to old things.

- The immediate is preferable to the delayed.

- People prefer more of a good thing to less of it.

- People tend to prefer what they think others prefer.

- What is real is preferable to what is artificial or imaginary.

- Truth is preferable to opinion.

- Certainty is preferable to uncertainty, so much so that sometimes people would rather a negative outcome than wait any longer in the hope of a positive one.

- Whatever produces a greater thing is preferable to whatever produces a lesser thing.

- What is useful in many ways is preferable to what has fewer uses.

- What is less painful is preferable to what is more painful.

- Of two goods, that which added to one makes the whole greater is greater.

- What is conspicuously valued is preferable to that which is valued without notice.

- Anything done with premeditation and care is greater (better or worse) than anything done accidentally or of necessity.

- What many prefer is preferable to what only a few care about, unless the few are more highly esteemed than the many.

- People prefer those things they think are uniquely theirs, or tend to belong to people like them or to the kind of people they wish they were or wish to someday be.

The topics of the preferable will reward constant practice. Work with them long enough, and you will start to see them at work everywhere. When you do, keep examples using an app like Evernote. Make sure you tag each entry so you can sort by relevant examples later on. Your goal with this kind of practice isn't so much to quote something, though you might want to, but rather to engrain the patterns in your thinking so that they will come quickly to mind when you need to make a decision or promote a course of action or keep people from making a mistake.

The topics of praise and blame

Here is another example of special topics. This list relates to *encomium* (praise) and *vituperation* (condemnation) of a person. These are two significant forms of discourse under the more general heading of epideictic or ceremonial rhetoric. This list comes from Cicero's character Antonius (*On the Orator*). Notice that this example is subtly different from the Aristotelian one in that, while we do get an assertion that might pass for a generally acceptable premise, "anyone . . . will realize" we aren't offered a definition. Cicero just jumps to the list:

> Anyone who intends to praise someone will realize that he must set out the advantages of fortune. These are descent, money, relatives, friends, power, health, beauty, strength, intelligence, and everything else that is either a matter of the body or external. If the person he is praising possesses these things, the speaker must say that he has used them well; if he lost them, that he bore their loss with moderation. Secondly he must relate what this person has undertaken or endured in a wise manner, or generously, or courageously, or justly, or magnificently or dutifully, or humanely, in short, in any way that showed some virtue or other. These strategies and others of this sort will easily be understood by someone wishing to praise, as will their opposites by someone wanting to blame. (2.46)

The argument for using these parts is only implicit rather than explicit like it would be in Aristotle. Here we are simply told that this is how you do it because everyone knows this is how it's done. It's an argument from tradition, nothing more. But there's nothing wrong with that if the purpose of the practice is to give you material to work with.

Do you recognize the list? Reminiscent of the *bios* section, right? It's offering the same idea, that, by having a list of the things everyone always talks about when called upon to praise or blame someone, all you need to do is come up with the details for that particular person, fit to the occasion and the audience. You know what questions to ask; all you need are the answers.

Following are a few more collections of special topics.

Topics of interpretation

Letter and spirit: argument over whether one should read a particular passage literally or figuratively

Ambiguity: argument over the precise meaning of a passage that could mean at least two different things

Disagreement between laws: argument over the meaning of a text as a result of the application of conflicting interpretive conventions

Definition and use of a specific word: argument over an interpretation hinging on the definition of a single word

Analogy: argument over whether or not a text refers to a subject in addition to the one it appears to discuss

Topics of last resort

Below is the set of special topics relevant to self-defense under the worst possible circumstances, when you've been caught red-handed (notice the cliché?), when all of the ways in which you can deny having done it have been proven wrong.

Confess: Yeah, I did it. Only a delusional person or an incorrigible liar would deny the truth in the face of overwhelming evidence. Some political advisors suggest that if you have any skeletons in your closet that might come out, own up before your opponent accuses you.

Deny intent: I didn't mean to do it. I'm not a doctor, and I'm not used to giving injections.

Deny wrongdoing: (When denying intent doesn't or can't work.) It was the right thing to do. It wasn't murder; it was mercy killing.

Deny responsibility: (When denying wrongdoing doesn't or can't work.) The doctor told me I could administer this drug myself, and anyway, this drug is legal.

Beg forgiveness, then appeal for sympathy: I'm sorry, but the agony of watching her suffer was unbearable; if you were in my position, you would have done what I did.

Go out with dignity: Well, I'm not ashamed of what I did. If it was illegal, it was not unethical. In fact, if there were any justice in this land, I would be considered a brave and honorable person.

Guilt trip or remorse: When all else has failed, make your accusers feel a twinge of remorse, as Jim Rocap, the lawyer for Teresa Lewis who was executed in Virginia for murder, did:

Tonight, the machinery of death in Virginia extinguished the beautiful, childlike and loving human spirit of Teresa Lewis," he said. "Teresa asked that I send her thanks and love to all of those who have supported her in this fight for her life. In her words, 'It's just awesome.' It is our hope that Teresa's death will cause a reexamination of the badly broken system of justice that could allow something as wrong and unjust as this to happen. (O'Connor)

Summary

So the topics, both general and specific, help you invent arguments by giving you an apparently unarguable assertion to derive a generally accepted definition and then enumerating the parts out of which you can construct a new argument. You simply have a list of available parts and patterns, and you plug the parts into the patterns until you get the right fit. You need judgment because the practice will generate both garbage and gold. You need to figure out what will work and what won't based on who you are talking or writing to, when, and why.

The advantage of the topical approach to invention over dialectic is that it saves you the trouble of asking questions, but its virtue, like nearly all virtues, can be a defect as well. If you make an assumption that isn't accepted by the audience or warranted by the evidence as you can demonstrate to the audience, then you will have set off at cross-purposes, and your rhetorical efforts may make things worse rather than better. Sometimes, as with dialectic, you need to scrutinize the questions carefully before piling up possible answers. The process of asking the right questions in the right order is offered by stasis theory.

Stasis

Stasis is the Greek word from which we get "static" as in "stationary." In rhetoric, *stasis* refers to a direct disagreement (a.k.a. an issue) that evidence can resolve. It also refers to a process of questioning that can lead to a better understanding of a complex disagreement or situation. Thus, stasis is both an inventional and an analytical strategy. It can also form a pattern of arrangement. Stasis theory takes Plato's idea that you have to answer some questions before asking others (definition before evaluation) and works out the details in great detail, associating each set of questions with a particular kind of discourse.

What is an *issue*?

A rational argument is a specific disagreement about a thing, event, action, or word that can be resolved by answering a set of questions in a specific order. Whenever any question can be answered in directly contradictory ways (one person says "yes"; one person says "no"), there is an *issue* that needs to be resolved before the argument can continue or the participants can move on if it's the last remaining issue. Sometimes the issue is simple and obvious to everyone. In such cases, you need to do nothing more than state the issue and then seek evidence to support either answer and then judge which answer has the better evidence:

> Should we have gun control?
> Yes!
> No, we shouldn't!

If you turn a truly static question into a statement, you have a thesis statement worthy of research because you have directly opposing viewpoints, a direct disagreement, an issue. If during your research you have evidence that adequately supports one position and adequately undermines the counter-position, then you have material worthy of an academic paper. Without the direct disagreement, all you have is a controversy. Without the evidence, all you have is a shouting match.

Sometimes, however, the issue is complex in the sense that something is agreed on, but underlying that agreement is disagreement or confusion:

> We should have gun control. (I think guns lead to violence.)
> I agree we should have gun control. (I'm an American selling guns in Mexico, and, if guns were harder for the average person to buy up north, I could sell even more of them down here.)

And sometimes the issue is obscured. People are talking at cross-purposes, or they have different definitions for key terms and don't realize it, or they are not listening closely, or they are trying to avoid an unpleasant consequence by denying what they should accept.

> We should have gun control. (I think guns lead to violence.)
> I disagree. (I'm not hurting anyone using my radar gun to measure the speed of my fastball.)

If the issue is not simple and obvious, then it needs to be located, simplified, and agreed upon before the evidence can be considered effectively. It is in these cases where the issue is obscured that stasis theory can be a helpful inventional strategy because, by walking you through some specific points of possible contention, stasis theory can help you clarify the disagreement and keep you from wasting time arguing about things already agreed on and things that are irrelevant to the conversation.

Once you have located the specific disagreement (the issue), the next thing you should do is discover the various opinions. There are always at least two sides to an issue (agree, disagree), but there may be more than two (agree, disagree, partially agree, occasionally disagree). The next step is to think about how people's beliefs and situations lead them to their conclusions. Only if you know how (not just what) someone thinks will you be able to persuade them. That may seem like a monumental task, to know how someone thinks, and it can be as the sections on characterization and personas suggest, but there is one primary question the answer to which will give you a handle on nearly any rhetorical situation: *What's in it for them?*

People will believe and do whatever they think is in their best (*what does "best" mean?*) interest, regardless of whether or not it really is. Most people don't quite understand this. They think their beliefs are real or true and not the result of a rhetorical process, a semiconscious reasoning from unspoken, unexamined, and in some cases unquestionable premises quickly leading to the belief they want to believe. Rarely, and often only in the most crushingly real situations, will people come to believe what they really don't want to believe. I'm talking, of course, about people who haven't read this book. Those of you who have read this far have been inoculated against rhetorical naiveté.

So, before you ask yourself, Do I believe in gun control? you have to answer a specific set of questions, most of which have to do with carefully defining the terms used in the argument. What is a gun? Seriously, a radar gun is not a gun, but is a bazooka a gun? Does any projectile-firing weapon qualify as a gun? What is control? What is gun control? What is the place of law in society? What is law? What is society? (*Yes, I am still being serious.*) And, then, when you know the exact meaning of these terms as defined by dictionaries, common use, and legal statute, you need to assemble as many positions on the issue as you can find, and then you need to psych the positions. Ask yourself, Why does this person believe this? or What would a person have to believe to believe this? Often it helps to know a person's situation. If you live in a rural area or a suburb and to you a gun is a shotgun, and a pleasant autumnal activity is sitting quietly in the woods waiting to pop a deer that you can take home proudly and feast on with your relatives, you're going to think differently about gun control than if you live in a deteriorating inner-city neighborhood where a gun is a Glock that the drug dealers use to keep you terrified in your house at night.

I'm not sure because I don't actually know you, but I'm guessing at this point that you are thinking something like, "Holy smoke, that's a lot of obvious questions and an unbelievably tedious way of thinking about something I already know what I think about." Yeah, true. But that's actually the point of learning inventional strategies. You want to think beyond the obvious. You want to start with what everybody always says, and then you want to get deeper into the disagreement and see if you can come up with something that will resolve the dispute. *Persuasion from a rhetorical perspective isn't about who has the biggest, loudest set of arguments. Truly persuasive people understand how arguments work and build their participation in those arguments on those understandings. Rhetors* don't shoot from the hip.

Below are five sets of stasis questions. Each set is tailored for a specific kind of subject. Read over each one, and then come up with as detailed an example as you can for each.

Thing

1. Does it exist? (Did it, will it, or could it? You have to be clear on whether it's conjectural, historical, or current.)

2. Is it simple or complex (analysis—iron, love)?

3. Stable or dynamic (never changes or changes depending on location or context)?

4. What is it (definition)?

5. What names does it go by (nomination)?

6. Is it good or bad, useful or not (evaluation)?

Concept

1. What is it called (nomination)? Is it simple or complex (analysis)?

3. Stable or dynamic (changes depending context)?

4. How is it defined? (We can't ask if it exists—see the following list.)

5. Is it referential or conventional? (Is there a corresponding thing in the world outside our heads, or does it exist only in language or as a byproduct of cognition?)

Event

1. Did it happen? (Could it, should it, will it?)

2. What is this event called (nomination)?

3. Circumstances that caused it (causation)?

4. What are the consequences?

5. Will it (can it, should it) happen again?

6. How can we prepare for the next time?

Action

1. Did someone do something (investigation)?

2. What was it (categorization)?

3. Who did it (interrogation, accusation, attribution)?

4. Was it good or bad, useful or useless, legal or illegal (evaluation)?

5. Did they mean to do it (intention)?

6. What were the circumstances?

7. What are the consequences?

8. What is the jurisdiction? (Who's responsible for taking action, if any?)

Word

1. What does it mean (definition)?

2. What does it mean in different contexts (variation)?

3. How is it used (application)?

4. What words are like it (synonyms)?

5. What are its opposites (antonyms)?

It is important to realize that not all issues are real issues. Sometimes people create controversy for the sake of creating public relations opportunities, for getting in the news and looking important. The academic version of this nefarious practice is called creating a straw dog, a fake opponent. The political versions of straw dogs take many forms and are often merely a misrepresentation or unfair simplification of an actual entity or group. People also sometimes exploit fake issues in order to distract others from important issues. Fake opposition is also sometimes used to increase sales by capitalizing on people's innate desire to compete (PC vs. Apple) and in some cases to create an identity. Some activities and organizations only exist in opposition to something and would cease to exist if the other thing went away. In such cases, winning would lead to death for the victor as much as for the vanquished. In these cases you have to figure the possibility of resolution is a source of anguish even though it looks like a goal.

It is also important to realize that sometimes we get into arguments with ourselves or with others about matters that seem like real issues and are not fake or pseudoissues but that nevertheless turn out to be non-issues. You can save yourself a great deal of time and frustration by learning to recognize non-issues when you encounter them.

Asystasis—non-issues

Asystatic issues interrupt discourse but do not prompt answers from which any useful agreement can be obtained. They simply spin a vortex in which agreement is lost and prejudices are condensed because they do not generate any new information or alter the participants' perceptual frames in any way. If you ask an unanswerable question, you may create an *asystatic* controversy. This might be useful, if you need to stall for time or distract people or exploit their unexamined assumptions. Most of the time, however, deliberately setting up an *asystatic* discourse is socially corrosive, while falling into one unaware wastes time and intellectual energy. Traditionally, there are four kinds of *asystatic* issues:

> *Monomeres* are issues that do not bear debate because the evidence is all one sided. The convicted parricide that begs the sentencing magistrate for leniency on the grounds that he is an orphan frames a *monomere*. There is no response to the claim, "I deserve leniency," but astonishment and derision.

> *Isazon* occurs when the evidence is perfectly balanced. An ancient example of this might be found in the lore surrounding Korax and his student Tisias. Korax guaranteed his teaching. If a student failed to win his first court case, Korax would refund his tuition. Tisias, who had gone into teaching rather than pleading, sued Korax on the grounds that he had never won a court case. Tisias argued that he could not lose because if the court ruled in favor of Korax then he, Tisias, had lost the case and won his refund, and if the court decided in his favor then the teacher would have to refund the tuition anyway. Korax argued the opposite. If Tisias won, then the refund would not be forthcoming because the condition of the guarantee was met, and if Tisias lost then the refund would not be forthcoming because he had sued for the refund and lost. The court is said to have dismissed the case with a pun on Korax's name: from a bad crow, a rotten egg.

> *Ellipes* is an issue that rests on inconclusive evidence. In a sense, any radical induction will ultimately be reduced to *ellipes*. While it is simple enough to prove to yourself deductively that you are mortal

(All people are mortal. I am a person; therefore I am mortal), it is impossible to prove it inductively. By the time the only necessary example is in place, the question is moot.

Aporon occurs when no solution or even end to the inquiry is possible. This *asystasis* is a staple of deconstructive rhetoric and of *elenchus*. It arises when the premises of an argument have been so relentlessly questioned that no deductive thinking is possible. The iterative *why?* of an inquisitive child and the ironic questions of Socrates both lead to a vertiginous moment when there appear to be no foundational beliefs, and therefore one is left to choose among faith, despair, anger, or *absurd laughter*. People sometimes create *aporonic* situations because they haven't framed the question correctly, but they also sometimes create them in order to distract an audience in order to delay a decision. This rhetorical strategy is known as filibustering.

There is another form of *asystatic* controversy that doesn't fall under any of these and which as far as I know does not have a name. These controversies occur when there is no common ground upon which to base a rational disagreement, no agreement about what the key terms mean or what counts as evidence or how to evaluate evidence. In such cases, every argument presented by one side necessarily falls on deaf ears and vice versa. These arguments are irrational and so don't really warrant the term argument, but they are prevalent today. The opinions that underwrite each side are all diametrically opposed, and thus there's no way to resolve the dispute. Even legislation won't resolve the dispute.

The debate over abortion is a prominent example. You either believe children come from God or from women and men (which is not to say that one side is populated entirely by atheists). The evolution-creationism debate is another. You either believe that science offers our best hope of understanding the physical universe, or you believe religion does. Climate change is a third. You either think that the demonstrably shrinking polar ice caps are evidence of the effect of greenhouse gasses on the climate or you don't.

It's not that you can't learn something about yourself by debating these issues. Indeed they include entire chains of values that are important for every person to ponder. But they are not resolvable through argumentation, nor can persuasion quiet all opposition. There are just too many underlying disagreements about the nature and purpose of life for issues like these to be resolved. To my mind, while it is okay to talk about these kinds of issues, any attempt to legislate in favor of one side or the other should be illegal. But now I'm waxing editorial.

It is also important to keep in mind that some issues are only relatively *asystatic*, that is for the people involved there's no way to create a rational argument because the essential information is missing or the emotional connections don't exist. In such cases groundwork in the form of research or education or experience has to precede argumentation for opinions to move. Some issues are only temporarily *asystatic*, the missing information coming soon. So when you seem to have reached an impasse, step back and ask yourself, What would I need to know in order to resolve this disagreement? and then go looking for what you just found missing.

Finally, people sometimes create *asystatic* issues for purely political reasons. Such groups have a purely oppositional identity in the sense that they would cease to exist absent the controversy and thus, rather than removing the disagreement, they do everything they can to entrench it. Whenever you hear the expression *the war on X*, consider the possibility that the controversy thus created is either ill formed or actually non-existent. But also keep in mind that by forming an adversary where no single enemy previously existed, it is possible to create the opportunity to change people's minds. In rhetoric, even a vacuum has potential.

Your Turn

You could argue that such non-issues are the inevitable result of any adversarial system that has only two necessarily opposing sides. You could. Try it.

Make a list of all of the *asystatic* controversies you can think of, and then share them with someone else. Does that person agree that each of the items on your list is *asystatic*?

Framing

People will sometimes try to control an argument's outcome by constraining the terms, trying to force people to see the issue as one way when it could be others. This is known as framing, and knowing how to frame and how to break a frame is one of a *rhetor*'s primary skills. The image on the left is a pixilated face. Look closely at it, and you will see clearly that what look like pixels are actually crayons. When it comes to framing, sometimes you need to step closer. Sometimes you need to step back. And always you need to be looking out for clandestine metaphors (step?), euphemisms, and dysphemisms, as well as oversimplifications and distortions.

The simplest frame is the false dichotomy: It's either X or –X. (What about Y? you should ask.) The sales version is using empty comparisons: 20 percent less salt (less than what? you should ask). You either support the president or you are anti-American, and so on. Whenever anyone offers you a choice of two, consider both and neither as well.

Here is a more complex example from *The Art of Framing: Managing the Language of Leadership.*

> A plumber we know used his backhoe to look for a broken sewer line under a neighbor's lawn and was successful in his search. When asked by the lady of the house, "How can you stand that stifling smell?" his reply was, "Smells like bacon and eggs to a plumber, ma'am." The plumber's frame of the situation, focusing on his economic gain, probably helps him tolerate a smell that most of us find repugnant. (Fairhurst and Saar, 7)

Think about how the effect would have been different (less effective) if the plumber had said, "Smells like money to me."

I had a high school teacher who had a cool example, too. She said she once scolded her seven-year-old son for doing something that annoyed her by saying, "You're a very bad boy," to which he replied, "I'm not a bad boy. I did a bad thing." Somehow this precocious kid had discovered that one possible defense from an unavoidable accusation is to separate the doer from the deed. He had also stumbled across the fundamental attribution error: smart kid.

Sometimes you can break a frame by dodging a question that's designed to frame you in. When President Obama was asked if life began at conception, he said, as I recall, "That's above my pay grade." While no one's mind was changed on that issue by that response, not answering the question was probably the wisest move at the time because the question is a leading one, designed to force him into a discussion about abortion framed in a particular way.

Another example, from Steven E. Landsburg's *The Armchair Economist*:

> I once heard someone say that we would have far fewer car accidents if we took out the seatbelts and the supplemental restraint systems and put a big spike right in the middle of the steering wheel. People are in the greatest danger when they think they are safe. (5)

Another common example has to do with the psychological difference between *cost* and *loss*. Because people hate to lose (psychologists call it *loss aversion*) but recognize that some things cost money, what people won't accept as a surcharge they will sometimes accept as a premium. So, to take a late night television example, Would you rather have one product for $10 or two for $25? What if they told you the product costs $25, but if you order in the next five minutes they will give you one for free? Ridiculous, I know, and so do you. But we will pay the extra. When credit cards first came out, they charged proprietors 1 percent to use them, and so proprietors thought to pass the 1 percent on to consumers as a surcharge. The credit card companies got legislation passed that allowed proprietors to offer a cash "discount" but not a credit card surcharge. What's the monetary difference? None, but the persuasive difference is big. When you buy groceries you may see at the bottom of the receipt something like, "You saved $3.27 by shopping with us today." Yeah, but I spent $100.00.

Here is an example to remember on your next visit to the grocery store. What's the mathematical difference between 90 percent lean and 10 percent fat? Nothing. What's the rhetorical difference? Lean is the preferred frame of reference. The grocery store is in fact a great place to think about framing. Why do you smell baked goods or rotisserie chicken when you first walk in? Why is the milk at the far back of the store? Why are the less expensive brands typically on the first shelf, well below eye level?

Here's a very different kind of example from Nobel Laureate[7] Daniel Kahneman, in his book *Thinking, Fast and Slow*:

> Adam switches from a gas-guzzler of 12 mpg to a slightly less voracious guzzler that runs at 14 mpg. The environmentally virtuous Beth switches from a 30-mpg car to one that runs at 40 mpg. Suppose both drivers travel equal distances over a year. Who will save more gas by switching? (372)

The first time I read this question I thought, well, the 40 mpg car, which is apparently what most people think. But Kahneman goes on to explain:

> If the two car owners both drive 10,000 miles, Adam will reduce his consumption from a scandalous 833 gallons to a still shocking 714 gallons, for a saving of 119 gallons. Beth's use of fuel will drop from 333 gallons to 250, saving only 83 gallons. The mpg frame is wrong, and it should be replaced by the gallons-per-mile frame. (372)

I'm guessing that when you read the question, "Who will save more gas by switching?" you did what I did, which was pass by without stopping. If the question were on an exam, I might have squinted at it, maybe even written it down and thought about it carefully before trying to supply an answer, but I didn't do that. I wasn't reading against the grain, and so I

---

7. Was that an argument from authority?

put something like "better gas mileage" into my working memory and kept going. Because I didn't stop to think I got it wrong. Kahneman's point is that we all do that, and it's the idea of mpg that's to blame. It's the wrong way to frame the problem. Because it's the customary way to think about the problem, however, as a culture we always get it wrong. If our goal is to reduce gas consumption, moving people from their V-6 twin turbo to a V-4 will do more than moving them from a V-4 gas engine to a hybrid. On the other hand, if the goal is to save energy, not just gas, then we should all buy very old cars that suck gasoline like a glutton sucks gravy because those ancient monsters had their environmental impact long ago, whereas whatever you buy new is hurting the environment now. Whatever energy you save driving your hybrid was offset by the energy consumption spent to build and ship it. It's all a matter of how you look at it. The frame determines the conclusion.

Here's another example, but this time the frame is caused by a fundamental psychological problem that most people suffer from constantly.

There's an urban legend among students that goes something like this: When taking a multiple-choice test, always go with the first answer that occurs to you. Never second-guess. Turns out this is bad advice. You are almost three times as likely to get it right if you work out the answer and change your mind. In other words, your gut is wrong more often than not (Benjamin 133–41).[8]

If it's wrong so often, why do we accept this bad advice so readily? The answer has to do with the fact that we register regret more strongly than success. We pay closer attention when we get burned, so, if you've ever second-guessed a gut feeling and turned the correct answer into a wrong answer, you probably felt it keenly when you realized what you did. Hindsight bias might be playing a role here, too. You might not have actually known the answer, but, either way, the fact that you think you would have gotten it right had you not stopped to think about it, coupled with a general preference for fast and easy decisions of the trust-your-gut variety, makes you (and me and everyone else) remember the far less common occurrence of changing a right answer to a wrong one, thus the common bad advice to go with our gut when we should do the math instead.

One last example of how a frame controls a debate. What would happen if Americans started calling the activities known now as *lobbying* by the name they are known as in other countries, *bribery*?

---

8. Wait a minute, Pullman. In the section on intuition you said that people who recognize patterns can draw accurate inferences quickly. I did. But there I was talking about experts with thousands of hours of experience and encouraging you to become one. Here we are talking about hindsight bias and misinterpreting the sting of failure as a pain to be avoided rather than a tool for better learning. Good catch all the same.

Frame-breaking strategies

Once you realize that as a general rule you should always look for a frame and consider breaking it when you find it, it helps to have some frame-breaking strategies at hand. The most general strategy is to shift focus from the object of attention to the context that object is in and vice versa. As with all things persuasive, always remember to think of the opposite. So, for example, remember the kid who fended off his mother's anger by saying, "I'm not a bad boy. I did a bad thing"?

Cause to effect: Sometimes when something bad happens, people will go straight to assigning blame. It might be a better idea to solve the problem regardless of the cause (or blame).

Consequence to accident: It happened, but it didn't have to happen that way. Things might have turned out differently. In other words, the event was accidental not consequential.

Process to product: If someone is focused on the product, consider the process that created it. That awesome pair of sneakers you're wearing: Were they made in a sweatshop?

Means to ends: If someone is arguing for a particular goal, consider shifting attention to the way in which a goal might be obtained. By showing what it will take to accomplish something, you might get people to reconsider the objective. How do you eat an elephant? But of course, if people are getting bogged down in the details of implementation, you might consider foregrounding the goal again, to keep everyone's eyes focused on the prize.

Request to demand: If you need something from someone, you need to ask for it, but asking can put you at a disadvantage by showing the other person that you have needs. So you might simply demand the thing you need, and they might just give it to you, especially if they don't see you as in need. And of course you could ask for something you have the capacity to demand because the indirect approach might make you seem less demanding and more accommodating, more of a team player or a gentler boss.

Object to function: It sometimes happens that we accept a tool because it's the only one available, not because it's particularly good or does exactly what we need. Sometimes we become so accustomed to the tool that even when its imperfections create trouble we learn not only to live with the problems but come to love them, as though they are features or benefits rather than problems. In other words, our love for the tool makes us romanticize our experiences with it. When this happens, we aren't inclined to give the tool up when something better comes along or even when we are really struggling with it. At such times the tool frames our understanding of our work, and that frame can keep us from finding better ways or even new things to do.

Many people, for example, prefer paper books to electronic ones because they find underlining with a pencil easier than with a mouse or a finger. Even though you can search an electronic book much more easily, and they take up no space in your house, and you can read them anywhere without taking them with you, some people are reluctant to give up the print book. "It's the smell, the feel," they will tell you. Romantics. Actually, if you wanted to be harsh, you could call them fetishists. But calling people names won't get you anywhere. You need to get them to stop looking at the object and focus on the purpose the object serves.

Object to context: Sometimes where something is can tell you more than what something is, and sometimes you can't tell what you are looking at unless you pan back and take in the whole scene. (*You noticed that as a metaphor, right?*)

Act to intention or purpose: Not what a person did but why they did it. Whenever we want to excuse someone or ourselves for doing something that turned out badly, we will consider shifting the focus from the act to the person's reason for doing it. If the reason we use to reframe the event is what a person was trying to accomplish, then we are talking about their intentions. If someone is speeding through a school zone because his or her house is on fire, that's different than if he or she is late for lunch. Or maybe it isn't. The same reframe can be useful if what the person did turned out well, but for some reason we want to undermine the achievement. Thus we would argue that yeah, it was a great thing, but they set out to do something else, or they were motivated by greed or lust or something.

Intention to habit: When a person claims they chose to do something, and for some reason you want to undermine that assertion, you could argue that the act was caused by habit rather than by intention; they only thought they meant to do it. They'd have done it in their sleep. The very idea of intention is debatable. It's a topic, remember? Thus, change the environment, and you change people's habits, and eventually you will modify their "intentions" because they will begin to think differently.

Individual to system: Is each individual responsible for his or her actions because each of us has intentions and free will, or do we each do what we do because of our place in culture and time? Obviously this is a wild and wooly philosophical conundrum and one worth pondering in detail with specific examples, pro and con, but it is also a rhetorical resource.

Moral failing to medical condition: Dope fiend versus addictive personality disorder.

Criminal justice to public health: Delinquency versus poverty, few creative outlets, few financial opportunities.

Past to present: That was then, and this is now. Things change. Or they should. Or they shouldn't. Rhetoric is about proving opposites, right? Psychologists sometimes talk about there being two selves, the current and the future self. The future self is the one that will save money and lose weight and read the classics and exercise every day, and the current self is the one that will wash a bag of donuts down with a bottle of wine, the one that can't or won't resist immediate gratification. Because we live in the current and only think about the future, we often don't remember exactly how we got to where we are—life can be a bit like forgetting what the last exit was (psychologists call that feeling *transient amnesia* when it is really intense)—and so providing people with a history can help revise their understanding of the present situation, which can help them change their minds.

Present to future: Look for unintended consequences, hidden costs, new inventions, and disruptive technologies; take the long view. And think of some great examples of past fears that turned out pointless. Back in the 1800s, New Yorkers used to worry about where to put all the horse manure that the ever-increasing number of horse-drawn carts was creating. "Just imagine what it will be like in a hundred years," they must have fussed. And it would have been awful, but then the automobile came along, and everything changed. And then again, we still have pollution, right? Also, given the present- and future-person idea, if you need people to do something difficult, set the bill to come due down the road—buy now, pay later.

Negative to positive: Anything that is bad for one person might be good for someone else. Death is good for the funeral business. War is good for munitions dealers. Cancer is good for the medical industry. Every complaint is an opportunity for improvement. Every failure provides data for a future success. The sunny side of the street. The dark end of the road.

Natural to habitual: Whatever seems like a natural thing to do might actually be something we learned to do so long ago we forgot we learned it. How did people listen to music before earphones? If you need to break a habit, form a different healthier one, and swap them out. Do the new habit long enough, and it will become "natural."[9]

---

9. If you are interested in the idea of habituation, have a look at *The Power of Habit: Why We Do What We Do In Business and Life*, by Charles Duhigg.

Natural to conventional: Maybe whatever seems natural is only natural to a certain group of people at a certain time and place. By pointing out that other people do the same thing differently, you might be able to get people to think past their ways of doing things. This won't work if the other people aren't somehow admirable to your target audience.

Normal to normalized: Whatever is familiar is thought to be normal, and whatever is normal is thought to be good or permanent or real, all of which are difficult to change. If you grew up swimming to school with everyone else, it might seem weird to walk or take a bus. If everyone you know works for a living, you'll think working is what people do. If you can show people the process that led them to do what they do, they may see what they do as optional or at least habitual and thus open to change, not normal but normalized. And the opposite, right? If somebody thinks something you are doing is weird, you can argue that it's actually common among people of your sort or where you came from or among people who are forward thinking. Everyone's doing it. If they don't jump at that, introduce the new behavior a little bit at a time, and over time the normalization process will make the novel normal.

Familiar to strange: While people do tend to prefer what they know, they also sometimes get bored with it, and so you can spice things up by focusing on a characteristic uncommonly observed about whatever it is they always do. Show them a side they haven't seen. Use the common thing or idea in an uncommon way.

Political to personal: Or public to private. Most people have two sets of beliefs or one set of beliefs but two hierarchies of value for them. The differences come out whenever we switch from thinking about something as a public matter to thinking about it as a personal matter (and vice versa). When things get personal, our attitudes sometimes change. And then too, when a topic feels like a matter of public importance, when our own personal feelings seem for some reason less relevant or are rejected by a dominant culture and we fear being outed, our attitudes differ.

Experience to data: Go stream the movie *Moneyball*.

I'm not sure where this example belongs. There's an episode of *The Big Bang Theory* (season 2, episode 23) where Raj, Howard, and Leonard are deliberating about joining Sheldon Cooper on a trip to the North Pole, and Leonard argues that they can't turn down a National Science Foundation grant (they are academics—grant money is everything to profs), and Howard reframes the proposition. Instead of focusing on the scientific enterprise, he focuses on being stranded for three months in a frozen environment with Sheldon.

The Big Bang Theory is full of examples of framing and reframing. It is one of the show's primary humor techniques, which makes sense because the characters are (parodies of) academics, and argumentative discourse is the standard form of academic communication.

If you find framing and reframing interesting, you might enjoy Kenneth Burke's *A Grammar of Motives*,[10] which offers a more abstract and therefore even more portable way of thinking about frames of reference.

See if you can come up with an example for each of the frame-breakers above. Then share them with someone else, and see what they think.

Conclusion

A couple general comments about framing: People who stick to rigid argumentative lines, who insist they stand on principle and by principle really mean unexamined assumptions, will be very leery of frame-shifting. They will insist that a principle is a principle, for example, and argue that any effort to shift perspective is dishonest and manipulative, rhetorical. You need to tread lightly here. You might want to start with a separate issue to see if you can make people more aware of how they are sometimes flexible, and, having gotten them to see that they aren't always completely rigid, that perhaps in this case another principle might apply. That way they can continue to insist on a principle and thus on principles, yet you've got them to think beyond where they were.

People who suffer from radical relativism suffer the same intellectual impairment but for the opposite reason. They insist on one principle, and that principle is no principle. By insisting that all opinions are equally valid, the radical relativist discounts the value of evidence and minimizes the importance of persuasion. With these people you have to find a stable frame, or at least a relatively stable frame, else they will just keep moving through frames like guests in a house of mirrors.

Commonplaces

A *commonplace* is a subject about which everyone has something to say, and most things said are more or less the same, with a few variations in style and with even fewer variations in perspective. In the next section I'm going to explain where the commonplaces came from and show you how to use them and how to avoid them when saying something distinctive is warranted.

The Greek word *topic* was translated into Latin as *locus*, as in *location*. In English the same idea is *place*.

---

10. Burke, Kenneth. *A Grammar of Motives.* California ed. Berkley: University of California Press, 1969.

Our intellectual predecessors, the Greeks and the Romans, more or less agreed on the meaning and content of the specific topics, but they used the idea of the common topics quite differently. While the Greeks, or at least Aristotle, defined the common topics, *koina*, as patterns of thought that apply to any genre of rhetorical discourse, like more of a good thing is preferable to less, the Latin expression *loci communes* refers to something more like a conventional and quite likely superficial representation of a common character or place.

If we take the expression *commonplaces* literally for a moment, we have something like tourist destinations, the famous locations anybody who ever visits a city will almost certainly see. Think Paris, think the Eiffel Tower; think New York, think the Statue of Liberty; think Rio de Janeiro, the giant statue of Christ the Redeemer; London, Buckingham Palace; Sydney, the Opera House; Beijing, Tiananmen Square. If you are ever a tourist in any one of these cities, you are almost certainly going to visit these landmarks and upload photos as a way of saying you were there. (If you live in one of those cities you probably don't even notice the landmark anymore.) Even if you've not yet seen these places in person, chances are you've seen photographs of them because everyone always photographs them. Because they are so widely known, they have come to represent the vast and complex cities where they stand. They are a kind of shorthand, a token, an icon for what would take a great many images and words to evoke for a reader. For most people, a trip to Rome without a visit to the Sistine Chapel would be incomplete, and a trip to the Sistine Chapel alone might be enough to say one had been to Rome despite the fact that Rome rests on the remnants of several civilizations and is far more than one church, however commonly visited. For most people, the tip of the iceberg is the iceberg. Thus you can evoke a vastly complex idea with a single, readily recognized image (or cliché like *tip of the iceberg*). The details, the nuances, are ignored in favor of the general impression: efficiency at the expense of precision.

The human equivalent of a city's icon is the stock character or stereotype: The Jock; The Artist; The Geek; The Gearhead; The Goth; The Gamer; The Frat Boy (Girl), The Nerd, The Hipster, The Digital Native, just to list a handful from a university setting. This list of types is long, and each one has variations. Sometimes a type is so well cast that it becomes the archetype for the type; Shakespeare's Iago from *Othello*, for example, is an iconic representation of the sociopath. The rhetorical tradition is filled with the practice of embodying a way of living or a profession in the figure of a person with specific traits that then becomes a pattern for all such people subsequently.

The practice of creating stock characters, perhaps as much for amusement as for rhetorical training, as you did in the *bios* section and again in a slightly different way in the section on personas, goes back a long way. Aristotle's successor Theophrastus left an interesting collection of such pieces in a book called *The Characters of Theophrastus*. Below is a piece on the "Flatterer":

> The Flatterer is a person who will say as he walks with another, "Do you observe how people are looking at you? This happens to no man in Athens but you. A compliment was paid to you yesterday at the Stoa. More than thirty persons were sitting there; the question was started, Who is our foremost man? Everyone mentioned you first, and ended by coming back to your name." With these and the like words, he will remove a morsel of wool from his patron's coat; or, if a speck of chaff has been laid on the other's hair by the wind, he will pick it off; adding with a laugh, "Do you see? Because I have not met you for two days, you have had your beard full of white hairs; although no one has darker hair for his years than you." Then he will request the company to be silent while the great man is speaking, and will praise him, too, in his hearing, and mark his approbation at a pause with "True"; or he will laugh at a frigid joke, and stuff his cloak into his mouth as if he could not repress his amusement. He will request those whom he meets to stand still until "his Honour" has passed. He will buy apples and pears, and bring them in and give them to the children in the father's presence; adding, with kisses, "Chicks of a good father." Also, when he assists at the purchase of slippers, he will declare that the foot is more shapely than the shoe. If his patron is approaching a friend, he will run forward and say, "He is coming to you"; and then, turning back, "I have announced you." He is just the person, too, who can run errands to the women's market without drawing breath. He is the first of the guests to praise the wine; and to say, as he reclines next the host, "How delicate is your fare!" and (taking up something from the table) "Now this—how excellent it is!" He will ask his friend if he is cold, and if he would like something more; and, before the words are spoken, will wrap him up. Moreover he will lean towards his ear and whisper with him; or will glance at him as he talks to the rest of the company. (2)

When we think of stock figures today we tend to focus on appearances rather than on behaviors or expressions; how a Goth dresses seems more pertinent than what she does or what he says. But to get the full effect one really needs to work out the standard details in detail. As with all things persuasive, it's the details that conjure the image and make what you are talking about *feel* real. The more specific you are, the more convincing you might be. If you can find an unexpected way to depart from the standard type without necessarily confusing your audience about what type you are playing on, you may have something even more vivid because you've altered people's expectations.

Whenever a person is falling in with a group of people who conform to a standard type in some ways, the newbie (the old word is *neophyte*) may play to the stereotype until he or she gets the nuances and subtle differences that only someone who has been around for a while can get. No one joins a fraternity, for example, to become a two-dimensional caricature of a hard-partying college goof-off in a frayed white baseball cap, but, in the process of becoming what a fraternity member really is (and each person inhabits the role a little bit differently), one will tend to overdo some elements of the stock figure and underdo others, thus inhabiting a caricature for a while. The commonplace character isn't merely a perception based on ignorance and prejudice; it's also a pattern, like footprints painted on a dance hall floor. If you choose to join a group, you select a range of options for behaviors, beliefs, expressions, clothes, accessories, and so on that persuade you to become the kind of person who is a member of the group you chose, which in turn helps initiate you into the group by helping the others recognize you as someone who wants in. Even if you choose the outsider role, you will likely conform to the "outsider." If you don't, no one will know you are rebelling, and what's the point of rebelling if no one knows?

The difference between *rhetors* and everyone else as regards playing roles is that *rhetors* know they are doing it, and they more or less consciously craft the role, which means they can move a little more easily from one group to another, without irony or parody and without appearing fake or inauthentic. While a tourist wears a black-and-white striped fishing shirt and a beret while sipping a Coke at Les Deux Magots in Saint-Germain-des-Prés, the *rhetor* wears a shirt she bought at Monoprix[11] and drinks a café au lait like everyone else.[12] A really effective *rhetor* can sense the principles upon which the original pattern is based and thus find a new feature, something there that hasn't yet been seen. Sometimes just twisting a known feature slightly, maybe even something so simple (*simpleminded?*) as wearing a baseball cap backward, can add a touch of difference and thus something special to the common. Of course, if you pick something really apropos of the form, others will immediately imitate it, and chances are you will have a hard time claiming ownership. That's fine. It's the group's identity anyway.

---

11. Monprix (http://www.monoprix.fr/) is a common department store in France; actually they are in China, too, and probably elsewhere. I mentioned it only as a detail, like the famous café Les Deux Magots. Details, details, details. Did you recognize the "tourist" as a common character type, the person who sticks out because she wants to fit in so badly? A few years back the Travel Channel had an amusing set of adds with the slogan "Don't be a tourist." Google it. There were some nice examples of layering stereotypes to create the illusion of something new.

12. Should we push back on that assertion? Look up the word *poseur*, and then write a brief essay on why the true *rhetor* always travels in what he or she wears at home.

Just as there are commonplaces for cities and people, there are also common emotions. People tend to have conventional responses to certain kinds of events and things. We might call this the *aww response* that a picture of a kitten or a puppy almost inevitably evokes, or the *eww* that people utter involuntarily when they hear or see something gross.[13] We cry at weddings and funerals, or try desperately not to, even when we hardly know the people getting married or buried. People mirror the people around them. When we don't mirror, or mirror unsuccessfully, we make others and often ourselves uncomfortable. Such is the power of convention and the reason why you need to make a careful study of as many conventions as you can find. When you find a new convention, describe it to yourself in detail. Make sure you look closely. Don't let a single observation pass for the whole story. As a *rhetor* you need to be able to recognize conventions, try them out, try them on, and modify them for specific purposes. The most important trait is to get the details right without taking anything too far. If you take it too far, you look outlandish, like the fanboy dressed head to foot in major-league game gear (unless of course you are going for that look).

The idea of the commonplace has a moral component as well as an anthropological one.[14]

The Latin expression *locicommunes*, or commonplace (all one word rather than modifier and noun), can be found among the traditional classroom exercises known as the *progymnasmata*, fourteen exercises that led the rhetorical novice up levels of complexity from telling a story using animals as characters, the fable, to presenting a court case. In the center of the process, at number seven, was the commonplace, an epideictic speech amplifying a virtue or a vice: on love, on licentiousness, and so on. This exercise led to encomium, praise of the virtues of a specific person, and vituperation, condemnation of the vices of a specific person, like we explored in the section on *bios*.

Quintilian explains the commonplace this way:

> Commonplaces (I speak of those in which, without specifying persons, it is usual to declaim against vices themselves, as against those of the adulterer, the gamester, the licentious person) are of the very nature of speeches on trials and, if you add the name of an accused party, are real accusations. These, however, are usually altered from their treatment as general subjects to something specific, as when

---

13. The word *gross* works here because it's the word we would use most commonly these days, but it really means "big" or "course," so *repellent* or *repugnant* or *disgusting* would have been more accurate, and yet *gross* is more appropriate because we are talking about commonplaces, and so the common is better than the accurate in this place.

14. Can you explain to me why I might want to invert that transitional sentence, putting "anthropology" before "morality"?

the subject of a declamation is a blind adulterer, a poor gamester, or a licentious old man. Sometimes, also, they have their use in a defense, for we occasionally speak in favor of luxury or licentiousness, and a procurer or parasite is sometimes defended in such a way that we advocate, not the person, but the vice. (2.4.22)

Though a little hard to follow taken out of context, what Quintilian is suggesting is that by practicing admiration and condemnation one will become adept at admiring virtue and condemning vice. Through constant practice these commonplaces became stock items in the warehouse of our collective memory, prefabricated modules that any of us can snap into place when the time comes. In addition to providing a handy collection of prefabricated things to say about a given moral or ethical subject, having children create commonplaces was also thought to serve a moral purpose because by praising good behavior and condemning bad behavior a young person might come to know the difference and thus choose good over evil. The common stock also provided a common morality, a shared set of immediate responses to events and behaviors that served as the foundation for cultural identity that made a cohesive community possible. What learning the commonplaces also did, however, was encourage people to always say more or less the same things on the same subjects in the same ways, creating a culturally cohesive set of moral standards but at the same time creating commonplace ideas in the pejorative sense of the word, the way we use it most often today, to mean trite or hackneyed or stereotypical or cliché.

The *rhetor*'s dilemma is how to say the expected in unexpected ways, to connect new ideas and commitments to people's preexisting beliefs and assumptions without just rehearsing the common, inevitable, same old clichés and stereotypes, which would be at best merely conventional and at worse boring and trivial. *To be persuasive you need to rework the conventional, make important unnoticed details stand out, invoke the senses, or distort a common detail to reveal something unexpected or previously unremarkable. Make your audience feel like they are there again for the first time.*

Knowing how an audience will likely respond, setting them up for that response, and then producing something slightly better will delight people. If you set them up and give them something slightly worse, you will disappoint, annoy, or scare them. Or you might make them laugh. The twist, the slight variation on the expected, can also be instructive if the conventional expectations lack insight into the subject or the place or the people involved.

Your Turn

What are some contemporary synonyms for a *flatterer*? Presumably they all have the same core meaning, but what differentiates each one? Can you visualize each as a different character?

Make a list of all of the villains you can think of. What do that they all have in common, and what unique features differentiate one from another? Take your list, and share it with others to see if you can assemble a really thorough understanding of the *villain* and from there a more nuanced understanding of *villainy*. Any specific embodiment of an idea is a metonymic representation of the whole. No one character can have all the attributes without becoming indistinct, blurry, over the top.

Now think of a character who has some of the characteristics of villainy but who isn't generally considered a villain, and write a denunciation of him or her.

Signs

A sign is a word, action, event, or thing the presence or absence of which indicates the presence or absence of something else. *Signs are the bridges between sensing (sight, sound, feeling, scent, taste) and knowing.*

Signs are important forms of evidence. They may convince people that unwitnessed events did or did not take place. Signs may also convince people that an event will or will not take place in the future. In ancient Greece, some people believed that the entrails of animals or the shapes of clouds indicated the course of future events. While augury is no longer widely credible, anyone who listens to the news knows that forecasting is acceptable, and such predicting is done by inference from signs. Rain will occur when a high- and a low-pressure system interact. If a weak company merges with a strong company, the weaker company's stock is bound to rise. If the dollar is weak, imports will decline, and exports will increase. If you are obese, sedentary, and a smoker, you are at a greater risk of stroke or coronary heart disease than if you are thin, athletic, and a non-smoker.

Following Aristotle, we can assert that there are two categories of signs: *infallible* and *fallible.*

Infallible signs *necessarily* indicate the presence or absence of something. The most common infallible signs are causes and effects.

> Fire → heat
> Ice → 32° Fahrenheit or less

The fallacy of *post hoc ergo propter hoc* occurs when temporality is confused with causality: Just because two things happen in sequence does not mean that the first caused the second or that the two are related in any way at all. A similar error in thinking occurs when we confuse contiguity with relationship. Just because two things arrive together or are found together doesn't mean they necessarily have anything to do with each other. Not everything taken for a sign necessarily signifies in the way we think it does.

The cognitive bias in favor of coherence over randomness makes it very easy for us to falsely attribute causes. You need to think carefully before you decide that one thing will bring another. And, if at all possible, you should try to experiment to prove the case before you try to make the case to others.

Here's a concrete example of what I'm talking about, albeit a silly one:

Hypothesis:[15] Opening a can brings my pug, Jake, running.

Variables: The place (kitchen) where I usually open cans, other sounds directly before I open a can (utensils rattling, footsteps in the kitchen, what else?).

Test: Open a can in another room having tiptoed into the kitchen barefoot and removed a can and the can opener without making any noise.

Control: Walk into the kitchen, and stand there. If Jake arrives unbidden by the sounds that signify the arrival of food, then my hypothesis that kitchen sounds cause Jake's presence is inaccurate. I need to refine my hypothesis and think of some new ways to test it.

Okay, so this is a silly example, but the practice of creating hypotheses, identifying possible variables, and designing tests to isolate them in order to determine what causes what is a key part of learning from evidence and thus a key part of learning how to use signs persuasively. You don't have to become a scientist to benefit from thinking systematically.

To get good at identifying physical evidence you have to practice, and the best way to practice anything is to make it a routine part of daily life. Generate enough silly examples, and eventually you will start generating less silly ones. If nothing else you will start recognizing false causes when someone offers them as evidence.

Fallible signs merely suggest the presence or absence of something; they are signs that provide evidence that may or may not prove (or disprove) something. In nearly all non-trivial matters outside of the physical universe, in most areas of human existence, in other words, only fallible signs are available.

Smoke → fire
Laughter → happiness

---

15. A *hypothesis* is a testable assertion, a statement about the world that can be proven or disproven (almost always a stronger proof) through some form of experimentation. A statement that can't be tested is just an assertion. A statement that doesn't need to be tested is a fact or a falsehood. A statement offered as fact without proof that isn't accepted by the audience is a provocation.

We might refine Aristotle's heading of fallible signs by creating a continuum from most convincing to least convincing: probable, improbable, prejudicial, superstitious, absurd.

A *probable sign* is a fallible sign where the connection between two events or things is nevertheless strong enough that we will feel somewhat secure in inferring one from the other.

Big house → big family
Corporate jet → rich person
Fifteen-year-old rust bucket → low income
Smiling face → pleasant person
University degree → educated person

You need to come up with your own examples, and think about the ways in which they may and may not signify correctly. I included the university degree in my list to remind you that often the definition of words makes for complicated correlations. You can buy a university degree from a degree mill and learn nothing. You can also spend a lot of time and money at a perfectly good institution of higher learning and learn very little, so degree doesn't necessarily equal educated. I included the smiling face example because there can be true and false smiles (if you don't see crow's feet in the corner of their eyes, they're faking it) but also because in some cultures smiling is a way of hiding embarrassment and thus a sign of something other than happiness. A new car costs money, and maintaining an old one can cost almost as much. So if you are driving a rust bucket, chances are you have better ways to spend your money, but that doesn't mean your income is low. Maybe it's just a priorities thing. Rich people tend to have fancy forms of conveyance, but of course you can rent time on a Gulfstream, not that that's cheap I imagine, but it must cost less than owning your own airplane. And what about the big house–big family correlation? Think about it. Don't mistake an expectation for a probable cause.

An *improbable sign* suggests that a connection between two things or events is possible but unlikely.

- Two people who grew up in the same city know each other.

- People who are classically trained musicians will have the same taste in music.

- Someone who didn't benefit at all from another's death didn't kill him.

A *prejudicial sign* is one where a stereotypical characteristic is perceived as an indication (a sign) that someone is or is not a certain kind of person.

- A thin, single man in his thirties must be gay.

- She's pretty, so she must be dumb.

- They are American, so they must be overly friendly and ill informed.

- He's a Southerner, so he must love college football.

- They wear Abercrombie and Fitch, so they must be from Jersey.

- She graduated from Harvard, so she must be above-average smart and an awkward introvert.

- The evil eye symbol on that person's door indicates he is Mediterranean.

Most of our errors in critical thinking come from believing in misleading indicators. Because they look like causes, these prejudicial signs can be very misleading, seeming to offer proof of that which we are predisposed to believe but which, if we insisted on more evidence or were more careful about scrutinizing our evidence, we would find lacking. Making connections and therefore predictions between appearances and events is a difficult impulse to resist. Creating connections makes us feel like we understand the world and therefore have a greater measure of control over it. But we should resist because such signs are all too fallible.

A *superstitious sign* is one where two separate things are linked by optimism and a desire for control over the outcome of events.

- If I mark my golf ball with a 1962 quarter, I'll sink the putt.

- The evil eye symbol will protect us from the envy and cruelty of others.

An *absurd sign* is one where two events are linked by imagination alone.

- A monstrous shadow on the wall indicates the presence of a monster.

━━━ Your Turn

Now make your own "sign → inference" list in descending order of believability, and share your list with someone else to see if they can find the fallibility in it, while you search for fallibility in theirs.

Proverbs, maxims, aphorisms: On the origin of sound bites

A sound bite is a sentence or two that attracts the attention of news media during an interview and gets rebroadcast repeatedly because it distills the essence of an entire press release or lengthy interview into a few carefully chosen words. It makes a great headline or video clip. It is memorable and easily repeated. If you want to make the news, give good sound bites. If you ramble when you speak, say "um" and "like" and "or whatever," the journalists will either ignore you or truncate what you said to make a sound bite, which may or may not help your cause. If you want to control the message, speak in short, memorable, information-rich sentences: make every word count. If you ever wondered where the rhetorical form of the sound bite came from, read on.

Effective communicators are skilled at saying complicated things in compressed and compelling ways. A single simple sentence can carry a great deal of evidentiary weight if it's the right sentence at the right time said by the right person. The fact that people have always known this is demonstrated by the existence of proverbs, wisdom bequeathed by word of mouth from one generation to the next. "A stitch in time saves nine," for example, explains the value of timely intervention using the (once) common experience of mending clothes. If you deal with a problem quickly, it won't have time to get worse. Interestingly, proverbs survive in language long after the common experience they leverage has left our consciousness. When was the last time you mended a garment? Or hoed a row or toed a line? We use many proverbs correctly for the most part without knowing their literal meaning. Many of them are in fact agrarian, and most of us have been living in cities for several generations now.

For a proverb to be effective it has to connect something known to something new. If the connection is obscure, it will be a riddle rather than a proverb, and it will create confusion or curiosity rather than a nod of admiration and a murmur of assent. If the connection is lost in the mists of time (a dead metaphor), then the proverb may still work but lack rhetorical power. It will be a cliché or worn-out idea, like a dead metaphor, capable of conveying received wisdom or common sense but incapable of elevating the *ethos* of the person who uses it because frequent use has worn it insignificantly thin, uninventive, thoughtless.

"Like father like son" is a common proverb. You could update it a bit by switching genders, "like mother like daughter," or mixing genders, "like father like daughter." Or you could switch out the proverb for an aphorism. Thomas Hobbes said, "From like antecedents flow like consequents." That sounds more scientific than the proverb, and it has the added weight of being attributed to a notable philosopher. Before you use it, however, you need to check the attribution. I'm quoting Taleb Nassim, *The Black Swan*. I've never read the Hobbes piece Nassim is referring to, and quoting at second hand is rarely a good idea.

Proverbs are rhetorically weak because they say nothing new, which means that, while they are easily understood, they are boring and trite. Worse yet, grabbing the first proverb that comes to mind might keep you from thinking deeply about a situation or problem by offering a ready-made answer, one that fits but doesn't offer insight or require you to reflect on your actions and decisions.[16] When writing or speaking, it's best to use proverbs rarely and even then only the less common ones. Sometimes a proverb from a different culture will make a more interesting point and make you seem like a more interesting person. Be careful when borrowing from other languages, however. Proverbs draw on cultural wisdom, and not all cultural wisdoms are shared. Thus many proverbs don't translate well:

> Don't let your daughter-in-law eat your autumn eggplants (Japanese proverb).

Nevertheless, trying to make sense of an exotic proverb can help you learn to think beyond your cultural comforts, force you out of your standard patterns of thought and expression, and thus help you think more sophisticated thoughts. Are autumn eggplants inferior and daughters-in-law preferred, or is it the other way around? Does one *forbid* one's daughter-in-law from eating autumnal eggplants or *protect* her from them? What are autumn eggplants to daughters-in-law?

One level up in rhetorical power from the proverb is the maxim. A maxim contains a great deal of practical wisdom in a brief and interesting (unless overused) expression, often attributed to someone famous. Aristotle talked about maxims as a form of evidence, as a way of turning an assertion into an enthymeme by connecting what you want people to believe with some short, sharp saying that adds to your credibility and sounds like an endorsement from the sages. Maxims can be rhetorically superior to proverbs because they are less common than proverbs, which belong to no one and are beyond ancient. Novelty carries weight. Maxims also offer some reflected rhetorical power in that quoting one occasionally might

---

16. There is a counterpoint worth observing here at some length. Sometimes a proverb, especially one that is not often used, can be a very quick way of saying something usefully insightful. The right one can even serve as a form of weak evidence in support of an assertion. As long as the assertion isn't terribly controversial the person using the proverb has the right kind of gravitas. Young people don't seem to pull off proverbs quite so easily, although there's certainly no rule against it. Weak evidence though they are, proverbs have survived over a hundred generations without having been written down and studied. Inherited wisdom might be wisdom worth considering. So don't just roll your eyes at proverbs. Study them. Think about how and when they can be used and the important abstract principle underwriting each one.

make you seem like the kind of person who reads and remembers things, but here you have to be careful not to sound pretentious or uncomfortably cultured.

The older you get, the more likely you can get away with using other people's maxims in conversation. Writers and politicians and lawyers and in general most people who make a living with words have collected maxims from other writers and made up their own. Here are two examples from a writer who is famous for practicing the form, seventeenth-century French philosopher La Rochefoucauld in *Maximes*:

> Good advice is something a man gives when he is too old to set a bad example.
> We all have sufficient strength to bear the misfortunes of others.

Here's one from a twentieth-century American writer, Dorothy Parker:

> They sicken of the calm, who knew the storm. (*New York World*, [20 January 1928] p. 13, according to WikiQuote.org)

A variation on the maxim is the aphorism, which is formally identical but is about abstract subjects rather than conduct or human behavior. The word *aphorism* first appeared in the *Aphorisms* by Hippocrates. Nietzsche published a great many of these: "In the end one loves one's desire and not what is desired" (*Beyond Good and Evil*, 100). The Renaissance scholar Desiderius Erasmus of Rotterdam did as well; in fact, his *Adages* is one of the best known of all such collections. Ben Franklin, Mark Twain, Dorothy Parker, P. T. Barnum, and of course Lawrence "Yogi" Berra ("It isn't over till it's over.") are among the most often quoted Americans when it comes to aphorisms.

One of my favorite aphorisms is from Arthur Schopenhauer: "Every nation ridicules other nations—and all are right" (from *Law and Politics*). Notice the unexpected twist at the end. This makes the idea more memorable and more interesting. You want your aphorisms to stick. You want your audience to think, I wish I'd said that. A gas station attendant once said to me when I declined to buy a lottery ticket: "Can't win if you don't play," he said. (Can't lose either, I thought, but I just smiled and said nothing.)

Collecting maxims and aphorisms as you read—or even just Googling lists of them—is an excellent form of rhetorical exercise because it helps you think about how best to say things, and it makes you strive to write and speak effectively, finding the best way and not just the first way to say something. But if you collect aphorisms, be careful using them directly. Quoting aphorisms in conversation or using them in writing for anything other than an epigraph can make you seem pretentious. And if you misattribute a maxim or aphorism (in front of someone who knows), you will look worse than pretentious. (*On the other hand, if they don't notice it won't matter.*)

If you think a maxim or aphorism really does distill the thought, then use it. If you are writing, make sure you attribute it correctly. In speaking, you can almost pass it off as your own or use the feint "As someone once said, . . ." That may sound a bit less pretentious. The virtue of collecting and appreciating maxims and aphorisms isn't so much in their use as in their inspiration: Learn to create your own maxims and aphorisms, and you will become a much more effective *rhetor*. So ask yourself, how can I sound the best plausible me? Reach out, but don't fall over.

While aphorisms and maxims have always been a popular way to show off your learning and your wit, they are even more potentially powerful today when the sound bite rules the information channels. *If you ever want your TV interview televised, or your blog quoted, you need to be able to sum it all up in some short, tight, shiny way and not just fall back on worn-out expressions and clichés.* A maxim or an aphorism of your own can also be a great way to summarize and make memorable a complicated paragraph or section of a longer discourse. Get it right, and you will sound brilliant. Get it wrong regularly and in a consistent way, and you might end up a YouTube meme of the stuff-these-people-say variety.

Your Turn

> I hear, and I forget; I see, and I remember; I do, and I understand (Confucius).

You can learn in a different way from collections of proverbs by exploiting the fact that being able to explain something concrete in abstract terms is a sign and therefore potentially a cause of cognitive development. Try it: Explain the moral principle behind the proverb, "The early bird catches the worm." (Don't use the word *early* in your explanation.) If that was too easy, try "A bird in the hand is worth two in the bush."

Here is an example assignment and an explanation of what we have just been talking about taken from *Advanced Course of Composition and Rhetoric*, an early American (nineteenth-century) textbook on rhetoric:

> Maxims Aphorisms Proverbs and Saws are often paraphrased [as a rhetorical exercise]. A Maxim is a proposition briefly expressed which teaches a moral truth and is susceptible of practical application [advice about how to act]. An Aphorism, which corresponds with the Apothegm of the ancients, is a speculative rather than a practical proposition embodying a doctrine or the principles of a science [advice about how to think]. A Proverb or

Saying, the Adage of the ancients, is a terse proposition current among all classes relating to matters of worldly wisdom as well as moral truth [a generally acknowledged truth]. A Saw is a vulgar proverb [home-spun wisdom].

The following examples will show the difference between them:

Maxim: Forgiveness is the noblest revenge.

Aphorism: Originality in Art is the individualizing of the universal.

Proverb: A word to the wise is sufficient.

Saw: A nod is as good as a wink to a blind horse.

Paraphrase the following Maxims, Proverbs.

Example: Wealth begets want. Paraphrase—The desires of man increase with his acquisitions. Every step that he advances brings something within his view which he did not see before and which as soon as he sees it he begins to want When necessity ends curiosity begins and no sooner are we supplied with everything that nature can demand than we sit down to contrive artificial appetites.

1. Either never attempt or persevere to the end.

2. Poor and content is rich, and rich enough.

3. Good news doeth good like medicine.

4. No pains no gains.

5. Fear is the mark of a mean spirit.

6. One swallow does not make a summer.

7. Nothing venture, nothing have.

8. Between two stools one comes to the ground.

9. One good turn deserves another.

10. Money makes the mare go.

11. It never rains but it pours.

12. Penny wise pound foolish. (Quackenbos 345)

Summary of invention

What you just finished reading is the longest and most complex part of this book. Invention is the name given to the strategies and practices used to come up with things to say that don't include research per se. That is, generating ideas by thinking about what's in the common stock of opinions, both from among the specific and the common topics but also from the commonplaces and maxims and aphorisms and even proverbs; using dialectic to test and organize those opinions; using maxims and aphorisms to add weight and power to commonly accepted ideas, not so much as evidence but as support; using signs to identify causes and to predict effects; using stasis theory to forecast the way an argument might precede and *asystasis* to locate the most important points while avoiding the irrelevant or improvable ones.

The power of rhetorical invention is that it shows you in detail how to harness commonly held beliefs to advance new ones as well as ways to critique other people's inventions. The downside of rhetorical invention is that when done badly it only rehearses received wisdom and the commonplace beliefs that people often accept without scrutiny. This is why I've included dialectic. Dialectic teaches us how to be skeptical about the obvious and how to question really any assertion at all. Practicing each of these elements of invention will make you a more critical thinker and a more persuasive communicator.

The other four canons—arrangement, style, memory, and delivery—are important, and entire books have been written about each one. Entire library shelves carry books about style, and even memory has some fine tombs dedicated to it. But I'm going to walk a bit more quickly now. My goal is to give you the basics and then point you in the direction of some really good books with which you can develop the basics into advanced competencies.

Arrangement

If invention is the process of coming up with things to say, then it makes sense that the next step in the persuasion process would be arranging the ideas in a manner best suited to the audience's needs and expectations. However, it doesn't always happen that you will invent first and arrange second. As you know from the section on dialectic, invention is a process of collecting and dividing, of putting like things together and separating them from unlike things, which is also what arrangement is about. During the process of invention it sometimes happens that you discover something you didn't anticipate, and it changes the way you understand everything you've written so far, and thus you have to rearrange what you have. At such moments it also sometimes happens that you suddenly see everything differently. So in practice, invention and arrangement are not always separate moments.

When you organize your ideas depends to some extent on how you write and how well you know the subject. If you know a subject well, have thought about it a lot, and have written about it before, you might start with an outline and then, after maybe pushing a line up here and another line down there, you've pretty much got the structure in place, and you are ready to fill in the blanks. When I have to give a lecture or make a presentation to a group of peers or business people, I often start with an outline and then practice what I'm going to say by either writing subheads under each heading in the outline or by just taking through each heading in my head. By doing this I am basically turning a topic sentence into a paragraph. Sometimes I write the paragraphs out to make sure I've really thought it through, but if I know the subject well I often just put the main ideas down and work through them repeatedly, making sure I know why they are in the order I put them in and that the order is the best one for the audience.

If I am new to a subject or unclear about it, however, I might write many paragraphs just to get possible ideas out onto a screen where I can examine them carefully before I start to think about what order to put them in. When I'm *writing-to-learn* (the technical term for that kind of writing), the structure won't be apparent until a great deal of inventing has happened.

Regardless of when you arrange your material, it matters that you do arrange it and don't just let the thoughts lay where they land because if you don't think about the structure you are likely to confuse your readers.

Order plays an important role in understanding. If you can't separate one idea from another you have a jumble of ideas that will tend to confuse your readers. Frustrated and exhausted composition teachers sometimes refer to this kind of prose as word salad, everything just tossed together. Salad isn't a great metaphor because you can almost always distinguish a walnut from a tomato no matter what the jumble. Word pudding might be a better metaphor. But the point is an important one. You need to sort and organize the thoughts in such a way that a clear relationship among the ideas is apparent. Like things go with like things. Related things go nearby. Distant things are set off at an appropriate distance. Importance is indicated by magnitude—you don't spend a thousand words on a footnote if the whole piece is only five pages. Magnitude is also signaled by the order of the ideas. Generally speaking the beginning and the end are the most important places when speaking.[17] You don't introduce new ideas before having completely dealt with the current ones. First things first. Second things second, and so on. Arrangement is obvious when you think about it like this. The problem is that ideas don't always occur to us in the order best suited for sharing them with others.

---

17. For written documents, the beginning and the end are important, but, because people don't have to read in order and can read for a few minutes here and there, wandering away as their mind wanders, you need to break up the idea into useful chunks.

If we just put them down as they occur to us, people won't be able to follow our train of thought because they aren't privy to all of it, to the pre or unconscious thoughts that surfaced the ones we wrote down. The result is that the audience is left wondering, Where did that come from? while we've already moved on.

There's an exchange in Plato's *Phaedrus* during which arrangement is discussed in some detail. I'll paraphrase this small section for you, although you really should read the whole dialogue.

> Socrates: But surely you will admit at least this much: Every speech must be put together like a living creature, with a body of its own; it must be neither without head nor without legs; and it must have a middle and extremities that are fitting both to one another and to the whole work.
>
> Phaedrus: How could it be otherwise?
>
> Socrates: But look at your friend's speech: Is it like that or is it otherwise? Actually, you'll find that it's just like the epigram people say is inscribed on the tomb of Midas the Phrygian.
>
> Phaedrus: What epigram is that? And what's the matter with it?
>
> Socrates: It goes like this:
>
> A maid of Bronze am I, on Midas' tomb I lie
> As long as water flows, and trees grow tall
> Shielding the grave where many come to cry
> That Midas rests here I say to one and all.
>
> Socrates: I'm sure you notice that it makes no difference at all which of its verses comes first, and which last. (264c–e)

I wish Phaedrus had asked Socrates why order matters instead of just acquiescing, but nevertheless, if you reorder the lines in that poem, you can see that the order is irrelevant. Whether or not that is actually a problem given that it's a poem might be debatable, but the point is generally useful.

Here's another example. This time, I've broken a paragraph up into sentences and scrambled their order. How would you order them?

1. The first skill area involves acquiring a writing system, which may be alphabetic (as in European languages) or non-alphabetic (as in many Asian languages).

2. Because of these characteristics, writing is not an innate natural ability like speaking but has to be acquired through years of training or schooling.

3.   The second skill area requires selecting the appropriate grammar and vocabulary to form acceptable sentences and then arranging them in paragraphs.

4.   Writing is a complex sociocognitive process involving the construction of recorded messages on paper or on some other material, and, more recently, on a computer screen.

5.   Third, writing involves thinking about the purpose of the text to be composed and about its possible effects on the intended readership.

6.   The skills needed to write range from making the appropriate graphic marks, through utilizing the resources of the chosen language, to anticipating the reactions of the intended readers.

7.   One important aspect of this last feature is the choice of a suitable style. (Swales and Feak 34)

Answer: 4, 6, 1, 3, 5, 7, 2.

How long did that take you? One of the nice things about that example is that some of the sentences began with numbers, which made it pretty easy to get started. Here's a different example. See how long this one takes you.

1.   After wiping her hands, she placed her heavy arms, as if they tired her, on the shelf.

2.   At the back of the room, on the lunch side, an oblong square was cut in the wall and a large woman with a soft, round face peered through at us.

3.   Beneath the racks were wire-back chairs, one of them piled with magazines, and between every third or fourth chair a brass spittoon.

4.   Near the center of the room, revolving slowly as if the idle air was water, a large propeller fan suspended from the pressed tin ceiling.

5.   Mabel's Lunch stood along one wall of a wide room, once a pool hall, with the empty cue racks along the back side.

6.   It made a humming sound, like a telephone pole, or an idle, throbbing locomotive, and although the switch cord vibrated it was cluttered with flies.[18]

Answer: 5, 3, 4, 6, 2, 1.

---

18. Adapted from a paragraph in *The World in the Attic*, by Wright Morris (Scribner's, 1949), and taken from http://grammar.about.com/od/developingparagraphs/a/placedesc.htm.

The organization here is spatial rather than temporal, and so you have to put yourself in the scene and scan the room with your imagination. So how did you put yourself in the scene? What's the most likely sentence to start with and why? Why wouldn't you start with sentence 6? Why does 4 have to precede 6? Why does sentence 1 make the best sentence to end on?

Let's try one more. This one is especially difficult, I think.

1. On the one hand, a decibel is a decibel is a decibel.

2. On the other hand, the reasons why an airport will affect its neighbors in different ways, leaving some depressed or hypertensive and others relatively unfazed, are as variable and invisible as sound itself.

3. At least one of them objects to eliminating human commotion at its source, and consequently a chosen few are able to step blinking from the ark into a temporarily quieter world.

4. Noise is both an objective and a subjective phenomenon: it comprises both common and uncommon ground.

5. Human noise is political from its inception, not only because it emerges with the polis—that artificial forest where the tree that falls always makes a sound—but also because it lends itself so well to political conflict.

6. Even the gods who confer with Enlil are not of the same party on the noise issue.

7. The fact that the human ear can endure about two continuous hours of a power drill but only thirty minutes of a typical video arcade before sustaining permanent hearing loss and the related fact that eighty-year-old Sudanese villagers hear better than thirty-year-old Americans are just that: facts.[19]

   Answer: 5, 4, 1, 7, 2, 6, 3.

Can you explain why this paragraph is so hard to unscramble?

Regardless of when you sort and organize (arrange) your ideas to suit your readers' needs, there are several principles of arrangement that will increase the readability of your writing.

1. Start where your audience is, not necessarily where you are. (Drafting is about talking to yourself; revising is about talking to others; so often the last sentence of a draft might make an excellent opening sentence.)

---

19. From "Sound and Fury: The Politics of Noise in a Loud Society," by Garret Keizer, *Harper's Magazine*, March 2001, p. 39.

2. Define things before you evaluate them.

3. Name things before you explain them (unless you are trying to create suspense or preparing your audience for something they don't want to hear).

4. Deal with each point completely before moving on, and then don't look back until you get to the end. (If you find yourself saying "as I said," maybe you need to move the section you are writing to the place where you said it before.)

5. Give the backstory only if it sets a necessary context. (Don't tell people things they don't need to know or tell them things they already know, but be sure you decide to include or exclude based on what they really know and not what you think they know; on the web you can provide links to all relevant information, and let readers choose for themselves. On paper you have to choose for your readers. It's better to be boring and complete than interesting but vague.)

6. Correct any misperceptions early, especially those concerning incorrect or unhelpful interpretations of words. You saw me do this when you read about critical thinking. Here's another example: Some people hear the word *question* as a synonym for *doubt*. If you really mean you want to ask a question about something rather than interrogate it or cast doubt on it, you might want to keep that difference of perceived connotation in mind.

7. Each sentence should begin with the subject, preferably a concrete noun, but rarely a word or phrase that points back to the subject of a previous sentence. That (*what does "that" refer to?*) makes your reader scan back to the previous sentence, which breaks their concentration, and that's not a good thing. Prepositional phrases are only good to open with if you need one to link the previous sentence. Otherwise, revise.

8. Each paragraph should develop only one idea.

9. Transition between paragraphs so the reader understands how what just happened connects with what is about to happen.

10. If possible, use a readily discernible, preferably visible, pattern of arrangement: chronological, hierarchical, geographical, geometrical, logical, proportional, antithetical, whatever concept of order lends itself to the subject and fits the audience's expectations.

11. Conclude by reminding your audience of the key points, and motivate them to act or at least decide.

In general, a well-structured English sentence has subject-verb-object word order. A well-structured paragraph develops only one idea and has every sentence in its place. A well-structured document has every paragraph and every section in the place where the intended readers would expect to find them. Keep in mind that the arrangement that best suits your audience is almost never the order in which the ideas occurred to you.

The classical rhetorical tradition offers patterns of arrangement, what today we call templates, layouts into which words can be poured. The typical pattern of arrangement handed down by rhetorical lore is the argument as it might be performed in a court case. Below is an example from Roman tradition, specifically an interpretation of what is offered in Cicero's *On Invention* (*De Inventione*), a textbook on rhetoric that he is said to have written while still a teenager.

But before I show you the standard template, I want to digress for a moment about formulas and the formulaic.

Socrates' point about prose being organic (having a beginning, a middle, and an end) so spoke to people that many have misunderstood the point. What you want is natural but not necessarily spontaneous because rarely do well-formed ideas tumble perfectly from our minds, especially early on in our careers. So a template is helpful early on because it relieves some of the cognitive burden as we write. We don't have to think about where to put things and come up with what to say at the same time. On the other hand, there are some people who find an overt structure distracting, and they may call what you've written "formulaic," by which they mean lacking in originality.

Here is a concrete example. A common five-paragraph essay pattern looks something like this:

> I think that everyone should spend three hours in the library every week for the following three reasons. Firstly, you might meet new people. Secondly, the internet connections are faster than wireless. Thirdly, they have great coffee.
> Firstly, . . .
> Secondly, . . .
> Finally (a little flourish there instead of just "thirdly"), . . .
> Therefore, you should spend at least three hours every week in the library.

Now the real problem with this essay is that it asserts that one should spend three hours in the library but proves that there are three reasons for going to the library. The duration of any given stay isn't discussed at all. If your goal is to meet people, presumably the longer you stay the better your chances, and so on. A more appropriate thesis statement for the evidence provided would have been, "There are at least three reasons to go to a library." But if you were to write an essay that looked like this, rather than getting some useful rhetorical advice, you might hear from some readers that it is too formulaic, that the structure is distractingly obvious. Such an obvious structure makes the essay seem contrived, unnatural, and so on.

Such an assessment is typical of people who have a romantic view of writing, that is people who think that conventions and forms are signs that the writer is just doing what everyone who came before her is doing and that all great writing breaks the molds used by lesser writers. This highly aestheticized view of writing is more appropriate for poets and novelists than it is for the rest of us, but it's not completely inappropriate because, if what we have to say isn't all that interesting and we say it in a less than interesting way, then really, what's the point? To render the structure a bit less obvious you need to replace "Firstly," "Secondly," and "Thirdly" with transitional phrases that tie the whole thesis statement together:

> I went to the library because they had great coffee, and while I was there I saw an open computer, and it was so fast I lost track of time. An hour later I ran into this person from my calculus class, and he introduced me to some friends.

Whatever. The point is that the second version tells a story that makes the three points the formulaic essay was making, but it seems more organic because it's a story. I made the whole thing up of course, but it sounds plausible because I used chronology to hold the parts in a perceptible order.

As a *rhetor*, you need to know formulas because they will help you get the right information down in the right order. You may eventually want to make the transitions from section to section less overt, to make the piece seem less formulaic, but that's very different from just rejecting all formulas and heading out on your own to see what comes along. Just as you wouldn't build a building without a scaffold or head into the woods without a map, so writing without a pattern in mind is ill advised.

Introduction (**exordium**)

All introductions state what the subject is, explain why the intended audience should care, and explain how the document is organized. Short documents may do away with the organizational part. There are basically two kinds of introductions: the direct and the indirect. The indirect method (sometimes called *insinuation*) is used when the audience is likely to find the subject matter objectionable or distressing, like when you have to give bad news or talk about something no one wants to talk about. The indirect may also work if you can lead your audience to what feels to them like an important discovery, as if they have decoded a secret or understood a complex game. This kind of indirection works because it makes your audience feel like they are in the know, which makes them feel good. Such a move is risky because you could lose your audience's attention or make them feel like you are wasting their time. In most circumstances, getting directly to the point is preferable to dancing around it.

The introduction is the most important part of any persuasive performance, and it is often best to write it last, when you know for sure what you are going to do and how you did it. When drafting, however, an initial introduction can help you stay on topic and remain organized. Just keep in mind that you will almost certainly need to change it as changes to your text help to evolve your thinking about the subject and how your audience will understand it. Below is a blueprint for a basic argumentative paper.

Division (*partitio*)

1. Establish a positive *ethos*, your expertise, credibility, goodwill.

2. State plainly what the disagreement is about and the various opposing opinions.

3. Give your position and how it differs from others (where you agree, where you disagree).

4. Present your argument in brief (just the propositions).

Background (*narratio*)

Who, what, where, when, and why? Only provide what is useful.

1. Define key words.

2. Use technical terminology correctly.

3. Do not define widely understood words or quote dictionaries.

4. If the key words contain technical applications of common words, make sure your audience understands the difference and isn't just substituting the common definition when the technical one is required.[20]

Confirmation (*conformatio*)

Present the evidence and arguments that support your position.

1. Probabilities

2. Enthymemes

---

20. Are these four list items in the right order?

3. Examples

4. Maxims

5. Signs

6. Data and evidence

Refutation (*refutatio*)

Present (fairly) the arguments the opposition will use to undermine the position you are advocating, then refute them.

1. Question the opposition's assumptions.

2. Deny the premises.

3. Grant the premises, but deny the conclusions.

4. Question the examples.

5. Provide counterexamples.

6. Reframe the arguments.

Conclusion (peroration)

Explain the benefits of your position using the topics of expedience, justice, practicality, and whatever else seems appropriate.

1. Remind the audience why your position matters to them.

2. Motivate the audience to decide, if necessary.

3. Add nothing new. (Stay focused.)

═══════ Your Turn

Techniques for learning effective arrangement
While you can take the above pattern and adapt it to your own needs, an even more instructive practice is to find a handful of examples of the kinds of work you want to do and see if you can identify an underlying pattern in them. If you can, then you can use that pattern of arrangement to guide you through the work. This will be much more efficient than trying to work your way to an organic structure relying on intuition and luck.

Another technique I find useful is to go through what I'm writing and highlight the one sentence that says what the paragraph is about (the topic sentence). If I find more than one sentence in a paragraph to highlight, which happens, then I know I need to break the paragraph into two (or three or more) and make sure each topic sentence is fully developed, explained, defended, and illustrated, whatever it needs. Once I have one topic sentence per paragraph highlighted, I reread the piece ignoring everything but what I have highlighted. If one of the sentences seems to appear at the wrong moment, I check to see if there's a better place for the paragraph. On longer pieces, I use Microsoft Word's style sheet to mark up the topic sentences and then generate a table of contents that includes those sentences. That way I can look at the whole without being distracted by the details.

I find that the color-coding process (a.k.a. tagging or markup) can be extended for different purposes. Look through the list of transition words at smart-words.org,[21] then highlight those word in your own document. Scan through your document to see if the transitions are the right transitions and if they are inserted in the correct places. Check to see if there seems to be a *transition desert* in the piece, where you go off on a riff and leave your readers behind.

For another way to think about marking up a text in order to learn more about it, have a look at the section "Toulmin's Model of Argumentation" in Chapter 1.

If you're not sure what order the sentences of a given paragraph should go in, try scrambling them, and see if the reorder tells you anything. You will find a handy tool for doing this at the following website: www.gpullman. com/phtp/paragraph_scrambler.php.

The most important thing to remember about arrangement is that the order you present things in influences how people understand what you are saying, what they will remember, and how much they will agree with you. The basic idea is to start and finish strong. Don't bury the weak or confusing in the middle; get rid of it, but keep in mind that often the last thing you say will be what people remember most, and the first thing you say will frame their attitudes toward you and what you are talking about.[22]

Style

The canon of style often vexes people who teach writing and speaking today. On the one hand, style is seen as a trivial part of writing, the polish added via editing after the construction is finished, and therefore as ancillary to

---

21. http://www.smart-words.org/transition-words.html

22. Have a look at the last clauses in that last sentence. Do you think it might be easier to read if the pattern was reversed: "the first thing . . . , and the last thing . . ."? Can you explain why?

invention, where the real thinking happens. On the other hand, style is seen as a sign of character and therefore not something to be experimented (tampered?) with because doing so might change a person's character or make them less authentically themselves. Style in this case is viewed as *voice* and therefore somehow naturally one's own. Learning a new style, or insisting on a "correct" style, might remove a person's ethnicity or even tamper with their gender, if it is true that men and women have different styles because they have different physiologies.

To complicate matters more, we could argue that style is also an indicator of class and social status. If this is the case, then learning how to emulate the middle and upper-middle classes' ways of talking and writing (again assuming they have them) might be a way to advance in society but also would be a way to leave one's place of origin, with all of the inner and interpersonal conflicts attending such a move. The idea of code switching, where you slip in and out of the relevant styles based on your context, is a way of trying to deal consciously with the relationship between style and identity.

In order to explore some of these ideas about style as more than superficial, read "Politics and the English Language," by George Orwell, and *Metaphors We Live By*, by George Lakoff and Mark Johnson.

One way to avoid (some might say *deny*) the vexation I described is to talk about the *plain* style, which is typically what you read and hear about when you take a writing class, especially academic or technical writing classes, and the ability to produce it is a valuable intellectual asset. The plain style uses the fewest words possible, with few or no rhetorical or poetic flourishes or personal idiosyncrasies. The information is front and center, the writer invisible. If two people wrote on the same subject in the plain style, it might be hard to tell who wrote what.

The plain style, even the idea of the plain style, is offensive to those who believe in authentic voices and writing for self-discovery and expression. For people who articulate the needs of corporations and businesses generally, having all employees write in a single voice can be very important. Personality in such a setting is counterproductive, at least in so far as it might be expressed in writing. This problem of the relation between style and context is one of the reasons, by the way, that what people learn about writing in many first-year composition courses doesn't transfer well into upper-level courses in other disciplines. Different disciplines want different styles and make different assumptions about the relevant presence or absence of an authorial voice, assumptions not typically shared by English professors who tend to love aesthetic compositions. For concrete advice about how to write in the plain style, see the last section in this chapter.

From a rhetorical perspective, *style is about choice and flexibility*, about fitting the words and expressions to the occasion, the audience's expectations, the way you want to sound or seem to your audience (your *ethos*), and the way you feel about what you are talking about.

Let's go through each of these ideas separately before we put them together.

Fitness for the occasion means thinking about the context of reception, when will what you are presenting be heard, at what time of day, at what point in the calendar, and at what point in the proceedings. Are you speaking first, in the middle, last? Will your audience be alert, tired, distracted? Will your work be read with a bunch of other works or separately? Will the readers be in a hurry or have time to ponder and appreciate? Will they care, or will they just be performing a job function? Will they be concentrating on what you've written, or will they be multitasking or otherwise likely distracted? Is the topic important to the reader, and if so in what ways?

Fit with the subject means using elevated language for elevated subjects (or the opposite if you want to be subversive or dismissive or insolent) and denigrated language (slang, colloquialisms) for low subjects. A high or elevated subject would be anything that people revere, like religion or art or significant moments in history. A low subject is mundane or terrestrial, ordinary, everyday, things that have to do with family or friendships or work on a non-professional level. Neutral language is for subjects where the information is more important than anyone's attitude toward it. Neutral language is typically preferred in all academic communications. It is also preferable in business communication and in fact at any time when there's work that needs to get done. Neutral language tends to lack adjectival intensifiers and editorial comments.

Fitness with your intended *ethos* is more than just sounding like yourself, authentic. It's about stretching your self-concept. It's about playing with possibilities in order to generate insights about the possibilities in order to make effective improvements in how you think and how you interact with others. For more about this, read the upcoming "Your Turn" section. At any rate, you want to choose words and expressions that will make you seem a certain kind of person to the people you are trying to communicate with. Do you want to sound educated or sophisticated or untutored? Do you want to sound passionate or detached? Do you want to seem like you are conscientious or nonchalant or somewhere in between? Do you want to appear funny or approachable or serious and superior? You can extend this list. How many attitudes can you think of? Now present them on a continuum from positive to neutral to negative.

Finally, you want to choose words and expressions based on your own feelings and attitudes toward the subject and the people you are trying to reach. Do you believe strongly about the subject, or are you non-committal? Are you writing or speaking because it's your duty or because it's your job, or is there some indirect motivation for your participation? Is it really you, or are you fulfilling an obligation? I asked about your own feelings last in this list of rhetorical elements of style because it's most people's default. We think about how we feel about the subject automatically and have to reach for the audience, but ultimately it is the audience that decides whether we succeeded or not, so we should foreground the audience's feelings and impressions, to the extent we can, when designing our sentences.

Generally speaking, the more ways you can think to say something, the more choices you have and therefore the more opportunity to pick the better way to go. In the process of generating alternative expressions you may actually discover a new thought or a new way of thinking about an existing idea, and thus stylistic revision may sometimes become inventional. Correctness (fit with standard conventions of usage and punctuation and grammar) and clarity (fit with audience expectations about the meaning of words and the way the world works) are important, but don't aim solely for them. Correctness and clarity are the minimum requirement for maximal persuasion.

Style shouldn't be an afterthought or a given.

As with anything, you should practice before you play. Most people write only when something is due, and that's too late because the cognitive load of keeping the grammar and the conventions in check make it harder to really develop your thinking or work on your style. If you practice every day, the conventional stuff will become more automatic, and that will free up some of your energy for the ideas and how you want to express them. You won't have to spend three minutes remembering when a semicolon is correct and looking up citation conventions.

You need to write every day the way you practice a musical instrument every day or train your body every day. You can't just sit around all week and then hit the field on Friday expecting to win. Write. Try on other people's voices. Do you have a favorite TV show? See if you can write something that sounds like what one of the characters would have said. Favorite author? Try to sound like her.

If you can't think of anything to write, write a single sentence, and then see how many different ways you can say essentially the same thing. If you'd like to see a virtuoso performance along these lines, Google "Erasmus De copia," and you'll find how the Renaissance rhetorician was able to say, "Your letter pleased me greatly," over eighty different ways. Pointless? Well, maybe not entirely. He was showing off in a way, but the point is a good one: Effective selection requires multiple options to choose from and the more accustomed you are to saying things in different ways, the more likely the best way will occur to you quickly. Perhaps more importantly, play is a catalyst for creativity. If you turn off your inner sensor and just write the same sentence in as many different ways as you can imagine, the intellectual equivalent of making up trick shots, you might discover something you wouldn't have noticed if you'd been tightly focused on saying just one thing.

Your Turn

Find an essay you wish you had written because of the author's style, and describe what you like about it and why. Then see if you can write something mimicking that style.

If the opposite of *authentic* is *inauthentic* in the sense of fake or false or forced, then such a style would likely be pointless practice, unless through practicing one might make it real. Fake it till you make it, as the saying goes. On the other hand, seeking a one true authentic voice might be restrictive to the evolution of yourself. What do you think? Do you have a style that is your voice? Will it be the same ten years from now? Could it keep you from evolving? If you don't think you have a voice, or a style that is your own, does it matter to you?

Diction

The expression "That's just semantics" is often said when people tire of an argument or are trying to discredit a statement they can't disprove. The underlying idea is that words are not important. Actions, behaviors, and things are real; words are just words. If that is true, then diction is just about selecting the word that denotes (refers to) the thing you have in mind. Your words should be transparent, a window on your thoughts. Problems arise when you don't quite know what you are talking about, or when what you are talking about is not a thing but rather a concept or abstract idea, a word that does not have a corresponding thing to be denoted, a non-referential word. The most important words are like this: love, justice, and the like. These words have no referent but other words. Because nearly every important discussion involves the important words, words with no concrete referent or with a disputed referent or with multiple referents, *nearly all arguments are semantic arguments.*

Because non-referential words do not point indisputably to some specific, verifiable thing in the world, they carry a great deal of rhetorical force, and so they need to be carefully scrutinized. Unless you are writing a technical manual describing how a machine works, writing is not just a matter of correctly naming the things you are talking about (getting the *denotation* right). It's also about getting the *connotation* right, about recognizing the range of rhetorical effects an expression might have, how it will sound differently coming from different people, and how it will produce different effects in different people.

Using the noun rather than an adjective makes it sound as though you are referring to something concrete, to a thing. To say that someone is graceful is to say something remarkably different from saying the same person has grace. By using the word *grace* you make grace seem like a thing; to use *graceful* you make it sound like an attribute of a person, an abstract idea, a quality. Now consider the difference of reception between someone who interprets grace to be a religious idea compared to someone who interprets it as a combination of strength, balance, and flexibility: same word, totally different rhetorical results. Even if the context clarifies the use, like you are talking about an athlete, not a priest, the nexus of connotations will still apply, just not so strongly. These subtle differences tend to accumulate quickly and go unnoticed. But in the end, the impact is felt. (Or not. If you are relying on subtleties your audience doesn't get, then either they will reject you for a pedant or they will miss the point entirely. This is why *rhetors* sometimes work on two levels at once, providing material out of which several interpretations are quite possible.)

You have to *choose your words not just for what they refer to but for what connotations they will carry*, and to do this you will need to consider what preexisting beliefs and attitudes they will jack into.

The words you choose can both produce rhetorical effects in others and suggest what rhetorical influences you are operating under, which in turn will alter how your words are heard. If I use the expression "liberal media" I'm signaling something about my affiliations and commitments, and I'm telling you something about how to interpret what else I say. I'm trying to establish a positive relationship with certain members of my audience and therefore must out of necessity establish an antagonistic relationship with others (not present more often than not). If I use the expression as if it refers to a thing in the world, as if it had a referent (a measurable quality that all members of the media possess), then I'm sending one set of signals. If I use it instead as a non-referential word, use it ironically, then I'm sending a different set of signals, but in both cases I'm being rhetorically naive. The phrase "liberal media" refers to a cluster of studies about what attitudes are typically represented by different television and radio networks. I've never seen any of these studies. I don't even know if they were actually done let alone done well. So if I am going to use the expression I have to find the studies. If I can't or don't find the studies, I have to reject the phrase, whether I'm inclined to accept it as a simple truth or a simple lie. If I just use it, then I am committing myself to an entire network of beliefs and therefore isolating myself from other networks. *If the word or phrase has an abstract referent, be careful how you use it, and keep in mind that it will mean different things to different people and change the way some people perceive you.*

Because an expression like "liberal media" is part of a clearly agendized discourse (conservative talk radio), it's not unexpected that it would carry ideological weight and therefore have a rhetorical force, instantly positive for some, instantly negative for others. But words that aren't a part of an identifiable agenda can also carry typically unobserved rhetorical force. Scott Plous explains,

> When people do not have deep convictions about an issue, they often respond to "catch phrases" that point them in [what they consider] a socially desirable direction. For example, *U.S. News and World Report* published the results of a poll in which 58 percent of the respondents favored aid to Nicaraguan rebels "to prevent Communist influence from spreading," but only 24 percent favored assistance to "the people trying to overthrow the government of Nicaragua." (68–69)

In other words "aid to rebels to prevent communism" seems like a good thing to the people who responded positively, while "overthrowing the government" seems like a bad thing to the people who responded negatively to it. The fact that they are different ways of saying essentially the same thing and yet lead people to draw different conclusions underscores the importance of careful phrasing. And that is why *you should never accept survey data unless the survey and the methodology of how it was administered are also offered into evidence* because clearly a clever person could trick anyone into saying nearly anything.

Another example, this one from the *New York Times* in 2001, indicates that nearly 70 percent of the people asked said "they favor allowing 'gay men and lesbians' to serve in the military," while only 59 percent were in favor of allowing "homosexuals" to serve (Sussman).

The connotations of even individual words can influence opinions. There is an often-quoted example how mere wording can control the outcome of a survey. Back in 1941 a researcher named Daniel Rugg asked Americans if the United States should allow antidemocracy speeches. He then ran another survey asking if such speeches should be forbidden. To the question of allowing, 62 percent denied that antidemocracy speeches should be allowed while 21 percent agreed, and 17 percent had no opinion. The numbers where different, however, when the question was rephrased using "forbidding." This time, 39 percent agreed and 46 percent disagreed with the statement while 15 percent had no opinion. Because to forbid something is the opposite of to allow something, you would expect that the results would have been mirror opposites, but they were not. From this experiment it was inferred that people have different affective reactions to the verbs "to forbid" and "to allow" even though they are opposites. So, if you want to show that people weakly oppose something, ask if they think it should be forbidden, and if you want to show a weak approval, ask if it should be allowed. More importantly, as far as critical thinking goes, whenever you read survey results, don't just look at the numbers. Look closely at the words that elicited the numbers. Always *beware statistical evidence.*

Even a word as apparently neutral as *because* has a remarkable rhetorical force because it signifies reason and thus adds to the speaker's or writer's *ethos.* There have been several sociological studies in *The Power of Persuasion: How We're Bought and Sold* that suggest that if a person makes a request followed by a reason for the request signaled by "because," it is more likely to be granted than if the word *because* isn't used, even if what follows "because" is irrelevant. While this may surprise sociologists, it's not so surprising for *rhetors* because adding "because" to a request creates an enthymeme, and enthymemes sound reasonable, and people who sound reasonable have more credibility and are therefore more persuasive.

There are a great many words and phrases that, like *because,* sound reasonable and thoughtful even though they aren't necessarily so: scientists have discovered, as history indicates, research has shown, common sense dictates, evidence indicates, technologically advanced, innovative, new, made in America, as Plous (*some supposed authority*) observed. Phrases like these don't stand up to careful questioning, but they are superficially reassuring and so can pass for reasonable. Even just speaking of a potential as if it were an accomplished feat ("Welcome to your new home!" says the realtor to the prospective buyers) can be persuasive.

God and devil terms

We have similarly autonomic (knee-jerk) responses to words like *motherhood* and *fatherhood* and *nature.* Most people don't stop to ask, What exactly do you mean by motherhood? because it would seem like only an idiot or a bad person (or someone trained in dialectical invention) would question what the referent for motherhood is. Conventional words and expressions are a facsimile of thinking, an expression of belief in and commitment to a set of ideas that have not been personally demonstrated or even examined. And the words and phrases you use, especially if you are un-self-conscious about your selections, reflect what rhetorical processes have influenced you.

In addition to assuming the meanings of commonly used words, we assume a value as well. *Motherhood* and *fatherhood* and *nature,* like *patriot* and *hero,* are unquestionably positive terms called "god terms" (Weaver 222–23). God terms can be powerful motivators because they jack into our basic needs and fears and thus forestall thinking. Even a company as apparently utilitarian as one that sells tires can jack into these resources. Look up Michelin Tires' "Because so much is riding on your tires" campaign on YouTube to see what I mean.

If there are god terms there are certainly also devil terms,[23] words that are accepted as unquestionably bad. *Un-American* is an obvious example. *Terrorist, fanatic, racist,* and *socialist* are some others. And then there are expressions like *big government* that are instantly repellent for some people but meaningless to others. Whenever you encounter words like these you need to remember that they get their power from remaining unexamined and also that one person's god is another person's devil.

God and devil terms can be useful resources for arguments when evidence or time are lacking, but they also tend to retard critical thinking and therefore may get in the way of really understanding something. If you choose to use them, use them carefully; and, whatever you do, listen carefully to the words other people use.

While god and devil terms, words with absolute values, are potentially powerful, *don't passively accept or reject either the meaning or the value of any word or phrase. Question the obvious.* God and devil terms are not as common as words that have mixed values. With mixed-value words, the connotation of a word or phrase is indicated by the context, the speaker, the occasion, the topic, and the audience.

Consider the word *liberal* for example. The word *liberal* was once neutral, meaning free. It was turned into a positive term by people who believed the government should help the people and recently turned into a negative term by people who believe the people should help themselves. The word *felon*, to take a completely different example, would seem to have nearly universally negative connotations, but if you are describing how you prefer your running shoes without laces, *felons* are a good thing.

━━━━ Your Turn

Make a list of god terms and a list of devil terms, and share them with someone else. Do they see devils in your gods? Does identifying a term as having an absolutely positive or negative connotation instantly demythologize it (*metaphorically speaking*)?

Do you think it's possible to escape rhetoric? If so, how and why? If not, why not, and what does the inescapability of rhetoric mean for human communication?

━━━━━━━━━━━━━━━

23. Did you notice the if-then construction and the god term *certainly*? Sounded awfully logical didn't it? Because there's a god term there certainly must be a devil term? Don't forget to read against the grain. I'm not lying to you, but all the same.

Positive, negative, neutral language

Effective writers and thinkers (rhetors) *notice distinctions others miss or ignore or deny.*

A good way to practice your facility with observing, avoiding, and when absolutely necessary (when for some reason you need to flame or troll) exploiting loaded language is to set out lists of three, more or less, synonymous terms with positive on the left, neutral in the middle, and negative on the right (or vice versa). The goal ultimately is always to think of possible alternatives because small faults can be presented as virtues and virtues as flaws. By the way, is a *fault* different from a *flaw* in denotation or connotation or implication?

Below is a list of similar if not exactly synonymous words arranged on a continuum. Read them from left to right, and ask yourself if you agree with the way they are laid out. Are the neutral terms really neutral to you, to others, to anyone, in all circumstances? If you read them slowly and think about them, I think you will see how unstable the positive and negative charges are in some cases. Consider especially the martyr, activist, terrorist triumvirate.

Positive	*Neutral*	*Negative*
Solicitous	Helpful	Meddlesome
Stalwart	Steady	Stubborn
Placid	Calm	Lazy
Generous	Giving	Profligate
Martyr	Activist	Terrorist
Improvement	Change	Deterioration
Traditional	Conventional	Old fashioned
Strategy	Plan	Plot
Whistle-blower	Informer	Snitch
Plenty	Many	Glut
Wink	Blink	Flinch
Praise	Approve	Flatter
Thrifty	Economical	Cheap

━━━ Your Turn

Now it's your turn. Create your own list, and then share it with someone else. See if they agree with your partitions.

Figures of speech

The rhetorical tradition has spent, in my estimation, an inordinate amount of effort labeling distinct departures from ordinary patterns of thought and speech. These are known as ~~figures~~ tropes and ~~tropes~~ figures,[24] and there are catalogs of them that go on for hundreds of pages. Richard Lanham's *A Handlist of Rhetorical Terms* is a good one. I've always thought knowing them, being able to observe and identify them, or being able to name and give an example of, say, zeugma is a trivial matter when it comes to knowing how to be persuasive. Minute knowledge of the figures and tropes is esoterica, as far as I'm concerned.

Still, there are a couple of important points to make about tropes and figures. The distinction between the literal and the figurative is critical to understanding rhetoric, and one could go on about it at great length. Some argue that in the end there is no difference, that everything linguistic is figurative. Others want to paint a bright line between them, insisting on a distinct division between language and ontology (words and things). It's enough, for our purposes, to agree that by *literal* we mean using common names for things (calling a stone a stone) and standard patterns of expression. *Figurative* means referring to things not with their proper name but with the name that is used for an attribute or a property or an accident of the thing itself (calling a stone a pain).

> We can't see the mountain because of the fog.
> The mountain is *obscured* by fog.
> The mountain is *shrouded* in fog.
> The mountain is *cloaked* in fog.

The important distinction between literal and figurative is obscured today by the fact that people often use the word *literally* as an intensifier meaning something like *very* but in cases where they already have a metaphor providing the intensification, with the result that while they mean to say one thing they say something different. *He literally exploded with rage*, does not mean he was very, very angry. It means he exploded like a bomb explodes. This transformation of the original meaning is akin to the fact that today many people use *really* instead of *very*. *She's really smart*, instead of *She's very smart*. Linguistic conservatives frown on such blithe substitutions; although there is certainly a backlash toward such people, evidenced by the fact that they are sometimes called "grammar Nazis."

Given that language is a medium of exchange held in common, people who know the difference between literal and figurative (or know that rage

---

24. Can you see why I made that revision? Think about arrangement and the idea that patterns shape understanding. I said "patterns of thoughts and speech" (a.k.a. tropes and figures) but then in the next sentence reversed the order to "figures and tropes" for no apparent reason. That's why I revised them. I didn't erase that revision in order to make this point: Don't change patterns randomly unless your goal is to confuse your audience.

can't cause combustion) will know what you mean when you say *literally* and mean *figuratively*, but they will suspect you don't know the difference, and the less kind among your audience might think less of your ideas because of how you expressed them.

Once a figure has been used for a few generations, we no longer notice that it's a figure of speech, if you "see" what I mean. These worn-out figures are sometimes called *dead metaphors*, and we are commonly advised to avoid them because they suggest a very conventional mind or a lack of thought. If you haven't yet read George Orwell's "Politics and the English Language," this would be a good time to read it.

If a figure has been around a long time but not long enough to have faded into invisibility, it's a cliché or a tired expression. We still recognize the figurativeness of the expression, but the connection it makes between the object it refers to and the quality of the object it uses as a way of referring to it is no longer vivid because it refers to a world unlike our own. Consider an expression like *a tough row to hoe*. We know it means a difficult life, but it's an agrarian metaphor; and, except for the few urban gardeners among us, very few of us have ever hoed a row, tough or soft. These tried-and-true figures suggest a lack of creative energy, but if the information is the main point of the discourse and therefore you don't want to call attention to the language then a cliché might suffice. And then again, you might prefer to appear conventional or boring. Just because you can smith words, doesn't mean you should do it all the time. The more often you do something, the less special it becomes. (But if you do it too rarely, it may seem a fluke.)

There are a couple of tropes that are especially important because they embed a world view in an expression that you may not notice if you don't question the obvious. The most important tropes are synecdoche, metonymy, irony, and metaphor.

Your Turn

Look up synecdoche, metonymy, and irony, and then come up with some examples of each.[25]

The editing checklist

Editing is the process of revisiting every word and every sentence to make sure each is the best fit for the audience, subject, and occasion. It's about fixing

---

25. Hey, Pullman, isn't that your job, to define and explain words like these? Actually, my job is to make you strong enough to replace me. Go look them up. I'll wait.

the grammar and the punctuation, but also the diction, the spelling, and the sentence structure. Sometimes in the process of editing you will encounter a moment of clarity that will make you revise an entire paragraph or even a section, but for the most part you are cleaning and polishing and straightening at this point, not building or remodeling. A well-edited piece of weak thinking will beat a badly edited piece of strong thinking more often than it should, especially if the audience is unfamiliar with the material. *A cover letter with a couple of typos in it will kill a career before it even gets started.*

That said, while most people wait until the draft is pretty much done before they start editing, some people edit as they revise because they prefer to get each sentence right before moving on to the next one. Most people worry about losing the train of thought if they stop to fix a typo or puzzle over the use of a comma and so would rather throw everything down first and then go back and tidy up. Regardless of what method you currently prefer, it is best to keep an editorial checklist and to make several passes through a paper looking for just one thing at a time, focusing especially on your weakest points. So if you know you often misuse commas, go through one time just looking at the commas and the coordinating and subordinating conjunctions because the latter suggest the need for a comma. Look at introductory phrases, also. When you are looking for needles in haystacks, it is often best to read backwards, from the last sentence up to the first, so you see each sentence clearly for what it is and don't let the sound in your head seduce your eyes. Once the commas are right, move on to homonyms, then capitalization or whatever you know you often get wrong. Run down your checklist. Proofread one time for each item. Use the search feature for words you commonly get wrong. (I can never remember *affect* versus *effect* so I search for each and look at the sentences they appear in and right-click and look at the synonyms list.) You can also use the search feature to check for things like pronoun antecedent agreement.

Keep a list of your common errors in a matrix, and check off each one as you accomplish it. Below is an example, although not a very complete one. You can start with this, but you should tailor it to your specific needs.

1. Sentence structure: Subject should be a concrete noun or at least a specific concept, and it should be the first word in the sentence. Adjectives are next to the nouns they modify.

2. Commas

3. Subject-verb agreement: If the subject of a sentence in singular, then the verb must also be in the singular form.

4. Number agreement

5. Pronoun agreement: If the subject of a sentence is singular, then any pronoun reference to the subject should also be singular. If you start out with one, don't switch to they (I tend to break this rule because keeping it can lead to inadvertent sexism).

6. Modification: Adjectives and adverbs should be next to the word or phrase they modify and not somewhere else in the sentence.

7. Capitalization

8. Italics: Titles of plays, novels, and TV shows should be italicized.

9. Homophones: There/their, affect/effect.

10. Citations

11. Redundant expressions

12. Verbosity

13. Diction: Use a dictionary and a thesaurus to ensure definitions and connotations.

14. Eliminate vague words: This, it, thing, some, people, society, culture.

15. Clichés

16. Identify and address unintentional and mixed metaphors.

17. Self-talk and finger-pointing: The word *this* and expressions like *that is to say* or *in other words* or *I will now*.

What's the opposite of *plain*?

Before I run through the standard advice about how to plain your prose style, here is an excellent explanation by way of contrast. Thanks, Constance Hale and *Sin and Syntax: How to Craft Wickedly Effective Prose*, for this:

> "People used to call me a good writer," mused John Ruskin, giant of the nineteenth-century essay. "Now they say I can't write at all; because, for instance, if I think anybody's house is on fire, I only say, 'Sir, your house is on fire.' . . . I used to say, 'Sir, the abode in which you probably passed the delightful days of youth is in a state of inflammation.'" (2)

You noticed the irony, I assume. George Orwell's essay "Politics and the English Language" offers more examples of how we puff up and thus distort our sentences. Much of the following advice about how to deflate sentences back to their intended form comes from Orwell, by way of Strunk and White (*Elements of Style*), and William Zinsser (*On Writing Well*). You want to read and practice using both of those books.[26] You needn't aspire to be, like

---

26. While you're at it, get a copy of *Sin and Syntax* and Christopher Johnson's *Microstyle: The Art of Writing Little* as well. Stanley Fish's *How to Write a Sentence*

John Ruskin, the greatest essayist of your generation to benefit from spending even thirty minutes a day honing your style. It will pay off in clearer thinking and better decisions down the road.

Editorial strategies for producing a plain style

- Don't inflate ideas with unnecessary words. Example: ~~call a halt to~~ stop.
- Don't say the same thing twice. Example: ~~aluminum metal~~ aluminum.
- Don't use vague words or clichés, such as *thing, some, a number of, any port in a storm.*
- Always be concrete, specific, and detailed.
- Put modifiers beside the words they modify. Example: ~~Lots of new exciting opportunities~~ Lots of exciting new opportunities.
- Avoid helping verbs such as *do, use, make, help, put, able, can, will,* and *take.*
- Avoid infinitive verb forms. Example: ~~she likes to think~~ she thinks.
- Avoid nominalization, or turning verbs into noun phrases. Example: ~~conducted an investigation~~ investigated.
- Begin each sentence with the subject, preferably a concrete noun.
- Use the shortest meaningful sentence.
- Use common words as they are commonly used.
- Remove all self-talk expressions, such as *as I said* or *as previously mentioned.*
- Name, don't point. Don't use words like *this* and *it.* Make your readers think; don't make them guess.
- Don't vary the terminology for the sake of variety; better redundant than obscure.
- Don't overuse the verb *to be.*

Basically, when editing to create a plain style, reduce the number of words in every sentence by at least 30 percent.

---

and Peter Clark's *Writing Tools: 50 Essential strategies for Every Writer* are also excellent.

━━━━━ **Your Turn**

Find an essay you wrote last semester, and edit solely for length. See if you can reduce it by 30 percent just by employing the plain style guidelines.

━━━━━━━━━━

Memory

Despite what we think, our memories are not like a video recorder. Our memory is more like a hard disk in that we store impressions and feelings and sensations and thoughts and words and whole speeches and music and everything we can remember in fragments in different places of our brain, and then, for reasons we often don't fully understand, we assemble the pieces into a vivid experience that we mistake for an image of an actual event. When we remember something, we are actually recomposing it out of these bits and pieces. When we encounter a gap, we supply the missing information with fragments of other memories, or we just make up stuff to fill in the gaps. (It's called *confabulation*.) This is why our natural memories are notoriously fallible and why eyewitness testimony convicts the innocent and why it is actually possible to make people believe they remember something that never actually happened (false memories).

Our natural memories are also powerful feeling generators. If we are stressed out by what's going on around us we can calm down just by recalling a happy or pleasant time in the past and focusing on what it felt like to be there then. When we do that, whatever is happening now recedes from conscious awareness a little bit, and we are transported for a moment or two. If we stay too long we might get nostalgic and long for things as they were, which won't be helpful. But a quick and vivid return to a lakeshore cabin or an early spring day or whatever you use to vividly represent a happy moment can help you rise above a current situation. This persuasion technique works for fear and its milder form anxiety. Just remember a previous success in a similar endeavor or even one unrelated, and the images will encourage you.

Memory is the handmaiden of persuasion.

Origins of the art of memory

Classical rhetoricians understood that there are two types of memory, natural and artificial. The natural memory is what we all just do as a matter of course. Artificial memory is something we construct on purpose in order to remember a great deal in great detail. The sophist Hippias is said to have been one of the first to teach an art of memory. It is the poet Simonides, however, who is usually associated with the origin of the art of memory. It is said, in *Rhetorica ad Herennium,* that one day he attended a banquet with a great many other guests. During dinner he was called outside, and, while he stood there conversing with a messenger, the banquet hall collapsed, crushing everyone inside. Simonides was able to reconstruct from memory who was in attendance and where each person was sitting. He was able to do this, he explained, because he had a visual image of the banquet hall firmly placed in his head.

Mnemonics

A standard sort of mnemonic device is to make a word out of the first letter of a list of words (or sentence out of the first word in a collection of phrases). To remember the five canons of rhetoric, for example, one can take the first letter of each and create a memorable word: MAIDS.

M̲emory
A̲udience
I̲nvention
D̲elivery
S̲tyle

Backgrounds and images

For more complex information, the classical tradition advises us to divide the matter into subject heads, print each on a card, and distribute the cards in a memorable pattern throughout a familiar room. By moving from place (card) to place throughout the room and practicing the part of the speech that each card represents as one stands before it, one can memorize a pattern that will be easily recalled and recall the information by association. During a public recitation, then, one simply returns to the room in one's head and retraces the familiar path. Using techniques like these, people have been able to memorize information of, to us, unimaginable complexity and magnitude. *The Iliad* and *The Odyssey* were recited from memory. Another memory technique is iconographic. One creates an image, mental or physical, that has memorable features, pictures that would remind one of the necessary topics.

The figure of Rhetorica, or Dame Rhetoric (right), is a mnemonic device for the art of rhetoric. The fold of sheep at the bottom right signifies Rhetoric's ability to lead even beasts; the fiery pot and the spurs at bottom left signify rhetoric's ability to move the passions and control the will. The caduceus in the right hand represents rhetoric's ability to unify opposing points of view (or hold both simultaneously); it might also remind one that Plato likened rhetoric to quackery. The three chains extending from Dame Rhetoric's mouth signify the three styles: low, middle, and high. The open left hand indicates rhetoric's ingratiating gift of words. The open hand might also remind one that Zeno is said to have contrasted rhetoric with dialectic by saying that, if rhetoric was an open

RHETORICA

hand, dialectic was a closed fist. The crown is to remind one that rhetoric was (for roughly fifteen hundred years) considered the crown or pinnacle of education.

ELOQUENTIA   LOGICA

A somewhat less complex application of the same method is to create separate icons for individual concepts. Zeno's idea of the open hand of rhetoric and the closed fist of dialectic is often depicted as the image on the left.

Stained glass windows are often mnemonic devices for scripture, particu-

larly useful for illiterate parishioners, but handy also for the clergy if they are struggling for something to say. The main concept here is that in the past at least, pictures really did tell stories, or rather reminded people of how to tell an oft-told story. One common example is the "Stations of the Cross," which is a representation of the passion of Christ as told in a sequence of fourteen images (an example is at right).

It is easy to understand how in an oral-culture memory would figure prominently in education. How else can you make use of what you learn when you can't keep a record of it except by remembering it? And how can you prepare a speech in advance if you can't memorize it. But is memory still important today? We can of course write things down and, better yet, write them into electronic tools that allow us to treat text as data, to recover anything we have come across in the past. Worse comes to worst, we can always re-Google something we can't remember. So why bother remembering anything at all? Well, of course if the power goes out, we're in trouble. Ever lose you phone and be unable to remember any of the numbers in speed dial? But there's more at stake when your memory fails.

The classical *rhetors'* artificial memory is an incredibly accurate analog of natural memory as neuroscience now understands it. Order provides access to content. Remember the order, and you can reconstruct the content with great fidelity. Focus on the content, and you will get lost. Think about it this way: Have you ever lost your keys? If you start by thinking about all of the places you might put your keys, you're sunk if you don't always put them in the same place, right? Pants pocket? Which pants? On the table by the door? On the desk? Now you are running all over the place looking practically at random. Try it this way instead: Where was the last place you had them? Now in your head retrace your steps from there. I opened the front door. So I had them then. I went to my room to change out of my workout clothes. I went to my office to read email. I left them in the pocket of my sweat pants. We forget things because we aren't paying attention when we do them. Or we are paying attention to something else while we do them. This is why, for example, we can't remember what we ate or what we wore yesterday.

Segmented hypergraphics—image maps

If you ever need to remember a complex set of ideas, visualization is a great way to go about it. Create an image, like Dame Rhetoric, and then add details. You can do this in Photoshop or Gimp or any graphics program. If you have layers of information to remember, you might try creating an electronic image known as a segmented hypergraphic, basically an image with pop-ups on rollover hotspots, like you see on websites. As with the traditional method, the idea is to associate what you want to remember with what you can readily call to your mind's eye. The more striking the image, the more memorable it will be.

You could use such an image on your tablet PC or your iPad or phone as a kind of teleprompter.

Plato and memory and writing

There's an interesting passage in *Phaedrus* where Plato's Socrates warns us about the dangerous impact of writing on learning:

> Among the ancient gods of Naucratis in Egypt there was one to whom the bird called the ibis is sacred. The name of that divinity was Theuth, and it was he who first discovered number and calculation, geometry and astronomy, as well as the games of draughts and dice, and, above all else, writing.
>
> Now the king of all Egypt at that time was Thamus, who lived in the great city in the upper region that the Greeks call Egyptian Thebes; Thamus they call Ammon. Theuth came to exhibit his arts to him and urged him to disseminate them to all the Egyptians. Thamus asked him about the usefulness of each art, and while Theuth was explaining it, Thamus praised him for whatever he thought was right in his explanations and criticized him for whatever he thought was wrong.
>
> The story goes that Thamus said much to Theuth, both for and against each art, which it would take too long to repeat. But when they came to writing, Theuth said: "O King, here is something that, once learned, will make the Egyptians wiser and will improve their memory; I have discovered a potion for memory and for wisdom." Thamus, however, replied: "O most expert Theuth, one man can judge how they can benefit or harm those who will use them. And now, since you are the father of writing, your affection for it has made you describe its effects as the opposite of what they really are. In fact, it will introduce forgetfulness into the soul of those who learn it: they will not practice using their memory because they will put their trust in writing, which is external and depends on signs that belong to others, instead of trying to remember from the inside, completely on their own. You have not discovered a potion for remembering, but for reminding; you provide your students with the appearance of wisdom, not with its reality. Your invention will enable them to hear many things without being properly taught, and they will imagine that they have come to know much while for the most part they will know nothing. And they will be difficult to get along with, since they will merely appear to be wise instead of really being so."

So writing creates forgetfulness, and reading provides only the illusion of knowledge. Learn to write and you will be an arrogant fool. Really, Socrates? Are you being ironic? Well, it's hard to say of course, and a few lines later he tells us why it's hard to say what a text someone left behind might mean:

> You know, Phaedrus, writing shares a strange feature with painting. The offsprings of painting stand there as if they are alive, but if anyone asks them anything, they remain most solemnly silent. The same is true of written words. You'd think they were speaking as if they have some understanding, but if you question anything that has been said because you want to learn more, it continues to signify just that very same thing forever. When it has once been written down, every discourse roams about everywhere, reaching indiscriminately those with understanding no less than those who have no business with it, and it doesn't know to whom it should speak and to whom it should not. And when it is faulted and attacked unfairly, it always needs its father's support; alone, it can neither defend itself nor come to its own support.

What do you make of that? I'm not sure I agree that texts always say the same thing. I've read a handful of books at different times in my life, and I've had different interpretations of them each time. True the words didn't change; only my interpretation of them did. So I agree texts are like paintings in that way. Well, we can argue all day about what a text means, and we should because that's a great exercise for the mind. From a *rhetor*'s perspective, however, such arguments are a means to an end, not an end in themselves.

I mention the "like paintings" point also because it tells you where the idea of reading against the grain ultimately comes from. Because we can't argue with texts, as Plato tells us, we have a lesser intellectual experience than if we were having a real dialectical conversation. Interjecting and critiquing in square brackets gives us a simulated dialogue. Not as good from Plato's perspective, I imagine, but better than thinking that just because we read something we learned something from it.

I reproduced the myth of Theuth for you also because it brings up an interesting point about memory and learning that is a part of many conversations today about the Internet and learning. Some people feel that having ubiquitous access to the vast majority of all texts written over the years gives us access to learning like no previous people ever had and that this information-rich existence enables advancement like never before. Others, however, argue that the deluge of information and that fact that we never have to remember anything because we can always look it up is leaving our minds empty of facts and therefore less capable of ideas and insights, turning us into perfect consumers and mindless automatons. This line of thinking looks also to ubiquitous video, to the fact that you don't really need to read anymore to keep up with current events because CNN and FOX and the lot provide video reports on demand. Nice bit of irony there for Plato: people today complaining that the negative effects Plato seemed to worry about are being caused by the decline of writing rather than by its advent.

━━━━━ ## Your Turn

What do you think? What impact does ubiquitous information have on how we think and learn? Once you've worked out a few pages, can you write the counterargument about the role of memory in persuasion?

━━━━━━━━━

Delivery

Delivery is about voice (intonation, pitch, and volume) and gesture (how one uses one's hands, holds one's body, moves, stands, dresses, makes eye contact). Rhetorics that focus on literate practices have tended to ignore delivery because written texts are disembodied, which is why all but the last part of this section is historical. Oral cultures, on the other hand,[27] have tended to emphasize delivery. The famous Attic orator Demosthenes is said to have answered the question What are the three most important factors of speech making? by saying, "Delivery, delivery, delivery."[28]

Aristotle also thought delivery was important, but he was ambivalent about it as a subject matter and as a rhetorical force:

> Delivery seems a vulgar matter when rightly understood. But since the whole business of rhetoric is with opinion, one should pay attention to delivery, not because it is right but because it is necessary, since true justice seeks nothing more in a speech than neither to offend nor to entertain; for to contend by means of the facts themselves is just, with the result that everything except demonstration is incidental; but nevertheless, [delivery] has great power . . . because of the corruption of

---

27. Think about the expression *on the other hand* for a moment. If you were speaking to a group of people about a decision they had to make, and you were presenting two ideas for comparison, you could mime a pair of scales with your hands and lower one and raise the other to signal which of the two ideas you thought was better. The expression *one the one hand . . . on the other hand . . .* is a textual expression of a visual cue. It helps the audience organize and evaluate the ideas being presented by helping them see the idea of comparison.

28. For further reading, check out Cicero's *On the Ideal Orator* (*De Oratore*), 3.213, as well as Quintilian, *Institutes of Oratory* (Institutio Oratoria) 11.3.6–7.

the audience. . . . Acting is a matter of natural talent and largely
not reducible to artistic rule. (*On Rhetoric*, 1404a)

There is no such ambivalence toward delivery in the author of *Rhetorica ad
Herennium*, a work attributed to Cicero:

Many have said that the faculty of greatest use to the speaker
and the most valuable for persuasion is Delivery. For my part,
I should not readily say that any of the five faculties is the most
important; that an exceptionally great usefulness resides in the
delivery I should boldly affirm. For skillful invention, elegant
style, the artistic arrangement of the parts comprising the case,
and the careful memory of all these will be of no more value
without delivery, than delivery alone and independent of these.
(3.11.19)

In *On Invention* (*De Inventione*) Cicero offers the following definition: "Delivery, is a regulating of the voice and body in a manner suitable
to the dignity of the subjects spoken of and of the language employed"
(1.7).

Quintilian considered delivery important enough to devote an entire
chapter to it in Book 11 of his twelve-volume set on rhetoric, *Institutes of
Oratory* (*Institutio Oratoria*):

There is no proof—that proceeds in any way from a pleader—of
such strength that it may not lose its effect unless it is supported
by a tone of affirmation in the speaker. All attempts at exciting
the feelings must prove ineffectual unless they are enlivened by
the voice of the speaker, by his look, and by the action of almost
his whole body.

His advice is far more specific and detailed than anything prior. Here is a
small piece, for example:

To secure grace it is essential that the head should be carried
naturally and erect. For a droop suggests humility, while if it be
thrown back it seems to express arrogance, if inclined to one side
it gives an impression of languor, while if it is held too stiffly and
rigidly it appears to indicate a rude and savage temper. (11.3.69)

For Quintilian delivery comes down to propriety, what is best suited to
the occasion and the circumstances. As typical of Quintilian, he warns

against excess: "In our attempt to ape the elegances of the stage, we shall lose the authority which should characterize the man of dignity and virtue" (349).

Quintilian's chapter on delivery in *Institutes of Oratory* (*Institutio Oratoria*) is worth reading in its entirety.

Interestingly, the sixteenth-century French humanist Peter Ramus (1515–August 26, 1572), who is often presented as a villain in the history of rhetoric for having excluded invention from the canons and having focused almost entirely on stylistic expression, nevertheless did see delivery, or "action," as important:

> His second main topic, action, deals with suitable delivery. Up to this time, it had been valued but not explicitly taught. With Ramus suitable delivery comprises the use of the voice and gestures. Under the head of vocal control he discusses how both in the case of single words and of sentences or combinations of words expression may be given through proper modulation to the various emotions such as fear, grief, and sympathy. Under the other division he deals with all the details of effective expression through gestures with the body, head, eyes, arms, hands, and fingers, and with the kind of gesticulation to be avoided. (Graves 137)

Several hundred years later, in eighteenth-century northern Europe and America, handbooks on delivery appeared with illustrations of all the supposedly appropriate ways to stand in order to evoke and express emotions: hands out, palms up for supplication, a raised fist for anger, and so on. This period is sometimes referred to as the elocutionary movement.

Here is a definition of elocution from one of the textbooks of the time, *Elocution and Oratory: Giving a Thorough Treatise on the Art of Reading and Speaking (1869)*:

> Elocution is the art of delivering with ease and propriety; written or extemporaneous composition.
>
> Good reading or speaking, therefore, may be considered not only as uttering the words of a sentence so that it may be distinctly heard, but also giving them all that force and variety of which they are susceptible.
>
> The prime qualification of an orator, is a pure and cultivated voice; therefore, knowledge of the right use of the breathing apparatus, together with the proper manner of disciplining and using the voice, is the first subject the student should notice. (Wiley 15)

It's interesting the lengths to which eighteenth-century scholars went to catalog hand gestures and postures. Below is a plate from Gilbert Austin's *Chironomia* (on the right) and one from John Bulwer's *Chirologia* (on the left).

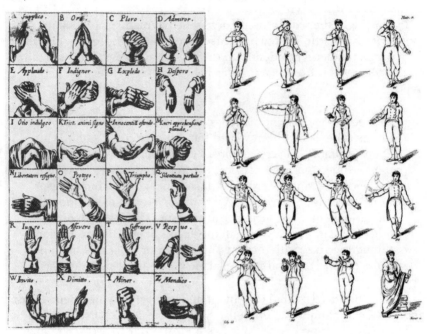

If these seem a bit alien, here's a still resonant example:

convicium facio—I provoke (an argument). The putting forth of the middle finger the rest drawn into a fist on each side . . . is a natural expression of scorn and contempt. This gesture is called *catapygon* by the Athenians that is, a fornicator and whore, because he is prone to obscenity and because he arouses a bad reputation and creates a noisy disturbance. . . . That is, if he calls you a fornicator you should cast the same aspersion on him and pay him back, raising your third finger which is the sign of a fornicator; for it is used not only to denote derision but also disgrace and weakness of any sort. (Bulwer 132)

Today it seems more than a little arcane to be concerned for pronunciation. In fact, were one to correct a student's pronunciation one might be denounced for an elitist, or worse. Still, an impenetrable accent is undeniably a rhetorical handicap. Demosthenes, by the way, is said to have perfected his pronunciation and the strength of his lungs while practicing declaiming with a mouth full of pebbles in a cave by the sea, where he had to strain to be heard over the crashing waves—apocryphal, no doubt, but an interesting indication of the traditions' value for enunciation and projection.

Your Turn

The importance of delivery when it comes to public speaking or even just speaking informally with colleagues is inestimable. If you can't get a sentence out without a dozen "ums" and "likes" and other verbal ticks you'll ruin your *ethos*. Even the pace at which you speak can make a difference; people think that quick (smart) people speak more quickly slow people speak. Tone, too, affects persuasiveness. The lower the tone, the more likely people are to listen. This is true for both men and women. One way to practice is to sit in front of your computer and just record yourself giving a summary of the day's events or your plans for the evening or for tomorrow. Then play it back and listen to yourself as you watch yourself. You don't have to aspire to being on camera to learn from this exercise, although that camera and actual performances are very different.

Body language

While traditional discussions of delivery seem dated because they were developed for people speaking to an audience from a stage, something few of us do anymore, we are a far more oral culture now than we have been for hundreds of years. Video chat is rapidly becoming mainstream, and Flash videos are a popular way of sharing interesting, and spreading viral, ideas. You can find many excellent examples of modern rhetorical performances at the website Technology, Entertainment, and Design (TED.com). If you are inclined toward becoming a renowned public speaker, getting on TED should be one of your goals.

When we talk of delivery today we are usually talking about body language, and the emphasis is, typical of many contemporary rhetorics, on decoding what others do rather than on perfecting our own performance. The basic idea is that we all have what gamblers call *tells*, things we do with our body, hands, feet, and face that "betray" our subconscious or unconscious or hidden feelings, beliefs, and attitudes, unintentional non-verbal communication in other words. People who interrogate others for a living have studied these behaviors closely. But business people too often rely on non-verbal impressions to make rhetorical judgments about salespeople, job candidates, even co-workers. Not just, are you telling the truth? But are you comfortable? Are you paying attention? Are you feeling confident, dominant, embarrassed, distracted, etc.? What a person says and what a person thinks are not always the same, and sometimes the body underscores the difference. This is why listening to both the words and the music, as the saying goes, is an important part of real-time rhetorical transactions.

The most important thing to remember when "reading" people is that, without a baseline understanding of a given person's mannerisms and habits, you don't really know exactly what anything they do means because unintentional communication isn't scientific. We are not robots producing certain outputs given certain inputs. And our behaviors are subject to cultural variations as well. In some places smiling and nodding means agreement and understanding, while in others it means embarrassment and confusion.

Changes in bodily disposition often tell an observer something, but change is a relative quantity, and thus without a baseline you can't tell whether the flushed face of the fair-skinned person you are talking to indicates embarrassment or arousal or nothing more than an autonomic response to environmental conditions. Dilated pupils are often said to be a sign of sexual arousal, but unless you know a person's unaroused pupil size you can't tell if they are larger now than when they first walked into the room. And looking that intently into someone's eyes is sure to change the other's presentation of self in some way. One last example: You have perhaps heard the expression *shifty-eyed* to describe an untrustworthy person. Looking a person in the eyes is thought to be a sure sign of openness and confidence, and thus if anyone avoids another person's gaze they are considered shifty. But eye gaze is more complicated than that. Looking too long at someone can be considered intimidating or just weird, and how long is too long varies by gender (men tend to glance and look away more often unless they are really intent on getting a message across) and setting. Also, some people are physiologically predisposed to avoid eye contact, people with autism and people with face blindness, for example.

The point I am illustrating here is that little, when it comes to non-verbal communication, is entirely reliable. You need soft eyes, as the saying goes: Contextualize whatever behavior you are inclined to interpret as signifying an inner state before you infer meaning from it.

Here is a synopsis of the standard advice about how to read people and therefore how to deliver your inner states to others (or hide them).

Common gestures and how they are commonly interpreted in the Western world

Oddly enough, if you try out these gestures some of them may actually make you feel the way they are said to signify. Try it. Stroke you chin. Do you feel pensive? Rub the back of your neck. Now how do you feel? I have no idea why that happens or if it will indeed happen for you. At any rate, we use these gestures to signal inner states, and we tend to interpret them as indicating inner states in others. You will see actors using them also. And that, of course, should alert you to the fact that, because one can affect these gestures, they don't necessarily signify an inner state. A person could be faking it. More often than not, however, most people are pretty un-self-conscious when it comes to how they hold themselves and the gestures they use. You should make a point of observing people in general but especially the people you work and live with. A sudden change from a standard posture might say something important.

Below is a list of common gestures and how they are commonly interpreted. As with all of the lists in this book, this list is partial. What's missing? Keep in mind here especially that different cultures employ different gestures and that in some cases the same gesture may be interpreted differently in different cultures.

stroking the chin, tapping the upper lip: contemplation, thinking, deciding

steepling the hands: judgment, command, control

hands folded over the stomach or on the table: composed, contrite

hands clenched or clenching and unclenching: angry, anxious, fidgety

feet up, hands behind the head: dominance, comfort, self-importance

hunched shoulders, curved spine: weak, stressed out, burdened, deflated, disappointed

leaning forward: focused, intent, listening

head tilted: flirting, submissive, but also possibly just listening carefully

arms folded across the chest: defensive, closed off, skeptical

arms akimbo: dominant, confident, defiant, angry

touching the throat or clavicle: fearful, threatened, self-conscious

rubbing the neck, pulling the ear: uncertainty, contemplation

self-soothing gestures, nail biting, lip biting, hair playing, thigh rubbing, feet bouncing: uneasiness, boredom, but a habit for some people and therefore akin to a normal state

touching the nose: lying, or a way to make a person think you might be lying, used by actors

flared nostrils: anger, exasperation, preparing to pounce

covering or obscuring the face with a hand or an object, rubbing the eyes: deception, embarrassment, unease, desire to forget or get past

collar pulling: stress, deception

mirroring: a general principle rather than a gesture, doing what the other is doing as a way of generating a sense of rapport

pinching the bridge of the nose, head down, eyes closed: disapproval, negative evaluation, sudden frustration, stifling a sneeze

chest out, chin up: confident, proud, in command

head down, shoulders rounded: submissive, depressed

suddenly raised eye brows: positive recognition, pleasant surprise

hand on heart: sincerity

When you are trying to infer someone's inner state of mind, don't just look at what they are doing, but look for changes in what they are doing. Without a stable frame of reference no single gesture can tell you much, but a sudden change might give you a clue. Pay attention and look for changes.

━━━━ Your Turn

Try doing each one of the gestures above, and see if it has any effect on your inner state.

Try doing each one in front of you computer's camera (or a mirror), and see what you look like doing them. Are any of these gestures "natural" expressions for you? If you were to start using them consciously, which ones would you use in what circumstances and why?

Putting the Canons to Work: From Writing Process to Rhetorical Practice

Open any handbook on writing and somewhere early on you will likely see the expression "the writing process." This is usually described as brainstorm, plan, outline, draft, revise, edit, submit. True, as far as it goes, but there is way more to practicing rhetoric than ticking the boxes in a linear process. To become persuasive you have to work on each of the elements regularly, and one of the best ways to work on all of them is to write every day. That may seem odd.

If you want to have ideas worth listening to, if you want to be a *rhetor*, you have to work on your thinking every day, and the best way to work on your thinking is to exteriorize it, put it down where you can see it clearly. Question it. Share it. Rethink it. Refine it. Throw some of it out, and start over. From a rhetorical perspective, writing is a means to an end, not an end in itself. Writing is a mental discipline, a set of habits and a way of being, not a manufacturing process. It might seem like spending a few hours a day writing is something only a would-be author would do, not a *rhetor* or anyone with other than authorial intentions. The confusion here is the concept of the author. What comes to mind when you hear that expression? I won't name names, but I'm guessing you are thinking of someone famous, maybe someone rich and famous, or dead and famous. We think of authors as geniuses, uniquely talented and gifted people. But that's the wrong way to think about writers. The difference between writers and everybody else is that writers write. Moreover, the vast majority of people who write don't qualify as authors at all. They are doctors or lawyers or architects or teachers or sales reps; name a profession, and I'll show you someone who writes regularly. It's not just that writers write. Professionals write. There's nothing mystical about writing. The poets and the novelists and the dramatists are no different from the rest of the world who make a living and a place for themselves with ideas and words. Writing disciplines the mind and refines our thinking. We don't write because we are smart. We get smart by writing.

When it comes to rhetorical success, practice, commitment, and reflection are far more important than talent. An interesting point about talent, by the way, is that people who think they are naturally talented often don't progress as quickly as people who think they are hard workers (Ericsson, Krampe, and Tesch-Romer). It's not that hard work trumps talent; it's just that talented people sometimes get complacent and slack off, or get distracted and otherwise don't fully live up to their tremendous potential. The most troubled talents are the prodigies. If you associate your talent with your identity, then you run the risk of underperforming because every attempt threatens your sense of self, even if you are extremely good at something and have often succeeded. People who consider themselves hard workers, on the other hand, remain focused and engaged because their identity is the hard worker. They are okay with making mistakes, not that they are willing to let the mistake stand, but they don't consider themselves perfect or even perfectible, so when they turn in an imperfect performance they aren't devastated by their failure because they aren't left wondering if maybe they aren't the genius everybody said they were. They just get back in and do it again, and again, and again. When it comes to talent and practice, it's a tortoise and hare thing.[29]

---

29. If you have your doubts about this (good, you are reading against the grain), check out Carol Dweck's *Mindset: The New Psychology of Success.*

There are well-known steps to becoming good at anything, whether a sport, an instrument, or an intellectual pursuit like chess or persuasion. The first and most important step is *constant, frequent, goal-directed practice right at the outer edges of your current skill level,* the place Lev S. Vygotsky called the zone of proximal development. The requisite skills for a *rhetor* are

1. the ability to make distinctions and connections that others don't see coming;

2. the ability to promote and defend decisions by selecting effective arguments and using them appropriately;

3. the ability to understand people, both individuals and groups (what motivates them, what inhibits them, how they want to be perceived by others, how they want to see themselves, what they are feeling);

4. the ability to organize information for maximum recall and utility (for him or herself and others);

5. facility with words, spoken and written—a wide and deep vocabulary and an array of sources for metaphors and analogies, as well as common and special topics, both those listed in books like this but also those that are implicit in a given subject but not listed anywhere;

6. and the ability to infer needs and opportunities from circumstances (kairos, or timing).

To become an effective *rhetor* you need to develop your own methods for practicing all six of these abilities. While advice about expertise always indicates that you should break each move into component parts and practice each part in isolation until you've perfected it, performance is ultimately measured by how well you can put all the parts together at the moment when the moment arrives. This is a tall order, so you need to commit yourself to exercising daily, preparing to write a paper that hasn't been assigned yet or make a presentation or otherwise organize information to make a point long before a specific task arrives in your inbox. Here are some specific ways to practice being a *rhetor*.

> **Create a browser home page** with links to information relevant to your intellectual and personal interests. That way every time you fire up Chrome or Firefox or Safari or Internet Explorer you will remind yourself to practice. My home page has links to fifteen newspapers from around the world and twenty-seven magazines covering the gamut of political persuasions as well as several dealing with learning and technology. You should make a point of looking for opinions you don't agree with. Most people want their beliefs confirmed and so consume only opinions like their own. Worse yet, many people cannot hear opposing viewpoints undistorted by their prior commitments,

which means they can't learn from people who disagree with them. Because of confirmation bias we are all prone to distorting what doesn't immediately appeal to us. As a *rhetor* you have to be more objective than your allegiances might incline you. If you are going to be able to argue both sides of a case, you can't be blinded by one of them. So make sure your collection of frequented news and magazine sites includes some sources you don't look forward to hearing from. You also want to make sure that the collection of sources includes a broad array of subjects so that you've got lots of different things to think and talk and write about. The more you know, the more readily you can learn, and the more readily you can find ways to connect ideas and people.

My home or landing page also has links to sites like Wired.com and Boing Boing and Reddit and LifeHacker and PopUrls, from which I seek new ideas and trends. But that's just me. You might want links to sites with statistical information, like the World Health Organization or the Census Bureau or any number of other sources of information. You can set up your smart phone in a similar way. The point here is just that you should develop and over time broaden a spectrum of resources for ideas and arguments and data. And you should make a daily habit of checking the lines to see if anything has come up that is worth writing and thinking about. Get curious.

The quickest test to know if something is worth writing about is of course to ask if you agree or not and then to argue *against* your inclinations. A more sophisticated approach is to write notes about what a person would have to believe in order to agree and what another person would have to believe in order to disagree. And then finally make some notes about how you could help one person become (*turn him or her into?*) the other.

Use news aggregators so you always have something to read and think about. CNN and NPR and WSJ are useful examples. There's an app called Zite that will pull blogs based on the subjects you give it to search for that can give you a pretty good collection of new things to read every couple of days.

Set up Google Alerts (www.google.com/alerts). You need to be informed so that you can make informed decisions but also so that you have something informed and interesting to say so that people come to think of you as informed and interesting—not a know-it-all or a pedant—just someone who is alive to the world happening around them. If you can take an interest in things, you will be more interesting. As the saying goes, if you're bored than you're boring.

Read for form and structure and style as well as content. Read many different kinds of texts (paper and electronic) and on lots of different subjects, paying attention not only to the ideas but the expression and arrangement. Ask yourself, how else could this be said? Can I say the same thing with fewer words? What about with more words? Why did they say it this way? If I scrambled the sentences in this paragraph, would it matter? When you get ten minutes to spare, sit down at a computer and literally rewrite something you've just read. Or use an app like Evernote and text yourself a few thoughts for further writing about later. The more you practice composing your thoughts, the more rapidly articulate thoughts will come. But speed shouldn't be your primary objective, especially not in the beginning. People who study the development of expertise like to say that expertise requires ten thousand hours of directed practice. If there's any truth to that, longer and slower is better. Tortoise, not hare.

Keep lists of useful phrases and word patterns, and practice them until you don't need to look at the list anymore. Constantly seek new sentence and paragraph structures as well new words and reusable phrases. Do a web search for "academic phrases," or Google "Academic Phrase Bank." If you prefer books, have a look at the book *They Say, I Say* (Graff and Birkenstein). Learn how your newfound pieces are used by creating examples, and keep an eye out for other examples as you read and listen to the world.

Develop an encyclopedic vocabulary, but don't use it for writing so much as for reading and understanding. The best word might be arcane (old fashioned), but if no one knows what it means anymore it's not the best word anymore. At the same time, the more words you have, the more options you have, and the greater your capacity to make careful distinctions among them, and this enables insight and innovation. Consider using a flash card app like Evernote Peek or Mental Case Flashcards HD or Flashcards Deluxe for your vocabulary exercises and fact memorizing. An app like Index Cards is great for sorting and organizing ideas, figuring out what goes with what and what needs to be kept separate. There are also very useful apps for brainstorming ideas and outlining papers and talks: MagicalPad and Total Recall, for example. Apps are constantly changing, of course, so by the time this paragraph reaches you there will certainly be other apps out there, and these may have gone away or have morphed into something else. The point is just that there are some very good tools out there for acquiring, organizing, recalling, and using information. Find a few favorites, and use them every day.

Write something, anything, every day. If you can't think of something to write about, get a book like Garry Poole's *The Complete Book of Questions* for inspiration. Or do a TIL search at Reddit.com. Or open a book at random, and write about whatever line pops out at you. If you're listening to a song, notice the hook, and explain to yourself why it works or doesn't. What about that billboard over there? Too many words or just the right number? Is the picture reinforcing the message? Think of an idea, and then see if you can find the perfect image to represent it using Google Images or Flickr or Creative Commons. This may not seem like writing, but it absolutely is. Writing is about distilling a concept to its essence. Of course you can also go the other way. Find an interesting image, and then see if you can describe it using only words. This practice is called *ekphrasis*, by the way.

Write in your head. If you aren't at a keyboard, instead of daydreaming, compose your thoughts as though someone else will hear or read them. Don't just say it; revise it. Don't just let the voice in your head run wild; tame it; tone it. Consider the best word, the best phrasing. Say it different ways, and listen to the differences. When you are not writing, read against the grain.

Keep a commonplace book. *Rhetors* make a habit of admiring what other people have written. Traditionally this admiration was expressed by copying down sentences and paragraphs that met the I-wish-I'd-said-that test. When books were expensive and rare and only the rich had their own libraries, writing down anything good you happened across was a good way of remembering it and at very least gave you the chance to look it up after the book was no longer available to you. People often used subject headings as a way to organize their quotations and to make searching the collection easier. Today, of course, we have thousands of texts at our fingertips, and we needn't write down what we read in order to copy it—although we should frequently because the act of reading something out loud while transcribing it helps us remember and think about what we are reading. Transcription also focuses our attention on how something is written, like chewing slowly rather than scarfing mindlessly. Today, gathering the information isn't as important as creating the connections among the many things we read and developing our own database of ideas to work from and expressions to learn from. We may choose to quote something someday, like when we have a particular assignment due, but we may also just benefit from stuff we read years ago if we can remind ourselves about it years later.

There are a number of electronic equivalents of the commonplace notebook, tools that make it more convenient to record your reading. Some of these tools enable you to use your phone as the interface.

Others facilitate clipping stuff from your web browser. The best allow you to use any screen and save the data on a server you can access from numerous devices. The best also have keyword tagging and search facilities so you can recover what you've recorded and mine your collection for information down the road. Below are several very useful examples of good commonplacing software. Each of them has a slightly different focus. Zotero, for example, is a web browser plug-in (and now stand-alone piece of software) that keeps bibliographic information for you and is especially good at mining library catalogs for resources to cite. You can use it to generate bibliographies in any format when your research and writing are done. Evernote is a great tool for clipping information and images and ideas from the web. Because it has keyword tags and is searchable, whatever you put in there can be rethought about later. Kindle is a great tool for highlighting and making notes in the "margins" as you read e-books. It doesn't currently function as a database; it isn't searchable across entries (it probably will be soon); but it does allow you to look at all of your highlights online, and you can copy and paste from it. Some books that you read on Kindle will provide the bibliographic information (title, author, page) when you cut and paste from them. Other rhetorically useful applications arrive on the scene almost daily. Keep an eye out for such things, but always keep in mind that you need to keep your collection long term. So make sure the format is portable, and keep a back up. At the same time, however, don't make a fetish object out of your information base. If a hard disk crashes or a company in the cloud bursts, you don't have your notes maybe, but you should still have the results of the practice of keeping them. Remember, we are talking about a means to an end here. We aren't archiving for the sake of the artifacts so much as archiving for the increased mental capacity the act of archiving enables.

Learn the rules of grammar and punctuation and usage so well that you no longer need to think about them to get them right.[30] This will lighten the cognitive load required to write and give you more time to work on the ideas and how you present them. It will also improve your reputation as a detail-oriented person, which can pay off in lots of positive ways. I have a friend who co-owns a company where, among other things, he reads job applications. When he finds one full of typos and spelling mistakes and garbled sentences, he likes to cross out the names and send it to me. It makes him laugh. It makes me sad for the applicant. Here's someone who has spent thousands of hours and tens of thousands of dollars getting an engineering degree in order to get a swingin' gig, and he or she neglected the key that opens the door.

---

30. I'm blushing as I type this. I never did become automatic with these things, but I really wish I had. I'm sure the editor of this book wished I had, too. [Ed.: This is true.]

Some writing teachers think grammar and punctuation and usage don't matter. They are wrong. Others think grammar and punctuation and usage are all writing is. They are nuts. Grammar, punctuation, and usage are preliminary and prerequisite to being a *rhetor*. You have to have them, which means reading the rules and practicing getting them right until creating grammatically accurate sentences composed with the right words in the right order is close to second nature. But there's way more to becoming a persuasive person than grammar and punctuation and usage. And nearly no one writes each sentence exactly right the first time. I don't even try. I try to make sure I've got it right before I send it out but not when I'm just trying to get it down or when I'm just practicing for the sake of becoming a better *rhetor*.

Keep a weblog. *Rhetors* need a public, a constituency. Find a subject that you think interesting and maybe even relevant to your future self, and start writing about it in public. You can set up a WordPress site for free. Blogger.com is another free option. Blogware is easy to use, and you can blog from your phone so you don't have to be tied to a desk.

Seek a community of like-minded folk, and write to them. Leave thoughtful comments on blogs. Actually say something on Facebook.

When someone gives you an assignment

Plan. How long is it? When is it due? How much research time will you need? How well do you know the subject, and therefore how much writing toward understanding will you have to do (i.e., how many drafts)?

If you have to meet a deadline, like for a term paper or for work, place the due date on a calendar, and work back to today. Then add 25 percent for the inevitable interruptions that life will throw at you. Set milestones. For example, by the end of week one I will have started gathering sources or doing the fieldwork or searching the archives or whatever activities are required to gather the relevant information, facts, opinions, and arguments. By the end of week two I will have X amount of information, and so on. Among your early milestones should be a list of key words, the subjects you want to talk about. You should also have a list of possible assertions you think you need to make and provide evidence in support of. (*This might be a good moment to review Toulmin's model.*) This list will become an outline over time. At some specific time in advance of your deadline you should plan to write a complete draft—something with an introduction, all of the main points, and a conclusion, with sources listed in a works cited page or however your discipline goes about providing the sources. This draft should be done far enough in advance that you can walk away from it for a few days and then pick it up again and revise it. Leave another whole session for editing—not that you can't edit along the way, but sometimes you will want to get the ideas down and then go back and rethink them and then, finally, go back and do the finish work. The finish work is critical. Don't underestimate its value. After all of the efforts you've made already, making the bright work shine (a car metaphor) may seem trivial, but it is not. Whenever people aren't entirely sure of their opinions on something, they will hang their doubts on the slightest visible imperfection.

When it comes to budgeting time for a writing project or a public presentation, you need to overestimate. Most people underestimate. Most people are unrealistically optimistic about what they can do, especially if the doing will happen tomorrow. That's why people have exercise equipment gathering dust in the garage and gym memberships they don't use and books they haven't read and software programs they don't know how to use and credit card debt and, well, this is getting depressing. Most people, in other words, procrastinate. You need to *set up a process that disables procrastination* and keeps you taking one small step after another. Don't put it off. Don't wait for inspiration. The muse will not descend unbidden.

If you don't have to deal with a deadline, create some artificial ones. Because most of us are hardwired to do what we say we will do—*cognitive dissonance is created when we declare an intention and then fail to follow through,* and most of us find cognitive dissonance really unpleasant—tell yourself you will have

something specific done by X date and X time. Write it down. Say it out loud. Tell someone else. Put it on your blog.

Beware self-defeating strategies like thinking, if I put this off until I don't have enough time and I screw it up it's not really a reflection of my true ability. I just didn't try. Don't be this guy.

Revising

You need to *develop your own revision checklist* because only you can figure out how the way you think and the way you write interact, interfere with, and support each other. That said, you might learn something from what I do.

I'm a drafter. When I start a project, I write out everything I can think of, and I just keep going. Then I go back to the beginning and rewrite from the top. Once the piece is longer than a few pages, I might start a revising session at a section heading rather than from at the top, but basically I'm sifting through words looking for the main idea until I locate it, and then I foreground that idea (make it the first paragraph) and subordinate everything else to it, either using each subordinate idea to support the main idea or getting rid of it entirely. I don't always know where I'm going when I set out, and I try to remain open to unanticipated consequences even after the draft has become something worth refining and tightening and smoothing and polishing, all useful synonyms for my experience of revising. Drafting is about getting it down. Revising is about getting it right. Editing is about getting it ready for public consumption and occasionally meeting the needs of the organization that is going to publish the piece. For me, the distinction between drafting and revising isn't a stable one. I'm always adding and subtracting ideas, moving sections around, rethinking what I've said and not just how I said it. I'm not a perfectionist. Perfectionism is a self-defeating mechanism, like self-censorship. I'm just naturally less precise than I wish I were. Maybe that's why I can't read anything I have in print. I'd want to start it all over again.

Because I'm a drafter and therefore always trying to locate what matters, I have a set of practices I employ to speed up the process a bit. Not that I'm quick. It's all relative, I suppose, but writing to me is like ironing corrugated tin. As I'm revising a draft I look for place-holder text, that is, words I threw down to remind myself to go back and refine the thinking later, when the idea was more clear to me or when I had finished whatever I was afraid of forgetting if I stopped to think that bit through. Some of my place-holder texts are obviously notes to myself, square bracketed phrases like, don't forget to talk about blah blah, or questions I can imagine someone reading against the grain might ask that I can't yet answer. But sometimes my placeholders are masquerading and finished products. Those are the hardest to find. I've all but said it, but I haven't actually said it yet. And then again, sometimes I've said the same thing twice in slightly different ways. When I notice this, I try to zero in on how the two forms are different, why one alone isn't enough and why just putting them together with a simple "and" won't get it. Some days I feel like a three year old who's just learned to tell stories: and, and, and, gasp, and then. . . . Sometimes the variant is actually irrelevant, and I can safely just remove it.

In addition to sentences that need combining and others that need dividing, my early drafts are full of vague modifiers (some, many, these days), vague nouns (thing, it, society, aspect), redundant expressions, clichés and stereotypes, unwarranted assumptions, and grandiose generalizations—thoughts not fully thought out. So when I'm revising I spend a lot of time looking for the vague and the common and the simplistic parts, and then I try to get closer to the point.

Clarity comes from precise diction, and so whenever I notice a word that doesn't seem fully thought through I ask myself, What kind of X is this X?

Do I need an adjective here to zero in on what I'm really talking about, or do I need a different word entirely? If I use the word *experience*, for example, what kind of experience am I talking about? Is it an emotional experience, an intellectual one, a vicarious one? If I use the word *point*, what kind of point is that point?

The original beginning is almost never the rhetorical beginning. This means that I am constantly moving paragraphs and sections around, and, whenever I do that, some paragraph I love suddenly becomes inconvenient at best and more often than not actually irrelevant. I have this problem with sentences, too.

The hardest part about revising is having the courage to delete a large section and start over. You feel like you've just gone backward. This hurts. Someone (*Was it William Faulkner?*) once referred to it as "killing your little darlings." Someone else once referred to excision as "knifing babies," an image so vividly violent that I've forgotten who said it. To cope with the misery excision brings, some *rhetors keep a second-thought file,* an electronic space filled with things you think you might want to say some time, but which don't fit the current occasion. I used to do that. But I never went back into the file, so eventually I stopped keeping one. Well, I do have twenty-three drafts of this document so far, so I guess I do still keep a second-thought file in that sense.

The most important thing (*"thing"? Vague word choice. Revise.*) to remember about writing is that your first draft will almost always be crap, a gross mixture of undifferentiated ideas, clichés, stereotypes, unwarranted assumptions, unintentional metaphors, and just downright meaningless drivel. That's just fine as long as you don't turn it in. Keep at it. Go back to the top, and revise each sentence for clarity and brevity. Question the assumptions. Locate the clichés, and think about why you used each one. Is there a less mundane maybe more insightful way to say it? Locate the subject of each sentence and ask, what kind of X is this X? Question your definitions. Look for words that can have multiple meanings, and make sure you and your readers know which meaning you are using. Ponder the connotation of words.

Keep in mind that, when you start to revise, a draft may get worse before it starts getting better. Writing, getting lost in the flow of your words, can be fun, even exhilarating. Revising, on the other hand, is hard labor on hot day. Unfortunately, most of the time it will take three or four drafts just to get a draft worth sharing. And then burdened with that feedback you're going to have to revise or maybe even rewrite it again to make it ready for a wider audience. If you want a simple *yes* from your audience, you're going to have to work hard to get it. The harder you work, the less work your audience will have to do, and therefore the more likely they are to approve what you've done. If you didn't have to work hard to get it, you need a more rigorous teacher.

Before you turn in an assignment

Reflect on what you have written as well as the process you used to write it. When you finish a piece, make a note of how long you spent on it, how much pre-planning you did, how many drafts you went through, how much feedback you got along the way, and note what you like about it now and what you would change if you had time to revise some more. Concentrate on the relationship between the process and the product. Don't just focus on the product. Even more importantly, if the piece was graded, don't focus on the grade. Focus on the comments.

Do a pre-mortem. Imagine that you get your finished piece back and you didn't get the grade or the result you wanted. Why would that have happened? If you can figure out why it might, fix the problem before you send it in. If you can't see any reason for it to fail but in the end it does, you need to rethink your process carefully.

Presentations: Putting the show in show and tell

Because I'm trying to convince you to become the most effective *rhetor* you can be, you must have been anticipating a section on giving public presentations. And here it is. But before we go through it, keep in mind that some *rhetors* rarely take the stage. They work behind the scenes, helping clarify positions and determine strategies and generally get the behind-the-scenes work done so whoever is the spokesperson knows what to say. You are also aware, however, that our goal with this book is to give you everything you need to succeed, and so, even if you aren't going to be the public face of your organization, you are going to have to give presentations along the way. In fact, the more successful you are, the more presentations you are likely to have to give. So you need to get the basics down, and you need to practice. You also need to know that most people are frightened by public speaking, and so if you are feeling your palms start to sweat right now you're not alone. You can get over that anxiety by preparing and rehearsing thoroughly. I'll show you how.

For good and ill, whenever anyone gives a presentation these days he or she will invariably consider using slides, PowerPoint or Keynote or Prezi. The reason for this is partially because this software is inexpensive and readily available but also because people think slides add pizzazz and professionalism to a presentation. They don't necessarily.

Not every presentation lends itself to slides. The size of the audience, who they are, who you are, the room, the kind of information, and the purpose of the meeting all play a part in deciding whether or not to use slides. Nevertheless, people often assume that a talk will be accompanied by slides, so whenever you have a talk to prepare one question worth asking is, Can what I'm talking about be usefully visualized? *People can't both read and listen at the same time.* If you put words on the screen and talk over them, people will either ignore you or the slide. If you put words up, shut up and let them read. Or you can say what you have to say and then shut up and put the words on the screen, so by reading them the audience may remember the important points. Better yet, don't use bulleted lists and chunks of texts at all but rather pictures and maybe a word or two. Visualize the information for your audience. They will remember it better, and you can set the mood and the tone more easily. *Use pictures to help your audience remember the key points.* Pictures simplify and therefore render a message more dramatic and more memorable. They do if you get the right pictures, that is.

Slides and the persuasion process

When the time comes to give a presentation using PowerPoint (or Keynote, the Mac alternative, or Prezi, the web-based alternative), don't use creating the slides as a method of invention or as a method of rehearsal. If you do, you will wind up with a slide show that is an outline of your talk, which is useful to you but useless for your audience. *The slides are for your audience not for you.*

First, compose your thoughts:

- What is your message?

- What do you want the audience to take home?

- How do you want them to feel?

- What do you want them to do?

Break the subject down into talking points with a memorable heading for each talking point. You might write the talking points down in an outline form. You might write each point on Post-it notes so you can push them around on the desk in front of you as a way of contemplating the best arrangement and to make sure you're not missing anything important. Some people like to use a whiteboard for this kind of brainstorming. There is also an app called Index Cards that provides a virtual version of the same process. Others prefer storyboarding. Some people write drafts. If you are a drafter like me, bold the key ideas as you realize what they are, so they jump out at you as you redraft.

Regardless of how you invent, once you have your talking points, practice elaborating on each one as if your audience were there in front of you. Once you have the presentation down to the point where you can do it without hesitation, then write the handout. Writing the handout will help you both condense the ideas and provide the details you want your audience to walk away with. If possible, a handout should be no more than one page, double sided. It should have your name, your contact information, the title of the talk, the place, and the event. If someone were to find your handout at the bottom of a drawer a year later, he or she should be able to figure out what they are looking at. Once the handout is done, create the slides. The slides come last in the presentation process because they provide a bird's-eye view of your subject, and to achieve that perspective you need to thoroughly know what you are talking about.

Distill the message to its essence, and put only the essence on the slides. When it comes to visualization, typically you want to *use graphs rather than tables* because you're trying to give the audience the big picture, the trends, and the relationships rather than the details. Whenever possible,

Beware of the competition

use images instead of words or in addition to words to help people remember the key points. Google image search can be very useful for finding photographic representations of ideas. Creative Commons is a great source as well because you can be sure that you have permission to use those images, which is not always the case with Google. If you are serious about a presentation, you might want to invest a few dollars in the permissions-granted images you can find at a place like iStockphoto.com. You might also want to take a course in photography or just practice using your phone to take pictures that represent ideas (in addition to the pics of your friends wearing funny hats that you always take anyway). If you go anywhere interesting, take a few iconic photos of the place. You never know when you might find a use for them.

If you do use words, use only one or two on a slide, and make the image dominate the screen.

Do not use cheesy clip art or common Microsoft PowerPoint themes. Everyone has seen these a hundred times. They are boring and redundant, and you don't want an audience associating those adjectives with you. Think of your slides as a set of exclamation points or as visually memorable distillations of

Pets for hard times

the content. Your slides are not the presentation. *Slides are the sauce, not the meat.*

Practice (rehearsal)

You should be able to manipulate the slides without looking at them. Most people find this difficult, and it requires a lot of practice. One effective approach is to have just one slide per talking point: make your point; change the slide. Another way to practice is to use the Slide Sorter function (in the View menu). This will set out the slides side by side, which will show you the flow of the talking points. You can also use this view as a way to refine your arrangement. This view functions kind of like a storyboard. If you are doing this, you should have finished the content already.

Some people use a key word as an internal cue to switch from slide to slide. Some people can visualize each slide without looking at them, and so they just know when it's time to move to the next. Others print an outline (something PowerPoint makes easy) and glance at it to keep them on track. If you have a laptop or a tablet as well as a screen, you can use it like a teleprompter or just mirror the slides on both and then, as you look out at your audience, you can see which image is showing by looking down for a second. *Never turn your back to your audience.*

PowerPoint has a Rehearse Timings feature. You click through the slides as you rehearse, and Microsoft tells you how long you were on each slide. That way you can judge how long to stay on each one. If you want a really spectacular performance, you can have the slides change automatically based on the time stamp, so you can forget about the slide show entirely and just speak at the same rate and for the same length as the machine expects you to. This is by far the best way to go because you are engaging with your audience directly and not being distracted by the slides. Can you imagine a newscaster looking down and clicking a button to transition from one story to the next? Not very professional. You don't want that. If using slides in whatever manner will distract you from your audience, don't use slides.

Be prepared

Nothing fails like technology. The room won't have a projector; the power cord won't be long enough; your laptop won't be compatible with the projector; you'll leave your jump drive in your hotel room. Don't depend on the visuals. Be ready to speak without them. Have a paper backup if people really need to see what you are talking about.

Remember that PowerPoint presentations usually consist of multiple files and that to get one to work properly the computer has to find all the files, which means that you can't just select Save As from the File menu, save the slides to a jump drive, and expect it to work on another computer. You have to select Publish then Package for CD and save the collection of files to a folder. (You don't have to burn the folder to a CD; you can use a flash drive.) Also, not all computers have PowerPoint, of course, so you may need to save the files in a compatibility mode. Know what technology you will have in the room where you are giving the presentation. If possible, bring your own. And always, *always* be prepared to present without your slides.

Anxiety—stage fright

There's an old story among public speaking teachers that says nine out of ten eulogists would happily trade places with the corpse. I don't know about the percentage, but the sentiment is accurate. Most people fear public speaking more than anything in life. This is partially because we overestimate how much anyone is paying attention to us. Think about the last lecture you attended. What percentage of the time was your mind wandering? Do you remember what your economics prof was wearing yesterday? Most members of your audience are either worrying about their own presentation or daydreaming. They want you to succeed. You are all in it together.

Have you ever seen anyone really melt down? In twenty-five years of teaching I've only experienced it once. There were about a hundred people in the audience, sitting in an amphitheater-like lecture hall. I said the first sentence all right, but my voice sounded kind of thin, and then all of a sudden my heart started racing, and I couldn't catch my breath. I know all the tricks (see the next section), and I went through all of them, and I still couldn't catch my breath. I talked the twenty minutes I was supposed to and sat down, sweating into my black shirt, my hands shaking. When the Q&A was over, someone came up to me and said the talk was the best paper they had heard at the conference, and they asked if they could publish it. Later I confided to a friend in the audience what I had had to endure, and he said, "Really? I didn't notice."

That was years ago, and it hasn't happened to me since. A couple of times I thought I was going to melt down again, but I remembered that time, and I calmed down. One of life's greatest achievements is to have survived a failure. You learn more from a failure than you can from any success.

The only way to deal with stage fright is to feel the fear and get on with it. You need to seek out opportunities to speak in public. And whenever you get one, rehearse at length beforehand. Even when you don't have an opportunity at hand, imagine giving a speech. Walk through the process; imagine the context. See yourself standing in front of an audience and moving them at will.

Strategies for dealing with stage fright

Take a few deep, centering breaths. This works in any anxiety-producing setting. Breathe in with your diaphragm slowly and consciously for six seconds, then hold your breath for two seconds, and exhale for eight. Don't think; just breathe.

Take a *power stance*, legs spread shoulder width, hands as fists resting on your hips. This stance is called *akimbo*. I know it sounds hokey. Try it. Stand akimbo right now, and feel how it makes you feel. You might want to do that *before* you go on—and then stand in a more relaxed manner when you are actually in front of people. Akimbo is an aggressive stance, and people might not warm to you if you come on that way.

Keep your hands just slightly above waist level, palms up and hands slightly apart or fingers interlaced. Try to move them naturally, but don't let them fly around or get tangled in your hair or start plucking at your chin or rubbing your neck or touching your nose or tapping your clavicle or pulling on your shirt. These are all gestures of distress, and they will tend to make your audience uncomfortable, just as they will make you even more uncomfortable. If worse comes to worst, hold onto the podium. Stuffing your hands in your pockets will make you look too casual.

Wear dark clothes if you're inclined to perspire—and don't wear anything brand new. It might not fit quite right, or there might be something wrong with it you didn't notice in the store. Don't get really dressed up unless you're participating in a formal occasion (usually after seven o'clock p.m.). Wear whatever people wear to work in your profession or intended profession. You need to be comfortable and confident. One exception: If you're giving a presentation for your class in college, you might want to dress it up a little bit. Flip-flops are for the beach. People (profs) feel slightly insulted by an overly casual appearance because they infer from that an overly casual attitude. Look like you care, and others may care about you.

Remember previous successes. If that doesn't inspire confidence, visualize your favorite place. Really go there in your mind. What is the quality of the light? What can you smell?

Step away from the right here and the right now. Listen for the traffic in the street, the sound of rain on the window, the air conditioner, a distant train, anything outside and beyond yourself. Whatever this is, it's temporary.

No one's listening to you. They are thinking about themselves. Okay, maybe I overstated that. You put all that work into this presentation, and you got dressed up a bit, and no one's listening? Well, there's something called the spotlight effect that's probably worth remembering if you find yourself getting really nervous. Have you ever spilled something on yourself and thought, Great, everyone's going to notice that. They're going to be staring at me all day and judging me for a klutz. Not really. We think everyone's looking at us, but they aren't typically. Even when you are standing up in front of people most of them aren't all that focused on you. Most of the time most people are focused on themselves. They are wondering how they look, how they'll sound when their turn comes. Or they're thinking about the test they have to write next week or whether or not they turned off the coffee pot. They will tune in and tune out. And when they are tuned it, they are rooting for you to do well.

Your Turn

PowerPoint is a cool piece of software, easy to use, totally absorbing, and a complete time-suck. *Don't let it distract you* when you have to prepare a presentation. Play with it in advance. Instead of watching yet another *Law and Order* rerun, fire up the computer, and mess around. Find some cool themes and background images. Create a template or two. (Don't rely on the default themes; everyone's seen them so much they are sick of them.) Make up a presentation about whatever, and just practice. Seriously. If you become proficient in advance of the need for that proficiency, when it comes time to do it for real you will have more time to concentrate on the speech itself. *Your slides are not your presentation.* They are merely visual aids for your audience.

You need to see some great presentations to see how to do it well. Go to TED.com, and look for a topic you find interesting, and watch the video. Watch how the people move and what they do with their hands and how they use the screen behind them. Most of these presentations are very polished, and they are all by people with something important to say, which helps, but they are not all equally great. Use your judgment. Consider what you think works and doesn't work, and then try to emulate the best things you see. If you find one you like, whether for content or form or both, share it with others in your class or with your friends.[31]

---

31. If you're tired of hearing people tell you to check out TED, you are not alone.

chapter 4
EVIDENCE-CENTERED FORMS
OF PERSUASION

Academic Argumentation

We have reached the penultimate chapter. To this point you have learned how to think critically, organize ideas effectively, develop useful intellectual habits, and practice the art of being persuasive. You have the foundational moves and a game plan. From this point on we are going to look more closely at the academic essay and some closely aligned argumentative forms. I'm thinking here in particular of cross-examination. You will certainly run into academic argumentation and negotiation. You may come across a few Machiavellians as well.

Academic argumentation takes place when assertions are presented with supporting evidence to an audience who will agree or disagree but won't vote or otherwise make a binding decision. If the only decision is who presented the better argument, then you have an instance of debate, which is different from academic argumentation in that in the former each participant is trying to win, while in the later there is a common enterprise; everyone is trying to get it right (although there is no shortage of ego in academic argumentation, and not all academics are above competition). Nearly every essay you have to write in college will be an argumentative essay.

The hallmark of academic argumentation is awareness of opposing points of view. Often we encounter discourses where the speaker or writer boldly asserts that his or her words are the truth and all others are lies or stupidities. These kinds of fake arguments often contain loaded language and ill-considered assumptions and are addressed to people who are incorrectly assumed to agree. They are the kind of ranting you are likely to hear on talk radio or read in the editorial pages of lesser newspapers, the kind of thing you will find also on many websites and weblogs. As you may remember from the discussion of Anne Coulter's piece on single mothers, this argumentative stance is sometimes called preaching to the choir. While a writer might preach to the choir because the audience is completely docile or because they completely share the speaker's beliefs, writers sometimes preach to the choir inadvertently, when the writer is oblivious or indifferent to the objections of an audience.

When you write academic arguments, you need to *assume a skeptical (not hostile) audience,* and thus you don't make an assertion without offering some kind of evidence to support it. The better the evidence, the better the argument.

Key point: After you write a sentence, ask yourself, Why do I believe this? Then ask yourself, Why should someone else believe this? What might keep them from agreeing with it? The answers may be very different. And the differences may be rhetorically instructive.

The blueprint for academic arguments

No matter how long they are, typically, academic arguments consist of at least two parts, *assertion* and *proof.*

> argument = assertion + proof
> (proof = evidence + support for evidence)

Assertion

An assertion is a simple (as opposed to compound) declarative sentence: X is Y. There are several kinds of assertions:

proposition: assertion offered for debate (Toulmin called them claims)

premise: assertion offered as already accepted, a given, may or may not be an actual fact

assumption: unstated premise (may be problematic)

fact: assertion accepted as true

opinion: assertion made without concern for agreement

contention: false assertion presented as true without evidence

metaphor: assertion that something is something it literally isn't

Basically, if a sentence ends with a period it is an assertion.

Any assertion that an audience doesn't require proof for is accepted (by that audience) as a fact.

All other assertions require proof to obtain the status of a fact for that audience.

Some sentences are so widely accepted as facts that one never needs to back them up with evidence and if one encounters resistance, usually instruction rather than evidence is required. Keep in mind, however, that *The world is the center of the universe* was once a universal fact. Now, of course, it's just a mistaken belief.

Proof

Proof = evidence + support for the validity, accuracy, and relevance of evidence. We are essentially reviewing Toulmin's model here but in an even more highly elaborated way because our goal here isn't to illustrate a model but to use the model and the scaffold for an argumentative paper. You aren't really experiencing déjà vu.

There are several kinds of evidence relevant to academic essays, and each kind of evidence has a kind of stasis theory accompanying it.

Evidence

Facts

- Is it really a fact?

- Is it always true?

- Are there exceptions?

- Could someone in the audience dispute the assertion or be inclined to object to my presenting the assertion I want to present as a fact is, in fact, a fact?

Observations—data

- Is it reproducible or otherwise verifiable (fact-check, cross-check)?

- Is it relevant?

- Is it valid?

- Is there an adequately sized, representative sample that is not cherry picked?

- Is it context independent? (Sometimes data proves something in one context that can't be transferred to another.)

Testimony—experts (authorities), witnesses

- Is the authority reliable on this subject?

- Was the witness actually there, in the right place (and fully conscious)?

- Is the testimony credible on its own?

- Is the witness properly motivated, intelligent, and knowledgeable. Is he or she truly an authority on the subject?

- Can the audience reproduce the same experience for themselves or readily imagine it?

Examples—historical, personal, imaginary
- Did the event or could it actually happen?

- Was it unique or context dependent?

- Is it relevant?

- Is it the best possible form of evidence under the circumstances?

Narratives—historical, personal, fictional
- Details, references to common experiences, events, feelings

- Deductions: inference from an assertion

- Are the conclusions formed from legitimate premises? Example: A = B, B = C, so A = C.

Definitions
- Some arguments rest on agreement on the definitions of the words involved. (Some are started by disagreement, usually unnoticed.)

- Rebuttals: refutation of counterarguments. It is important that when you represent other people's opinions you do it as they would, fairly, in other words, using expressions that show you take the opposition seriously and that you don't dislike them just because you disagree with them. The overt appearance of reasonableness is critical for academic discourse.

- Answers to possible questions

- Responses to possible objections

- Concessions when necessary or expedient

Conclusions
Ideally you want the audience (or reader) to supply the conclusion. But almost always you have to say it yourself. When you do say it, make sure that you do so with the amount of force (a.k.a. modality) that the evidence warrants. Don't say something like, "And therefore only an idiot would disagree" when in fact someone might disagree and be offended by being called an idiot.

Modality

Modality is the level of expected commitment to the argument. Below is a list of the most common levels of commitment, from strong to weak.

- necessarily

- definitely

- probably

- possibly

- maybe

- sometimes

- hope so

- ha—yeah right!

The shortest possible argument is a debatable assertion followed by a fact that proves the assertion true. For example, "We need to stop for gasoline in the next few miles; the indicator light just went on." In the rhetorical tradition this form of argument is called an enthymeme.

Arguments that can be laid to rest with a single enthymeme are rare. Most arguments require a series of assertions and proofs. In fact, even this example could elicit further questions. Is the light working? How many gallons remain when it comes on, assuming it's working? How many miles to the gallon? What does "next few" mean? Why didn't you fill the tank before we left?

How much proof do you need?

The amount of proof required varies a great deal depending on the audience's level of skepticism and their commitment to beliefs that oppose the one you are presenting. If they are indifferent to the topic or have no investment in conflicting viewpoints, then you might not need a great deal of evidence. On the other hand, if they perceive what you are proposing or defending as somehow conflicting with their prior beliefs, goals, or plans, then they may require a great deal more evidence. Given sufficient prior commitment to a conflicting belief, no amount of evidence will change some people's minds. In fact, for the most dogmatic among us, all facts to the contrary are assimilated into the preferred viewpoint or dismissed as untrustworthy. There are people who doubt that NASA ever landed a man on the moon. There are people who think the Holocaust never happened either.

Often the timing of the presentation of the evidence can determine how much evidence is needed. If you are dealing with a hot subject, something that people are eager for a decision about, then you may be able to present just preliminary evidence. If the subject is well worked over, you will likely need a great deal more evidence to capture anyone's attention. And if people are tired of a subject, it may be impossible to interest them no matter how much or even how convincing your evidence is.

Who is presenting the evidence can also influence the quantity and quality of the evidence required. Someone with a long-standing track record of great accomplishments can get away with really mediocre work. The cognitive bias known as the *halo effect* distracts people from really scrutinizing what's being offered this time around. But the opposite, of course, is also true. If you have presented a series of blunders in the past, you will need to overcome negative expectations and so need both really good evidence and a careful presentation of it. When it comes to writing papers in college, you want your first impression to be a really good impression. Your reputation for being thorough and on time will help out if life throws you a curve before you graduate.

Common argumentative errors

When it comes to argumentation, there are a number of errors that people often make, either because they don't really know what they are doing or because their evidence isn't really up to the task of fully supporting their assertions. You want to seek out and eliminate these errors in your own arguments and be wary of them in what you read.

1. Providing arguments for unprovable assertions (review "*Asystasis—non-issues*" in Chapter 3)

2. Forgetting to support the proof of an assertion (supporting an assertion with another assertion that looks like a form of proof but actually needs a proof of its own)
    "There must be life on Mars because there are riverbeds on Mars." [*Are we sure those are riverbeds? Even if there was water in them once, what now?*]

    Anyone who has driven an American car knows why the industry should be allowed to die. [*Anyone? Any American car? Ever? What proof can you offer to support corporate Darwinism?*]

    George Bush left office with the lowest approval rating of any president; therefore he was the worst president. [*How was the approval rating determined and by whom? Does public opinion determine value? What about presidents before public opinion polls? What about future presidents?*]

    Here, you'll like this; it's good for you. Breakfast cereals and other "healthy" products tend to offer arguments not much more highly evolved than this.

3. Using unfair or misleading or loaded language
    Calling the accused a "felon"

    Calling an economic policy "corporate Darwinism"

Calling a fee a "tax" (*Really? How can you tell the difference?*)

Saying of someone accused of a heinous crime that he is in serious trouble. (He isn't in trouble no matter how serious the charge if the evidence is no good.)

4. Making disparaging comments
   That's just dumb.

   As any serious person would agree . . .

   Clearly . . .

5. Offering incomplete evidence
   A recent study shows that . . . [*Just one study is enough?*]

   Scientists say that . . . [*Who are these "scientists," and do they all agree? Were they all on their game when they reached their shared conclusions?*]

6. Offering misleading evidence
   It hasn't happened yet, so why would it happen now?

   You can't prove that ghosts exist; therefore, they do not.

   You can't disprove that ghosts exist; therefore, they do.

7. Ignoring reasonable objections
   An economic downturn is a good time to increase public spending.

8. Presuming analogies
   We bailed out the banks; why not the auto industry?

9. Ignoring important problems
   The Chevy Volt will rescue GM.

10. Ignoring or downplaying significant risks
    You can't win a lottery if you don't buy a ticket.

11. Making inaccurate observations
    Any error in detail can significantly undercut your *ethos*.

12. Overstating the case, overgeneralizing
    Saying "absolutely" when the evidence only supports "probably."

13. Ignoring cultural differences
    Just because someone smiles and nods doesn't mean he agrees or understands.

14. Assuming a specific meaning for a key term that has multiple meanings
    Taking advantage of (or ignoring) someone's situation or emotional state

Putting it together

Basically an argumentative paper is a series of paragraphs, each one containing an assertion and proof to support the assertion. For arguments longer than a memo, you also need an introductory and concluding paragraph. If the paper is relatively short, less than five pages, the introduction and conclusion should be very brief and to the point. It's the argument that really matters, as long as the readers know what you are talking about and why you are talking (writing) to them.

Introduction

Introductions to academic argumentative papers tend to follow a single pattern, although each discipline tends to have its own variations. You announce the topic, review the recent literature in such a way that it's clear why you are writing what you are about to write about, state your claim (hypothesis to be tested, thesis to be proved), and finally forecast how the paper will proceed. Regardless of how you do it, your readers should finish the first paragraph knowing what they are about to read and why they want to read it. The why part, which is sometimes called the so-what part, is often the hardest part to write. We write papers in school because we have to, and profs read them because it's their job. There's rarely more reason than that. Beyond school, there are lots of reasons to write something: to solve a problem, to add to a growing body of knowledge, to resolve a controversy, to stir up interest, to promote yourself or your company or your industry. Keep in mind, however, that the best reason for writing is that you can do something for your intended audience: What's in it for them?

One of the standard pieces of advice about introductions is that you need to capture your reader's attention. This makes the most sense if what you are writing will appear in a context where lots of interests are competing for attention, like in an old-fashioned newspaper. As always, consider the context of reception before selecting a plan of action. If you know the person has to read what you've written, you already have their attention, so don't go after that; just reward them for granting it to you by getting quickly and correctly to the point.

Another common suggestion is to open with a joke. Great if you can do it, but dangerous, and rarely is the risk-to-reward ratio compelling. A related piece of advice is to say something provocative. Make a bold assertion, or say something controversial; peak interest. This might be worthwhile if the topic and occasion warrant it. But again, consider the potential downside. Maybe a direct opening is the better way to go.

Suspense, creating a sense of longing for resolution by walking right up to your main point and then leaving it hanging until later is a bad idea for academic papers. Your goal is to enlighten not entertain.

Don't bury the lead

Introductions are hard to write because you have to know exactly what you are going to say and why you are going to say it to the intended audience as opposed to anyone else. That's a tall order. Just knowing exactly what your evidence says is difficult, primarily because you are so close to it that often it's hard to see the larger picture, the implications, and the consequences. The trees obscure the forest. In *Made to Stick*, the brothers Heath offer a great example of this problem:

> Kenneth L. Peters, the principle of Beverly Hills high school, announced today that the entire high school faculty will travel to Sacramento next Thursday for a colloquium in new teaching methods. Among the speakers will be anthropologist Margaret Mead, college president Dr. Robert Maynard Hutchens, and California Governor Edmund "Pat" Brown. (*Made to Stick*, 75–6)

What should the headline be if this is a Beverly Hills school paper story? Your answer will reflect your understanding of your audience's needs given the context in which they will receive the information. Given this is a school newspaper, who will your primary audience be, and what will be the most important element of this story? Who will be the secondary audience, and what will they care most about? (Here's a hint: both will care about the same thing.)

When writing for an academic audience, the focus should be on the data and the methodology—the data, because that's where knowledge resides and that's what academics care about, and the methodology, because that's what tells the academics what value the data has. Outside academia, what matters most are the consequences of the data, not the data or even how it was generated but what should be done based on the data.

Given what I just said, what would the headline be if the audience were academics? (Hint: data rather than inference.)

Interior paragraphs

Interior paragraphs can, of course, take many different forms. Nevertheless, below is a fairly effective pattern that you can use in a wide range of circumstances.

1.   Begin each interior paragraph with an assertion.

2.   Follow that with evidence.

3.   Back up the evidence with reasons to believe the validity of the evidence.

4.   Deal with possible objections if there may be any.

5.   And then transition to the next paragraph.

If the paper is dealing with a controversial topic (when there are members of the audience who vehemently oppose what you are arguing for), there may be several separate paragraphs that refute specific counterarguments. In cases like these you need to be careful to represent the opposing viewpoints fairly and with insight into why a person would accept what you reject. Representing beliefs you reject in a correct and fair way almost always challenges your own beliefs, and such challenges can be very threatening. This is one of the reasons people construct straw dogs, counterarguments that are so weak that no one would agree with them. You don't want to construct a fake opposition. The purpose of argumentation is to test the validity of assertions, and if you shrink from the task you will weaken the value of your own opinions. Argumentation, like dialectic, takes courage and rewards risk.

The last paragraph of a typical argumentative paper is a conclusion that restates the main point, summarizes the key arguments (and briefly restates the primary evidence), and finally motivates the reader to take action.

Conclusion

If the paper is short (less than five pages), the conclusion should be a brief paragraph. Longer papers may require more summary, and, if the topic is very abstract or the audience can't clearly see the importance of the topic, you may need to spend more words on motivation. For an academic paper, concentrate on further avenues of research while talking briefly about the strengths and limitations of the research presented in the paper.

Plagiarism

Plagiarism is passing off someone else's work as your own, which means cutting and pasting or otherwise reproducing another's work and not indicating that you have. It's an ethical infraction that can get you thrown out of college or fired from your job. More importantly, plagiarism is intellectually lazy, like wimping out on a workout or slacking off at work. You weaken your mind, and over time you fall behind. You don't have the intellectual stamina or capacity to keep up with your peers. The future seems far off, and all you need right now is to graduate. But there are tens of thousands of people with university degrees graduating every year. No one is impressed by the piece of paper. It's the capacity for intellectual labor that paper is supposed to signify that people are looking for, and if you make a habit of cheating and passing off other people's work as your own people will see you for the fraud you are, and you won't get a job, or they won't notice right away, and you will spend a few miserable months cowering in a cubicle until someone does notice you can't do the work and fires you on the spot.

That said, plagiarism hasn't always been a clear-cut infraction of intellectual labor laws. By way of example I'd like to cite at length the Bishop of Hippo, St. Augustine:

> There are, indeed, some men who have a good delivery, but cannot compose anything to deliver. Now, if such men take what has been written with wisdom and eloquence by others, and commit it to memory, and deliver it to the people, they cannot be blamed, supposing them to do it without deception. For in this way many become preachers of the truth (which is certainly desirable), and yet not many teachers; for all deliver the discourse which one real teacher has composed, and there are no divisions among them. Nor are such men to be alarmed by the words of Jeremiah the prophet, through whom God denounces those who steal His words every one from his neighbor. For those who steal take what does not belong to them, but the word of God belongs to all who obey it; and it is the man who speaks well, but lives badly, who really takes the words that belong to another. For the good things he says seem to be the result of his own thought, and yet they have nothing in common with his manner of life. (29.62)

If it weren't for the caveat "without deception" everything in this quotation would seem to completely contradict modern copyright law, which makes sense considering when it was written and by whom and why. If words descend from God, the concept of intellectual property is empty, hubristic really. The rhetoric of ownership is an interesting topic to ponder. For all it may seem outlandish now, Augustine's position was more or less maintained by writers and thinkers for many years after his death.

When books were rare and incredibly expensive, people who made a living with words didn't just read casually; they poured over the few books they could find and committed passages to memory. They would also copy out whole sections and keep compendiums of useful expressions organized by topics. These books were known as commonplace books, and *rhetors* of every generation have kept them. Especially good collections were sometimes printed and sold, thus allowing the compiler to profit from others' thoughts. The practice of keeping a commonplace book had the effect of filling the *rhetor*'s mind with the ideas of others, and because there were so few books many people were acquainted with those same ideas; an important part of being an effective speaker became weaving those notable passages into your own writing and speeches but doing so in a way that, while the innocent of learning might think you a brilliant inventor of ideas, the learned members of your audience would hear an echo of a famous common ancestor and see what you were doing as an homage to tradition, not a form of theft.

The problem when you are just starting out is that it takes a great deal of talent to pull off this kind of oblique reference, a nod in the direction of a past master if done poorly winds up just being a cheap copy, unoriginal, thoughtless. Good artists copy; great artists steal, as Picasso is said to have said.

That last sentence was an object lesson. If I hadn't mentioned Picasso you might have thought I said it first, whereas in fact hundreds of people have echoed it since the first time it was said. So before you quote someone, make sure you've got the attribution right. But my Picasso example is an object lesson beyond "Know who you are stealing from." It turns out that not only did Picasso not say that famous phrase, but even the person who did didn't either. The phrase comes from an essay by T. S. Eliot, apparently, and the original is a bit subtler than the paraphrase that is misattributed:

> One of the surest tests [of the superiority or inferiority of a poet] is the way in which a poet borrows. Immature poets imitate; mature poets steal; bad poets deface what they take, and good poets make it into something better, or at least something differ-ent. The good poet welds his theft into a whole of feeling, which is unique, utterly different than that from which it is torn; the bad poet throws it into something which has no cohesion. A good poet will usually borrow from authors remote in time, or alien in language, or diverse in interest. (Eliot 1.6)

The point here is that all work, great and menial, derives from previous work, and the artistry and the impact come not from originality of thought but from originality of expression and from providing the previously thought to people who haven't yet thought about it in that way. *Persuasive power comes from connecting the preexisting dots in novel and interestingly useful ways.* For the most part, the dots already exist. You have to connect them in new ways or connect to dots people hadn't noticed yet. You don't have to make it all up yourself, but at the same time you can't just pass off others' work as your own or even just string together properly attributed quotations. You have to own your predecessors' work. You have to fit your perspective into the kaleidoscope of perspectives that make up reality.

The importance of the reappropriation of previous work has become an important part of current creativity. Mashups, sampling, and tributes are all forms of intellectual borrowing that, as long as the original work is identi-fied in some way, are not considered unethical uses. But you have to be care-ful here, especially as regards just image leaching and idea poaching. Some bloggers, for example, don't write their own material so much as report on what others have written and link to it, making an echo at best. This kind of intellectual effort can be useful for your own learning, but if you pass yourself off as a *rhetor* and yet only report others' work you won't have accomplished much, and you won't be any closer to doing so a year from now than you are now. Put in the time. Sample only if you've really got an ironic insight worth sharing. Leach only to make a more important point or to leave a trail for yourself to get back and do a better job in the near future.

Imitation is an often-neglected element of learning, and fears of intellectual property theft tend to alienate learners from the real task of learning, which is to fake it until you can make it on your own. At the same time, this fact of learning certainly *does not give us license to pass off other people's work as our own.* It only serves to remind us that work is always a shared experience, even when done in the solitude of one's own mind constrained by the limitations of one's own words. First we trace. Then we copy. Then we freehand from memory, and then and only then do we face the blank page alone, and even then we aren't really alone.

So, plagiarism is both a simple law—don't pass off other people's work as your own—and a complexly dynamic issue. Digital files can be endlessly replicated, and as a result intellectual property is a constant legal battle. Ultimately, if you have to chose, you'd rather sue than be sued.[1]

Cross-examination

Interrogation

Probably the most alienating thing you will find in the rhetorical tradition are the topics to employ when arguing for or against the admittance of evidence from slaves under torture (Aristotle, *On Rhetoric*, 1.15). It seems that the Greeks thought that if you needed the testimony of a slave you had best torture him or her, as they would only speak reliably under extreme duress— bizarre by modern standards, any relatively recent talk of enemy combatants notwithstanding. At any rate, while most of us will rarely be forced to force someone else to speak, we may occasionally suspect someone isn't really telling us the truth, and so knowing something of how interrogation and deception work might prove rhetorically useful.

Body language and deception—tells

There's a lot of folklore about lie detection. You've heard it. (And you read about it in the section on delivery.) If people don't look you in the eye, they are lying. If they touch their nose or pull at their collar they are uncomfortable and therefore lying. If they have an exaggerated reaction or suddenly

---

1. See *Writing with Sources*, by Gordon Harvey (Hackett Publishing Co., 2008), for more detail on what constitutes plagiarism, how to avoid it, and how to properly cite sources.

stop moving (freeze) you know you've caught them in a lie. And so on. Most people who research deception and detection are quick to point out that without a baseline understanding of a person's normal behavior it is impossible to interpret any behavior as proving a specific mental state, whether lying or anything else. Some people are just sweaty and shifty eyed. Some people can look you straight in the eye and lie like a rug (cliché). To make matters even less clear, the so-called *tells* of deception are so widely known that people who have to get by in the world by lying learn how to do the opposite and thus throw the rhetorically naive off the scent. Even lie detection machines, which monitor pulse and perspiration and blood pressure and heart rate, can only indicate agitation, from which one might *infer* but in no way truly detect deception. That is why their "evidence" is inadmissible in court. They are typically used as leverage on a suspect, or as a way to frighten employees into compliance.

Two approaches: Ingratiation and intimidation

Unless you are a detective, your best bet for getting at the truth is to be disarmingly friendly and non-threatening, the kind of person there's no reason to lie to because you have nothing to hide and nothing to give and no power to assert: just another one of the lads or gals or, if you are much older than the other person, a sweet old lady or a harmless old man.

If you do have some authority, if you aren't just another one of the lads or gals, then you are still probably better off using the soft touch, also known as *ingratiation*.

All ingratiating rhetorical techniques attempt to build identification with other people, to make them feel that you are just like them. Meet them on their turf. Show respect, even deference. Your goal is to make them see you as friendly and maybe even a bit dull witted or off the scent. If they are agitated, seem concerned for them, and do what you can to soothe them, empathize, sympathize. Conspire, normalize, create hope, offer rewards for participation, and veil your threats. Make the person trust you and see you as a friend who will help them get out of trouble or minimize the damage if getting out is impossible.

If the soft touch doesn't work, and there is something really important at stake, and you have the authority to truly interrogate people, then set up a more intense interview. Make them come to you. Control the scene, the time of day, the environment, the light, the furniture, everything. They need to see that you are in absolute control. Make them wait; keep them isolated, uncertain. When they come in, have them sit in a chair that is lower than yours, or have them sit while you stand over them. Don't let them see where your questions are going or where you are coming from. You don't necessarily have to appear menacing but all business for sure and in complete control of the situation. You want them to think you know everything already. And change it up. If you start out hard, soften a bit if they give you a piece of what you want; harden if they resist. Frighten the interviewees, catastrophize the situation, destabilize and confuse them. Make them uncomfortable, uncertain. Make requests seem like demands, opportunities like threats; encourage helplessness, panic. Just as you would mirror during an ingratiating interview, do the opposite now. If they get angry, get cold. If they seem indifferent, escalate the intensity in your voice. Your goal is to seem more frightening than the punishment that awaits them if they confess.

Keep in mind, however, that in nearly all organizations there are people specifically employed to interrogate others, and if it's not your job you ought to make sure someone else does it. If you need to question someone closely, and you have the right to do it, then consider the tactics outlined above, but be ready to deal with the consequences as well.

You also need to ask yourself, are you really this kind of person who can pull the "bad cop" off? I know I can take the ingratiation approach—I'm good at disarming and friendly—but I could never intentionally intimidate any-one, and I'm six feet tall and, well, let's say "heavy set." I have a deep voice, too, but I can't do menacing. I'm so not a scary person that I couldn't even pretend to be one, so I would never use those tactics. Plato got that right for sure: know yourself.

Examination versus cross-examination

When examining a witness, as opposed to cross-examining a witness, one asks simple, specific questions that will elicit detailed answers so that the witness can tell the full story of exactly what happened. One leads the witness to the truth but in a way that seems un-pre-meditated. And then what happened? And then what did you do? You want to appear interested, as if you are hearing this for the first time, and you use your questions to get the person to highlight the evidence most use-ful to your case. They are, after all, testifying to the advantage of your case. You might even ask a question that comes close to something prob-lematic with the story, so you can do a little pseudo-cross-examination in advance, to forestall perhaps a real cross-examination. If they use a vague word, get them to specify. If they say something hard to believe, ask them to explain how they know it is true (assuming of course you know they can). If there are credibility issues in general, bring them up, and deal with them directly unless you have good reasons to believe your adversary won't bring them up (because they will somehow be more damaging to the opposition, not because you think the person doesn't know about them. Never assume they don't know.), in which case con-sider ignoring them completely. You can't ask the witness to speculate or interpret or describe things they couldn't possibly have seen.

When you cross-examine, on the other hand, the testimony that was just given has damaged your case, otherwise you wouldn't cross, and so you have to ask questions that will undermine the truth of what the witness has just said. Because the witness knows you want to discredit their testimony and thus prove them either mistaken or a liar, they will be wary and inclined, as Socrates' "partners" were, to evade your questions. So the primary strategy of cross-examination is subterfuge.

The first technique is to disarm the respondent by being friendly, non-threatening, and reassuring. Deny that you are adversaries. Insist that you are friends, or at least emphasize that it's the truth not victory that is at stake. Then, begin asking the questions. The questions should be phrased in such a way that *yes* or *no* are the only possible answers, and the implications of each aren't obvious to the witness. The goal is to control the witnesses' testimony, so they can't say anything you don't want the judge and jury to hear and so that they can't figure out how best to hide the truth, if indeed they want to.

If you were to ask them directly, "Were you at the scene of the crime?" they could instinctively deny being there. If you were to ask, "Where were you at 12:30, January 2, 2009?" they might put themselves in the neighborhood without thinking about it. In cross-examination, or whenever you are questioning someone who might lie or say something untrue (not all untruths are lies exactly; sometimes a person will say something because they think that's the right thing to say, or because they think that's what they saw), the question isn't as important as the implication of the question. So, when trying to "death qualify" a jury, a prosecutor might ask if a prospective juror is in favor of gun control because there's a statistical correlation, apparently, between being for gun control and against capital punishment (Lieberman, 38). Another approach is to ask an abstract question that correlates to a concrete one: "Under any circumstances would it ever be ok to take advantage of one's spouse?" is a way of getting at whether or not a married person is happily married because people would answer a question like that from personal experience. A happily married person would almost certainly say, "No, of course not." But a less than happily married person might have thought about lying or hiding something from their spouse and so might be much less emphatic (37).

There's a famous example of this kind of trickery where the prosecutor said to the person receiving disability insurance for a shoulder injury, "How high can you raise your arm now?" And after the witness raised it to shoulder level, the prosecutor asked, "And how high could you raise it before the accident?" and the fool raised it over his head (Wellman 48). The witness was so worried about saying the wrong thing that he focused on the answer instead of listening carefully enough to the question to recognize the implication.

Another way to hide the point is to ask questions that seem to be going in one direction and then change course. One has to be careful here, however, as one isn't allowed to ask questions at random, and the judge will intervene if she can't see the relevance of the questions. It's ok if the witness can't. Wellman advises another form of misdirection: "Ask [the question] as if you wanted a certain answer, when in reality you desire just the opposite. 'Hold your own temper while you lead the witness to lose his' is a Golden Rule on all such occasions" (61).

One might hide the implication of a question not to uncover a lie but to dramatically reveal a mistake. One technique for accomplishing this is to play on people's general desire to say the socially acceptable thing. Most people don't want to appear rude or uneducated or biased. Making use of this, Leonard E. Davies offers the following example:

> After some preliminary questions that give me a sense of rapport
> with the jury panel I ask the following question:
> "Mr. Winston do you have an opinion as to the guilt or inno-
> cence of the defendant as he sits here at this moment?"
> Not wishing to show any bias and believing he should be open
> minded the jurors' response is always "no." The same question is
> then put to others with the same response.
> [Mr. Davies then talks for a paragraph about the concept of
> presumption of innocence] . . . Having hammered home the con-
> cept of presumption of innocence *adopt a sense of appearing to
> come to a conclusion myself* [emphasis added] and return to Mr.
> Winston with the following.
> Mr. Winston I know you've been listening to this very carefully
> and I feel that having heard all this you may realize now that your
> earlier answer with respect to having an opinion as the defen-
> dant's guilt or innocence may be different now. (62)

A revelation is more powerful than an assertion (show, don't tell). Mr. Davies might simply have asserted, "A person is innocent until proven guilty, is that not so Mr. Winston?" and Mr. Winston would have agreed, but he would not, perhaps, have seen the implication that the court is supposed to be biased in favor of the defendant and that in this case being biased is a good thing. The destination is the same, but the journey creates a completely different experience, and now "presumption of innocence" is dramatically affirmed for the jury, which should serve the defense counsel well. The juror might even feel a little guilty himself.

It seems generally agreed that how one performs a cross-examination should be determined in part by what kind of witness one is crossing. Are you trying to catch a liar? Are they an honest person who has made a mistake? Are they an expert? And under each of these main headings there may be subheads as well. Despite this general awareness that techniques should suit the nature of the witness, there are some widely offered general guidelines, and among them the most common are Irving Younger's 10 Commandments, as quoted from Michael Tigar's *Examining Witnesses*.

Irving Younger's 10 Commandments

Among law professors, Irving Younger is remembered as an outstanding advocate, judge, and teacher. His books on courtroom practices are widely read and admired. He is perhaps best remembered for his 10 commandments of cross-examination. The commandments are as follows.

1. Be brief.

2. Short questions, plain words.

3. Ask only leading questions.

4. Never ask a question to which you do not already know the answer.

5. Listen to the answer.

6. Do not quarrel with the witness.

7. Do not permit the witness to explain.

8. Do not ask the witness to repeat the testimony he gave.

9. Avoid one question too many.

10. Save the explanation for the summation. (Tigar 203)

The first two commandments remind me of Plato's insistence to ask only simple questions, that is, questions with a single predicate. The idea is that the respondent should be able to answer with a simple *yes* or *no*. But if one is advised also to be brief, assuming that means not just asking short questions but not asking hundreds of them, how does one keep the first commandment from breaking the second? According to Tigar, "You can ask compound questions to move things along, but when you get a 'no,' consider dividing the inquiry" (258).

Item number three, "Ask only leading questions," advises the cross-examiner to embed the answer in the question. This is the opposite of advice given to people designing questionnaires or other kinds of human-subject research tools. This makes sense because leading questions help you control the respondents, which you want to do if they are a witness but don't want to do if they are a research subject providing data. Small differences in phrasing can make a big difference in the results of the testimony. Consider the difference between *What did the defendant say?* and *What did you hear the defendant say?* The former actually leaves open the possibility that the witness will testify to hearsay. The second pins the witness down to saying only what he heard. But there is a problem even with that much more precise phrasing; it is too open ended. The witness has to answer more than *yes* or *no*. And if the answer is "I wish that jerk was dead," you have a problem. The leading question would be "Did you hear the witness say he would kill the deceased?" This is better because the answer can only be *yes* or *no*, and you are not letting the witness say anything in their own words. If the answer is no, you still have a problem, but then you should have known the answer was no before you asked the question, and in that case you should not have asked it.

The most famous rule, "Never ask a question to which you do not already know the answer," leads to a common piece of advice about phrasing questions: Turn a simple declarative sentence into a question by adding something like "Is that not right?" at the end, or better yet by raising the intonation in your voice at the end of the sentence—"You own a gun?" Again, the point is to limit what the witness can say and to keep the testimony moving in the direction you need it to move.

A corollary to this rule is "If you aren't prepared for the answer, don't ask the question" (Davies 130). They aren't exactly the same thing. Obviously if you don't know the answer you can't be prepared for it, but the expected answer may come back in unexpected ways or have an unexpected impact on the jury or the judge. So before you ask a question, know the answer, but know also how the answer will sound, how it will play. Also, if you are surprised by an answer, and eventually you have to be because courtroom discourse is unscripted, don't hesitate or let anyone see your surprise because it will undermine your *ethos*, making you look unprepared. On the other hand, if what the witness says is self-evidently contradictory, you could use a dramatic pause and a look of surprise to convey to the jury what words alone could not.

In writing it is difficult to acquire the capacity to know how words will play out because you're not there to see the effects. The audience is an abstraction. So you might ask yourself, What would a kind person who didn't agree with my position say to this? and What might a hostile opponent say? and What about someone who isn't really paying attention? *When you are writing you are both examiner and cross-examiner.* And the best way to do this is to voice the opposition, but you must do so fairly (no straw dogs). If you can't convince your opponents they are wrong, you can at least convince them you are reasonable.

According to Tigar, there are four defects in evidence that cross-examination is intended to uncover: meaning, perception, memory, and veracity (209). Tigar's primary point here is that a witness does not have to lie in order to say something questionable, and you don't have to risk alienating anyone in the room by calling a witness a liar in order to render the testimony doubtful. "There is a marked distinction between discrediting the *testimony* and discrediting the *witness*," as Francis Wellman puts it in *The Art of Cross-Examination* (24). Generally speaking it's best if you can keep it impersonal because, as Wellman also says, "The sympathies of the jury are invariably on the side of the witness" (26). You can discredit testimony without impugning the witness by questioning the meaning of what was said, finding ambiguities. Perception is notoriously unreliable so you can ask questions of the witness to show that he or she might not have heard or seen exactly what he or she thought. Memory, too, is fallible, and people often fill in the gaps with expectations and embellishments without intentionally lying. But finally, if these other techniques are ineffective, get the witness to say things that undermine his or her credibility, and let the jury draw the conclusion that the testimony is unreliable. Don't call the witness a liar or a fool; make them say unreliable things. In other words, *as with all things rhetorical, show don't tell.*

Tigar points out that the famous ten are often broken to positive effect and that they are also often added to. One addition he advocates is "Have a point"—don't ask questions at random, and make sure you are headed toward a specific point. Davies takes this principle even further when he advises that *one should start developing the trial's closing arguments the first time one meets the client* (86). In essence, work backwards in preparation for the event, and then make sure along the way that each step leads to the next one and that the outcome is inevitable. So, think of the answer, then phrase the question.

Another common addition to the ten is "End strong." Save the best for the last. Make the revelation dramatic. And then stop.

Alternatives to cross-examination

Cross-examination is so much a part of television courtroom drama that many people assume that every witness must be cross-examined, but trial lawyers are advised to always consider alternatives and to cross-examine as a last resort. Davies lists the alternatives as follows: "leave the issue alone and deal with it in . . . [the] argument; . . . wait and rebut the matter with another witness; . . . answer through silent cross-examination" (103). Silent examination is using body language and tone of voice: irony, exasperation, disbelief, contempt, and impatience.

How does one dismiss evidence in writing? Excluding it may work, but those who know about the evidence will disapprove. One option is to bring it in and then undermine its validity, or accuracy, or relevance. As a last resort one might cast doubt on the authority of whoever assembled the evidence, but this runs the risk of encouraging animosity, and it's rarely a good idea to antagonize strangers and so make enemies of their friends.

The purpose of "testimony" in written arguments, and now I'm speaking more broadly than courtroom rhetoric, is to endorse a position, but one might also use testimony (quotations) to contrast a position or even just to show that you have a thorough grasp of everything said relevant to the topic, whether it's directly relevant or not, so that your readers will see you as an equal. We might call this use of quotations character witnesses for the writer.

The bottom line

Assume the witness is distrustful and that the spectators and jurors are inclined to side with them. Assume that the witness will not willingly say what you need them to say and that they will try to anticipate the implications of your questions and avoid saying anything that they might need to contradict later. As a result, ask short, leading questions (Plato would likely object to this), accept only yes or no answers—don't let the witness elaborate—and hide the point you are trying to establish from the witness, to make it harder for them to avoid it. Keep a friendly, professional demeanor, and don't let your emotions or anyone else's distract you. Make your point as quickly as possible, make sure the jury noticed the point (without gloating), and move on. It is enough to raise doubts in the jury's mind to undermine most witness testimony. So don't demolish a witness just because you can. It will only create hard feelings, and the jury may sympathize against you for doing it.

Your Turn

It's hard to practice cross-examination because it is an overtly adversarial form of persuasion and as such unpleasant. You can make it less unpleasant by turning it into the game of twenty questions. This is a game played by at least two people where one thinks of something, an event or an act or whatever, and the others try to guess what it is by asking questions that that the concealer can only answer yes or no to. If the answer can't be either yes or no, the concealer tells the asker to rephrase. Because this is a game, it's competitive not adversarial. One tries to win, but that doesn't entail the destruction of one's opponent; and since the quality of the game has to do with the experience of the questions and answers, it's possible for everyone to win in a sense. On the other hand, the absence of real threat makes twenty questions very unlike cross-examination.

A variation on the twenty questions game is the lying game. You have someone give an autobiography in which they are to say a bunch of true things and one thing that is a lie. And then the other people have to figure out which thing is the lie. You can make this game more like interrogation by having someone announce they think they know what the lie is, and then have them ask yes-no questions to determine the truth. The fewer the questions, the higher the score.

Another way to practice cross-examination is to search YouTube for examples of cross-examination, and analyze them for structure and plausibility. My favorite example is from the *The Wire*, "Omar Testifies Against Bird." Part of the fun is that the witness turns prosecutor, and if I hadn't just spoiled it for you you wouldn't have seen it coming. Hiding the outcome and then revealing it in dramatic fashion such that it seems inevitable, and therefore true (not the same thing), is what makes cross-examination a dramatic art as well as a persuasive technique. You can use it in many settings, not just courtrooms, but keep in mind that it hurts feelings by exposing weaknesses. Be mindful.

Decision making: Deliberation, justification, and intuition

Traditionally, deliberative rhetoric refers to the speeches a *rhetor* would make before a body charged with setting laws and making decisions for the community, where the goal would be to persuade or dissuade the group from making a particular decision that would directly affect the future welfare of the city-state and thus every citizen directly. Aristotle is credited with having come up with the division of rhetorical genres based on the *rhetor*'s purpose, and you encountered much of what he had to say about deliberation in the section "Invention" in Chapter 3 where you read about happiness and its parts.

In this section we are treating deliberation as a part of decision making in general, not just political discourse. *Deliberation*, for our purposes, is any conscious thought process you engage in when trying to decide what to do or say. *Justification* is deliberation in reverse, a process of finding reasons for doing what you did. Because they are both conscious processes, they are available to inventional strategies. *Intuition*, on the other hand, is a preconscious decision-making process, and as such it just happens. Traditionally *rhetors* have referred to this moment as inspiration—having spirit or breath blown into you—or as the moment when the muse descends. As we will see, there are explanations other than metaphysical available for how it happens that thoughts just come to us and how we might prepare ourselves to receive inspiration.

Let's deal with each of these rhetorically significant practices separately, keeping in mind that they are often mixed together in reality.

Deliberation

In everyday usage, deliberation means deciding, as in a jury deliberates over a verdict and then presents its decision to the court. When we are deliberating over a verdict, we are trying to decide if the evidence proves beyond a reasonable doubt that what the prosecution said happened did in fact happen. Used in this way, deliberation is about weighing evidence and then rendering a verdict. There is no need to justify such a verdict. We might choose later to explain how we arrived at the decision, but we don't have to. We just decided, and that's that.

We also use the word *deliberation* more broadly to refer to choosing a course of action. When deliberating in this broader sense you are focused on the future, with an eye on outcomes and consequences, both intended (what you are trying to accomplish) and unintended (the good but also the bad that might happen because of what you do). Deliberation is a difficult form of critical thinking because the future is unpredictable in many ways and because we use self-delusion and denial and wishful thinking to protect ourselves from uncertainty. Any of the cognitive biases may come into play when you are trying to decide what to do.

There's a distinction between choosing and deliberating that is worth maintaining. Choice is about making an immediate, short-term decision between obvious competing alternatives. Do I eat pho or Korean tacos today? Well, I had pho yesterday, but I do love it. Hmm. Decision making in this narrow sense is merely making a quick decision about something where the outcome will either please or displease you. It isn't critical thinking in the same way deliberation is, because you aren't questioning the outcomes closely. You are just weighing options in a semithoughtful way and then going with what feels right. Intuition and current emotional state play a big part in simple choosing. These kinds of decisions are only semiconscious, although that's not to say irrational or unreasonable. Emotion plays a part in all thinking. If, instead of deciding between pho and Korean tacos, you think, "Maybe I'll make my lunch today—and from now on—because that's cheaper and less caloric, and I'll put it on my calendar every day to remind myself, and I'll tell my friends that I'll meet them for coffee at 3 instead," then you are not choosing but deliberating.

When deliberating, as distinct from choosing, you are looking down-range, into the future, not focused on the here and now but rather on the event horizon; what's coming up, and how do you get ready for it? How do you position yourself and your groups to maximize your returns? Because you are looking downrange, you want to try as much as possible to keep your intuition and your current emotional state out of the process. You can't remove them entirely because, as we saw in the section on emotions, thought without motivation is paralytic and because we don't have direct access to whatever is happening in our preconscious. Because we don't have any access to the preconscious thoughts of others, and we only feel their emotional states indirectly, we can more clearly deliberate for others, which is a good reason for seeking advice from others when you are deliberating for yourself.

When deliberating, you need to decide on a goal, develop a strategy, and choose your tactics. If you don't have a strategy, the decision can't be put into practice, which makes it more of a wish than a decision. If you have a strategy but it's impractical, too expensive, or requires commitment from too many people, you have a dream at best. Deliberation requires seeing the goal, the path, and every step on the way. However, because the future is unpredictable, the best plans are those that can be modified quickly if circumstances change. On the other hand, putting off making a decision is also a decision, and you have to be careful you don't wait too long.

Between the need to resist the impulse to choose quickly and the unpredictability of the future, deliberating is the most difficult persuasion process. So let's lay it out one piece at a time and then walk through a few examples together before you walk through your own.

When it comes to deliberating, the most general goal is to do the right thing, of course. But the word *right* is complex like the word *love*. Review Chapter 3, the section on "Dialectic" and then apply the technique of division to "the right thing."

How many kinds of "right thing" can we think of?

Leads to the best outcome: What is "best"—what we want the most, what will benefit the greatest number of people, what will cause the least harm in a bad situation?

Maximizes a good: Saves energy, money, and time; increases value, utility, and options later on. (What is "good"? To whom?)

Maximizes a principle: Reduces taxes, obeys the laws strictly, helps others in need, gets the biggest piece for yourself, does no harm. (Whose principles?)

Provides emotional impact: Has a positive emotional impact on us, making us feel useful, virtuous, honorable, smart, connected, capable; has a positive emotional impact on others.

What other kinds of "right" can you think of?

Right, so now we have selected a meaning for "the right thing" in a particular case, and we are ready to operationalize our goal. Now we need strategies and tactics.

A *strategy* is a general plan of action that you have reasons to believe will achieve your goal—neutralize the dominant player, strengthen your weaknesses, get a marketable education, do what you love and let tomorrow take care of itself, procrastinate until there's little chance of real success but also no great risk of failure. These are examples of deliberative strategies.

Tactics are the steps that implement the strategy—double-team the dominant player, practice your forehand two hours a day, do a double major (something practical and something theoretical), carry your instrument everywhere you go and play it every chance you get, spend all your time hanging out with your least promising friends. These are examples of deliberative tactics.

Because we don't always know what our goals are (they are away down the road in the future somewhere), and our tactics are things we are doing and are therefore more available to consciousness, it is sometimes possible to figure out what our goals are by looking carefully at our tactics. What you do from day to day isn't quite so inconsequential as you might think. If you're not sure I'm right, good. Starting this coming Monday, keep a list of all of your activities for seven days. When you are done, look at the list to see which activities were just maintenance of your physical and mental well-being (eating, sleeping, etc.) and which were teleological—that is, headed in a predictable direction (learning, thinking, playing, overindulging, etc.). And finally, what things were you doing that you have no conscious reason for doing at all? What do all these things tell you about your goals?

Can you think of an example from, say, the end of last semester where you put off doing something that you might have done better if you started earlier but were willing to settle for good enough? Were you making a pragmatic decision or just protecting your ego from the pain of possible failure? Aiming for an A and getting a B is unpleasant. Setting yourself up for safe but mediocre by procrastinating frees you up to pursue more immediately gratifying objectives, and it also protects you from the possibility of failure, but it also minimizes the chances of greater achievement. Procrastination is an example of a deliberative strategy, the operationalization of a decision to avoid the risk of failure. There's a similar deliberative strategy that is actually productive of achievement, which we might call *goofing off*.

Sometimes if you concentrate too long or hard on a problem, you start to slow down, or you get confused or frustrated, tired basically. At such times, doing something else, like going for a walk or taking a nap or talking with friends is really helpful, which is why whenever you have to do something that will take a long time it's best not to wait so long that you will have to get it done in a single sitting. You need to build goofing off time into every project so that, when focus fails, there's time to let the ideas work their way around in the preconscious part of your brain. A lot of writers find that rereading what they've written before they go to bed helps them write more efficiently in the morning, the assumption being that overnight the mind keeps working, and that preconscious or perhaps even unconscious thought contributes to conscious thought. At any rate, build some slack into your processes in order to accommodate the intellectual equivalent of cost overruns and contingencies. (Be careful what you choose for slack-time activities. They may become habits. Stopping work every two hours for a donut and an energy drink will mess you up over time. I'm not even going to talk about cigarette breaks.)

▬▬▬▬ Your Turn

See if you can explain to someone else my distinction between choosing and deliberating, and give them a couple examples of each.

Justification

Justification is deliberation in reverse. Some negatively weighted synonyms are *excuse* and *rationalization*, and some positively weighted synonyms are *reason*, *explanation*, and *rationale*. While it might seem like you should never choose a course of action without reasoning through everything, we rarely make decisions in this way. It takes too long, and it's hard. Also there are so many variables to factor in that the possible combinations of outcomes overload our minds. Most of the time we just decide and move on, and we don't work out why we did what we did unless it goes wrong and we want to figure out why or if someone demands we explain our actions. Often, in fact, it's a good idea to avoid justifying a decision. If you have the authority to issue commands or directives, or if you don't but people will let it slide, you should consider saying nothing about why you decided to do what you did. This is because we decide, most often anyway, using what psychologists call the intuitive part of our brains, the lower limbic system, but we justify our actions using the rational part of our brains. Because the two parts work differently—we are not directly aware of the intuitive system while logic and rhetoric and statistics and arithmetic and all of the systems we use to construct arguments require some conscious effort—it is often counterproductive to insist on a justification because justifications are hindsight biased and likely to confuse or distract people. On the other hand, if you are thinking about doing something that will inevitably require a justification, you might want to work out the justification in advance before you do what you're planning to do. If you can't find a good justification, you might want to reconsider the decision.

The nature of the justification you use is determined by the context in which it is called for. If you are talking to yourself then it's different than if you are being told to explain something by a superior or an authority figure. If you are talking to yourself, you need to be careful that you aren't protecting your ego by rationalizing, explaining away your actions, ignoring significantly inconvenient details like evidence to the contrary. If the justification was required by someone else and you have to comply, then you need to make sure that the details are consistent and the reasoning seems sound. You are looking for a chain of thoughts that is analogous to a chain of events—one thought led logically (reasonably, legally) to the other.

We don't really know why we do some of the things we do so our justifications and our decisions are necessarily different even though they are two sides of the same coin.

Intuition—pattern recognition

Intuition is a mental process that is a bit hard to pin down because it isn't available to consciousness. We can't really reflect on it. Psychology and neuroscience have been able to determine that there are preconscious mental events happening in our brains all the time and that we can become aware of their effects even if we aren't aware of the processes themselves. It's important to keep in mind that when I use the word *intuition* I'm not referring to a sixth sense or clairvoyance, which I discuss in a later chapter. By intuition I'm referring to wordless, preconscious thought. If you practice rhetorical invention regularly and persistently, you can engrain the habits of mind they provide and thus become a more intuitive *rhetor*, that is, one who doesn't have to analyze every situation before initializing a rhetorical response. Habitual rhetorical responses will enable you to seize the moment when such moments arrive, whereas if you have to stop to analyze the rhetorical situation the moment will pass, and you will be left standing there slack jawed and heart broken.[2] On the other hand, it is also important to remember that some rhetorical practices require conscious reflection, and so even when you become rhetorically adept you will be switching back and forth between responding and planning.

Heuristic—the Greek word for "invention"—is used today primarily to refer to patterns of thought or habits of mind that help a person quickly connect a set of data points into a recognizable pattern and thus, using that pattern, quickly decide on an effective (or ineffective) course of action. Heuristics are especially useful when time is critical, like in an emergency room in a hospital. If you have ever watched the TV show *House*, you've seen doctors working at the limits of heuristic thinking. The patient presents with a set of life-threatening symptoms that only partially fit the known patterns for disease, and in the process of testing the doctors come up with a new way to understand the pattern, and thus they solve the medical problem and save the patient's life in the last ten minutes of the show—while reassuring us that the world makes rational sense, and we can know it.

Here's a concrete, if simplistic, example of how a heuristic works. How many black dots are there on the board on the right? And how many black dots are there on the board on the left?

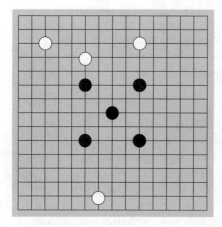 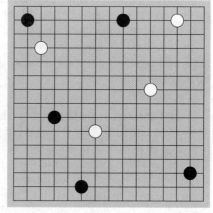

---

2. Was that melodramatic? What would be a calmer way to put that?

It probably took you a nanosecond longer to answer the first question than it did the second one. That's because you had to count the dots to answer the first question, whereas you didn't have to count the second time because the dots form a recognizable pattern.

Nearly all businesses and professions have heuristics. Sometimes they are called *decision matrixes* or *algorithms*, and each one is designed to quickly choose a course of action based on an identifiable pattern. Do we lend this person money? Do we grant this person bail? Do we have bottomless data plans for everyone or just the people in the field? Do the spark plugs need replacing? And so on.

Heuristic thinking is powerful because it is rapid, but it is dangerous for the same reason, and because we aren't really conscious of the pattern we have invoked we may have done nothing more than drawn on convention or tradition or mere prejudice. You have to train your instincts. Gary Klein has a number of excellent examples of intuitive expertise in *Sources of Power: How People Make Decisions*. One of the most memorable examples is of a fire commander who enters a burning building with his team, and together they start spraying water on the flames they can see, but the fire isn't reacting to the water the way the commander expects based on his experience, and he realizes that the room is even hotter than a room burning in that way should be. Instantly he realizes something is very wrong, and he shouts, "Get out. Get out!" Seconds later the building collapses into the basement. The firefighters were fighting a secondary blaze while standing on a floor that the primary blaze had burnt through to the point just before complete failure. The commander, Klein asserts, was able to make the life-saving decision in an instant because he didn't stop to reason his way through a logical process. He took a scene in through his senses, matched that scene against previous similar scenes, and realized something was wrong. He didn't know what was wrong, but he knew intuitively they were in danger. And he had the wit to decide without stopping to think it through.

Now of course, because you are reading against the grain, you have to wonder, okay so this is a vivid example of a successful application of a heuristic way of thinking, but isn't it possible that there are other examples where someone made the wrong decision in the same way and we just never heard about it because they didn't live to tell the tale? (Good for you. Klein has a few great examples. If you are interested in this topic, check out Kahneman's *Thinking, Fast and Slow*.)

Can you improve your powers of intuition?

In order to develop intuitive expertise, it helps to have a scaffold to practice on. This is why we spent so much time on patterns in the section on invention. I want to offer you another pattern here. This one is specifically tailored for decision making, persuasion with an eye toward the future. Because it's forward facing, it can't possibly predict what will actually happen in any given instance or how past events will be perceived once hindsight kicks in. This pattern is designed to be as portable as possible, and therefore it is very general. The downside of portability is that it won't address specific concerns well. So read what follows with several grains of salt, and try it out on a few real-world examples before you decide to adopt it. Consider what follows the intellectual equivalent of footprints on a dance floor, but keep in mind that in life there's more than one way to dance.

Internalizing the inventional strategies to the point where they become habitual—until the pattern five comes so quickly to mind that you don't have to stop to count—is what makes it possible to think quickly on your feet. Pattern recognition is the essence of rhetorical activity. So practice, reflect, and practice some more. You want to train your instincts to ask the right questions and look closely at the answers that come back.

When it comes to making heuristic decisions, you have to take context carefully into account. There's no one pattern that fits all situations. Most people learn how to make decisions effectively only after years of experience in a given field, and often what they know about one field doesn't transfer well to others. This is why a great CEO might make a lousy basketball coach, or why Michael Jordan couldn't play professional baseball. Experience offers a great deal of tacit knowledge, what one knows but can't fully articulate or even sometimes draw on explicitly. If you know how to do something really well, and someone asks you to explain it, you might struggle for a while and then just say, "I don't know how I do it; I just do." Try to explain how you ride a bicycle, if you don't believe me. If you did believe me, remember to read against the grain.

Steps for generalized decision making

Keep in mind that while it is possible to lay these questions out in a hierarchical fashion, the answer to one question might render subsequent questions moot (meaning you need to jump to a subsequent question) or end the process entirely. So as you answer these questions, keep your eyes and mind open. Keep the cognitive biases in mind as you scrutinize the evidence offered as an answer to any of the following questions.

Basic deliberative pattern: Problem–solution

Most of life's problems are ill defined, amorphous, fuzzy. For the people caught up in the situation there's no recognizable pattern, and thus there's no clear problem to solve. Sometimes people who have a problem don't even see that they do. A *rhetor*'s greatest contribution to a community may lie in being able to clearly define an amorphous problem, or in convincing people they have a problem when they don't believe they do. This is why communication is more important than knowledge. You have to ask insightful questions and listen carefully to the answers. You also have to keep in mind that people aren't always aware of what they need or what they are doing, caught up in the moment as they are. At any rate, until you really understand the problem, you are unlikely to offer a good solution. This may seem obvious, but we so often encounter advertisements where the "problem" that the product "solves" is a pseudoproblem that we are accustomed to focusing on solutions and passing over the problems. Frequently the problem is the problem, and once it is correctly understood the solution is obvious, no problem at all.

In a nutshell, if you can't think of the answer, try asking a different question.

Problem

One of the problems with learning to be a rhetor in a schoolroom is that there are no real problems, no people who really need something fixed or explained or worked around. Thus in school we spend all our times trying to come up with interesting questions to ask and imaginary problems to solve. In the "real world," the problems of invention are different. Often the problem is only vaguely understood and often it is very complicated, fuzzy, the sort of situation that can be described in multiple ways with outcomes that will differ based on the description and not just the solution offered. So you need to learn to be systematic when it comes to thinking about problems and solutions. Below is a blueprint to get you started. You will want to develop this blueprint as your experience with real problems grows.

1. Is there a problem?

2. How do you define the problem?

3. Is the problem
   a. simple (one cause, one effect)?

   b. complex (multiple causes, multiple effects)?

   c. complicated (multiple, interconnected contributing factors and outcomes)?

   d. stable (recent, long-standing, permanent)?

   e. dynamic (temporary, periodic, intermittent)?

4. For whom is it a problem?

5. For whom is it *not* a problem?

6. Who currently benefits or thinks they benefit from this problem (resistance)?

7. What are the direct and indirect consequences?

8. How bad are the consequences (irritating to lethal)?

9. What happens if you do nothing?

10. What happens if you wait?

Solution

1. Is the proposed solution possible? (Can it be done? If done, will it solve the problem without causing others?)

2. Is it legal?

3. Is it ethical?

4. Is it honorable? (Will solving it reflect positively on us? Are we properly motivated to get involved in the first place?)

5. Is it practical (time, expense, materials, people, hours, personnel, maintenance, opportunity costs)?

6. Is it durable?

7. Are there competing alternatives?

8. Are there any unintended consequences?

9. If there are, are they bad?

If you have read the section on stasis theory, you will notice a distinct resemblance here. It's the same idea presented in a slightly different way, connected to a specific kind of rhetorical thought, deliberation. The idea, however, is basic. Given a rhetorical goal, there are a set of questions you can ask to guide you through the discovery process from which you can begin to assemble the draft of an argument, or, given an argument, you can follow the process to discover how complete and how compelling the argument is.

Obviously this pattern is a bit superficial because it's designed to be as portable as possible. You need to refine the pattern by rethinking it each time you use it, adding questions and providing examples until you have a rich history of problem solving to draw on. If you do this, over time you will develop much greater decision-making skills.

The setting matters

We deliberate alone differently than we do in groups. When we are alone, thinking for ourselves, we don't necessarily think about what others are thinking. We may wonder what others will say or what others might do if they were deciding, but basically we ask X or Y and then try to generate reasons for each one and then either add the number of reasons up to see which option has the longer list or weight each item in the list to get a more carefully considered data set to base our decision on. This would be a reasonable model of self-deliberation. But of course most of us don't really do this, or at least not all that consciously.

Most often most of us don't actually deliberate; we justify. We choose, and then we come up with a rationale for the decision. How we choose must be the result of some kind of process, but we aren't always aware of what it was. Sometimes it's just a series of daydreams about what the future might be like if we, for example, go to the pastoral land-grant college and then another series of daydreams about what it would be like if instead we go to the gritty, urban state university. Once we've chosen, everything changes.

If you'd like a dramatic representation of the afterward-everything-changes effect, go to YouTube, and type in "Shawshank Redemption Red Released." You'll find (if it hasn't been taken down) the scene where the parole board asks a man who has been in prison for decades if he has reformed, and he schools them on the meaning of remorse. What he offers, by the way, is a beautifully dramatic example of a functional definition. Remorse is wishing every day you could stop your former self and tell 'em what's what. . . . I'm paraphrasing. Go stream the bit.[3]

As I was saying, once you decide, everything changes, and you will never know whether or not you made the right decision because there will be no way to go back and run the other option through to see what the outcome would have really been. You chose the college you did, and now you are going to meet people you wouldn't have if you'd gone to another one. And those people there aren't going to meet you. The permutations are disturbingly numerous when we look forward, which is why most of us don't look forward; we look back. We don't really deliberate; we justify.

When we are in a group and trying to decide what to do, the dynamics alter the processes because self-interest isn't the only interest to consider. If we are in a group and we all have the same goals and we will all suffer the same consequences from a bad decision and benefit equally from a good one, then we will all be pulling together (a rowing metaphor, in case you didn't notice). But if our interests diverge, we may try to game the process or try to trick each other in order to get what we think is to our advantage. We might form alliances and sneak around. We might strategize and anticipate, or we might get ego involved and think only about winning. We might also just let the dominant person pick and then fall in behind them because that's just easier and we're tired or hungry or spotlight averse.

---

3. That was an example of a digression, the part where you step off the track for a moment to relax or entertain or distract your audience. Digressions are good if they are done intentionally, but you don't want to digress by accident. When you are drafting, however, there are no digressions yet because you don't yet know the destination for sure, and so what looks like a digression might actually be a course correction. Stay nimble.

Groups often don't really deliberate either; they pick, and then they justify. Or they just pick and move on. What comes is what comes.

The role of luck

Because we are all meaning-making beings, because we can't resist trying to explain why things happen and aren't content with random as an explanation, fearing, I suppose, the lack of control we would feel if we embraced chaos, most of us like to focus on success stories and try to learn from them, as though if we were to emulate the successful we would also become successful. The problem with this way of thinking is that for everyone who did X and got rich (or whatever measure of success you want to employ), there was probably a bunch of people who did the same thing and got nothing. You've heard of Darwin. Have you heard of Alfred Russell Wallace? You've heard of Edison. Have you heard of Tesla? You know who Gates and Jobs are. Do you know the names of the people at Stanford's Xerox PARC who invented the graphical interface? Those are just three examples. I should give you more, but the point is that our data set is largely incomplete when looking to the past for understanding the current situation and trying to imagine the future. In the highly unregulated world we live in outside of the physics lab and the elegantly rigorous world of mathematics, sometimes things happen. And when good things happen to good people, we celebrate them, and thus we remember them. When bad things happen, we celebrate them, too, for the opposite reason, as cautionary tales. But the vast majority of the time, nothing remarkable happens. And this data we don't remember.

Here's a concrete example. Imagine that you are selling stuff over the Internet. You've got a shopping cart, and you've set cookies so that you can see what path a person took to buying which products. So far so good, but what happened on those occasions when a person got right up to the point of pushing the Submit Now button and then didn't? You don't know what happened because the result was a non-event. All you know is nothing.

How we evaluate decisions depends entirely on our assessment criteria. If we look to the outcome, then we can make good decisions for bad reasons. We did everything wrong, and it still turned out well. And we can make bad decisions with good reasons. We did everything right and boom. On the other hand, if we decide to evaluate decisions based on the process rather than the outcome, then we can avoid the unfortunate consequences problem. We can say without irony or contradiction that the operation was a success and the patient died. But if we go that way, we also have to admit that we can't control the outcomes of our actions. We decide, and then we hope.

Confidence is an attractive trait, so much so that you will do well to practice the walk and the baring of one who has faith in her decisions and a clear plan in mind, chin up, chest out. You should also write clearly and directly, hedging only to show proper care for the value of the evidence rather than suggesting a lack of commitment. *Ethos*, remember? At the same time, however, don't let your swagger override your critical thinking or lessen your preparation.

The sources of bad decisions

According to Joseph T. Hallinan, author of *Why We Make Mistakes*, overconfidence is the primary cause of decisions with undesirable outcomes. Overconfidence is sometimes referred to as the *above-average effect*. We simply have a great deal more faith in our senses and our opinions than they warrant, and thus we don't stop to question the obvious. Here's how the brothers Heath in *Switch: How to Change Things When Change Is Hard* put it:

> Our brains are positive illusion factories: Only 2 percent of high school seniors believe their leadership skills are below average. A full 25 percent of people believe they're in the top 1 percent in their ability to get along with others. Ninety-four percent of college professors report doing above-average work. People think they're at lower risk than their peers for heart attacks, cancer, and even food-related illnesses such as salmonella. Most deliciously self-deceptive of all, people say they are more likely than their peers to provide accurate self-assessments. (114)

We don't ask questions. And even when we do look for evidence, we look for confirmation rather than contradiction. We seek out like-minded people, and together we reinforce each other's prejudices and presuppositions instead of seeking out people whose opinions will make us refine our own. We need a real opposition (hopefully a loyal one), and we need to read ourselves against the grain if we are to avoid overconfidence.

A corollary of the need to embrace contradictions and counterexamples is the fact that we should embrace failures and mistakes as well. We learn by making mistakes, by failing rather than succeeding. People who are afraid to fail do everything they can to minimize the risk of failure, and thus they decrease their chances of ever learning or achieving anything. Daniel Coyle offers a vivid example in *The Talent Code*:

> The staggering babies embody the deepest truth about deep practice: to get good, it's helpful to be willing, or even enthusiastic, about being bad. (94)

When it comes to life-long learning, people are sometimes divided into two types, those who have a "growth mindset" and those who have a "fixed mindset."[4] We touched on this idea briefly early on when I advised you that if you think that writing in particular but persuasion in general is an innate talent then you'd best quit reading. That was well over a hundred pages ago, so I presume you identified with the idea that you can improve. Belief in your ability to become more persuasive; a more diligent listener; a more accurate thinker; a more vigilant reader, writer, and speaker are directly connected to your commitment to reach beyond your current skills, to seek opportunities for improvement that necessarily entail the possibility of failure.

If you're not entirely sure that last description matches your self-concept, here is a simple test. Which of the following statements best applies to you?

a.   I work hard.

b.   I'm talented (smart, a good writer, a naturally persuasive person, etc.).

If you answered B, you're laboring under the fundamental attribution error, and your chances of success are diminished because criticism blows your ego. Perhaps even worse you may actually expect praise and learn nothing from it because you got what you expected. You need to take whatever feedback you get as a chance to reassess your practices. If someone says you are good, translate that as "I did a good job in this instance," and think about why you did, what worked and what didn't. Don't just spike the ball or run a victory lap. And if someone says you are awful, don't listen to them either; listen instead to the specific ways in which you can improve. If they weren't specific, write them off as inept, and walk away, but don't assume therefore that you are in fact good. They might suck as a critic, but they may have judged your performance accurately.

Becoming persuasive, becoming a *rhetor*, means looking past each particular performance to see how any given instance is evidence of your progress to date. It's about incremental and persistent improvement, not immediate success or failure. Take the long view. You are better at it today than you were three months ago, and you will be even better five years from now as long as you don't slacken your pace or become content with good enough.

When it comes deciding what to do now so that you get what you want down the road, the biggest mistake you can make is to believe in fate. True, random happens, but you have much more control over the opportunities that may come your way than you might realize: chance favors the prepared.

Learned helplessness

Oddly enough, while overconfidence can get us into trouble, underconfidence can as well. If we are constantly engaged in loosing battles, we will

---

4. Carol Dweck offers interesting insights into these two identities in *Mindset: The New Psychology of Success*.

begin to feel helpless, and if we let that feeling set in we will stop trying. We will just accept that we can't change what's happening and sink to the bottom. There have been a number of fascinating psychological studies confirming this piece of common sense. Charisse Nixon at Penn State, for example, asked a group of students to play with anagrams. What's another word you can make out of "bat?" And for "Cinerama"? In this study, some students were given easy examples first followed by harder ones, while other students were given just hard ones. The subjects who got the easy ones first were able to solve the harder ones more often or more quickly, whereas the subjects who got the tough ones first either gave up or took a longer time. Nothing succeeds like success. And nothing fails like failure.

Learned helplessness is a useful concept to remember when you are deciding whether or not to bail or go on because it gives you a concrete way to think about the context of the decision. Is the setback that's got you contemplating quitting the first one you've had after many successes? Is the setback the result of a sudden increase in degree of difficulty, or is the task the same as prior ones? Was there something different in the setting of this task that caused the setback, or was it the same as the others? In other words, is this setback an obstacle to be overcome or a limit to be respected? If you keep straining against a limit, you may become hopelessly frustrated and angry and quit entirely, whereas if you accept your limits you might go on enjoying and doing reasonably well. The result is all in how you talk to yourself about it.

Learned helplessness is also a helpful concept when contemplating a new course of action or activity. It's important to set the first bar low, either for yourself or for others if you are trying to lead the way. You need to build confidence so that when the going gets tough you can recall past successes and use those memories to hang tough. If you can't remember past achievements, make some up, or borrow inspiration from others' achievements. If that doesn't keep you moving in the desired direction, you may need to rethink your initial decision. Maybe it's time for a new plan or possibly even a new goal. At the same time, however, it's also important to keep resetting the bar just a little bit higher after each success so that over time you will continue to improve. The greatest improvement happens when you set a challenge for yourself that is just a little bit beyond what you are sure you can accomplish, what the famous educational psychologist Lev S. Vygotsky called the *zone of proximal development*.

Because we are so quick to trust our instincts, it's important to train them carefully, and this means cultivating the rhetorical conditions that are most likely to most often lead to success. So pay attention to how you are talking to yourself, and learn from that self-talk. Are you deliberating, or are you justifying a decision your instincts compelled you to make? And how well trained are your instincts?

Probabilities

Whenever you want to make a conscious decision, you will likely wonder about the chances of a desired outcome. This is where the idea of probabilities comes in and where thinking can get complicated. The word *probability* has two meanings, the non-technical sense of what people expect will probably happen and the technical meaning of what the statistical likelihood of an outcome is.

The common usage of *probability* is really just a generous way of saying "assumptions" or "prejudices" and means essentially what people expect to happen in a given situation. That said, because we humans depend so completely on our expectations and assumptions for understanding our worlds, expectations are an important persuasive resource. It is easier to connect what you need people to believe to what they already believe, even if those beliefs are inaccurate or even untrue, than it is to overcome their expectations before moving on.

Probably (*Did you notice that hedge?*) the best place to get a handle on the way the rhetorical tradition has used "the probable" in this sense is in Aristotle's *On Rhetoric*, which offers an awesome array of things to say in different situations. Here are two examples I've cherry picked:

> Wrong doers are likely to be unsuspected if [their appearance and condition in life] is inconsistent with the charges; for example. A weak man [is likely to be unsuspected] on a charge of assault, and a poor and ugly man on a charge of adultery. (1.12.5)

Obviously by modern evidentiary standards these are horrendously simple-minded ways of thinking, stereotyping in the pejorative sense of the word. Making arguments about a person's guilt or innocence out of pieces like this is what perpetuates the bad name Plato gave rhetoric. And yet, not all appearances are superficial. If you wanted to hire a body guard, to protect you from the paparazzi, let's say, would you hire a person of average build and slim physique or the biggest tough-looking beast you could find? The latter, I imagine, because you would think, like others would, who wants to mess with that?

Just a couple more examples of "the probable" from Aristotle, these on the subject of intentional wrongdoing. I'm paraphrasing here. You should look up the section (1.12) for yourself. He says that people do wrong who think the benefit outweighs the punishment or if the gratification will be immediate and the consequences delayed. Also, those who have money and influential friends and means of escape (the rich and the powerful) are inclined to do wrong, since they have reason to believe they can get away with it. And those who can do wrong on a grand scale are inclined to do it because they can sway public opinion in their favor later on. His list of the sources of wrongdoing goes on like this, including the ideas of vice and weakness and opportunity as motivation for doing wrong.

Now think about how our modern court dramas play out. What are the topics of forensic analysis, means, motive, opportunity? If a person has a reason to wrong another and they have the opportunity and the means, they will, we think, right? That's the same kind of reasoning. It's circumstantial, not definitive, but it will get you locked up on TV. And it could get you locked up for real. This is why "senseless" crimes are so hard for us to understand. They don't fit our rhetoric of wrongdoing.

At any rate, such is the traditional and still current use of the probable, what people and common sense assume happened or predict will happen. A married person is dead? The spouse did it. Kids missing? The estranged spouse fled the country with them. Something valuable missing from a house and no forced entry? The drug-addicted kid did it.

Not all such reasoning is about wrongs, of course. Who's more likely to succeed in business, someone with a Harvard MBA or a college dropout? If you're going to hire someone, do you want a person with experience or someone straight out of college? The probable in this sense is important because when we try to convince people of anything we have to start with their prevailing beliefs. We can change people's minds, but we have to start where they are, and so what they think will or did happen tells us how they are persuaded. While rhetoric of this kind may strike you as superficial because it is, don't underestimate its persuasive power. And keep in mind that if you are dealing with a situation for which no better evidence is available, which happens all the time in real life, reasoning like this may be the best you have to work with. If exploiting people's expectations is undesirable or unhelpful (or feels unethical to you), then you need to help people exceed their expectations and overcome their assumptions, or you need to abandon the goal of persuading these people on this point.

Probability in the second sense, statistical likelihood, is of course an important rhetorical resource but one that is often misused and misunderstood. While the most common source of misunderstanding comes from the way we use the probable in everyday life, we are also confused by statistical likelihoods because of a number of cognitive biases that directly affect how we come to predict the future.

Take, for example, the bias of availability. If you are constantly made aware of something that is statistically unlikely, then you will come to think of it as a common occurrence even though it isn't. Consider the local news. Because the news reports frequently on violent crimes, one might quickly and easily conclude that a given neighborhood or city is a dangerous place. But, if you contextualize the evidence and look at the incidences as per-capita events rather than just letting the accumulation of specific incidents resonate in your head, you might come to a very different conclusion.

I have a very smart friend who once told me that a certain brand of automobile was unreliable because he drove by a dealership every morning and every morning there was a lineup of that brand waiting in front of the service bays. What's wrong with that argument?

How many people take brand X to brand Y's service department? How many cars does it take to make a "lineup" in a parking lot of that size? How many cars of that brand are on the road in that area every morning, and what percentage of that number does the lineup represent? These are the kinds of question that would lead you to realize that the sample from which my friend was generalizing was not a representative sample. He's a smart guy; he just said a simple-minded thing. I do it all the time, too. I probably wouldn't even have noticed if he hadn't been talking about the brand of car I was thinking about buying (did buy). We are all persuaded by simple-minded uses of probabilities from time to time because we don't ask questions.

"Buy now, buy now, buy now!" is not an argument, but repetition creates a sense of familiarity, and we are more easily persuaded by the known despite the fact that familiarity and knowledge are different.

People often confuse what they expect to happen based on their past experiences with an accurate prediction about what will happen in the future. We think the past explains the future. And we are wrong. But most of the time we don't notice because of the way we persuade ourselves and others.

Which animals are more dangerous, sharks or deer? If you are like most people, and you don't remember reading this example in the section on cognitive biases, you're first answer will be something like, "Jaws vs. Bambi? Come on."[5] But statistically you are far more likely to be injured by a deer than a shark. Cars run into deer more frequently than people swim into sharks because fewer people swim in the oceans than drive through wooded areas. Fewer shark encounters, more deer encounters. My sharks-or-deer question was designed to trick you. If you were reading *with* the grain you visualized a huge mouth full of jagged teeth flying up out of the water, and then you visualized a soft almost doglike big-eyed doe. If you were reading *against* the grain you would not have visualized an image but rather have asked, "What do you mean by 'dangerous'? Do you mean, which am I more likely to encounter in a way that won't end well for me?" How a question is phrased can profoundly affect what kinds of answers are generated and therefore what you decide to do. See the section "Framing" in Chapter 3.

People also often think they saw an outcome as inevitable before it happened when in fact they only think so retrospectively. This is known as the *hindsight bias*, and it goes a long way toward explaining the proverb that hindsight is 20-20.

---

5. Was it not? Well good for you. The preceding paragraph should have made you suspicious that something was coming. Keep reading against the grain. The questions are more important than the answers.

Here is another example of how the two kinds of probability collide. This one is from *The Psychology of Judgment and Decision Making*, by Scott Plous:

> Linda is 31 years old, single, outspoken, and very bright. She majored in philosophy. As a student, she was deeply concerned with issues of discrimination and social justice, and also participated in antinuclear demonstrations. Please check off the most likely alternative:
>
> a. Linda is a bank teller.
>
> b. Linda is a bank teller and is active in the feminist movement. (110)

Ninety percent of respondents chose the second option. Statistically speaking, however, the first option is more probable because, as Plous explains, "The conjunction of two events (e.g., 'bank teller and feminist') cannot be more likely than the probability of either event alone (e.g., 'bank teller')."(110) The results of this experiment and others like it suggest that, according to Tversky and Kahneman and quoted by Plous,

> As the amount of detail in a scenario increases, its probability can only decrease steadily, but its representativeness and hence its apparent likelihood may increase. The reliance on representativeness, we believe, is a primary reason for the unwarranted appeal of detailed scenarios and the illusory sense of insight that such constructions often provide. . . . for example, the hypothesis "the defendant left the scene of the crime" may appear less plausible than the hypothesis "the defendant left the scene of the crime for fear of being accused of murder," although the latter account is less probable than the former. (111)

Vivid details are compelling even when they are irrelevant. I have a theory that the longer the sales pitch the more expensive the item. People will pay for words because they create a context, a scene, and they transport a person from the here and now (reality) to some other place where things cost more in proportion to how buying them makes a person feel. Ever see the *Territory Ahead* catalog? They will show you a cotton shirt against the azure sky and stunning white walls of cliff houses on the Greek island of Mykonos and then ask you to pay $80 for it. For the shirt? No, for the idea that you are rich enough to bask in the sun in Mykonos. And, oh yeah, you get this shirt to go with the daydream. As the marketers say, it's the sizzle you're selling not the steak. While we are used to sales pitches in the market place, we are less aware that they are used by politicians and statisticians, sometimes inadvertently but often with the intent to manipulate naive information consumers. As Darrell Huff, the author of *How to Lie with Statistics*, says,

> Averages and relationships and trends and graphs are not always what they seem. There may be more in them than meets the eye, and there may be a good deal less. (8)

Another common error in probabilistic reasoning is sometimes referred to as the *gambler's fallacy*. If you were to toss an unbiased coin five times, and the first four times it came up heads, what are the chances the fifth time it would be heads again? Fifty-fifty. It's either going to be heads or tails, and what happened before no more affects the toss than the outcome causes what will happen next week. The problem is that the odds of throwing heads five times in a row is 1 in 32, and most people focus on the context rather than the event. We are typically more interested in the story than the fact. This is why detailed stories (and outright lies) can by so devastatingly persuasive.

While we sometimes use our own reasoning to lead ourselves astray, often others are willing to do it for us. The people who do opinion polls can profoundly affect public opinion. This seems backwards. They are supposed to be describing, not persuading. Done correctly, of course, surveys can be powerful ways of understanding reality. But they can be done poorly more easily than you might imagine. There is a social phenomenon known as pseudo-opinions, opinions people hold about demonstrably non-existent things or events. I'm not talking about UFOs or swamp monsters. I'm talking about people having an opinion about some purely fictional House bill or some such thing concocted by the experimenters. The existence of pseudo-opinions does not prove that people are stupid; it proves that we don't like to appear stupid, which leads us to say and do stupid things.

Canadian comedian Rick Mercer has exploited our fear of being embarrassed by our ignorance in a bit he has done repeatedly called "Talking to Americans."[6]

There are ways to inadvertently create pseudo-opinions. If you present people with a questionnaire that does not offer an "I don't know" option, they will tend to answer either *yes* or *no*. So it is possible to create bogus statistics simply by failing (or refusing) to provide more than two possible answers. This is the survey equivalent of the logical fallacy of the excluded middle. Whenever anyone offers two exclusive options, either A or B, you should read the options against the grain and ask yourself, what about neither A nor B and both A and B?

---

6. "Talking to Americans" was a segment of the popular (in Canada) Canadian comedy TV program *This Hour Has 22 Minutes*. If you do a Google search for "Rick Mercer, Talking to Americans," you will likely find video clips.

Negotiation and sales

Negotiation

Negotiation is different from argumentation. When you are arguing, you are trying to prove an assertion true by presenting sound evidence and addressing objections. When you are negotiating, you are trying to *make a deal*. Negotiation is a process of exchange: give and take. A consequence of the process of negotiation will be a relationship, either positive or negative depending on how both parties feel about the deal. Often people feel that negotiation is a competitive or even an adversarial process, where one person is trying to beat or trick the other person, but, because long-term relationships are almost always better for people than short-term relationships and very few people are willing to be taken advantage of repeatedly, it's beneficial to think of the person you are negotiating with as a partner rather than as a competitor or adversary: no winner, no loser, no victor, no vanquished. Just people who struck a mutually beneficial bargain. Even if you are not in a business that relies on return customers and positive word of mouth, even if you are not in business at all, fair dealing pays off over time because reputation is part of *ethos*. If you are around people who get by taking, you are around the wrong people.

Research is crucial

To be an effective negotiator you have to know what you are talking about. You also have to know what the other person is talking about, and you have to know what you (and they) don't know as well. Ignorance on either side may lead to regrettable decisions. Ignorance also encourages deception, manipulation, and theft. *The un- and ill-informed make everything worse for all of us. So do your homework.* Know who you are. Know who they are. Know what you can (and will) do for them, and they can (and will) do for you. *Keep an open mind, but be disciplined.*

Price and cost

At its most basic level, research prior to negotiation is comparison shopping. When considering the price of an item, there's a great deal more to consider than just the price tag. For one thing, what's on the tag may be negotiable. And over time it may change. Things go on sale at certain times of the year. There are discounts for bulk buying. And there are special deals for special people. You may also need to consider what the price of credit adds to the price tag. In addition to what's on the price tag, you have to consider the *cost of ownership*. What does it cost to run, to fix, the upgrade? How fast will it depreciate? Will it last the right amount of time? Will you need to factor in training, downtime, legacy systems, interaction with other devices (or people)? What alternative products are there? And what would happen if you just said no?

Here's a simple example: Do you ever shop at a big-box store like Costco? Fans like to tell you that you can save 30 percent off your standard grocery bill by shopping at one of these stores. And that may well be true if you compare unit prices. Let's say you can pay thirty cents per ounce of coffee at a warehouse store and ninety cents per ounce at a standard grocery store. That seems an obvious savings. But in order to get that discount you have to buy maybe ten times as much coffee at the warehouse as you would at the grocery store. Are you still saving if all the extra coffee goes stale before you can drink it? What if you start drinking more coffee to avoid waste? What if we're talking cheese instead of coffee? The price of an item is not the cost of the item. The special topic of economies of scale, that the more you can make of something the cheaper each unit is, is great for production but unhealthy for consumption in most cases. Consider the context. Consider the frame.

In addition to the cost of ownership you need to consider the *opportunity cost*. What won't you be able to buy if you buy this? Keep in mind that *buy* is sometimes a metaphor because relationships are also negotiated agreements. I'm not being cynical. If you take a job at one place, you are not only not taking a job at some other place, but you are also missing out on whatever relationships and opportunities that other place would have provided. So to make an effective deal you have to know yourself above everything else.

You are always negotiating with yourself

Keep the big picture in mind. Don't get tunnel vision or sucked into thinking that whatever you want right now is what you will always want or that you can't live without it. There will always be another opportunity, another option, another other. If you don't keep the big picture in mind, you may get overly excited or anxious and decide too quickly. Good negotiators know how to let people talk themselves into a deal. Salespeople, too. It's better for them if you talk yourself into it because you go away feeling good, and that makes you want to tell other people about it, and that's word of mouth. So listen to them, and listen to yourself listening to them.

Negotiation experts have an acronym that they base much of their advice on: BATNA (Best Alternative To a Negotiated Agreement). Whenever you enter a negotiation, you need to have an exit strategy that includes walking away with nothing. So, for example, when you go to buy a car don't give away the keys to your car until you have agreed on a price for the new one. You need to be able to leave easily. (No one needs hours to inspect your car. Dealers use a published system of values based on year, make, model, and mileage. They might run an accident report but probably not. They know in five minutes what they will "give" you for your car.) My car example, while literally true, is also a metaphor. Make sure you can walk away in an emotional and financial sense. Don't hang your future on someone else's needs.

Negotiation basics

Do your homework. (Know what you know *and* what you don't know.)

Do their homework. (Know what they know *and* what they don't know.)

Knowledge trumps trust. Trust is a lot like faith. You have it until you don't anymore. Trust is an attitude you take toward people based on your belief in their honesty, and that belief is more tenuous if it rests only on what they say because people lie and they also make mistakes about what they believe and what they can accomplish. If, on the other hand, you assess a person's trustworthiness entirely on their behavior, or by comparing what they do with what they say, then you can't be misled by lies and errors.

Make sure you understand the real value of everything at stake, not just the prices but also the hidden costs and the costs of ownership as well as the opportunity costs.

Listen actively. When a person speaks you need to communicate that you understand what they are saying, not necessarily that you agree but that you understand. Repeat in your head what they say. Offer it back using expressions like, "so if I'm hearing you correctly. . . ." Don't think ahead to what you are going to say next or daydream or get distracted.

Listen to the words and the music, as Fisher and Shapiro advise in *Beyond Reason* (28). Listen carefully to the tone and to the voice and to the body, if present, of the person you are talking with. If a person is saying positive things but acting shifty, you have to wonder. Maybe their shoes are too tight, but, then again, maybe they are hiding something. Sometimes the way something is said conveys a metamessage, a nuance added to or even a refutation of what the words actually mean. What a person says isn't always what they will or even can do. Sometimes hard criticisms are couched in kind words.

Don't assume that what's happening here and now is everything that matters or even everything that's happening.

Keep the big picture in mind. Try to think of creative ways for both of you to get more than what seems to be on the table. But be aware of fake choices involving bogus options.

Don't confuse what you imagine the future holds with what the future will actually be once it arrives. Be careful what you wish for.

Do the math. I rented a car for two weeks once. The guy said, "Do you want to pay $10 a day for unlimited mileage?" I was driving to Canada so I figured without thinking, uh, sure. Later, as I was driving away it occurred to me I should have asked, how many miles do you get if you don't pay the extra? It turns out two hundred miles a day. Two weeks, fourteen hundred miles. I was doing twenty-two hundred, so it worked out for me, but I didn't think to do the math on the spot, and the guy didn't offer to do it for me. Salespeople rarely have much latitude. And I doubt it mattered to him if I took the unlimited mileage or not. Maybe he did the math in his head and did me the courtesy of figuring I'd done it, too, since it was in my favor and trapping me into paying more by going over would have left me with a bad impression of the company. My point is, think it all through from start to finish. Do the math.

Be aware of metaphors that may be blinding you to opportunities. If you think negotiation is a game, then you are focused on winning and worried about losing. But you are not playing a game, and therefore there is no winning and no losing. There are better and worse deals, certainly. But the better deal isn't necessarily the cheaper one or the one you thought you wanted when you started out. It's even possible that the last thing you want is actually the best possible thing for you.

Pay attention to your emotional state. If you find yourself breathing fast, slow it all down. Change it up. Get a broader perspective.

Know your BATNA. Know when to walk away, and don't lose sight of that moment.

Know their BATNA. You need to know at what point the deal is no longer a deal for your partner as well so that you don't push too far.

Be flexible but disciplined. Negotiation is about give and take, so you need to give some things up in order to get others, but you also need to stay focused on what is truly important and not let your emotions or your competitive spirit lead you to give away what matters in the pursuit of something that doesn't.

Be prepared (and able) to walk away with nothing but a smile.

Ready, set, negotiate

If you played the game described below, did you win? Did the winner overpower the loser? As Fisher and Shapiro point out in *Beyond Reason* (52), often when they have their clients play this game the clients fail to recognize the significance of list item 6: It does not matter how many points your partner gets. The best way to get the most points for yourself is to get as many points also for your partner—don't compete, coop- erate. When the ref says go, relax your arm and pull your hand slowly down so the back touches the table. You both then have to return to the upright posi- tion. Your partner should let you put their hand down, if they are smart. If they are stupid and try to force your hand down again, let them but try to do it in such a way that they get the message

> **Ready, Set, Negotiate: The Game**
> 1. Sit facing the person next to you.
> 2. Grasp your partner's right hand in yours, elbows on the table.
> 3. Don't let go.
> 4. You get one point each time you touch the back of your partner's right hand to the table.
> 5. The goal is to get as many points for yourself as you can.
> 6. It doesn't matter how many points your partner gets.
> 7. I'll give you 30 seconds.
> 8. Don't speak.
> 9. Close your eyes, and go!

that the best way to make points is to alternate as fast as you *both* can go, like you're playing at being windshield wipers or something. Item 6: it does not matter how many points your partner gets. Negotiation isn't an adversarial game. Life isn't a competition.

Take a look at the language of the negotiation "game" again. Did I lead you down a path? I didn't call the person you were playing with your adver- sary. I called them your partner. On the other hand, I said "grasp," which is suggestive of games,[7] and the posture you were asked to adopt is that of arm wrestling. So, yes, I set you up a bit by exploiting your expectations and assumptions. *To win you needed to see quickly beyond the expected and assumed and then quickly communicate to the other person what lies beyond.* On the other hand, if you both arrived at the same conclusion at once, you'd be back to arm wrestling, this time backward: you'd both be trying as hard as you could to lay down your arms. Someone needs to lead, then follow. Life isn't a game. It's a dance. Well, negotiation is anyway.

The rhetoric of retail

No book on persuasion would be complete without at least some discus- sion of advertising because advertising is arguably the premiere arena for rhetoric these days. Advertising is where the greatest amount of creative energy and research is focused because, of course, that's where the money is. Even our public officials have public relations campaign managers, and

---

7. If I were writing in the high style instead of the plain style I would have said "ludic situations" instead of "suggestive of games." Can you explain why?

many have the equivalent of a brand manager. In fact, if you went looking for a book on *ethos* today you would find instead books advising you how to manage your "personal brand." It's the same advice, just a twenty-first-century package.

Retail is also an important arena because we encounter its techniques far more often than any other techniques. Advertising is ubiquitous, and ever since network TV has given way to cable, as cable gives way to Internet viewing, advertising has become ever more subtle and more targeted. Rather than a 30-second spot clearly marked off from the show you were watching, now you have product placement and targeting messages sent to you specifically. The largest Internet companies, Google and Facebook primarily but others as well, have real-time information about your viewing and shopping habits, and they can send you messages accordingly. They don't know it's you exactly. Most of the data is anonymous, but they have the equivalent of a persona with real-time data rather than invented and generalized data. Your email messages, your Facebook updates, every credit card purchase, and every debit card transaction leave a trail, and that trail is bought and sold. Your viewing and purchasing behavior is a known commodity.

So it is critically important that you understand how you are marketed to and how you respond to advertising. We don't have enough space to cover this area of persuasion in depth, but we can cover the basics and give you a place to start further inquiries if the subject appeals to you. Even if it doesn't appeal to you sufficiently to pursue further research, pay (*metaphor alert*) close attention to what follows because it may save you a great deal of money in the near future.

Psychological math—shell games with numbers

> Money isn't money in a casino. At home, you might drive across town to save a buck on a box of Tide, but at the table you tip a waitress five dollars for bringing a free Coke. You do both these things on the same day. (Barthelme, *Double Down: Reflections on Gambling and Loss,* 25)

As you may recall, the most insidious cognitive bias is naive realism, thinking that the world is as you see it and that people are as you perceive them. Life isn't that simple. Our understanding of our world is something we create. That doesn't mean, however, that we have conscious control over all aspects of that creation. We can intervene in the construction here and there, but the opportunities are not always apparent to us, and even when we see an opportunity the psychological and cognitive effort required to revise our opinions is so great that often we just follow our friends and family. We are not purely rational consumers any more than we can be purely rational thinkers. Rhetoric is inevitable. Here are some common ways in which how you decide to buy things is influenced by how our minds typically work.

The principle of separate gains and losses: If you could win at a game four times for a total of $100 or once for $100, which would you prefer? If you are like most people, you would rather win four times than once even though the financial outcome is the same. And the same is true for losses; most people would be less upset if they lost $100 all at once than if they lost $25 four times in a row. Do you rip a bandage of quickly, or pull it slowly? The psychological effect of winning or losing affects us more than the money. Oddly enough, a small gain can offset a big loss. When you go shopping, are you tempted by the buy-one-get-one-half-off signs? If so, then you are willing to spend more than you were willing to spend in the first place. If they had just reduced the price of the one item by 25 percent, would you have been as tempted? Getting people to think about how much they "saved" instead of how much they spent is a very common application of psychological math. Take a look at the bottom or your receipt next time you go grocery shopping.

> People are more willing to gamble on avoiding a negative outcome than on receiving a positive one even if the odds of either are the same. In other words, people are not very good at calculating the odds of an outcome, and they are loss adverse. When it comes to gain, people tend to prefer a small certain gain over a less secure larger one. We might call this the "bird in the hand" principle. When it comes to the threat of a loss, however, people are more willing to gamble on a big loss rather than accepting a smaller certain loss. You might call this the let's-get-this-over-with principle. . . . Our aversion to loss not only makes us vulnerable to manipulation but often leads to just-plain-stupid decisions. For example, almost every stock market investor has heard the widely cited portfolio advice to cut your losses short and let your profits run. But, in fact, investors usually do the opposite. (Levine 121, 127)

This is sometimes referred to as the *sunk-cost fallacy*. Most people will hang on to a loser hoping it will come back because they hate to lose or hate to admit they were wrong, which often means they will lose more and at the very least means they don't have the opportunity to make money on a better option because their money is tied up in something not making money. A related error in judgment is explained by the proverb *better the devil you know*. People will stick with a bad situation, an unhappy marriage or an unfulfilling career, rather than get out because to quit would be to admit defeat or to seem disloyal (and because the unknown is often more frightening than the miserable is miserable). In other words, don't throw good money after bad.

The power of a perceived discount is almost irresistible for most people. This is why nearly no one pays retail and why every catalog you get has a "list price" and a "sale price." Some catalogs will even admit that the list price, or the manufacturer's suggested retail price (MSRP), is for reference purposes only and that the item may never have sold at that price. In other words, the rule of contrast makes paying 20 percent more for something than you have to seem like a great deal when compared to paying 50 percent more. I'll admit that I'm a sucker for this. I'll grin all the way to the checkout line to pay $20 at a TJ Maxx for something I wouldn't buy for $40 at Macy's. In effect, it cost me $20 to "save" $20. If what you are buying isn't a necessity, then it's always cheaper not to buy it at all.

Common sales techniques

False comparisons: "You can get with this, or you can go with that" (Black Sheep Kia Hamsters Ad). Low fat, reduced sodium, less sugar, 30 percent more. All of these are false comparisons because none offers the basis for comparison: less sugar than what, a ten-pound bag of sugar?

Price contrast: A salesperson presents you with an outrageously overpriced "option" with the expectation that by contrast the next step down will seem like a really good deal. Next time you are in a fancy restaurant, look at the price structure of the items on the menu. Chances are you will find an item far more expensive than the others. This makes the other items more attractive. These items are often more cost effective for the restaurant to produce and therefore preferable to them from an accounting perspective. Even a list can have *rhetor*ical power.

Bait and switch: You are presented with an inexpensive but inferior item which, while the low price brought you in, you quickly abandon for something better that costs more than you were planning to spend.

Lowball: The price of the item is $10, but shipping and handling is $20, and there's a restocking fee of $5. That means, of course, that the actual cost of the item is not $10 but $35. A slightly more sophisticated version of this is the "But wait, order now, and we'll give you a second one for free; just pay shipping and handling," which of course they don't tell you is equal to the price of the item. Banks also lowball us. They give us interest on our savings but charge fees for every interaction we have with them. Buying anything on credit is the lowest ball of all. A bargain paid for with a credit card is almost never a bargain at all.

Highball: People are willing to spend more for an item than they need to because doing so makes them feel superior to everyone else. The item need not be better in any significant sense, although it often will be in a superficial sense, better constructed, better material, better shine, and so on. We are even willing to pay extra for the name printed on an item because that name signifies something to us; it triggers a set of associations and a self-narrative that makes us feel better about ourselves. It may also make others feel better about us.

Scarcity principle: People more highly prize things that are uncommon because having one then sets a person apart from everyone else, even if it doesn't really at all.

Urgency principle: People are more likely to buy something if they think the item or the opportunity is rare. This is why you see "Going fast," "Only two items at this price left," and "One day only" signs everywhere. The urgency principle is also why we are given ultimatums by people who are trying to manipulate us.

Upselling, add-ons: Offering accessories to go with the thing you just bought. Once a person has spent a large some of money, it's easy to get them to spend an additional, lesser amount. This is why car dealers sell floor mats for $200 a piece, either so that they can take that in addition or to seem like they are being magnanimous when they sweeten the pot by throwing them in.

Foot in the door: A small gift or concession to start a process moving forward. The sales version of this is sometimes called a *loss leader*. You can buy milk for 30 percent below the current price, but on your way to the back of the store to get it you pass hundreds of overpriced items, only one of which needs to attract you to make up the store's loss.

Door in the face: Pique a person's interest by suggesting they aren't good enough, or rich enough, or tough enough, or whatever for whatever you want them to beg for.

Social proof, or the bandwagon: Everyone else is doing this; you want to, too. If you have been to a hotel recently you may have seen a sign that says something like, "We, like many of our guests, are concerned with the environment. If you would like to join us in helping to save energy and water, please leave your towels on the rack." Apparently the "like many" part is the hook. We want to be like others. Another example is the "If lines are busy" ploy. You think, wow, there must be a lot of people getting in on this. I don't want to miss out.[8]

Third-party endorsement: A.k.a. the *wing man* or the *shill*. This technique piques a person's interest by having someone else around who is showing interest. Oddly enough, if you walk up to someone and say, "Hey, I'm wonderful," they are less likely to believe you than if you send someone else over to say, "Hey, see that person over there? He is wonderful." The minute somebody wants something, others want it, too.

There is a high-end shopping mall in Atlanta, Georgia, as there are in all large cities, with marble floors and soaring, glass-domed atriums. And often at the intersection of the different wings you will find a convertible Bentley, an Aston Martin, a Maserati, or a tricked-out Lincoln Navigator. These high-end automobiles are for sale, but that's not why they are there. People don't buy $200,000 automobiles in shopping malls.[9] They are there to anchor an incredibly luxurious sale point in the minds of shoppers. There's no way you are going to buy a $200,000 car on impulse, but having just seen one you might pay $75 for a polo shirt of the same quality as one you could get literally across the street for $40. Luxury is a state of mind, which encourages people to spend whatever money they have as if they had twice as much. One of the greatest modern sources of happiness is a perceived increase in discretionary (*disposable?*) income. Once you have enough for the basic necessities of life—food, shelter, transportation, insurance, and enough for your family—small gains go to pleasant experiences, and from pleasant experiences, the anticipation of them and the memory of them, comes a sense of fulfillment. It's the difference between what you need to live and the financial means to acquire what

---

8. See *Yes! 50 Scientifically Proven Ways to Be Persuasive*, by Goldstein, Martin, and Cialdini.

9. Did you notice the enthymemic structure of those last two sentences? The second one is offered as a justification of the first.

you can imagine wanting that is your discretionary income. For most of us, as our incomes rise so do our imaginary needs. That's why you will occasionally run across a story of someone who makes a deep six figures a year but feels or actually is broke. We let our things define us. This is what it means to live in a consumer society. This is the rhetoric of retail.

> Advertising is about slogans, brand names, and images. A company may devote less attention to promoting the actual qualities of its products than to suggesting social images it wants you to associate with its product. If you're attracted to the image—if you want to play the role—the product becomes a prop in your performance. (Levine 153)

Aspirational thinking is what leads people to identify with practices and activities and beliefs and products that are beyond our actual resources. It's the kind of thinking that makes credit cards seem necessary and why so many people are willing to pay finance charges on things they don't need. The concept of *taste*, when mixed with advertising, plays a huge role in getting people to spend a great deal more on products than they need to in order to obtain essentially the same good. Middle-class people, especially those with some higher education, who are making more money than their parents did, and in some cases more than their childhood friends, often like to show off their elevation by having "discriminating" tastes in food and drink. The wine or scotch connoisseur has a story that goes along with that $100 bottle of whatever that makes the buyer feel as though he or she is knowledgeable, worldly, better. Having such "evidence" of money and insider knowledge makes a person feel that they have arrived. Further up the income chain the same thing happens with cars and houses, with vacation houses and yachts and club memberships and so on. But the same thing happens down the income chain as well. There are beer devotees, after all. The person who is intentionally buying the cheapest beer on the menu, by the way, is doing the same thing, only with a wink that gives him the same sense of superiority that the guy who just spent $20 on a Belgian ale is feeling. *In the end what we buy enables us to tell ourselves stories about who we want the world to believe we are.* We are buying the sizzle, as the advertising slogan goes, not the steak.

Identity and identification also play a significant part in how we respond to advertising. We are much more likely to buy something that we think people like us buy. If you are a parent, your sense of motherhood or fatherhood is a rich source of symbols and beliefs that advertisers and politicians can tap into. Life insurance is sold to married couples using the stereotypes of father-provider and prudent mother, with an added helping of simple fear to combat our tendency towards optimistic thinking, in order to get us to buy what statistically we don't need. The house always wins.

As with all other forms of persuasion, subtlety begets success. You have to disarm before you can charm. (*Advertising language, Pullman?*) The affordances of the media through which we consume advertising have a larger than commonly noticed impact on how we receive messages. In the days of network television, thirty-second, even sixty-second, ads were possible. Once the channel changer arrived and we all started surfing past ads, those spots shrank, and of course with DVRs the ads became imbedded in the content, in the shows we watch. Further changes are happening as a result of our moving to Internet viewing. The TV, you could argue, is really a relic of the pre-Internet age. Any TV you buy today is closer to a computer than a TV, and so, if it hasn't happened already for you, your entertainment and advertisement experiences will all be web based.

Forms of indirect marketing

Product placement: If you've watched TV you've seen this, products as props. Sometimes they are just there, on a shelf in the background, and sometimes the characters interact with the products, to call attention to them and make them seem desirable. The more subtle the interaction the more unnoticed the effort and thus, for some kinds of products, the better. But as with many things rhetorical, sometimes the best subterfuge is open acknowledgement, where you use irony to make the point you are pretending not to make.

Behavior placement: Writing in story lines that reinforce your product's *ethos* by suggesting that it's used by people to do the things you need people to do if they are going to buy your product or mimic the behavior you are trying to reinforce.

Sweepstakes: Giveaways that make people feel good about the company and hopeful enough to buy lots of product to improve their chances of winning.

Competitions: Motivating people to buy (or sell) your product by promising a prize for the most bought or sold.

Sponsorships: Logos on anything that generates excitement or enthusiasm that you can tap into, to share in the achievement or fame.

Events: Brought to you by . . .

Scholarships: Paying people to learn what you need them to learn if they are going to use your products or further the enterprises your products benefit from.

Research institutes: The same as think tanks. Essentially these are organizations designed to promote a product or an idea under the guise of scientific analysis. Some actually do research; others really just shill for the product or industry they were created in the service of.

Non-profit organizations: As with the research institutes, many of these organizations do good work. But many are also working for interests, their own and others. For every dollar you donate, a percentage, in some cases a large percentage, goes to running the organization that solicited the donation. In that sense, you are supporting the operation as well as the cause.

Publications: A lot of magazines today are little more than targeted advertising efforts, as are a number of cable networks. You can't watch a moment of DIY Network without thinking Lowe's and Home Depot must be major sponsors. The same is true of most magazines with a lifestyle or hobby focus.

Gifts to celebrities and taste makers: There's nothing better than getting collateral press out of your product showing up with a celebrity when he or she steps out onto the red carpet, and a good way to ensure it does is to give them one.

Naming sports arenas: And sponsoring sporting events. Anything that many people watch is an obvious way to increase brand recognition. Obviously only for companies with a lot of advertising money to spend.

Lobbies (councils): To get a really vivid image of how these organizations have exploited our beliefs over the years, read Edward Bernays' *Propaganda*.

Viral videos: These days corporations love to release versions of their advertisements on YouTube and elsewhere, hoping to generate buzz or even fandom. If you wanted to, you could easily spend an hour just watching entertaining ads on the web, often the less entertaining versions of which will interrupt your TV watching and therefore have less positive results.

Rivalries: Like controversy, rivalries can be good for everyone concerned. They help define brand identity and provide a potential excuse for press coverage. When Florida plays Georgia, a lot of money changes hands. When Apple "took on" PC (a fictional rival, as there is no PC brand), they helped their users feel hip and different and knowledgeable by making them feel like anyone other than the dorky guy in the bad pants and golf shirt. And of course, Microsoft felt compelled to offer a counterstatement with a "I'm not a dork, and I'm a PC" campaign. There are rules about colluding in business, but it's easy to create a rivalry, and both parties may win by the effort. You can tell a true rivalry from a fake one by the possibility of an outcome where one side actually loses, is run out of business, or is otherwise silenced. When real threats exist, there's less bravado and flag waving involved.

Scandals: No press is bad press, as the saying goes. You can get some collateral press if some of the people in your organization can get caught up in a controversy or personal disaster. But of course you don't want to take the disaster too far or let the scandal undermine the business or distract the leaders to the point where they can't do their job.

Stunts: Red Bull and other "excitement" brands often stage events that look like competitions, like swimming to Cuba or whatever, where the real point is not the athleticism but the advertising opportunity. I suppose if you wanted to be cynical you could argue the Olympics are little better now.

Narrative

When logic and even rhetoric in the forms of enthymemes and vivid examples fail, either because they are too complicated to follow or what we are trying to "prove" actually defies available evidence and explanations, then we can bring a great many people with us by telling a good story. We do this to ourselves all the time. We spin a scenario with ourselves as the protagonist and how it seems to play out is what we go with. If we think it will end badly, we choose not to. But if it seems like it will be exciting or just the sort of thing that we see ourselves a part of, we might go for it even if we think it will end badly. Most of us, however, don't tell our stories to the end. We set the scene and then jump in, heedless of where it will go and then retell it retrospectively to help us deal with and make use of the consequences.

Narratives are neat, symmetrical, unified. Everything is explained, all the loose ends tied up, the good rewarded, the bad punished. Everything that happens in a story happens for a reason. Random is not a narrative technique. In fact it may be that human beings created narratives as a way of dealing with the obvious lack of order and purpose pacing restlessly in the gloom beyond what our ancient campfires could illuminate and warm. Narratives have nothing to do with reality but everything to do with how we create meaning out of selected details as a way of creating communities and fostering beliefs and actions. Narrativization, in other words, is a critically significant form of persuasion because it works best when all else fails.

Here's an analogy for how storytelling works. Computers operate on several different levels at once. At the core, they are streaming 0s and 1s across circuits. One level up from there is machine code that determines how the 0s and 1s stream. One level up from machine code is the operating system that tells the machine how to integrate all of the mechanical and digital parts to perform tasks using the streams of 0s and 1s. Up from the operating system are programming languages that a person with technical skills can use to make the machine do different things with input from users and from other machines. Up from the programming languages you have programs themselves overtop of which lie graphical user interfaces that the average computer user uses to do what they want to do using the computer as the medium but more or less unaware of everything going on below the interface.

The stories we tell ourselves about ourselves and each other are like the graphical user interface; they enable (*and therefore disable, right?*) certain kinds of interaction. They are dependent on the processing going on down below, but we are mostly unaware of the processing, and few of us have the technical skills that allow us to hack the processes. The information coming in through our five senses and the autonomic impulses of our bodies are like the 1s and 0s beneath the operating system. Only under extreme conditions do we become aware of their functioning, but we have programs that make use of the information our bodies provide. These cognitive programs are written by rhetorics (*Remember I'm talking analogically here*), organizational schemas that filter and focus and organize our information in ways that make it possible for us to arrive at some conclusions quickly, others eventually, and still others never at all unless somehow we can change the rhetoric we are using to interact with our information sources (the human equivalent of 0s and 1s). New information running on the old rhetoric rarely enables significant changes because cognitive biases tend to discount and diminish or assimilate and dismiss new information that doesn't fit our prior expectations. Our archaic metaphors, holdovers from our past ways of being, also restrain new ways of thinking by forcing new meanings into archaic forms. Why did we call the first automobiles horseless carriages? Why do we persist in calling pocket computers phones? Every heroine of her own story is a villain in somebody else's.

If you can change the story, reorganize the interface, you may be able to change the rhetoric, reprogram the software.

Learn how to tell a good story, and you can persuade anyone (and yourself) of anything. Realize that all stories are just stories, however, and you may have an existential crisis on your hands. If you can come through that crisis still convinced that positive differences can still be made, you will be a *rhetor*—not necessarily an effective one, but a *rhetor* nonetheless.

Elements of a persuasive story

We're not talking here about full-on storytelling, with characters and set-tings and plots and images and so on. We're talking about the bare-bones narrative with most elements assumed and unsaid. The characters are you and the others involved in the persuasive act. The setting is *now* projected perhaps into the more or less immediate future. Nevertheless, there is one element of storytelling that all persuasive stories have: resolution. You create tension, and then you resolve it.[10]

Tension comes in various forms: frustration, resistance, obstruction, any emotion created when what the protagonist wants is delayed or temporarily denied—not permanently denied because that would be the end of the story. Narrative is a process of creating, amplifying, and then relieving tension— giving your audience what it wants, in other words, by making sense of or eliminating whatever is distressing them. Sometimes what you are eliminat-ing isn't what's actually bothering them. Sometimes you may be creating a distraction or a pseudoproblem that you can solve because the real prob-lem is something you can't fix. Narratives of consolation and narratives of triumph over adversity are two examples of narratives that perform these rhetorical functions.

Most of the stories we tell ourselves we tell so fast that it's really more like a series of images flashing across our fields of vision than it is a story fully worked out, with details and intrigues and plot twists and surprises, changes of pace and reversals of fortune. We just sort of straight-line the stories we tell ourselves, especially if we know where we want to be in advance.

We tell stories to ourselves about the past as well. We use them to explain why we did what we did, to explain how we got where we are, to correct, or justify, or motivate, or hide. The more flexible our stories, the more options we have. The more rigid our stories, the fewer options we have. Just as the computer interface controls how we interact with the software by organizing our perceptions of how to use it, so the stories we tell ourselves control our perceptions of the world and thus our places in it. We know a tiny fraction of what there is to know, and yet somehow our ignorance isn't a problem for us. We are simply oblivious to the vast majority of what's going on because our stories protect us from our ignorance, until they don't anymore and we have to flip the script.

And of course we tell other people stories, too, tales of disaster and heart-break when we are trying to stop someone, tales of happiness and fulfill-ment when we want to spur them on. Occasionally we might use a more elaborate technique, like mystery by being briefly absent without explana-tion, or heroism by doing something grand—throwing a big party, organiz-ing an outing, finding a cool restaurant no one knows about. By "grand" I

---

10. Or you exploit an existing tension.

just mean relatively bigger than the ordinary, something extraordinary. To a person who's really hungry, half of your sandwich (if it came in two parts, not just whatever's left) is a grand gesture. Humorous reversals of fortune or astonishing subversions of the expected are useful when we are trying to implant the idea that what is maybe something other than what it seems. But most of the time we tell simple narratives that structure and organize the otherwise chaotic welter of details and random events that are what experience is if we just experience it without a narrative overlay to make sense of it.

When it comes to narrative, the "trick" is to let your participants write their own parts. You create the tension and hint at or gesture toward the resolution. Then you get out of their way. If you set it up right, they will get from tension to resolution on their own. If they get stuck, you can prod them a bit or cheer them on. If you are too precise with the details, there's a greater chance they won't like what you're giving them. But of course if you are too vague they won't see there's a story there at all.

Humor

> One must destroy one's adversaries' seriousness with laughter, and their laughter with seriousness. (Attributed to Gorgias in *Ancilla to the Pre-Socratic Philosophers*; Freeman 138)

Being able to tell a joke and take one, as Aristotle observed when he was enumerating the characteristics that make people feel friendly toward you (*On Rhetoric*, 2.4), is a significant rhetorical skill. If you have a good sense of humor, people tend to feel good around you, and that means they are more likely to trust you, which means they are more likely to listen to you. You seem generous and non-judgmental, slow to accuse and slow to feel slighted, strong, secure, in control. (*Is this why "a good sense of humor" is so high on compatibility charts used in online dating sites?*)

The opposite, of course, is also true. Being completely humorless is often interpreted as a sign of oppression or weakness. If you can't take a joke, people may think you are impotent or frustrated, lacking self-esteem, or just ill humored and therefore unlikable. And yet, in some settings letting people laugh at you can have disastrous consequences for your status and credibility. Some jokes you should take; some you shouldn't stand for. Making fun of other people can elevate your status, but, again, the consequences can be disastrous. Humor is inherently risky.

Humor is rarely discussed in the rhetorical tradition,[11] primarily because of all the rhetorical skills it seems the most natural and therefore the least

---

11. Cicero has a rare section on humor in *De Orator* (chapters 54–73), and that's about it.

teachable. You can memorize jokes, but if you don't deliver the punch lines correctly, after waiting a beat for the full effect, you won't be funny.

There are two kinds of humor that rely primarily on words. Set pieces, jokes of the *a duck, a cat, and an antelope walk into a bar* variety, are hard for most people to work into normal conversation, even harder to pull off in writing. If you don't select the right kind of joke for the people and the setting, you might be worse than just not funny. Because most of these jokes make fun at a group's expense, anyone who identifies with that group will be offended. Even people who don't identify might be offended by your taking shots at others. So if you are going to teach yourself how to be funny in this way, curate your material carefully, and pay attention to who is going to pay for each joke.

The other kind of verbal humor, contextual humor, where you get a laugh by using what's happening at the moment, what's being said or done, is even harder to learn by studying others do it. And while it is possible to theorize a bit about how contextual humor works, as you will see as I fumble it in the following paragraphs, having a sense of how it's done does little to help you do it better.

There are many different levels of intensity of humor, everything from a grin to a fit (of laughter) or a spasm so intense one loses bodily control, tears and worse. (*Division, right?*) The level of intensity you might try to go for of course depends on the setting and the circumstance. You don't typically want people laughing uproariously in church. A mere smirk during happy hour is disappointing as well. One of the reasons it's so hard to get humor right is that laughter is caused by excess, and so the tendency is to go over the top, take it too far, or make fun of something too soon.

The best example of the latter I can think of is Gilbert Gottfried's telling of "The Aristocrats" at the Friar's Club roast for Hugh Hefner that took place three weeks after the World Trade Center bombing. Given what had just happened, the event probably should have been cancelled, but given the show-must-go-on attitude of show business they went for it anyway. Gottfried, once the voice of the Aflac Duck, gets up and tells a joke every comedian knows, a joke that is generally considered the most inappropriate joke ever told. It's the joke comedians tell each other between sets and after hours, a kind of insider's thing, where the way you tell it is what determines if you're funny or not because everyone's already heard it.[12]

I suspect Gottfried just couldn't resist; the setup was just too obvious to ignore. Here he was with all these people hoping to distract themselves from the misery of what had just happened literally just down the street with some good-natured raillery at Hugh Hefner, a guy whose persona is laughable

---

12. You can find Gilbert Gottfried and "The Aristocrats" by searching YouTube. But if you want to learn something about humor, and you're not horrified by staggering vulgarity, stream the documentary called *The Aristocrats* (2005).

anyway. The tension must have been intense. He opens with something like "I couldn't get a direct flight to New York because they'd have to stop at the Empire State Building," and the audience hisses and boos, "too soon!" And then he launches into the joke. The effect is both stunning and instructive. The general audience is horrified, and the comedians who are there to participate in the roast and sitting in the front rows of the house are all writhing in pain, trying so hard not to laugh at what is truly appalling and yet funny—not the joke so much as the fact that he's telling it at this particular moment. Humor comes from excess, but so does monstrosity.

The more solemn the circumstance the more compelled some people feel to laugh because laughter can relieve tension and create a sense of relief. The wedding scene of *Four Weddings and a Funeral* is a much more positive example of how to exploit this phenomenon.[13] The incongruity between the solemnity of the occasion and the unintentional hilarity of what the priest wants so desperately not to be saying provokes laughter.

Here is a literary example of humor by incongruity:

> It was the day my grandmother exploded. I sat in the crematorium, listening to my Uncle Hamish quietly snoring in harmony to Bach's Mass in B Minor, and I reflected that it always seemed to be death that drew me back to Gallanach. (Iain Banks 1)

The unexpected and the incongruous. The bigger the difference between what the audience expects and what you deliver, the bigger the effect.

There is a kind of violence to nearly all forms of humor. This is why comedians say they "killed" when a show went well. Humor is rhetorically indispensable because it can lighten the mood and bring people together, but it is also rhetorically dangerous. There is something of the paradox about all humor as well because the less apparently amused the *rhetor* the more amused the audience. Don't laugh at your own jokes.

Quintilian put it this way:

> Nothing is more silly than what is offered as witty. Gravity, however, adds much to the force of jests, and the very circumstance that he who utters a joke does not laugh, makes others laugh; yet sometimes a humorous look, a cast of countenance, or a gesture may be assumed, provided that certain bounds be observed. (6.3.26)

A great, and silly, contemporary example can be found in season 5, episode 16 ("The Vacation Solution"), of *The Big Bang Theory*, when Sheldon Cooper, a theoretical physicist, is trying to tell his friends about a Mad Libs

---

13. Search YouTube for "Four Weddings and a Funeral Scene."

game he's invented but is laughing so hard at his own wit he can't get the words out.[14] His friends of course don't think he's funny. Part of what we, the audience, laugh at here is Sheldon's persona. He's a precocious physicist who lacks social skills and knows it. He doesn't understand sarcasm and so keeps a running score of how often he gets and fails to get it, which is exactly how one becomes an expert at anything, define the parameters and then track your progress, but it's funny to us because humor seems like a "natural" quality, not something one can learn by keeping statistics and generating hypotheses. Sheldon's struggles to comprehend what most people feel like they were born understanding come from a psychological phenomenon. Asperger's is a syndrome with known traits, one of which is a problem understanding and executing interpersonal skills. So when we laugh at Sheldon we are laughing at someone who has a psychological condition, so in a way we should be ashamed of ourselves. But his condition seems more like a set of foibles and weirdnesses (his friend Leonard says they call him "quirky") than some kind of namable disorder. He has other characteristics that make him admirable (he is generous with money), as well as others that make him just sort of dorky (he loves Halloween because he can dress up as his favorite comic book characters). Basically he's adorkable, so we don't feel badly laughing at him. Nevertheless, his character clearly represents a psychological condition, and if you work at a university and know that Asperger's is also known as the "little professor's disease" and that one of the best definitions of the *academic* is "those people who no one would dance with in high school," your right eye might twitch a bit watching him. (See the upcoming paragraphs on self-deprecation.)

One of the primary rhetorical purposes of humor is to make a group of people feel superior either to another group or just superior in general. The kind of humor that makes people feel better by feeling superior to another group is usually (Sheldon Cooper not withstanding) ugly and small minded and ought to be avoided on ethical grounds alone. Now that any live event can find its way onto YouTube, if the ethics argument doesn't move you, consider the unintended consequences that might happen if whoever you made fun of found out about it or everyone found out about it. You don't need to denigrate one group to elevate another. If you feel compelled to go for the ugly, try to denigrate everyone equally by denigrating the idea rather than the people who represent it. Someone once defined suicide as permanent solution to a temporary problem. And I said, "Oh, I thought that was marriage." For some reason my wife never laughs at this joke.

While making fun of people can provoke laughter, it's a laugh at the expense of others, and so it's rarely the best way to go. The more rhetorically sophisticated form of humor makes the audience feel superior not at the expense of another group but in a general sense. This form works by giving

---

14. Search "Sheldon Cooper Mad Libs" on YouTube.

people what feels like a flash of insight. We might call this the *Oh, I get it* phenomenon. By making your audience draw an inference that is slightly different from the expected inference, you get a laugh that can serve a wide variety of purposes: to diffuse tension (surprise, relief); deflect criticism (deflate, distract); encourage optimism, generosity, even magnanimity.

The rhetorical effect of this kind of laughter is to lighten the mood. When people are in a good humor, they are likely to make less harsh, less self-righteous decisions. They are more likely to let a slight pass or an incompetence slide. You can't measure the rhetorical effectiveness of a joke by the size of the laugh it gets but rather by the nature of the decision or verdict. If the outcome was better than you hoped, humor might have helped. If worse, then it probably didn't. But more often than not you won't really know.

A secondary rhetorical purpose of humor, after making people feel good about themselves, is to make people feel good about *you*, to see you as smart, entertaining, easygoing, fun, maybe even just a little bit wicked or dangerous, or at least the sort of person who will occasionally color outside the lines. Aristotle defined wit as well-bred or cultured insolence (*On Rhetoric*, 2.12), a healthy disrespect for all things too readily admired. As always, however, know your audience. If the people you are with are painfully earnest, coloring outside the lines won't do much for you in their eyes. And if the people you are with feel as though their place in the world is threatened or undervalued, they may think you aren't serious enough or are too light hearted.

Another form of humor is self-deprecation, lifting people up by putting yourself down. Self-deprecation only works if you are "superior" to them or they feel "inferior" to you or are intimidated by you, and you will be better off if they feel more equal. I saw a T-shirt recently that said, "I'm no rocket surgeon." Years ago there was a presidential candidate running on an independent ticket named Ross Perot who had inordinately large ears. During one of the debates an opponent tried to shut him up by saying, "Listen to me!" and Perot put his hands behind his big ears and said, "I'm all ears." If you have a personal characteristic that you know some people might use to try to rattle you, you might want to get there first; that way they will think it won't work, and they won't bother. And then of course there is the always reliable Homeric allusion, "I am so smart, s-m-r-t."[15]

---

15. There were two jokes in that sentence. Did you get both of them? The misspelling was fairly obvious. The Homeric allusion was a reference to Homer Simpson of *The Simpsons*, not the blind poet of ancient Greece. I was trying to be funny. And also trying to demonstrate one of the problems with humor. If you've never seen *The Simpsons* or don't know who wrote the *Odyssey*, then you didn't get the joke. You might have gotten it and thought it unfunny, too. I admit it wasn't great. Like I said, humor is difficult.

Obviously you can take self-deprecation too far, and if you do you're in a really tough rhetorical spot. People will think you have low self-esteem or that you are insincere or really needy, searching for praise and affirmation. People don't like to be around people like that, unless they are the kind of person who feeds off of people like that. If you find yourself with someone who wants to put you down, who feels best about themselves when they make others feel worse, walk away, and don't look back.

The broadest form of humor is physical, mimicry and mockery (voices and gestures) and clowning (sustained physical humor). Playing with a foreign accent or impersonating someone famous can get a laugh, but it can also create enmity or just make you look foolish. Don't sacrifice your credibility for the sake of a laugh or let nervous tension turn you into a buffoon. "Whatever a good man says," said Quintilian, "he will say with dignity and decency, for the price of a laugh is too high if it is raised at the expense of propriety" (6.3.34).

Cicero is said to have had a self-destructive penchant for saying humorously cutting things about powerful people in earshot of others who would bring the comment back to the target (Everitt 122). This is a kind of passive-aggressive behavior that can and did eventually make powerful enemies. You can get a laugh from your co-workers by making fun of the boss, by playing up one of his or her idiosyncrasies. You can get the same laugh from your fellow students by clowning your teachers. But at what cost?

Conclusion: Be careful with humor. If you try to be funny all the time, people may stop taking you seriously. And if you try to be funny and fail, rather than laughter you might provoke anger, ridicule, or disgust. Even a good joke can destroy your credibility if you tell it at the wrong time or to the wrong people. A bad joke will set the audience against you. A really bad joke can destroy your career. Nevertheless, if you can make people laugh or even just smile good naturedly, you can accomplish a great deal more than if you have to approach everything without any levity. Flat bread fills the stomach but dulls the senses.

Charm and wit are powerful rhetorical tools. They are, as people have often said, like salt: just the right amount and the good gets infinitely better; too much and the whole dish is ruined. You are a *rhetor* not a clown.

━━━━ Your Turn

Having said a dozen times to be careful, now I want you to ignore me. You can't get better if you don't fail, and it's a good idea to fail in a safe space, where your reputation isn't on the line and nothing's at stake. So, make a list of all of the jokes you can think of in ten minutes or so. Then head out on the Internet, and go looking for jokes. What makes you laugh and why? How do those jokes compare to the ones you remembered? Now, locate what you think is the funniest joke, and share it with some other people. What's their reaction? Did you share the funniest thing you found or censor yourself in favor of something funny but less potentially offensive? Or is it just me who howls at aristocratic vulgarity?

The dark side

I hope you got a few laughs out of the last section because the next section is no laughing matter. The next several sections are about how rhetoric is used (*notice the passive voice?*) to manipulate and control people. You need to know these things to better guard against them. You may need to use some of them on occasion as well, but be careful if you do. If you mess up your grammar, people may think you poorly educated. If you mess up this kind of rhetoric, you may find yourself in jail.

Power and persuasion

One of the commonplaces of classical rhetoric is that rhetoric is a positive alternative to violence. If you can persuade someone you needn't intimidate, constrain, or repress them. But if we look more closely (*notice the optical metaphor there?*) at the tradition, we can see that persuasion was often plan B. A Greek historian named Herodotus put this idea in the mouth of a Melian ambassador who was sent to Athens to negotiate peace, or, more accurately, the terms of surrender.

> You know as well as we that what is just is arrived at by human arguments only when the necessity [for doing so] on both sides is equal; but the powerful do whatever they want, while the weak yield. (Thucydides 5.89)

Rhetoric in the Western tradition (we will look at Eastern in a minute) is predicated on the idea of equality, that any citizen should be able to address any other citizen freely. As a result, little is said about how to behave with one's social superiors. It is important to realize, however, that Greek culture was not truly egalitarian. Only men whose parents were both born in a given city had voting rights in that city. Women, children, non-citizen freemen, and slaves, in other words the vast majority of people, had no rights. So the classical idea of equality was nothing like we would recognize today.

Despite the actual imbalance of power, most of the classical handbooks on rhetoric neglect rhetorical advice that might apply between people of different social status and rank because there was no need to persuade one's inferiors. You issued orders or just took what you wanted. To provide someone with reasons and arguments was to accord them the status of equality, and that you would do only if you had to. Even today there is little rhetorical advice about how to get what you want from people more powerful than you. We prefer to imagine that truth can speak to power and that "reason" transcends rank and social status.

From a rhetorical perspective, the idea that anything rhetorical is necessarily tainted, either by experience or power or corruption, is itself a rhetoric, a belief founded on generalizations and amalgamations of several of the topics of preference, not an accurate depiction of reality but a partisan construction of opinions aimed at replacing one authority with another. The rhetoric of truth *is* a rhetoric of power. Nietzsche taught us this ("On Truth and Lie in an Extra-Moral Sense"). He also taught us, however, that knowing how persuasion works doesn't liberate us from it. Language is an onion, as he said, layer upon layer upon layer upon nothing. I'm not being nihilistic here. Our perceptions are unreliable, our opinions change, and our understanding of the world is constantly being renovated and remodeled. This is a good thing. At least it is a prerequisite to being a *rhetor* because being able to see ideas from many perspectives, speak in many voices, and think from different angles is what enables a person to make the most persuasive case possible in the most compelling way. A rigid commitment to a single set of unquestionable ideas is anathema to persuasive thinking. There's nothing wrong with having some principles upon which we will always insist, but calling these principles "the real" or "the true" is a rhetorical effort to hide the rhetorical nature of the principles. If you do that unknowingly, then you are being rhetorically naive. If you do it knowingly, then you are being insincere.

> It is the mark of an educated mind to be able to entertain a thought without accepting it. (Aristotle)

The no-spin zone is a spin zone. Anyone who says, "trust me," is almost certainly lying to you. Don't believe me? Good.

At any rate, such is my justification for what I am about to do. I am about to show you the dark side of persuasion. I'm going to show you how to manipulate people. (*Would it be better if I put that in the passive voice and said I'm going to show you how people are manipulated?*) I could of course provide a parental advisory warning here or offer something of a *don't try this at home* disclaimer, but I'm not going to. (*Why?*) Because not every relationship you encounter in life will be honest and open and based on equality, and on those occasions you need more options than much of what we've considered so far affords.

If equality can be defined as mutual need and mutual benefit, then whenever one person has more or needs less than another, he or she is more powerful than the other. So when it comes to rhetoric and power, your options are either to eliminate all desire and minimize your needs (self-control) to the point where you do not need to communicate with others because you have no need of them or obtain enough persuasive power to live happily among others. You need to approximate either Alexander or Diogenes.[16]

As far as I can tell, the best place to come to an understanding about rhetoric among unequals is a piece called the "The Difficulties of Persuasion," written by a Chinese scholar named Han Fei. This piece was apparently written in what the Western calendar refers to as the second century BCE and what is known in China as the Warring States Period. This was during the time when what is now China was a collection of independent states organized by warlords who were constantly fighting for territory and fealty. Prior to unification there were a number of men who for various reasons left their home states to go live in another state, and while there they developed a relationship with the reigning power. Han Fei was such a man, and his "Difficulties of Persuasion" is advice to one who would follow in his footsteps. You need to read it and talk with others about it and write about it for yourself to really start to feel a rhetoric of absolute inequality, but I will summarize some of the key points for you here.

The primary principle is that the reigning power, the emperor, has absolute power over everybody. He can kill at will. He can promote at will. He answers to no one. His word is law. You cannot argue with this person. You cannot offer advice directly. If you offend him, you are dead. If you make him suspicious, you are dead. If you make yourself seem wiser or better or kinder or any positive quality more than he is, you are dead. In addition, there are others at court working under the same conditions who also harbor some ambition to get close to the emperor, and every one of them is your potential enemy because you want what they want, and you can't be sure all of you can have it. Given all of these dangerous conditions, why get involved?

Fei suggests that you do so because you know what the emperor needs to know in order to ensure the peace and security of the land. The difficulty, the ultimate difficulty of all persuasion, is that you can't come right out and say it because it's not your place to do that. You have to be subtle, indirect, say things in a way that makes it seem like maybe you didn't say it or that you were actually saying something else. Your goal is for the emperor to think the ideas were his from the start.

---

16. The very richest and most powerful people are oddly similar to the poorest and most detached in that both are beyond need. There's a famous *chreia* about Diogenes of Synope, the original cynic, and Alexander the Great: Alexander came across Diogenes lying in the gutter as was his custom, and Alexander, not knowing who he was and wishing to make a show of magnanimity to his followers, walked up to Diogenes and said, "I am Alexander the Great. I will grant you anything you want." And Diogenes said, opening one eye, "You're blocking the sun; step away." Later, it is said, that Alexander remarked, "If I could not be Alexander I would be Diogenes."

Given these conditions, certain principles of persuasion apply. "The Difficulties of Persuasion" begins in the following way:

> On the whole, the difficult thing about persuading others is not that one lacks the knowledge needed to state his case nor the audacity to exercise his abilities to the full. On the whole, the difficult thing about persuasion is to know the mind of the person one is trying to persuade and to be able to fit one's words to it. (73)

This dismissal of knowledge is astonishing, from a Western rhetorical perspective. The idea that knowledge is a given would make Plato rage and Aristotle blink in disbelief. The second part, however, that one must fit one's words to the other person's mind, would inspire a sagely nod from both.

From here Han Fei makes a distinction between the public and the private that Plato might have accepted but Aristotle would have excluded by definition because for him rhetoric is public discourse. Regardless of how it might have played out in the ancient Mediterranean, the advice holds up, I think. People will agree to something in private that they would not accept in public because of peer pressure or conventional standards of decency. The expression *political correctness* is sometimes used to denote a discrepancy between public and private beliefs. Although when that expression is used, typically the user is asserting that all reasonable people privately share his attitudes and beliefs even if they lack his courage in admitting them in public.

Kahneman tells the story of how office workers were persuaded to contribute more often to the general coffee fund simply by having a picture of a pair of eyes taped to the wall over the coffee pot (57). Even though the workers were alone while getting a cup of coffee, and had in the past been disinclined to toss a quarter or a dollar in the jar, the eyes made them less inclined to freeload.

Fei puts it this way:

> If the person you are trying to persuade is secretly out for big gain but ostensibly claims to be interested in a virtuous name alone, and you talk to him about a reputation for virtue, then he will pretend to welcome and heed you, but in fact will shunt you aside; if you talk to him about making a big gain, he will secretly follow your advice but ostensibly reject you. (73)

Conflicting values create treacherous conditions. If you add to this idea that most of us are unknowingly hypocritical, that what we think and what we do don't match consistently because we tend to think different things in different contexts, then you've got a pretty good idea about why this kind of persuasion is so dangerous. (*Good for you if you read the previous sentence against the grain—have another look at the section on cognitive biases.*)

Fei also advises the would-be advisor that the speaker's relation to the listener is more important for persuasion than the truth of what he is saying.

> Once there was a rich man of Sung. When the dirt wall around his house collapsed in a heavy rain, his son said, "If you don't rebuild it, thieves will surely break in," and the old man who lived next door told him the same thing. When night fell, thieves actually broke in and made off with a large share of the rich man's wealth. The rich man's family praised the son for his wisdom, but eyed the old man next door with suspicion. (77)

Fei doesn't come right out and tell us what the meaning of the parable is. He leaves us to draw the appropriate conclusion for ourselves, which is an example of the technique he is encouraging us to use. Just in case you missed it, I'll do the Western rhetorical thing and come right out and say it. The son can say what the neighbor can't because his own interests are aligned with the family's interests while the neighbor could gain from the family's loss and so must be mistrusted.

The difficulties continue. The emperor's attitude toward you will determine how he hears what you tell him. When you are in his favor, you can do no wrong; if you fall out of favor, not only will everything you do be wrong, but every past success will be turned against you. You must never incur blame nor do anything to push yourself from favor, but expect the worst if you fall.

Play up what the emperor is proud of and play down what he dislikes, but at the same time try to attach at least two sets of reasons for any given action, those that are idealistic and consistent with public policy and another more expedient and consistent with the emperor's inclinations and personal commitments and belief, if they vary from his public opinions, but never do this in public. If you do it in earshot of anyone, the emperor will have to kill you.

You need to maintain secrecy at all costs; conceal your actions; don't inadvertently discover others actions (if you come across someone else's plans, don't let anyone know you know); don't expose the emperor's plans or thoughts or show him that you know what you know. While the Greeks understood that "naturalness" as opposed to overt, contrived, or feigned behavior was an important element for rhetorical success, and Aristotle says in several different places that concealment is necessary, Fei takes the need for secrecy to a much higher level, partially because the stakes are higher. If you mess it up, the best you can hope for is having your feet amputated. I'm not making this up. But you also need to be secretive because speaking directly about anything important isn't an option whenever the person you would persuade is infinitely more powerful than you are, which happens whenever you need them more than they need you.

The emperor must always come to the conclusion you want him to come to on his own, unaware that you led him there. He will take credit for it anyway if it is successful, and if it's unsuccessful he may not realize it's you he needs to kill for being wrong. You have to be invisible. If you are right, he will kill you. If you are wrong, he will kill you. You have to influence the emperor's decisions the way gravity influences orbiting objects.

You lay out the thoughts, circle around, suggest possibilities, and let the other person decide. It would be considered incredibly rude to take the you-want-this-for-the-following-three-reasons approach.

As Fei says, "It is not difficult to know a thing; what is difficult is to know how to use what you know." (78)

It's important to realize that being indirect is not a geographical (West vs. East) but rather a social phenomenon that is a consequence of hierarchically arranged societies. Thus indirection plays a part in any culture or subculture where one person or group is "superior" to another because indirection is a way of showing deference and thus a way of granting superiority to someone, just as giving orders and bossing people around is a way of trying to assert superiority.

Power is about who needs whom more. The rhetorical choice between direct and indirect forms of expression demonstrate a power differential, whether you are in Beijing or Washington or Ottawa or Sydney.

Despite Western rhetoric's commitment to the rhetoric of equality, it has always been aware that a soft touch is sometimes invaluable.

One might argue, in fact, that even for the Greeks *subtlety is the fundamental rhetorical principle*. As Aristotle explains, "Naturalness is persuasive, artificiality is the contrary; for our hearers are prejudiced and think we have some design against them" (*On Rhetoric*, 3.2, 1404b). Quintilian is even more emphatic about the need for subtlety in *Institutes of Oratory* (*Institutio Oratoria*):

> Sometimes, too, the judge must be misled and wrought upon by various artifices, that he may suppose something else to be intended than what is really our object. (4.5.5)

Ingratiation

Ingratiation refers to the set of techniques one uses to fit in and get along with people. Some people are adept at ingratiation, others not at all. Among those who don't get it are some who are oblivious to others, egocentric types. Others disapprove of ingratiation generally; these are irascible people or people who want above all to be left alone, who think that any attempt to reach out to another person is flattery, while trying to blend in will destroy one's identity and autonomy. Among those who are adept at ingratiation, it's worth noting, are those people who can't help but fit in, to the point where their sense of self and their autonomy are indeed compromised. The vast majority of people simply seek to fit in where they feel they belong, and they don't venture out often once they've found their place. But even there they spend some time ingratiating themselves to others, to cement their place in the group and to support the community in general. Rhetors see ingratiation as a technique, an option, when fitting in will be more effective than standing out.[17]

A common form of ingratiation is *asking a question instead of making a demand*. "You wouldn't happen to have a bottle of water, would you?" is obviously quite a bit different from "Get me some water." A variant of this is making a statement from which you hope your listener will draw the correct inference. "I'm thirsty," for example. The advantage of such an indirect approach is that it may give you a chance to see if your listener is paying attention to you, is on the same page as you, as it were, and it may also help to hide or minimize a difference in status. You are in a position to make demands, but you're a nice boss, and you don't want to pull rank. The downside of asking when demanding is that you may not get what you want. If you make someone infer your needs, they may infer incorrectly or miss the point entirely. They may think you are weak or that you don't know what you want. Or they may be so focused on their own needs that they don't notice yours. In any setting, whenever you make your audience infer, you cede control. As Fei reminds us, sometimes you have to. But even if your audience isn't an emperor, you may want to. When you are trying to teach people, for example, when you want the "aha!" moment of insight to reinforce an important idea, you might want to walk right up to the point and then say nothing.

On the other hand, if you frequently play *guess what's on my mind* you may alienate people. Men and women often get into relationship difficulties because women sometimes tend toward rhetorical acts that require inference (a rhetoric of community) while many men tend toward direct rhetorical acts (a rhetoric of autonomy), with the mismatching result that she thinks he is insensitive and he thinks she is vague. If you find the idea of gendered rhetorics appealing, there are dozens of texts to pursue, but you might want to start with Deborah Tannen's *That's Not What I Meant*.

Perhaps the most powerful form of indirect persuasion is to *lead by example*. By doing the things you want others to do, and making it appear that they can do them, too, you indirectly encourage compliance. People tend to do what the people they admire do, but they also tend to do what the other people around them are doing, so even if you are not in a position to get people to follow your lead you can lead by taking the lead. Show enough enthusiasm for a course of action, and do it successfully for a while, and people will start doing it, too. So, for example, if you want to help someone lose weight,

---

17. Can you identify the structure of that paragraph? It's a form of division, where I took a word, said there were two types, then divided the types into types. It's a standard opening move. Notice also how the last sentence ties the set of ideas to the main idea, how to be a *rhetor*.

get into some kind of interesting exercise program or some aerobic sport, and talk about how much you are loving it.

The indirect form of gift giving is doing someone a favor. Doing someone a favor can have both positive and negative effects. Everything depends on whether the receiver feels gratitude or humiliation. To help someone in front of their friends or family or business associates is likely to cause humiliation, especially if you are helping someone who has a big ego or whose ego excludes the idea of getting others to do favors for him or her. Doing a big favor for someone greater than you can be very dangerous, while doing a small one will seem only like flattery or even tribute. The opposite is also true, doing a favor for someone lower than you in the hierarchy can cause trouble as well, making the beneficiary feel more important than they are, or ungrateful.

To avoid embarrassment and resentment or ingratitude, it is sometimes a very good idea to do a favor indirectly, so the receiver does not know immediately where their good fortune came from. If you want them indebted to you, then they need to know it was you, but you may not want to tell them yourself, although perhaps it will be enough if you don't tell them until you are alone. An even less direct method would be to have someone else (whom you trust) tell them, or to leave a clue or two lying around so that your beneficiary can infer it was you. There are times, too, when you might prefer your beneficiary never knows it was you—when it's really about them and not about you.

Perhaps a minute version of the favor is *politeness*. Being conscious of someone else's state and making small efforts to make them feel respected or even appreciated can go a long way toward creating a situation favorable to persuasion. At the very least it will reduce the risk of inadvertently creating resistance. Arthur Schopenhauer put it this way (pay attention to the dialectical topic of the opposite at the beginning of the quotation and the argument from analogy at the end):

> It is a wise thing to be polite; consequently, it is a stupid thing to be rude. To make enemies by unnecessary and willful incivility, is just as insane a proceeding as to set your house on fire. For politeness is like a counter—an avowedly false coin, with which it is foolish to be stingy. A sensible man will be generous in the use of it. . . . Wax, a substance naturally hard and brittle, can be made soft by the application of a little warmth, so that it will take any shape you please. In the same way, by being polite and friendly you can make people pliable and obliging, even though they are apt to be crabbed and malevolent. Hence politeness is to human nature what warmth is to wax. (Schopenhauer, *The Wisdom of Life*, 108)

By contemporary stylistic standards, Schopenhauer's prose might be a bit long winded. Certainly wouldn't fit in a Twitter feed. See if you can say the same thing in half as many words. Hint: wax.

Saying to someone "I really like you" is a direct form of ingratiation and thus potentially embarrassing for both parties. This is why we have flattery, which is an indirect form of ingratiation. Telling someone you like their shoes or their suit is an indirect form of flattery. Being appropriately indirect is the key to successful flattery, typically. Saying something like "Look at those shoes! You have great taste in fashion; you must be crazy rich!" is a slobbering sort of way to suck up to someone, whereas "Oh, cool! Prada?" is much less likely to come across grossly (assuming the shoes are Prada or some aspiring but less expensive brand). You don't have to actually care about shoes (or football or physics or anything else) to do this well, but you have to know about whatever the subject is. If you lack knowledge of something someone else obviously prizes, either because they talk about it all the time or seem to have invested in it, figuratively or literally, then you can show an interest yourself. That's fascinating; tell me more.

I did the opposite of ingratiation once, by accident, although in retrospect I was less ashamed of it than I probably should have been. Many years ago, a young woman whose family was rich enough to buy her a sports car gave me a ride to a restaurant, and as I was getting into her Maserati in the semidarkness I said, "Hey, cool car; is this a Mazda?" She did her best to pass it off as the faux pas of a Canadian rube, but she was clearly unimpressed.

The most common kind of indirection is perhaps *irony*. The "Is this a Mazda?" question would have been a kind of irony if there had been someone there who liked to make fun of the rich and undeserving. The humor for the cynical observer would have been in our collective but hidden (indirect) stance against the unsuspecting snob. This might be a good moment to read the section on humor, but let me summarize the main ideas for you right now. A "good" sense of humor is rhetorically important because having one draws people to you by making them feel comfortable around you. Take humor too far, though, and people will think you aren't a serious person or that you are neurotic in some way. Also, humor is potentially alienating so you need to be careful about how you go about it. Using set pieces, *Have you heard the one about the penguin and the nun?* is especially dangerous in a crowd, because you are either likely to offend someone or fail to get a laugh at all. Set pieces are also premeditated and therefore seem contrived. Contextual humor, on the other hand, where you get a laugh out of what's going on right now can have a very positive effect on your *ethos* because you will come across as witty, quick witted, and smart. Again, get it wrong and you're just a jerk or a dork. Humor is dangerous because it is powerful. You can learn a great deal about people by what makes them laugh how.

Allegory

Allegory is a more elaborate and sustained use of indirection than irony, obviously, and one that enables a wide range of audience responses. Political allegory (think Orwell's *Animal Farm*, for example) can protect both the author and the knowing audience by distracting or confusing those in power and those too naive to realize they are being abused by those in power.

Indirection is also a dialectical technique (think cross-examination), where in the game of question and answer one asks a question at one or two removes from what one really wants the opponent to admit, to keep the opponent off balance and unable to prepare a defense. If you ask, "Were you at the seen of the crime?" you're less likely to get an admission you can use than if you ask, "Were you at the Corner Tavern on Halloween last year?"

Here's a better example. I found this in *You Can Read Anyone*, by David J. Lieberman:

> The question is, "Are you happy in your marriage?" The primary correlated statistic is: people who are happy in marriage are grateful for their spouse. The secondary correlated statistic is: a person who is grateful for his spouse tends not to take advantage of her [sic.] The question is, "Do you think taking advantage of your spouse is simply part of marriage?" (37)

He also offers the example of a trial lawyer who wants to know if a prospective juror is pro–death penalty. Not wanting to ask directly, and knowing that most people who are pro–death penalty are anti–gun control, the lawyer might ask whether Smith and Wesson should be held accountable for deaths caused by their guns (38).

Another form of indirection relevant to cross-examination is what is called a complex question, where the answer necessarily incriminates the answerer: Have you stopped beating your spouse? That looks like a yes-or-no question, but either *yes* or *no* are equally incriminating. Obviously the respondent has to object to the question. There are far more subtle forms of a complex question, of course.

Nearly all political campaigns are organized around expressions that are designed to make opposition appear unreasonable. If the opponent accepts the terms of the debate, he will lose automatically. This is why so much political discussion is fruitless. There is no stasis upon which to build a real argument. Someone who is pro-life is not therefore antichoice, just as one who is pro-choice is not therefore antilife. Those expressions disable real debate by excluding the opposition from the realm of reasonable beings. A shouting match like the kind engendered by such *asystatic* arguments is also a form of indirection. If you find yourself cornered by two opponents, set one against the other, and while they are fighting you can slip away.

Clairvoyance: The art of cold reading

How well does the following quotation describe you?

> You have a need for other people to like and admire you, and yet you tend to be critical of yourself. While you have some personality weaknesses you are generally able to compensate for them. You have considerable unused capacity that you have not turned to your advantage. At times you have serious doubts whether you have made the right decision or done the right thing. (*The Skeptic's Dictionary*, Barnum Effect)

THE FOOL .

If you are like nearly all people encountering this series of assertions for the first time, your first thought was probably something like "Hmm, that's actually pretty close to me." I'm guessing you said something like that because the statement above is crafted for the broadest possible appeal. Most people want to be liked, and most people have doubts and feel underappreciated. If you identified with the above statement, it's not because it describes you but because it describes everyone, and you took it personally. There is an important lesson about persuasion here. In some rhetorical situations, the audience does most of the persuading, and the *rhetor* just facilitates the process. These kinds of rhetorical acts are all about saying as close to nothing as possible.

Cold reading is a perfect example. Cold reading is a highly elaborated and contextualized kind of flattery designed to charm people, typically willing participants, out of their money. Cold reading is how psychics "read minds" and "predict the future." They use a set of rhetorical tricks, carefully crafted vagaries and leading statements, out of which the person being read can construct meaning and significance. When we think of rhetorical acts we tend to think of the speaker creating meaning for the audience, but here the audience creates meaning for themselves and attributes it to the speaker.

There are several well-known techniques that you can discover online if you do a Google search for "cold reading." I will describe some of the most common.

The first step in cold reading is to acquire the target's complicity by under-playing your ability so as to reduce expectations and give you an out if you say something they reject. One way to do this is to say that there's a lot of static in the air today and so the messages you are receiving are fuzzy, merely meta-phors or impressions that may seem a bit obscure at first but will become clearer if the client helps interpret the messages. You then increase the level of participation by saying something like "I can tell you are an unusually perceptive person who has a natural capacity for understanding the super-natural," or whatever you can think of that will make them work harder to see meaning in what you are about to say, since if they fail to find meaning they are in a sense blaming themselves for the failure.

Another common technique is to use a prop like tarot cards or a crystal ball or an astrological chart. The prop gives the client the impression there is some magical or, if you prefer, supernatural technology involved, and it gives you time to ponder what you will say next. The prop may also distract your client's gaze so you can steal glances at them to see how they are affected by what you've just said. Obviously, as a rhetorician you are not going to set yourself up as a psychic or palmist, but you can, if you need to, use charts, tables, images, and iconography to create a mood and provide your audi-ence with objects out of which to create meanings. The harder the audience works, the greater their commitment to the result will be—to a point. If you are too obscure they won't consider you oracular; they will consider you inscrutable or deceitfully vague. You have to get the balance of transparent to opaque just right. One way to get the balance right is to say things anyone not reading against the grain would be inclined to accept.

Forer statements, more commonly known as Barnum statements, are gen-eral assertions that sound like individual assessments of a person's character or inner being. The idea comes from the psychologist Bertrand R. Forer who, in 1949, gave his students the following passage and asked them to judge on a scale of 1 to 5 whether they felt the description fit them personally.

> You have a great need for other people to like and admire you. You have a tendency to be critical of yourself. You have a great deal of unused capacity which you have not turned to your advantage. While you have some personality weaknesses, you are generally able to compensate for them. Your sexual adjustment has pre-sented problems for you. Disciplined and self-controlled outside, you tend to be worrisome and insecure inside. At times you have serious doubts as to whether you have made the right decision or done the right thing. You prefer a certain amount of change and variety and become dissatisfied when hemmed in by restrictions and limitations. You pride yourself as an independent thinker and do not accept others' statements without satisfactory proof. You have found it unwise to be too frank in revealing yourself

to others. At times you are extroverted, affable, sociable, while at other times you are introverted, wary, reserved. Some of your aspirations tend to be pretty unrealistic. Security is one of your major goals in life. (Forer)

Each student thought he or she was given a unique description, whereas in fact they all received the same description. The average rating was 4.26 out of 5. In other words, the vast majority of the students felt the passage accurately described them personally even though the passage was composed of statements Forer had gotten out of the horoscope pages. Forer's point was that people are often poor self-judges, and thus would-be psychologists should be careful of self-reporting as a starting point for analysis. In the context of cold reading, however, the construction of readily acceptable assertions presented to a gullible audience as observations about unique character traits go to the heart of the rhetorical practice.

Another technique common to cold reading is sometimes called *fishing*, where you say something just to get a reaction and then go from there based on what the client says. If they look surprised or offer a refinement of what you just said, you know you are on to something. If they remain unmoved or look indifferent, you've gotten colder. If they look annoyed or upset, you might be on to the opposite of something, so reverse directions. If worse comes to worst, fall back on the ruse that perhaps you were getting a message from someone close to them, perhaps a close friend, or maybe a new acquaintance. Disarm by deflecting.

Some statements are perfect for this because they are intentionally contradictory, allowing the speaker to have it both ways. This technique is sometimes known as the *rainbow ruse*. (The alliteration makes it more memorable.) For example, *You have a tendency to be very self-critical, but other times you just want to be you. You are basically a generous-hearted soul, but you get angry when people get better than they deserve. You are basically an honest person, but you will lie to spare a friend's feelings.* Rainbows work because they offer both ends of the spectrum at once, and the client will likely pick up on one end of the spectrum, and then you can go from there. At the very least you've said something that can't really be denied because it is so broadly inclusive.

Here is another widely applicable example of a rainbow statement: *People don't fully appreciate you. You have a great deal of unrealized potential.* This rainbow works because of what psychologists call the *above-average effect*. Most people think they are smarter and harder working than other people. That's not just because most of us are egotistical; well, actually it is. All of us are very aware of what's going on in our own experiences and not very aware of anybody else's experiences, with the result that we tend to think of ourselves as unique and everyone else as much less so. Even our close friends and family members are not as vividly knowable to us as we are to ourselves.

There's a neat experiment that the brothers Heath relate in *Made to Stick* that might make this point more clearly than I can. Hum the song "Happy Birthday" in your head while you tap out the rhythm on the desk or the arm of your chair or edge of your e-reader. What are the chances that someone hearing you tap out the rhythm could guess what song you are humming in your head? Many people think it might be quite high, like 50 percent. Elizabeth Newton, the psychologist who first performed this experiment, discovered that it's actually more like 2.5 percent. In other words, the chances are very poor that someone can guess what you are humming based solely on your tapping, but that's not obvious to you because you can hear yourself humming, and it doesn't occur to you that someone can't infer from the outward manifestation (tapping) what's happening in your head (humming). You have way more information than the other person, but you don't stop to think about that (Heath and Heath, 19–20).

Egocentricity, a tight focus on one's self, is a natural way to be because we have way more information about ourselves than we do about anyone else. Some people have gone so far as to assert that our understandings of others are merely hallucinations. The people are real, but what we think about them and their internal mental states are entirely our own fabulations. (*Do you buy that? Why and why not?*) At any rate, any general statement about how we are more X or Y or Z than others is one we are likely to accept if the trait is a positive one or even if it is negative but balanced by a positive.

The fact is we are not as unique as we think we are, compounded by the illusion of self-perception which makes us susceptible to rainbow statements. Another common technique is the pseudorevelation. This technique exploits people's ignorance of known facts and phenomena. If you know, for example, that an eclipse will happen at a given day and time, as you can if you know about astronomy, but your audience doesn't know about astronomy, you can amaze them by "predicting" the future.

Here is a mathemagical (*did you notice that?*) example:

- Pick a number between 1 and 10.

- Multiply that number by 9.

- You now have a two-digit number.

- Add the two digits together.

- Subtract 5 from the sum.

- Associate that number with a letter: 1 = a, 2 = b, 3 = c, 4 = d, etc.

- Now write down a country that begins with that letter.

I'll bet you a dollar you wrote down Denmark

The result is always 9: $2 \times 9 = 18$ ($1 + 8 = 9$), $3 \times 9 = 27$ ($2 + 7 = 9$), and so on. And $9 - 5$ always $= 4$, and $4 = d$, and not many countries begin with *d*. Unless you knew about the rule of the number nine and saw the inevitable conclusion coming, or thought of Dominican Republic instead of Denmark, you were probably surprised that I was able to predict Denmark. But the game was rigged. The evidence was faked. I narrowed your options, and you didn't notice me doing it. You were diligently doing the math while I was picking your pocket. (*Or were you reading against the grain?*)

All forms of rhetorical chicanery are made possible by the fact that nearly all of us are compelled to find meaning everywhere. From images of religious figures in toast to the man in the moon, we fabricate intention out of random because that gives us the illusion of control and understanding. Think about it. If someone told you life is meaningless, would you breathe a sigh of relief? And yet, much of the evidence out of which we build our meanings is of our own devising, often with the witting and unwitting collusion of others. Life may not be meaningless, but meaning is socially constructed. We tell ourselves and each other stories we want to hear, and many of them are persuasive because they make better sense of the available evidence than the evidence warrants.

Cold reading uses rhetorical techniques that are perfectly designed to exploit our compulsion to create meaning and significance out of anything at all. If the person doing the cold reading makes the person being read feel good about themselves or happy with the experience, and in return receives a commensurate compensation (like $5 for 10 minutes), then perhaps no real harm is done. But of course people use these same techniques to rob people of fortunes, and we sometimes use them on ourselves, often with unfortunate pseudobeliefs and false insights as a consequence.

Your Turn

Find a willing participant, and read them cold. Based on their age, dress, and demeanor, offer a few rainbow statements, and see if you can follow their reaction in a meaning-making way. Remember you are not really trying to predict the future so much as provide a description of the person that makes them feel good about themselves and then "predict" a few positive and statistically very likely future events. If they are wearing a wedding ring, talk finances. If they aren't wearing a wedding ring, talk romance. If they are carefully dressed, talk about how conscientious and diligent they are. If they are wearing yesterday's T-shirt, talk about how they are a deep thinker who can't be bothered by normal social conventions and superficial distractions like fashion and blah, blah, blah. . . .

Machiavellian rhetoric

Niccolò Machiavelli was a Renaissance diplomat, political philosopher, historian, playwright, novelist, and poet (a *rhetor*) who lived from 1469 to 1527. He spent much of his life fighting for the political independence of his city-state Florence from marauding foreign powers like France and Spain and from the Medici, a powerful family that sought dominion over the collection of city-states that eventually became Italy. In the end the Medici managed to capture Florence and, after being tortured as a form of interrogation regarding whether or not he was conspiring against the Medici, Machiavelli spent the remainder of his life exiled from political involvement, writing.

His most well-known book, *The Prince*, offers advice to someone who had seized power rather than having inherited it and who would need to exercise great imagination, strategy, and force if he was to remain in power and would seek to remain in power at all cost. Machiavelli's advice to the would-be leader clearly reflects the violent and chaotic quality of the times in which he lived. Everything from religion to warfare is performed in service to the maintenance of the prince's power. There is neither right nor wrong except insofar as it increases or decreases the prince's security. Everything is subordinated to that one goal. Machiavelli's prince comes to us as the stereotype of the military strong man, the power maven, the person who manages to take everything his neighbors' have and turn it into an empire of his own. Machiavelli's rhetoric, if we can call his maxims about power that, offers advice to those who seek dominion over others and thus a lasting place in history.

There are only a handful of books that offer advice about persuasion in this vein. Baldassare Castiglione's *The Courtier* is a much gentler version of the same advice about how to get and hold power through art and artifice. The "Difficulties of Persuasion" also clearly belongs here. As does Sun Tzu's *The Art of War*. Nietzsche's *Thus Spoke Zarathustra* is also sometimes bundled with this crowd, though there is some dispute about whether or not it really belongs. More recently we have Ralph Gun Hoy Siu's *The Craft of Power* and Robert Greene's *The 48 Rules of Power*. What all of these books have in common is advice about how to maintain and increase power once you have seized it. As someone now fully equipped with a dialectical sensibility you are no doubt looking for a definition of power at this point.

Power is the ability to get work done or the ability to orchestrate the efforts of many for the achievement of a single purpose. Ralph Gun Hoy Siu offers an interesting alternative definition: "Power is the intentional influence over the beliefs, emotions, and behaviors of people. Potential power is the capacity to do so, but kinetic power is the act of doing so. . . . The techniques of eliciting empowering responses of the kind and at the time desired from targeted individuals constitute the craft of power"(31). A far more common understanding of power is found in the commonplace *Power corrupts, and absolute power corrupts absolutely*, which is of course an evaluation rather than a definition, the definition of power being taken for granted. At any rate, power is commonly viewed with negative platitudes on the one hand and giddy aspirations on the other. It is also often assumed to be a personal trait or a set of cultivated practices that imbue the politically ambitious with the capacity to dominate others. A third, and in many ways more compelling, perspective on power is that it is neither good nor evil nor the attribute of a single individual but rather a function of the social systems we live in. From this perspective power passes among and through all of us. A French philosopher by the name of Michel Foucault popularized this systemic view of power. You might want to start with *Discipline and Punish* if you find the idea intriguing.

At any rate, a Machiavellian rhetoric would identify power as the primary rhetorical objective and define power as dominion over others. Machiavellian *rhetors* care nothing about people's feelings, are willing to wrong others, are deeply concerned with appearances, and dissemble constantly. They are superficial, charming, fascinating, and completely unreliable. They are the psychopaths among us. When we hear the word *psychopath* we tend to think of Ted Bundy and Jeffrey Dahmer, crazy loners with twisted sexual compulsions. But recent research into psychopathy suggests that it is a neurological condition that doesn't entail violent sexual preferences or anything that would necessarily land a psychopath in the news.

The majority of psychopaths aren't killers. They are, however, morally detached because while they are capable of a theory of mind, capable of understanding what other people feel and think, they don't mirror those feelings. They don't sympathize. They don't care. They are focused on whatever it is they want, and they are willing to do anything necessary to get it because they aren't constrained by norms of moral behavior and they live in the present moment, focused on the here and now and indifferent to the future. Thus if a psychopath fixes on obtaining something good, good may well follow, just as bad will if the object is bad or crazy if the object is crazy. Some of the psychopath's traits are actually admirable, especially when focused on obtaining something good. If you're interested in this view of psychopathy, have a look at *Snakes in Suites: When Psychopaths Go to Work*, by Paul Babiak and Robert D. Hare, or *The Sociopath Next Door*, by Martha Stout.[18] An even more provocative interpretation of the phenomenon is offered by Kevin Dutton in *The Wisdom of Psychopaths: What Saints, Spies, and Serial Killers Can Teach Us About Success*.

In case you are wondering (*and you should be because you are reading against the grain*), I brought up the subject of psychopaths because some

---

18. The words *sociopath* and *psychopath* are used, as far as I can tell, interchangeably. Perhaps there's a distinction to be made between those whose neurological condition excludes nearly all social integration and those who pass for normal most of the time. Still, I haven't seen the distinction made.

kinds of *rhetors* are clearly psychopaths, and anyone who has conceived a desire to become rhetorical will need to cultivate the laser-like focus, the charm, the flexibility, and the impulse to succeed that are the positive characteristics of the psychopath. At the same time, however, there are related traits to be scrupulously avoided. Chief among them are impulsivity (*rhetors* are hyperintentional), superficiality (*rhetors* know surfaces are important, but they take the long view always), and tunnel vision.

By way of an extended tour of Machiavellian rhetoric, I'm offering a relatively detailed discussion of Greene's *The 48 Rules of Power*. That may strike you as perverse. (*Good. You are still reading against the grain.*) If you are going to talk about Machiavellian rhetoric, why not engage *The Prince*? We could do that. In fact *you* should do that, but Machiavellian rhetoric has taken on a life that far outstrips its namesake, and to cover the full range of strategies in a short time, without getting bogged down in political philosophy or Renaissance history, it might be more effective to look at a more recent and fittingly superficial book, one that synthesizes much of the advice in the tradition that both preceded and followed Machiavelli.

If anything in *Persuasion: History, Theory, Practice* needed a preface, it would seem to be this collection of maxims about power because they sound dangerous, primarily because they are clearly addressed to someone who has conceived a desire to be dangerous. Anyone who would seek power, who would try to create his or her own destiny by manipulating others, needs to be cautioned, for their own and everyone else's sake. But I'm not exactly sure what to say. The most common platitude is that until you have power over yourself, in the forms of self-control, self-knowledge, and practical wisdom, you should never seek power over others. This idea has probably occurred to nearly anyone capable of reflective thinking, but those familiar with rhetorical traditions tend to attribute it to Plato, to *Gorgias* in particular. While there's nothing wrong with asserting that one must first seek self-knowledge before seeking power, most people change over time, and so knowing yourself is an endless struggle. Twenty years from now you won't be who you are today. Twenty years from now you might have more money, more influence, more responsibilities, and more options. Your ambitions, in other words, may have started to materialize. What you think of these rules now may not be what you think of them in the future. If you begin to invoke them now, you may have to deal with the consequences for a long time to come.

You don't have to be Machiavellian at heart to learn from these maxims of power. If you don't exercise some power over yourself for your own good, then others may step in and exercise it over you for their own purposes; they may anyway. You can't avoid power, either using it or being used by it, but you can avoid victimization without seeking victory. If you think you are a Machiavellian, then start slowly, lurk, listen, and learn. If you reveal yourself for an ambitious person without first acquiring demonstrable skills, people will think you are merely an ambitious idiot (which is an *ethos* that can work in some settings, but I'm not recommending it). Once you really do have something to offer the group, then proceed. Never seek to achieve anything for it's own sake. Every achievement must lead to and facilitate the next challenge. Don't take either your successes or your failures personally. You don't have to hurt people along the way. And even if some day you have to, never take pleasure in it.

Acquiring needless enemies is reckless. As you progress, consider the moral, social, and financial costs you are accruing. Don't spend $100 to win $99. Don't make an enemy if you can make a friend; a friend is someone who wishes good things for you; an enemy is one who wishes bad things for you. Obviously acquiring enemies is counterproductive more often than not. (Although because your friend's enemies are your enemies, there may come a time when you will need to pick a fight to secure a friendship.) From the perspective of power, friendship has nothing to do with how you feel about a person or how they feel about you; it has to do with what they can and will do for you and what they think you will do for and to them.

True Machiavellians think themselves amoral, but the rest of the world thinks them psychopaths, so if you are willing to break moral codes make sure the gain is truly significant, and keep the potential backlash in mind. If nothing else, make certain you are in fact a Machiavellian and not just an arrogant young fool like Dostoevsky's Raskolnikov. Avoid being too useful to people much more ambitious and powerful than yourself. There are lots of sharks in the water; it's the one that passes silently unseen that will eat you. As Siu says, "Fortify yourself against the likes of you. . . . Expect foul play" (6).

I'm not going to reproduce *The 48 Rules* verbatim here. I'm simply going to quote each maxim in bold and then read each one against the grain. You might want to buy a copy of the book or get one out of a library. It has some very entertaining anecdotes about court intrigue and military machinations.

Law 1: Never Outshine the Master. If you are certain your skills have truly exceeded your master's, then look for a new master. Don't try to kill and eat the one you think is standing in your way. All the same, more senior people do sometimes feel threatened by junior people of talent, and you may benefit from camouflaging your talent or giving someone above you credit for something you've accomplished, assuming you've got more where that came from.

Law 2: Never Put Too Much Trust in Friends; Learn How to Use Enemies. There are a number of interesting assumptions about the nature of friendship and the social milieu in which a person who would say this or believe it must have. Clearly, the world this advice comes from is fluid and unstructured, where friends and enemies are resources. I assume that he thinks that friends are those who might do you a good turn because they would benefit too somehow, while enemies are those who can only advance at your expense. These are purely functional understandings of the terms and they may not have occurred to you before. For most people, friends are people we hang out with and with whom we share more of ourselves than with others. Most of us don't have enemies, per se. The would-be power maven, however, is looking for leverage, and people, all people, are therefore a potential source of power.

Law 3: Conceal Your Intentions. As you know from the sections on dialectic and cross-examination, it's much harder to defend against something you didn't see coming, and thus keeping your goal hidden from someone who might stand in your way is a plausible strategy. On the other hand, everybody is standing in your way and if you conceal your intentions from people who don't have any reason to object they may not notice you standing there and so fail to help even though they would be inclined to if they knew what you were trying to do. And as we have also observed, by stating your intentions out loud you increase your chances of following through. So as with all advice, you have to consider the context in which you would employ law 3.

Law 4: Always Say Less Than Necessary. As you know from the section on clairvoyance, people tend to read into vague or leading expressions and thus given the right people in the right situation, the less you say the more powerful you may be. Your minions will pick up whatever scarps you offered and run with them. This of course assumes you've already been granted some power within the group. If you are just another member, being vague or incomplete will get you ignored or abused. The other value of economy when it comes to communicating is that you leave less evidence behind if things go badly. I would revise this law to read, Say only what is necessary. If something is necessary, then by definition it needs to be said. After that, however, say nothing more and let them fill in the gaps for themselves.

Law 5: So Much Depends on Reputation—Guard It with Your Life. While it is true that if something horrible must be done you can protect your reputation by hiring someone else to do the wet work, guarding your reputation isn't just for mafia dons and the princes of Wall Street. You can guard your reputation by doing only good things and by publicizing the good work you do. Some people are really good at milking their accomplishments. Others tend to downplay their achievements. "Don't be so humble," my father once told me, "you're not that good." (He was quoting Golda Meir.) Taken to an extreme, law 5 is prison-yard logic. *You lookin' at me?* But taken in the correct dose, paying attention to how people perceive you is likely a very good idea. Thinking about how what you do will be perceived is thinking like a *rhetor*. But choosing to do the wrong thing because the right thing won't be well received is failure of imagination and courage.

Law 6: Court Attention at All Cost. Well, yes. Be seen. But don't look like you're shouting, "Look at me, look at me!" Some people can get away with wearing spectacular clothes or driving an outrageously extravagant and flashy car. Some people can share courtside seats graciously. Some people can't. The "at all cost" addition strikes me as too much, but then I'm no power broker, and I'm an introvert anyway. All the same, you are your own PR agent until you've accomplished enough to hire a professional.

Law 7: Get Others to Do the Work for You, but Always Take the Credit. Well, I'm not sure how to put a positive spin on this one. The executive chef gets all the glory; the sous and prep chefs do the work. I get that. Maybe it's just my stuck-in-the-middle-class mentality, but taking credit for other people's work strikes me as hideous. Whatever you do, don't take credit in front of the people who actually did the work without having a bodyguard standing by.

Law 8: Make Other People Come to You—Use Bait If Necessary. Hmm, more flies with honey. Well, if people see others flocking to you, they will want to know what's the fuss about. Meeting people on their turf or on neutral ground has a very different rhetorical effect than making them come to you.

Law 9: Win through Your Actions, Never through Argument. I can't improve on this. Show, don't tell. Or in the words of a contemporary poet from Detroit, "It ain't bragging if you back it up." On the other hand, there are times when arguments are actions. Whenever people are deciding on the best course of action, for example, it's the people with the compelling plan that get the nod.

Law 10: Infection—Avoid the Unhappy and Unlucky. Well, yes, I guess, but don't abandon your friends when they fall on hard times or surround yourself with lying Pollyannas. Still, a drowning man can take you with him, and we do tend to become more like the people we associate with. Remember that study about how obesity might be contagious? At the risk of sounding like a parent with teenagers (I'm not), you really do need to pick your friends wisely.

Law 11: Learn to Keep People Dependent on You. No, I just can't accept this no matter how I spin "dependent." I'm a teacher. My goal is to make myself unnecessary. I also value autonomy, so for me this maxim would be counterproductive of power.

Law 12: Use Selective Honesty and Generosity to Disarm Your Victim. Well, honesty and generosity are tools that disarm, but do you really have to frame your colleagues and friends as potential victims? What does that get you? More importantly, perhaps, what does it get Greene?

Law 13: When Asking for Help, Appeal to People's Self-Interest, Never to Their Mercy or Gratitude. That's really just common sense. You don't have to debase yourself to get help. But it's worth pointing out that Greene is assuming that weakness necessarily encourages others to attack and that you look weak if you need help, and appealing for mercy makes you look even weaker.

Law 14: Pose as a Friend, Work as a Spy. Don't really know how to spin this one either, except perhaps to say that you can learn from what others are doing and maybe make good use of it, too, without harming them in the process. You might do well to keep in mind that unscrupulous people will use what you give them, and even decent people will gossip. "Can you keep a secret?" is the first step toward destroying yourself, doesn't matter who you ask it of. Again, consider the context. If you are working in a place of high intrigue, where secrets are power and common knowledge is useless, law 14 might come in handy.

Law 15: Crush Your Enemy Totally. Well, what does "enemy" mean? If the person in question will inevitably take up arms against you first opportunity they get, then yes you probably don't want them ever to get the opportunity. On the other hand, a reputation for clemency served Caesar well, at least for a while. Gratitude in the mind of the right kind of person can make a lasting "friend." Everything depends on whether or not your one-time enemy feels empowered or disempowered by an alliance with you. In other words, you would need to ensure that their gratitude doesn't eventually morph into resentment.

Law 16: Use Absence to Increase Respect and Honor. Works as long as people think you're actually off doing something important and not just off playing tennis or coaching little league. It's generally a bad idea to hang out with your subordinates or be too approachable. It is much harder to "boss" your friends because you may be overly concerned for their feelings, assuming you have real feelings for them. And they may try to take advantage of your friendship. Inevitably you will have to choose between their feelings and your needs. Nevertheless, until you do rank, you will likely benefit more from being constantly present than curiously absent. Arrive early. Stay late.

Law 17: Keep Others in Suspended Terror: Cultivate an Air of Unpredictability. Please. I guess if you are a big shot, you can pull this off. But be careful doing it around even bigger shots than yourself. Or at least limit your acts of disequilibrium to eccentricities. There's a big difference between being perceived as unconventional and being perceived as nuts.

Law 18: Do Not Build Fortresses to Protect Yourself. Taken metaphorically, this is an interesting piece of advice. If you withdraw behind a single source of strength—if you only have one way to make money, for example, or only one or two friends—you will be more vulnerable than if you have multiple sources of strength. The best defense is a good offense. (Yes, I know that's backward, but all advice cuts both ways.)

Law 19: Know Who You're Dealing With—Do Not Offend the Wrong Person. Certainly it is important to have a clear sense of the personality and character of the people you are dealing with, who is easy going and who is quick to offend. It's also a good idea to accord respect to everyone regardless of rank or power on the grounds that you don't always know for certain with whom you are dealing or who is watching. I frankly can't see what offending anyone could get you unless you are trying to pick a fight or you think trash-talking will distract and thus diminish a greater opponent. If this is your idea of how to get ahead in business, you may need to go back to school.

Law 20: Do Not Commit to Anyone. Hmm. *Keep your options open* seems like generally good advice, but can you really remain forever uncommitted? Won't there come a time when you have to throw in with others or go it forever alone?

Law 21: Play a Sucker to Catch a Sucker. Another form of dissembling. Whatever resources you keep in reserve are resources you can spring on the unsuspecting. I think a better way to put this is that, if there will in fact be a contest of some kind, letting people underestimate you in advance might make them slack off or become overconfident and unfocused. But hiding your light under a bushel, as the saying goes, wont' be effective if there's no opportunity for a big reveal. If people think you're a bit dim, they may invoke the rule about contagion and stay away from you.

Law 22: Use the Surrender Tactic—Transform Weakness into Power. Well, this is clearly a tactic of last resort, but under certain circumstances it might be wise. If you can't beat 'em, join 'em. But again, in a modern business setting, how does this work? You sell your company to a potentially hostile, larger conglomerate and then ingratiate yourself with their board of directors? I have no idea. This is way beyond my realm of experience.

Law 23: Concentrate Your Forces. I don't like the way he put it, but play to your strengths and don't dilute your energy by going off in all directions at once is sage advice. Find your focus, and stay focused. But of course, that principle can lead to tunnel vision if taken too far or if the climate changes drastically.

Law 24: Play the Perfect Courtier. Sigh, ugh. Still, a competent but annoying person will be passed over in favor of a competent person who's easy to deal with. If you want to see this law fully spelled out, in a relatively entertaining way, read Baldessare Castiglione in *The Courtier*.

Law 25: Re-create Yourself. Sure enough, but what does it mean, and how do you do it? What can you do today and tomorrow that will ensure that you won't be the same person you are now five years from now? I'm serious about that. If five years is still too far out, what about one year from now? Pick something relatively concrete and measurable, like an ideal weight or an exercise goal or a new programming language or a new instrument. What it is probably doesn't matter as much as that you get in the habit of trying to improve. That way if something drastic happens and you have to really change, you'll be better ready to do it.

Law 26: Keep Your Hands Clean. It's the idea of having others do your dirty work that makes this rule reprehensible. I can't positively spin this one without rewriting it. Maybe you can think of a scenario where this would be good advice.

Law 27: Play on People's Need to Believe to Create a Cultlike Following. People do want to look up to their leaders. You have to look impressive, which is easier if you actually are impressive. But what does it mean to "look" impressive, come to think of it? And how can you be sure that whatever symbols of power and success and accomplishment you decorate your life with won't just be interpreted as pretentious or intimidating? Even that harmless picture of your two smiling children will alienate a few of the people who see it. Why do you think Steve Jobs wore nothing but black turtlenecks and blue jeans? Do you think the answer might be connected to law 4 in some way, the rule about understatement?

Law 28: Enter Action with Boldness. True this. Hesitate and die. But always? Which of the laws contradicts this one?

Law 29: Plan All the Way to the End. Also obviously true and very easy to get wrong, since it's hard to know where the end may really be. Every ending is another beginning.

Law 30: Make Your Accomplishments Seem Effortless. This can backfire. If people think what you did was really hard, and you made it look easy, then yes that will be impressive. But if people really don't know how hard something is and you make it look easy, they may think it is easy. If someone thanks you and you say, "It was nothing," they may actually think it was nothing. On the other hand (there are always at least two hands, eh?) I know people who have an annoying habit of making the mundane seem spectacularly difficult, like they had to move heaven and earth to find an email from last year or summarize a document. Being in a constant sweat isn't very compelling. I guess I would say, know the real value of the work you do, and make sure others do as well.

Law 31: Control the Options. True. All too commonly true. Most people find even more than a couple of color choices an overwhelming experience. Add in a bunch of different features, and they are likely to freeze with indecision. In my experience people really do prefer a carefully orchestrated illusion of choice to the real thing.

Law 32: Play to People's Fantasies. This is the source of everything wrong with the world. I think there's a big difference between believing that the world is a rhetorical construct, or more accurately a nexus of rhetorical constructs, and saying the world is a fantasy. Rhetorical constructs require evidence, not just wishful thinking and well-tuned symbolism.

Law 33: Discover Each Man's Thumbscrew. I don't think this knowledge has to be used for evil purposes. When it comes to teaching writing, for example, knowing where a person's insecurities lie enables you to bolster their self-esteem and get their courage up. But I suppose my revision here just willfully disregards Greene's premise that we are talking about people who aspire to being the boss of bosses.

Law 34: Be Royal in your Own Fashion. People will tend to treat you the way you seem to want to be treated, sure enough. Appear dignified, and people are more likely to treat you with dignity. One can learn a great deal about this from watching Cesar Millan, the Dog Whisperer.

Law 35: Master the Art of Timing. I agree with this maxim completely. The relevant rhetorical concept is kairos, timing. Timing is critical to rhetorical success. You have to know when to engage, when to disengage, and when to wait. People don't often add this point, especially when they are feeding you the illusion of control through learning, but luck probably plays a greater role in timing than planning ever could. Anyone who says they can show you how to master the art of luck is definitely selling you snake oil.

Law 36: Disdain Things You Cannot Have: Ignoring Them Is the Best Revenge. I'm not sure ignoring and disdaining are the same activity, but envy is an incredibly destructive emotion. Sour grapes?

Law 37: Create Compelling Spectacles. Not everyone can afford to put on a circus, but it's amazing what the occasional awards ceremony can do for morale. Even a dinner party can produce positive impressions.

Law 38: Think as You Like but Behave Like Others. Seems to contradict law 34.

Law 39: Stir Up Waters to Catch Fish. I suppose this can work, but I'd have to think more about it to figure out how to assimilate it to the world of the non-power-hungry, and I can't be bothered. This more than perhaps any of the other laws strikes me as a trait of a psychopath. Most of the others at least suggest some fear of getting caught or some concern for reputation. Psychopaths are fearless, and they don't tend to distinguish between good and bad attention.

Law 40: Despise the Free Lunch. True this. Don't take the free lunch. There are probably a hundred scenes from art and literature to illustrate this principle, but my favorite at the moment is one you may be able to find on YouTube if you search for "The Wire: Michael and Marlo," from 1:06 forward. Warning: explicit language. The power is more in Michael's unwavering gaze than in his refusal, but the refusal got him the face-to-face time with the boss.

Law 41: Avoid Stepping into a Great Man's Shoes. The contrast effect will be profoundly unflattering.

Law 42: Strike the Shepherd and the Sheep Will Scatter. Either this is obvious or I'm tired of reading at this point.

Law 43: Work on the Hearts and Minds of Others. True, I think. But you have to be careful here. Consider law 16.

Law 44: Disarm and Infuriate with the Mirror Effect. Seems childish. *I know you are, but what am I?* There is a commonplace among people who like to speak cynically about business that you can't tell the difference between an executive and a screaming baby. You know it's their problem, but you're still going to have to deal with it.

Law 45: Preach the Need for Change, but Never Reform Too Much at Once. I wish someone had told me this twenty years ago.

Law 46: Never Appear Too Perfect. Easy for me.

Law 47: Do Not Go Past the Mark You Aimed For; In Victory, Learn When to Stop. Precision in all things, definitely.

Law 48: Assume Formlessness. Hmm, this one relates to laws 3 and 4, but of course it's a bit vague, formless. I imagine the point here is that if you are too obviously one way or another you are easy to predict and therefore easy to manipulate. By constantly changing and adapting, by constantly learning, to put a positive spin on this, you have a better chance of constantly improving and less of a chance of stagnating.

Your Turn

Can you think of a person or a character from literature or film that embodies one or two of these laws? Or a character that embodies a cluster of these character traits? Maybe someone who always seeks the center of attention. Or perhaps someone who is overly concerned with his or her reputation? (*Did you just notice how "reputation" has a slightly different meaning depending on the gender of the pronoun preceding it? Like all rhetorics of power, rhetorics of gender often pass unnoticed.*)

Another way to make sense of the rules of power is to come up with the rules of weakness, either as a parody or as a counterpoint. The list would include such things as *Never choose a plan of action, Always follow, Blend in, Pile on, Always be available, Never say no, Seek a protector in every situation, Never do anything alone, Beg from everyone, especially those less fortunate than yourself*. See if you can flesh out the list, and then compare the two ways of being. What's wrong with the either-or setup of powerful and powerless?

Here is another opportunity to have your say: Read my "against the grains" against the grains. Do you agree with my implicit ideological stance that one should get one's way but not at any cost, or do you think I'm being immoral?

chapter 5
CONCLUSION

So I have been trying to convince you that you are a *rhetor* and to give you the insights and techniques that will help you become the best *rhetor* you can be. I have been trying to make you think critically, seek evidence, question the obvious, and judge the value of what evidence is presented by others and the value of the evidence you can find on your own. I've been trying also to encourage you to see yourself as a member of intersecting and overlapping communities who has a positive contribution to make and an obligation to participate usefully and consciously, not just for yourself but for others as well.

Assuming you're basically content with this book's designs on your character because you've read this far, in the next section is a breakdown of the specific treats I associate with the term *rhetor*. Perhaps I should add at this point that I never refer to myself as a *rhetor*. Technically I would have to say I'm a rhetorician because I teach others how to be *rhetors,* but when people ask me what I do for a living I say I teach writing and leave it at that. Sometimes I'll add "rhetoric" and then say, "Like Plato and Aristotle and Cicero." I never say *rhetor* because it's just too arcane a word. I chose it deliberately for this book, however, because it doesn't come with a whole lot of vivid presuppositions, and thus I was hopeful I might be able to make it meaningful for you without having to empty it first. Below you'll find the ideas I hoped to invest the word *rhetor* with. The ones you wish to identify with are, of course, entirely up to you. If nothing else, having come this far, you should have a much clearer sense about what it takes to be persuasive in a given situation and an outline for a life plan if you think you might want to pursue a persuasive way of life.

Character Traits of the *Rhetor*

You are keenly aware of irony because you can see many different explanations for similar things, some of which conflict and yet carry equal weight. (*You are reminded of the section on clairvoyance just now.*) This doesn't mean you are constantly being ironic or winking at one side of your audience while condescending to the other. You just understand that the literal and figurative are constantly at play and that the same evidence can almost always serve conflicting purposes.

The dialectical impulse is part of your ironic intellectual landscape; everything that is also isn't or could be said in a slightly different sense not to be. The dialectical impulse is a consequence of habitually reading against the grain. Nevertheless, you are not, like Socrates, a perpetual pain to the people you encounter, incessantly undermining their beliefs and questioning their understanding of things routinely, but only when it seems helpful or even necessary for the proper functioning of the group. You aren't out to prove yourself smarter than others; in fact you know full well that *smart* is a complex word like *love* and *justice*, a word with multiple-context variant meanings and no true referent.

You are aware of your own and everyone else's cognitive biases, and you understand how they are exploited.

A strategic impulse governs your communications. Not that you are devious or double dealing at all, just that you are aware of both the message and how it will be understood based on how it will be conveyed and to whom and when. You don't just say the first thing that comes into your head. And sometimes you don't say what you are thinking at all. You can be quick and apparently spontaneous in that you don't always stop to think each move out, but you are working from patterns gained by experience and study, not just extemporizing.

You are diligent in your daily pursuits of opinions and ideas worth listening to because you realize keenly that you have a constituency; you are a part of several communities of people who have overlapping interests who can benefit occasionally from your efforts. You aren't necessarily in search of a leadership position, but you could lead if you needed to. You know how to follow the chain of command. You also know how to whisper in the emperor's ear. And you are prepared if necessary to move on. You don't have tunnel vision. You remember what BATNA stands for, and you've always got one in mind. You can change.

You have a disciplined mind. You read (against the grain) and write every day—not just when something is due or even as something is about to become due—every single day. Your intellectual capacity is a function of your general well-being, and well-being is improved through careful and constant diet and exercise. For the body that means eating right and exercising regularly, and for the brain that means reading and writing and questioning and pondering. You work your brain every day because you want to be effective when the big opportunities arrive, and you know they will arrive because you've diligently paved the way.

Your discipline includes cultivating and maintaining specific attitudes toward criticism and an internal locus of control. You don't take either positive or negative criticism personally, and yet you own your efforts, the good, the bad, and the mixed. You reframe failures as learning opportunities, and so you don't fear or avoid failure. Indeed, because you are constantly seeking new challenges you are keenly aware that failures are inevitable. You know that if you've stopped failing you've stopped pushing yourself. You also don't fully accept or fully reject other people's characterizations of your efforts.

You have developed your own universal inventional heuristic that includes the following questions: What do I know, and how do I know it? What don't I know, and how can I find out about it? What do I believe, and how have I come to believe these things? Who do I know, and what do I know about them? Who do I need to meet? How can I present what I do know so that it will have the most powerful positive impact for a given audience? (*For those of you who, like me, are introverted, who get your energy from separation and reflection rather than group participation, knowing lots of people doesn't mean spending a great deal of time among them. Not all* rhetors *are gregarious.*)

In addition to a consistent set of ready questions, you also keep an electronic notebook that you fill with everything you come across as you read. You make a conscious and constant effort to develop and expand your key words so you can effectively tag and cross-reference entries, but you also keep these lists because you realize that your capacity for learning expands as your lists do. Your notebooks are notes to your current and future self. While you take some pleasure in the craft you use to develop them, you know they are a means to an end, a warehouse, not a place of worship.

Before you turn in an assignment or otherwise engage in a public act of persuasion, you make a note to yourself about what you did and how you feel about the results and what you might have done differently, what result you expect to get, and what likely will have gone wrong if you don't get what you expected. Keeping notes to yourself like this refines your practices and thus improves your outcomes. These kinds of reflective moments help build your metacognitive capacities and your ability to plan, acquire and use resources efficiently, and predict outcomes within a reasonable margin of error, mindful that luck (good and bad) is always possible, while reminding yourself constantly that when it comes to luck whether it was good or bad isn't always immediately apparent.

In addition to your notebooks, you also keep a separate reading journal filled with quotations from the books and articles and online posts you read, with page numbers or URLs, so you can mine your past reading for ideas and provide direct quotations and proper attributions when those ideas are not entirely your own.

You maintain a blog, a public space where you hone your ideas and reach out for an audience. You need to develop your constituency. You also make a habit of socializing your ideas, that is, figuring out how they will play to whom before you broadcast them. You are constantly mindful of the fact that becoming a *rhetor* is a long-term and constantly morphing practice. What's possible is always changing. You also understand that your electronic past directly affects your current options, so you think ahead.

Glossary

You could argue that persuasion is a lexicon, a collection of important words that help you understand how to craft and understand how others craft opinions. You've encountered a great many new words throughout this text that I've explained at some length in the place where you encountered them. What follows here is a list of words that I've not defined at length before or, in a few cases, a quick reminder about the meaning of some of the more important words. If you need, for testing purposes, to lean these definitions, then you might want to consider making flash cards of them. Reduce the longer ones to three or five sentences, and then memorize them. Better yet, practice re-creating the definitions based on what you've learn about persuasion.

Absolute value: The value placed on an idea or activity remains the same no matter what happens around it. Another way of saying this is that it is context invariant. For example, *doing the right thing* is an absolute value for anyone who is willing to suffer physical or emotional injury as a result of doing the right thing. For that kind of person, even self-interest doesn't trump duty or honor or truth or whatever concept underwrites what he or she decides is "doing the right thing." To take another example, for some people paying taxes is so repugnant that they will take on a tax-deductible debt even if once the interest payments are subtracted from the tax savings the net result is a loss. Such a person holds *not paying taxes* as an absolute value. Absolute values are separate from a person's hierarchies of value because the absolute never shifts while all other values reorganize themselves a bit depending on circumstances. There's an instructive cliché here. You sometimes hear people say "God, family, work," indicating an inviolable triumvirate of values. But what if a child is very ill, say with pneumonia? Would this person miss church that Sunday morning by explaining (*rationalizing?*) to himself that the house of God is optional when it comes to piety? Or would they go to the house of worship and leave the child alone? If your hierarchies of value are rigid, if you are intellectually and morally inflexible, you will find it hard to adapt to change, both to make use of opportunities and get out of unfortunate circumstances. If you inhabit a completely stable world, this may be advantageous, since for you things are as they are, and you need to make due. If you inhabit a changing world, rigidity won't serve you well.

Affordance: From usability studies, the form of a thing should tell you immediately how to use it. So, for example, a door with a handle on it ought to be pulled rather than pushed, and a door that has to be pushed should tell you where to push. In other words, a well-designed door has a handle on one side and a push pad on the other, unless it swings both ways, in which case it should have a push pad on both sides and a window so people can see if anyone's coming the other way. Here's an example from *Nudge*:

The nozzles that deliver diesel fuel are too large to fit into the opening on cars that use gasoline, so it is not possible to make the mistake of putting diesel fuel in your gasoline-powered car (though it is still possible to make the opposite mistake). (Thaler 88)

My favorite example is pink ceiling paint that turns white when it dries. Painting pink over white leaves little room for doubt about coverage. If it isn't pink, it isn't covered. Anything that has good affordances makes skillful use of conventions and expectations and circumstances to seamlessly provide what's needed at the moment it's needed in a way that makes it very difficult for a person to make a mistake or get confused. As a metaphor for persuasion, the concept of affordance is extremely apt.

Analogy: Two different things are treated as similar enough that what is true (or false) of one can be said to be approximately true (or false) of the other. How approximately depends on how similar the two things really are.

Analysis paralysis: Failing to act quickly enough because one is preoccupied with data or searching for more evidence or trying to work out every possible outcome, overthinking. Analysis paralysis is related to option paralysis, where you can't decide because you've got no way to prioritize many equal alternatives, and you wouldn't be so undecided if you had fewer alternatives. Differences that make no difference can slow decision making.

Arete: The Greek word for "excellence," often translated as "virtue," although that has later Christian connotations that are anachronistic. Basically it means the ability to get good and useful things done on time and on budget, a good decision maker, a reliable member of the community. *Arete* is a goal of *ethos* construction, which means that you not only want to do things that will be perceived as possessing this quality so that you will be associated with it and thought by means of the fundamental attribution error to possess it, but you will want to make sure the world knows about the good work you are doing.

Axiom (axiomatic): An axiom is a statement accepted as true for the sake of argument. Often the expressions *Given that . . .* or *Granted . . .* are used to signal that a sentence is offered axiomatically. You might accept the axiom to see what follows, or you might say, "Wait a minute . . ." and ask for clarification or some sort of reason to accept the statement before moving on.

Both sides of a case: One of the primary tenets of persuasion is that you need to be able to argue both sides of a case, to see what can be said for and against a position so that you can anticipate objections and test the relative merits of different perspectives. (Often there are more than two sides to a case, despite what stasis theory tells us. The idea that there are two sides comes from the predominance of forensic or courtroom persuasive acts in the rhetorical tradition.) People who present only one side or hear only one side often give it more credence than it deserves, which is good if you are trying to sell something but bad if you are trying to make a decision or anticipate how someone might object to what you are promoting or defending. So even if in the end you take a one-sided approach, you must carefully consider the plausible alternatives before you engage. If the people you need to persuade are skeptical by nature (professors, lawyers, people who are going to dislike what you have to say), it will serve your *ethos* to show awareness of objections, else they may think you are being dogmatic or pushy or worse, simpleminded.

Chunking: Try to memorize the following letters: ibfiafnlcnab. Now try to memorize these letters: nbanflciafbi. Easier, eh? That's chunking: creating meaningful blocks out of meaningless details. It is even easier to memorize the letters if you visualize their chunkiness: NBA, NFL, CIA, FBI. Here's a culinary example. Think about the difference between memorizing a list of ingredients to buy at the store versus going to the store with the idea of the dish itself in your head. It's easier to remember cacciatore than it is to remember each of the ingredients individually, assuming you've made cacciatore enough times to know what goes in it. For more on chunking, have a look at the *Ideas That Stick* blog.

Cliché: What everybody always says or thinks in a given situation. Why we think and speak clichés may be a matter of culture or a habit of mind or cognitive overload—too overwhelmed by emotion to look for an alternative. Or it might be ignorance; we just don't know we are using a cliché. Clichés are related to stereotypes in that they are both default patterns, words and ideas we go to without stopping to think. When your teachers tell you to avoid clichés, they are actually asking you to think. That's good of course because that's their job, but as a *rhetor* you should be able to decide when to use a cliché and when to choose an alternative form of expression or pattern of thought. In some settings, clichés can be useful.

Cognitive bias: The cognitive equivalent of an optical illusion, like the famous Müller-Lyer illusion on the right. The line on the left looks longer than the one on the right even though if you measure them you will see they are the same length. Our eyes can fool us if we don't invoke our critical thinking skills and question our perceptions. (Thanks to *Thinking, Fast and Slow* by Kahneman for this analogy.) Similarly, our minds tend to make mistakes that we may not notice are mistakes. See the section "Cognitive Biases" in Chapter 1 for a list of some significant cognitive biases.

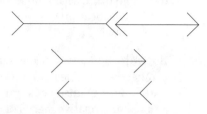

Cognitive dissonance: People like consistency. If we say we are going to do something, most of us will feel uncomfortable if we don't follow through. That sense of discomfort is called *cognitive dissonance,* and it's the reason people make public decisions to lose weight or sign letters of agreement or make public declarations of faith before other members of the community. We make unkept promises to ourselves all the time, but when we make a promise public it's harder to renege. The reason we make ourselves unkept promises is that we have two selves, our current self and our future self. Our future self is purely rational and strict and focused. Our current self seeks immediate gratification, daydreams, gets distracted, and generally lacks the ability to remain completely consistent because it lives in the moment, no past, no future, just right now. When we make a promise to our current self—never again—we feel little cognitive dissonance when we fail to keep it because in a sense we aren't that person sometimes even moments later. Some people are more consistent than others of course.

Cognitive Load: Strain put on your thought process as a result of having to keep an uncomfortable amount of information in your working memory. The more you have to remember, the harder it is to think, speak, or write. Not sure about this? Good. Try doing a basic arithmetical procedure in your head (what's 37 × 13?) while continuing to read this paragraph. Or make a grocery list in your head of, say, fifteen items, and then when you get to the store send a few text messages before starting to shop. Did you remember all fifteen items? Multitasking is a myth. Computers now routinely have enough RAM to keep several programs working simultaneously so you can keep your email and your Internet browser and your word processor and your music app all running at once, but you can't use them all at once without having to switch focus from one to the other, and the more you do that the less efficient you become. It gets worse as you get older, too (sigh).

Connotation: Words evoke feelings by association and convention. These feelings are a word's connotation. Two different words might denote or refer to more or less the same idea but evoke different feelings by alternate associations, like *cheap* and *frugal* or *attractive* and *seductive*. When it comes to reframing an argument, think about the connotation of the words being used. See *denotation*.

Context: Situation, circumstances, background. All of the elements that go into creating the place and time where whatever is happening is happening. Context can be naturalistic in the sense that everything relevant is just there, but it can also be perceptual in the sense that what is relevant appears so because of how you are talking about it or what you are doing. Change the context, change the meaning. See Chapter 3, "Framing".

Counterfactual: Something that isn't true but allows you to test the validity of an idea nevertheless. If X were the case, then Y. But X isn't, so not Y.

Counterintuitive: Something unexpectedly true. You should buy things only when you don't need them: heaters in the summer, air-conditioners in the winter, because things are cheaper off season.

Deliberate practice: Having a specific goal and a defined unit of measurement that allows you to accurately chart your progress toward that goal. Deliberate practice is different from play in that when you are playing you're getting lost in the flow of the activity, not trying to refine a skill so much as use the ones you have to your fullest current potential. Play is fun; deliberate practice is work. Play is about getting out of your head, unconscious and yet super-aware. Deliberate practice is about reflection and analysis and testing and evaluating. You need both if you are going to get better at anything, whether it's waterskiing or playing chess or computer programming or writing or speaking.

Deliberation: Any decision-making process, deciding on the best course of action based on an estimation of achieving a desired outcome and perhaps avoiding undesirable outcomes. Because we deliberate with an eye on the future and no one can predict the future, the results of our decisions are rarely completely predictable. Things change, unforeseen events transpire, unintended consequences provide new challenges and sometimes new opportunities.

Denotation: Words refer to things or ideas. The particular thing or idea that a given word refers to is its denotation. See *connotation*.

Dialectic: A form of discourse and a form of invention, where the validity of an assertion is tested for consistency and implication. Dialectic hinges on absolute definitions and therefore careful distinctions. Dialectic is a good mental exercise and a good way to test the strength of your opinions. And if reading just this definition is enough to get you full marks on a test, demand your money back.

Docile: Teachable. The characteristics of a learner are important to cultivate if you want to get better at anything at all, but especially if you want to become a *rhetor*. You have to accept criticism without taking it personally. You have to challenge yourself to the point where failure is a real possibility. And when you fail, you have to accept responsibility completely. Don't make excuses after the fact ("The professor doesn't like me") or build excuses into the process; procrastinating until there isn't enough time for you to make your best effort is a self-protecting but self-defeating strategy. You need to see each attempt regardless of outcome as an opportunity for improvement. You need to motivate yourself, without regard for what's on the test or how other people are doing. Think beyond the present situation.

Enthymeme: A statement supported by a reason to believe it. Often the word *because* signals the reason being offered. (For example, you should graduate from college because if you do you will make on average a million dollars more over your lifetime than if you drop out.) The enthymeme is the shortest unit of argument. Its brevity provides its power by leaving some of the relevant ideas unsaid. The audience then has to either infer them or assume them. The least experienced among the audience might fail to notice anything missing. By letting the audience fill in the missing parts, you offer them the chance to feel smart the way one does when one has an insight or gets a joke. You also have the opportunity to avoid an argument you don't think you can win or one that might delay the more important matters at hand if you have to discuss what you left out. But you also run the risk of getting push-back from an audience if what you leave out is something they are unwilling to assume. The enthymeme can be a very efficient form of reasoning, especially if everyone involved shares the same context and has the same attitudes. In such cases you don't have to spell everything out. In fact, if you did spell everything out you would bore your audience.

So, for example, if you were having a picnic and it started to rain, you could easily make the following enthymemic argument: *We need to move inside because it's raining*. But of course, under the circumstances, you don't need to make the argument because no one would disagree. Everyone runs for cover when it rains because we don't like wearing wet clothes and because we think we might get sick. Both of those two assertions might form part of a longer argument, each providing an enthymeme. But again, you don't need to bother because they are widely held beliefs. Now let's say you and your friends aren't having a picnic but are planting a garden when it starts to rain. What if you were delivering the mail? The deeper the disagreement, the less effective an enthymeme is likely to be.

Ethos: How you represent yourself to others. If your goal is to be credible, the three primary positive qualities you want to embody are good sense, goodwill, and effectiveness. As your goals change, so the qualities you need to embody change. If, for example, you want to be liked, then you would take an obvious interest in the things that interest those you want to befriend, showing yourself to be as like them as possible, consistent, and humorous. If you want people to rely on you, be consistently conscientious, useful, and effective. If for some reason you want to be feared, then you might choose to appear irascible, aggressive, and unpredictable. For every way you wish others to perceive you there is a set of characteristics to embody and an appropriate level of intensity for each element in the set. *Rhetors* can be chameleons; they can change as the context changes and new needs arise. This doesn't mean they are inauthentic (not truly themselves). It means their self-concept is adaptive because they are situation aware.

Event horizon: How far into the future you can see. No one can predict the future, but we live our lives according to circular calendars, which means that the same events come around the same time every year. Taxes in April (in the United States), planting in the spring, the Olympics every four years, and so on. This regularity allows us to plan. The further up the ladder you are, the further ahead you need to see. The people on the ground can only see what's directly in front of them. If you want to succeed, you need to think about how to extend your event horizon so that you can act instead of react to things as they come up. But if you are ambitious to climb the ladder, you need to stay always conscious of the fact that you cannot predict the future and so your plans have to be maximally flexible.

Fallacy: An argument that looks and sounds reasonable but is illogical.

Figurative: A word or expression that does not refer directly to a thing in the world or a concept in the mind. An indirect form of expression that refers to an attribute or quality of a thing or concept rather than the thing or concept itself.

Heuristic: From the Greek *eureka* which means "I have found it." It's the word the Greek rhetoricians used to name *invention*, or the process of coming up with the right things to say. Today it means a pattern or template that enables rapid decision making, sometimes suggesting less than rational, sometimes extrarational, depending on the user's attitude toward intuition.

Hierarchies of value: We all have a set of things we value, and we don't value each of them equally. *God, family, work* is a standard formulation that makes the point. Most people have more than three values, and for many they don't always take this order. When an argument hinges on values consider their relative importance and how that relation might change as the context changes. Remember that what you know about framing can help you change the context and thus the hierarchies of value. See Perelman and Olbrechts-Tyteca, *The New Rhetoric*, for more on hierarchies of value.

Icon: A sign or object that resembles the thing it signifies. The curvy line on the highway sign that indicates a curvy road ahead is an icon. So is the image of a leader.

Inference: An idea that directly follows from an observation or assertion, as when you infer it must be raining outside because the person who just got in the elevator is carrying a wet umbrella.

Intention: What someone means or meant to do, the purpose of an action or the goal. We use the idea of intention to explain what motivated a person to act and to decipher their current actions if they aren't explaining them to us. When persuading others, sometimes you want your intentions obvious, and sometimes you want them hidden, and sometimes you want them only partially revealed. If someone will try to stand between you and something you want, don't let them know what you want. If someone is only out for their own gain, and your goal isn't the same as their goal, but your plans are compatible, then reveal the part that fits their needs, and keep your other goals to yourself. No need to make the other feel you're not entirely on board or suspicious because your goals are complex. When issuing orders or otherwise leading, making your subordinates know what you want is critical to success. This form of intention is sometimes referred to as *commander's intent*, as it is in the armed forces. You want people to know what the goal is, but you don't want to explain step-by-step how to get there because it would take too long, or because you aren't close enough to the situation to know what the material conditions of implementation would be; you simply convey the goal, and leave it at that. If the subordinates know the commander's intent, then they are free to obtain it by whatever means they see likely to succeed, and the commander doesn't have to be omniscient. Leaders who can't leave the details of implementation alone are called *micromanagers*. It's not a compliment. The goal has to be clear even if the reason for obtaining it is never stated. (Such thinking is said to be "need to know only" so as to minimize leaks, to forestall second-guessing, and to keep subordinates focused on their tasks.) If the goal is vague or ambiguous, the subordinates won't know what to aim at.

When it comes to persuasion, your commander's intent is your primary goal, the point you need to make, the message you need to stay on. Everything is subordinate to that. In life, your commander's intent will vary over time. At some points in your life you may have a single intent, like graduating from college or getting an awesome job. At other times you may have a less targeted approach to life. Just remember that if you have to enlist other people's help you need to be very clear about what you need from them. Avoid mixing your messages.

Intuition: A form of semiconscious or even automatic thinking, where the chain of ideas passes so rapidly it's as if it never happened, and yet you clearly know what to do or say. Psychologists often describe intuition in terms of heuristics, patterns of thought created by years of experience from which one can instantly infer the correct course of action. Remember that the Greek word for "invention" is *heuresis*. Intuition in this sense is something that you learn and then forget you learned it, which is helpful because if you had to work out every step you wouldn't have time to react or you might even "choke," get so focused on the details of implementation that you can't execute properly.

Invention: A set of practices (heuristics, rules of thumb) for coming up with what to say and do, often organized by occasion or circumstances. The traditional practices include general patterns of thought (a.k.a. general topics—*more of a good thing is better than less of it; what the wise prefer is preferable to what the ignorant prefer*), patterns, in other words, that might work in any setting. There are also specific patterns of thought (a.k.a. special topics) that apply primarily to a single domain or field of study, such as *what a person intended when they set out a will should be the guide to interpreting that will*, or *as supply increases, prices drop*—patterns, in other words, that apply to a specific domain primarily but might analogically apply to other domains. In addition to general and specific topics we also have commonplaces or what today we might call stereotypes in the sense of conventional or culturally embedded expectations about people, places, and things. As someone trained in persuasion and therefore critical thinking, of course, you know that stereotypes are questionable and that often real insight comes from seeing through the stereotype to the expectations and beliefs that enable it. We also have stasis theory (a series of questions to ask in a given situation) and dialectical conversation.

Justification: The process of finding reasons for doing what you did.

Literal: A word or expression that directly refers to an object in the world or a concept of the mind. The word *literal* is often confused with *figurative* today despite the fact that *literal* is the opposite of *figurative*.

Logos: Word, argument, story, speech. Of the three Aristotelian artistic proofs (*ethos, pathos, logos*), *logos* refers to those proofs that use enthymemes or paradigms to provide evidence to support an assertion.

Maxim: A ready-made piece of weak evidence in the form of a brief, memorable, compelling statement that just sounds true and that might make a less compelling assertion more believable. When the assertion and the maxim appear together, you have an enthymeme. But often the more compelling use of the maxim is as a way of summing up a situation. We can use proverbs for the same purpose. Clichés too, but they are the weakest way to go, typically.

Memorization: Using constant repetition to readily recall a text or poem or speech or musical passage or physical move (muscle memory) verbatim at a later date. As a form of learning it is much maligned these days because it seems to exclude insight and understanding. Being able to recite a passage from a book or poem doesn't seem to prove you understand it. Getting a song stuck in your head isn't the same thing as being able to perform it.

Metacognition: Thinking about thinking. Being able to explain to yourself or others why you just thought what you thought or said what you said. Metacognition is sometimes associated with the idea of executive mental functions, planning, organizing, keeping track of details, and having what's needed readily available when it's needed.

Metaphor: A figurative expression where a word that refers to one thing is applied to something analogous, suggesting that one thing is the other thing, not just similar to it (that would be a simile, a comparison using *like* or *as* and thus drawing attention to the figure) but interchangeable with it. Most of the time we notice metaphors, which suggests both the user's sophistication and our own for noticing, but sometimes we fail to notice that an expression is metaphorical because it has been used that way so often the effect has been lost, in which case we have what is known as a dead metaphor.

Mnemonics: Techniques for connecting what you already know to what you want to be able to remember, using your innate capacity for association to learn new things.

Motivation: The set of characteristics and experiences that keep a person moving toward a goal. The characteristics are being able to visualize the outcome, believing you naturally are what you intend to become, a sense of destiny, identifying strongly with those who have succeeded before (role models, mentors), experiencing incremental achievements along the way, enjoying the challenge represented by setbacks, and responding to negative feedback with renewed effort and increased enthusiasm.

Pathos: Emotional appeal. One of Aristotle's three forms of proof, *logos* and *ethos* being the other two. With this form of argument, you try to increase or decrease your audience's emotional involvement in the argument by directly addressing their values, commitments, and beliefs. While many people today believe that emotional appeals are flagrant abuses of argumentation, the very essence of what is wrong with rhetoric, belief in the importance of dispassion in decision making is a value itself. And while exciting people may seem reprehensible to the people who prefer quiet contemplation of the fact, even these people must admit that being able to calm an audience must be something a speaker or writer can do.

Persona: A fictional character composed of attributes from real people designed to stand in for an actual person.

Phronesis: Practical wisdom, knowing what and why but especially how. *Phronesis* is the kind of smart that gets good things done. It's the most important kind of intellectual capacity, not averse to theoretical contemplation but always with an eye toward the practical world.

Premortem: In *Sources of Power: How People Make Decisions*, Gary Klein suggests that after a decision has been made it's a good idea to imagine the plan has failed and to come up with some explanations for why it did. The premortem helps to combat the natural optimism one feels after having made a decision. After all, no one intends to fail, but failure is always possible. In the context of becoming a more persuasive communicator, imagine how your plans might go wrong, and having anticipated those mistakes correct them in advance. If you are turning in a paper, estimate what grade you think you should get; imagine you get it back with a letter grade lower than expected, and see if you can explain why it happened. Then keep it from happening.

Price/cost: The *price* is the money you spend up front, but the *cost* is money spent subsequently on upgrades and add-ons and upkeep and training and support and maintenance and ultimately disposal. You also need to consider opportunity costs, that is, what you can't do with the money you spent because you spent it. Every decision you make opens some possibilities and closes others.

Probability: In a rhetorical sense, what people are likely to expect or assume, not necessarily what is statistically probable. In fact, expectations are frequently at odds with statistics. While you might want to teach an audience what the actual, statistical probability of an event might be, you always need to take into account people's expectations and assumptions.

Psychagogy: Plato minted this word in *Phaedrus* to signify a true rhetoric, one that he said essentially was possible but didn't yet exist. The word's derivation is instructive. *Psyche* is Greek for "mind," although it is often translated as "soul," a translation that strikes me as somewhat anachronistic or at any rate one that has for us irrelevant Christian overtones. *Agogue* is Greek for "lead," although literally "to mold with wax," and so psychagogy would be the discipline of leading minds in the right direction, tailoring a speech to the mind of the recipient with an eye toward the circumstances of reception. To be a psychagogue, you would need to know the types of soul (there are nine, Plato says; *Phaedrus*, 247a–d), the types of speech, and the ways each kind of soul is affected by each kind of speech. It's not entirely clear, of course, how serious Plato was about the types of mind, and he never defines the types of speech. But the concept left a mark on many subsequent discussions of rhetoric, including Aristotle's, because it indicated that careful knowledge of how our minds work matters a great deal. My thinking about psychagogy is what led me to spend so many words in this book talking about contemporary psychology.

Rationalization: Justifying an action without concern for evidence to the contrary. Wishful thinking is the deliberative equivalent.

Reciprocity: The psychological foundation of the Golden Rule. We tend to respond in kind. If someone is nice to us, we want to be nice back. When you give somebody something, it's the rule of reciprocity that inclines them to feel indebted and therefore compelled to return (reciprocate) the favor. As with all things rhetorical, the opposite is also true. Do something unkind, and unkindness will come back on you.

Rhetor: See Chapter 5, "Conclusion."

Rhetorical naiveté: Believing that language can accurately articulate experience, accepting simplistic dichotomies like reality/appearance, true/false, right/wrong, fact/value. Believing that adjectives are entities (the good, the bad) rather than attributed qualities. Failing to recognize common metaphors as metaphorical expressions. Using unintentional expressions. Not caring what your audience thinks. Thinking you don't have an audience.

Sign: An object that indicates the presence or absence of something else. If the indication is certain, unquestionable (fire means heat), then the sign is a cause or an effect of the other thing. If the indication is only likely (smoke means fire), then you have reason to believe you are looking in the right place but need to keep looking for more evidence. Some of the standard signs of guilt, for example, are motive, means, and opportunity. If someone wanted to do something wrong, had the chance to, and was capable of it, then you might be looking in the right direction.

Stasis/*asystasis*: A direct disagreement that forms the problem an argument is supposed to resolve. *He is falsely accused / No he isn't. We should do X / No we shouldn't.* Strictly speaking a static disagreement has to line up exactly, so *We should do X / No we should do Y* is a malformed disagreement. You should first prove that X is the wrong course and then offer Y as the best possible alternative, but because people are impatient, and proving Y by implication disproves X, you might skip the step. However, don't skip the step when you are inventing arguments. Think it through.

The opposite of *stasis* is *asystasis*. *Asystatic* arguments are hopeless disagreements, where the best outcome would be to move on as quickly as possible. If there's no evidence, if the evidence is all one sided, if the evidence is inconclusive for any reason, you have an *asystatic* situation. No reason to argue.

Theory of mind: Although we can't directly observe and therefore imperially know what someone else is thinking or even that they are thinking at all, most of us are extremely adept or imagine we are at inferring other people's inner states based on the situation, our knowledge of the person, and the way the person seems to be behaving—body posture, expression, voice, and so on. Sometimes we infer from how we would feel what the other person is likely to be experiencing. We sometimes call this ability emotional intelligence, and being able to theorize what another is thinking and feeling is a key rhetorical capacity. It is of course possible to provide a persuasive case using evidence alone, but especially in face-to-face settings, even over a computer monitor, this is much more difficult without a sense of how the words and examples you pick with play. You could argue that rhetoric was the first highly elaborated theory of mind, descending as it does from Plato's psychagogy and Aristotle's ideas about how enthymemes affect different audiences. Fei Tzu also observed that the difficulty of persuasion is knowing the mind of the one you would persuade.

Tunnel vision: When you look intensely at one thing, you don't see everything around it, like your mind is a camera and you are focusing on something, bringing it to the foreground, and blurring out all surrounding objects, blocking all other inputs. Having intense focus can be useful, but it can be harmful as well. If you are too single-minded you may miss other opportunities, and you may not fully understand the object of your focus because by staring at it in isolation you lose track of its context. A single focus can also negatively affect your emotions, making you anxious because everything depends on only one thing. Tunnel vision is especially bad when negotiating since it blinds you to opportunities that a wider view of the situation might reveal.

Writing process: You need to develop a robust writing discipline, one that incorporates the standard process of draft, write, revise, repeat into a larger practice. You need to develop a daily learning regime that you follow even before a specific writing task is assigned. You want to think about how you take notes, highlight the key points in what you are reading, make outlines, draw sketches, create concept maps, everything you can do that helps you learn the key concepts, arrange them in relation to each other, and discover what you need to learn next. You might well want to use an app for each or several of these tasks. In addition to developing a learning plan, you need a way to test the success of any given writing or speaking assignment. So before you turn anything in, do the premortem, and whenever you get anything back make the changes the reviewer suggests, regardless of whether or not you can resubmit it. Keep a portfolio of your work, not just to show to potential employers and possible clients but so you can measure your progress over time. You are taking the long view here. What you are doing now is preparation for life. It's not personal. Whether you do well or badly on any given assignment you can always improve, and that's always your goal.

Appendix: Selections on Rhetoric and Writing from Plato and Aristotle

Plato, *Gorgias*, 466a–481a

(Reprinted from Plato, Gorgias, translated by Donald J. Zeyl, Hackett Publishing Company, 1987.)

Polus: What is it you're saying, then? You think oratory is flattery?

Socrates: I said that it was a part of flattery. Don't you remember, Polus, young as you are? What's to become of you?

P: So you think that good orators are held in low regard in their cities, as flatterers?

S: Is this a question you're asking, or some speech you're beginning?

P: I'm asking a question.

S: I don't think they're held in any regard at all.

P: What do you mean, they're not held in any regard? Don't they have the greatest power in their cities?

S: No, if by "having power" you mean something that's good for the one who has the power.

P: That's just what I do mean.

S: In that case I think that orators have the least power of any in the city.

P: Really? Don't they, like tyrants, put to death anyone they want, and confiscate the property and banish from their cities anyone they see fit?

S: By the Dog, Polus! I can't make out one way or the other with each thing you're saying whether you're saying these things for yourself and revealing your own view, or whether you're questioning me.

P: I'm questioning you.

S: Very well, my friend. In that case, are you asking me two questions at once?

P: What do you mean, two?

S: Weren't you just now saying something like "Don't orators, like tyrants, put to death anyone they want, don't they confiscate the property of anyone they see fit, and don't they banish them from their cities?"

P: Yes, I was.

S: In that case I say that these are two questions, and I'll answer you both of them. I say, Polus, that both orators and tyrants have the least power in their cities, as I was saying just now. For they do just about nothing they want to, though they certainly do whatever they see most fit to do.

P: Well, isn't this having great power?

S: No; at least Polus says it isn't.

P: I say it isn't? I certainly say it is!

S: You certainly don't, by . . . !, since you say that having great power is good for the one who has it.

P: Yes, I do say that.

S: Do you think it's good, then, if a person does whatever he sees most fit to do when he lacks intelligence? Do you call this "having great power" too?

P: No, I do not.

S: Will you refute me, then, and prove that orators do have intelligence, and that oratory is a craft, and not flattery? If you leave me unrefuted, then the orators who do what they see fit in their cities, and the tyrants, too, won't have gained any good by this. Power is a good thing, you say, but you agree with me that doing what one sees fit without intelligence is bad. Or don't you?

P: Yes, I do.

S: How then could it be that orators or tyrants have great power in their cities, so long as Socrates is not refuted by Polus to show that they do what they want?

P: This fellow—

S: —denies that they do what they want. Go ahead and refute me.

P: Didn't you just now agree that they do what they see fit?

S: Yes, and I still do.

P: Don't they do what they want, then?

S: I say they don't.

P: Even though they do what they see fit?

S: That's what I say.

P: What an outrageous thing to say, Socrates! Perfectly monstrous!

S: Don't attack me, my peerless Polus, to address you in your own style. Instead, question me if you can, and prove that I'm wrong. Otherwise you must answer me.

P: All right, I'm willing to answer, to get some idea of what you're saying.

S: Do you think that when people do something, they want the thing they're doing at the time, or the thing for the sake of which they do what they're doing? Do you think that people who take medicines prescribed by their doctors, for instance, want what they're doing, the act of taking the medicine, with all its discomfort, or do they want to be healthy, the thing for the sake of which they're taking it?

P: Obviously they want their being healthy.

S: With seafarers, too, and those who make money in other ways, the thing they're doing at the time is not the thing they want—for who wants to make dangerous and troublesome sea voyages? What they want is their being wealthy, the thing for the sake of which, I suppose, they make their voyages. It's for the sake of wealth that they make them.

P: Yes, that's right.

S: Isn't it just the same in all cases, in fact? If a person does anything for the sake of something, he doesn't want this thing that he's doing, but the thing for the sake of which he's doing it?

P: Yes.

S: Now is there any thing that isn't either *good*, or *bad*, or, what is between these, *neither good or bad*?

P: There can't be, Socrates.

S: Do you say that wisdom, health, wealth and the like are *good*, and their opposites *bad*?

P: Yes, I do.

S: And by things which are *neither good nor bad* you mean things which sometimes partake of what's good, sometimes of what's bad, and sometimes of neither, such as sitting or walking, running or making sea voyages, or stones and sticks and the like? Aren't these the ones you mean? Or are there any others that you call things *neither good nor bad*?

P: No, these are the ones.

S: Now whenever people do things, do they do these intermediate things for the sake of good ones, or the good things for the sake of the intermediate ones?

P: The intermediate things for the sake of the good ones, surely.

S: So it's because we pursue what's good that we walk whenever we walk; we suppose that it's better to walk. And conversely, whenever we stand still, we stand still for the sake of the same thing, what's good. Isn't that so?

P: Yes.

S: And don't we also put a person to death, if we do, or banish him and confiscate his property because we suppose that doing that is better for us than not doing it?

P: That's right.

S: Hence, it's for the sake of what's good that those who do all these things do them.

P: I agree.

S: Now didn't we agree that we want, not those things that we do for the sake of something, but that thing for the sake of which we do them?

P: Yes, very much so.

S: Hence, we don't simply want to slaughter people, or exile them from their cities and confiscate their property as such; we want to do these things if they are beneficial, but if they're harmful we don't. For we want the things that are good, as you agree, and we don't want those that are neither good nor bad, nor those that are bad. Right? Do you think that what I'm saying is true, Polus, or don't you? Why don't you answer?

P: I think it's true.

S: Since we're in agreement about that then, if a person who's a tyrant or an orator puts somebody to death or exiles him or confiscates his property because he supposes that doing so is better for himself when actually it's worse, this person, I take it, is doing what he sees fit, isn't he?

P: Yes.

S: And is he also doing what he wants, if these things are actually bad? Why don't you answer?

P: All right, I don't think he's doing what he wants.

S: Can such a man possibly have great power in that city, if in fact having great power is, as you agree, something good?

P: He cannot.

S: So, what I was saying is true, when I said that it is possible for a man who does in his city what he sees fit not to have great power, nor to be doing what he wants.

P: Really, Socrates! As if you wouldn't welcome being in a position to do what you see fit in the city, rather than not! As if *you* wouldn't be envious whenever you'd see anyone putting to death some person he saw fit, or confiscating his property or tying him up!

S: Justly, you mean, or unjustly?

P: Whichever way he does it, isn't he to be envied either way?

S: Hush, Polus.

P: What for?

S: Because you're not supposed to envy the unenviable or the miserable. You're supposed to pity them.

P: Really? Is this how you think it is with the people I'm talking about?

S: Of course.

P: So, you think that a person who puts to death anyone he sees fit, and does so justly, is miserable and to be pitied?

S: No, I don't, but I don't think he's to be envied either.

P: Weren't you just now saying that he's miserable?

S: Yes, the one who puts someone to death unjustly is, my friend, and he's to be pitied besides. But the one who does so justly isn't to be envied.

P: Surely the one who's put to death unjustly is the one who's both to be pitied and miserable.

S: Less so than the one putting him to death, Polus, and less than the one who's justly put to death.

P: How can that be, Socrates?

S: It's because doing what's unjust is actually the greatest of evils.

P: Really? Is that the greatest? Isn't suffering what's unjust a greater one?

S: No, not in the least.

P: So you'd want to suffer what's unjust rather than do it?

S: I certainly wouldn't want either, but if it had to be one or the other, I would choose suffering over doing what's unjust.

P: You wouldn't welcome being a tyrant, then?

S: No, if by being a tyrant you mean what I do.

P: I mean just what I said a while ago, to be in a position to do whatever you see fit in the city, whether it's putting people to death or exiling them, or doing any and everything just as you see fit.

S: Well, my wonderful fellow! I'll put you a case, and you criticize it. Imagine me in a crowded marketplace, with a dagger up my sleeve, saying to you, "Polus, I've just got myself some marvelous tyrannical power. So, if I see fit to have any one of these people you see here put to death right on the spot, to death he'll be put. And if I see fit to have one of them have his head bashed in, bashed in it will be, right away. If I see fit to have his coat ripped apart, ripped it will be. That's how great my power in this city is!" Suppose you didn't believe me and I showed you the dagger. On seeing it, you'd be likely to say, "But Socrates, *everybody* could have great power that way. For this way any house you see fit might be burned down, and so might the dockyards and triremes of the Athenians, and all their ships, both public and private." But then *that's* not what having great power is, doing what one sees fit. Or do you think it is?

P: No, at least not like that.

S: Can you then tell me what your reason is for objecting to this sort of power?

P: Yes, I can.

S: What is it? Tell me.

P: It's that the person who acts this way is necessarily punished.

S: And isn't being punished a bad thing?

P: Yes, it really is.

S: Well then, my surprising fellow, here again you take the view that as long as acting as one sees fit coincides with acting beneficially, it is good, and this, evidently, is having great power. Otherwise it is a bad thing, and is having little power. Let's consider this point, too. Do we agree that sometimes it's better to do those things we were just now talking about, putting people to death and banishing them and confiscating their property, and at other times it isn't?

P: Yes, we do.

S: This point is evidently agreed upon by you and me both?

P: Yes.

S: When do you say that it's better to do these things then? Tell me where you draw the line.

P: Why don't you answer that question yourself, Socrates.

S: Well then, Polus, if you find it more pleasing to listen to me, I say that when one does these things justly, it's better, but when one does them unjustly, it's worse.

P: How hard it is to refute you, Socrates! Why, even a child could refute you and show that what you're saying isn't true!

S: In that case, I'll be very grateful to the child, and just as grateful to you if you refute me and rid me of this nonsense. Please don't falter now in doing a friend a good turn. Refute me.

P: Surely, Socrates, we don't need to refer to ancient history to refute you. Why, current events quite suffice to do that, and to prove that many people who behave unjustly are happy.

S: What sorts of events are these?

P: You can picture this man Archelaus, the son of Perdiccas, ruling Macedonia, I take it?

S: Well, if I can't picture him, I do hear things about him.

P: Do you think he's happy or miserable?

S: I don't know, Polus. I haven't met the man yet.

P: Really? You'd know this if you had met him, but without that you don't know straight off that he's happy?

S: No, I certainly don't, by Zeus!

P: It's obvious, Socrates, that you won't even claim to know that the Great King is happy!

S: Yes, and that would be true, for I don't know how he stands in regard to education and justice.

P: Really? Is happiness determined entirely by that?

S: Yes, Polus, so I say anyway. I say that the admirable and good person, man or woman, is happy, but that the one who's unjust and wicked is miserable.

P: So on your reasoning this man Archelaus is miserable?

S: Yes, my friend, if he is in fact unjust.

P: Why of course he's unjust! The sovereignty which he now holds doesn't belong to him at all, given the fact that his mother was a slave of Alcetas, Perdiccas's brother. By rights he was a slave of Alcetas, and if he wanted to do what's just, he'd still be a slave to Alcetas, and on your reasoning would be happy. As it is, how marvelously "miserable" he's turned out to be, now that he's committed the most heinous crimes. First he sends for this man, his very own master and uncle, on the pretext of restoring to him the sovereignty that Perdiccas had taken from him. He entertains him, gets him drunk, both him and his son Alexander, his own cousin and a boy about his own age. He then throws them into a wagon, drives it away at night, and slaughters and disposes of them both. And although he's committed these crimes, he remains unaware of how "miserable" he's become, and feels no remorse either. He refuses to become "happy" by justly bringing up his brother and conferring the sovereignty upon him, the legitimate son of Perdiccas, a boy of about seven to whom the sovereignty was by rights due to come. Instead, not long afterward, he throws him into a well and drowns him, telling the boy's mother Cleopatra that he fell into the well chasing a goose and lost his life. For this very reason now, because he's committed the most terrible of crimes of any in Macedonia, he's the most "miserable" of all Macedonians instead of the happiest, and no doubt there are some in Athens, beginning with yourself, who'd prefer being any other Macedonian at all to being Archelaus.

S: Already at the start of our discussions, Polus, I praised you because I thought you were well educated in oratory. But I also thought that you had neglected the practice of discussion. And now is *this* all there is to the argument by which even a child could refute me, and do you suppose that when I say that a person who acts unjustly is not happy, I now stand refuted by you by means of *this* argument? Where did you get that idea, my good man? As a matter of fact, I disagree with every single thing you say!

P: You're just unwilling to admit it. You really do think it's the way I say it is.

S: My wonderful man, you're trying to refute me in oratorical style, the way people in law courts do when they think they're refuting some claim. There, too, one side thinks it's refuting the other when it produces many reputable witnesses on behalf of the arguments it presents, while the person who asserts the opposite produces only one witness, or none at all. This "refutation" is worthless, as far as truth is concerned, for it might happen sometimes that an individual is brought down by the false testimony of many reputable people. Now too, nearly every Athenian and alien will take your side on the things you're saying, if it's witnesses you want to produce against me to show that what I say isn't true. Nikias the son of Niceratus will testify for you, if you like, and his brothers along with him, the ones whose tripods are standing in a row in the precinct of Dionysus. Aristocrates the son of Scellius will too, if you like, the one to whom that handsome votive offering in the precinct of Pythian Apollo belongs. And so will the whole house of Pericles, if you like, or any other local family you care to choose. Nevertheless, though I'm only one person, I don't agree with you. You don't compel me; instead you produce many false witnesses against me and try to banish me from my property, the truth. For my part, if I don't produce you as a single witness to agree with what I'm saying, then I suppose I've achieved nothing worth mentioning concerning the things we've been discussing. And I suppose you haven't either, if I don't testify on your side, though I'm just one person, and you disregard all these other people.

There is, then, this style of refutation, the one you and many others accept. There's also another, one that I accept. Let's compare the one with the other and see if they'll differ in any way. It's true, after all, that the matters in dispute between us are not at all insignificant ones, but pretty nearly those it's most admirable to have knowledge about, and most shameful not to. For the heart of the matter is that of recognizing or failing to recognize who is happy and who is not. To take first the immediate question our present discussion's about: you believe that it's possible for a man who behaves unjustly and who is unjust to be happy, since you believe Archelaus to be both unjust and happy. Are we to understand that this is precisely your view?

P: That's right.

S: And I say that that's impossible. This is one point in dispute between us. Fair enough. Although he acts unjustly, he'll be happy—that is, if he gets his due punishment?

P: Oh no, certainly not! That's how he'd be the most miserable!

S: But if a man who acts unjustly doesn't get his due, then, on your reasoning, he'll be happy?

P: That's what I say.

S: On my view of it, Polus, a man who acts unjustly, a man who is unjust, is thoroughly miserable, the more so if he doesn't get his due punishment for the wrongdoing he commits, the less so if he pays and receives what is due at the hands of both gods and men.

P: What an absurd position you're trying to maintain, Socrates!

S: Yes, and I'll try to get you to take the same position too, my good man, for I consider you a friend. For now, these are the points we differ on. Please look at them with me. I said earlier, didn't I, that doing what's unjust is worse than suffering it?

P: Yes, you did.

S: And you said that suffering it is worse.

P: Yes.

S: And I said that those who do what's unjust are miserable, and was "refuted" by you.

P: You certainly were, by Zeus!

S: So you think, Polus.

P: So I *truly* think.

S: Perhaps. And again, you think that those who do what's unjust are happy, so long as they don't pay what is due.

P: I certainly do.

S: Whereas I say that they're the most miserable, while those who pay their due are less so. Would you like to refute this too?

P: Why, that's even more "difficult" to refute than the other claim, Socrates!

S: Not difficult, surely, Polus. It's impossible. What's true is never refuted.

P: What do you mean? Take a man who's caught doing something unjust, say, plotting to set himself up as tyrant. Suppose that he's caught, put on the rack, castrated, and has his eyes burned out. Suppose that he's subjected to a host of other abuses of all sorts, and then made to witness his wife and children undergo the same. In the end he's impaled or tarred. Will he be happier than if he hadn't got caught, had set himself up as tyrant, and lived out his life ruling in his city and doing whatever he liked, a person envied and counted happy by fellow citizens and aliens alike? Is this what you say is impossible to refute?

S: This time you're spooking me, Polus, instead of refuting me. Just before, you were arguing by testimony. Still, refresh my memory on a small point: if the man plots to set himself up as tyrant *unjustly*, you said?

P: Yes, I did.

S: In that case neither of them will ever be the happier one, neither the one who gains tyrannical power unjustly, nor the one who pays what is due, for of two miserable people one could not be happier than the other. But the one who avoids getting caught and becomes a tyrant is the more miserable one. What's this, Polus? You're laughing? Is this now some further style of refutation, to laugh when somebody makes a point, instead of refuting him?

P: Don't you think you've been refuted already, Socrates, when you're saying things the likes of which no human being would maintain? Just ask any one of these people.

S: Polus, I'm not one of the politicians. Last year I was elected to the Council by lot, and when our tribe was presiding and I had to call for a vote, I came in for a laugh. I didn't know how to do it. So please don't tell me to call for a vote from the people present here. If you have no better "refutations" than these to offer, do as I suggested just now: let me have my turn, and you try the kind of refutation I think is called for. For I do know how to produce one witness to whatever I'm saying, and that's the man I'm having a discussion with. The majority I disregard. And I do know how to call for a vote from one man, but I don't even discuss things with the majority. See if you'll be willing to give me a refutation, then, by answering the questions you're asked. For I do believe that you and I and everybody else consider doing what's unjust worse than suffering it, and not paying what is due worse than paying it.

P: And I do believe that I don't, and that no other person does, either. So you'd take suffering what's unjust over doing it, would you?

S: Yes, and so would you and everyone else.

P: Far from it! I wouldn't, you wouldn't, and nobody else would, either.

S: Won't you answer, then?

P: I certainly will. I'm eager to know what you'll say, in fact.

S: So that you'll know, answer me as though this were my first question to you. Which do you think is worse, Polus, doing what's unjust or suffering it?

P: I think suffering it is.

S: You do? Which do you think is more shameful, doing what's unjust or suffering it? Tell me.

P: Doing it.

S: Now if doing it is in fact more shameful, isn't it also worse?

P: No, not in the least.

S: I see. Evidently you don't believe that *admirable* and *good* are the same, or that *bad* and *shameful* are.

P: No, I certainly don't.

S: Well, what about this? When you call all admirable things admirable, bodies, for example, or colors, shapes and sounds, or practices, is it with nothing in view that you do so each time? Take admirable bodies first. Don't you call them admirable either in virtue of their usefulness, relative to whatever it is that each is useful for, or else in virtue of some pleasure, if it makes the people who look at them get enjoyment from looking at them? In the case of the admirability of a body, can you mention anything other than these?

P: No, I can't.

S: Doesn't the same hold for all the other things? Don't you call shapes and colors admirable on account of either some pleasure or benefit or both?

P: Yes, I do.

S: Doesn't this also hold for sounds and all things musical?

P: Yes.

S: And certainly things that pertain to laws and practices—the admirable ones, that is—don't fall outside the limits of being either pleasant or beneficial, or both, I take it.

P: No, I don't think they do.

S: Doesn't the same hold for the admirability of the fields of learning, too?

P: Yes indeed. Yes, Socrates, your present definition of the admirable in terms of pleasure and good is an admirable one.

S: And so is my definition of the shameful in terms of the opposite, pain and evil, isn't it?

P: Necessarily so.

S: Therefore, whenever one of two admirable things is more admirable than the other, it is so because it surpasses the other either in one of these, pleasure or benefit, or in both.

P: Yes, that's right.

S: And whenever one of two shameful things is more shameful than the other, it will be so because it surpasses the other either in pain or in evil. Isn't that necessarily so?

P: Yes.

S: Well now, what were we saying a moment ago about doing what's unjust and suffering it? Weren't you saying that suffering it is more evil, but doing it more shameful?

P: I was.

S: Now if doing what's unjust is in fact more shameful than suffering it, wouldn't it be so either because it is more painful and surpasses the other in pain, or because it surpasses it in evil, or both? Isn't that necessarily so, too?

P: Of course it is.

S: Let's look at this first: does doing what's unjust surpass suffering it in pain, and do people who do it hurt more than people who suffer it?

P: No, Socrates, that's not the case at all!

S: So it doesn't surpass it in pain, anyhow.

P: Certainly not.

S: So, if it doesn't surpass it in pain, it couldn't at this point surpass it in both.

P: Apparently not.

S: This leaves it surpassing it only in the other thing.

P: Yes.

S: In evil.

P: Evidently.

S: So, because it surpasses it in evil, doing what's unjust would be more evil than suffering it.

P: That's clear.

S: Now didn't the majority of mankind, and you earlier, agree with us that doing what's unjust is more shameful than suffering it?

P: Yes.

S: And now, at least, it's turned out to be more evil.

P: Evidently.

S: Would you then welcome what's more evil and what's more shameful over what is less so? Don't shrink back from answering, Polus. You won't get hurt in any way. Submit yourself nobly to the argument, as you would to a doctor, and answer me. Say yes or no to what I ask you.

P: No, I wouldn't, Socrates.

S: And would any other person?

P: No, I don't think so, not on this reasoning, anyhow.

S: I was right, then, when I said that neither you nor I nor any other person would take doing what's unjust over suffering it, for it really is more evil.

P: So it appears.

S: So you see, Polus, that when the one refutation is compared with the other, there is no resemblance at all. Whereas everyone but me agrees with you, you are all I need, although you're just a party of one, for your agreement and testimony. It's you alone whom I call on for a vote; the others I disregard. Let this be our verdict on this matter, then. Let's next consider the second point in dispute between us, that is whether a wrongdoer's paying what is due is the greatest of evils, as you were supposing, or whether his not paying it is a greater one, as I was.

Let's look at it this way. Do you call paying what is due and being justly disciplined for wrongdoing the same?

P: Yes, I do.

S: Can you say, then, that all just things aren't admirable, insofar as they are just? Think carefully and tell me.

P: Yes, I think they are.

S: Consider this point, too. If somebody acts upon something, there's necessarily also something that has something done to it by the one acting upon it?

P: Yes, I think so.

S: And that it has done to it what the thing acting upon it does, and in the sort of way the thing acting upon it does it? I mean, for example, that if somebody hits, there's necessarily something that is being hit?

P: Necessarily.

S: And if the hitter hits hard or quickly, the thing being hit is hit that way, too?

P: Yes.

S: So the thing being hit gets acted upon in whatever way the hitting thing acts upon it?

P: Yes, that's right.

S: So, too, if somebody performs surgical burning, then necessarily something is being burned?

P: Of course.

S: And if he burns severely or painfully, the thing that's being burned is burned in whatever way the burning thing burns it?

P: That's right.

S: Doesn't the same account also hold if a person makes a surgical cut? For something is being cut.

P: Yes.

S: And if the cut is large or deep or painful, the thing being cut is cut in whatever way the cutting thing cuts it?

P: So it appears.

S: Summing it up, see if you agree with what I was saying just now, that in all cases, in whatever way the thing acting upon something acts upon it, the thing acted upon is acted upon in just that way.

P: Yes, I do agree.

S: Taking this as agreed, is paying what is due a case of being acted upon or of acting upon something?

P: It's necessarily a case of being acted upon, Socrates.

S: By someone who acts?

P: Of course. By the one administering discipline.

S: Now one who disciplines correctly disciplines justly?

P: Yes.

S: Thereby acting justly, or not?

P: Yes, justly.

S: So the one being disciplined is being acted upon justly when he pays what is due?

P: Apparently.

S: And it was agreed, I take it, that just things are admirable?

P: That's right.

S: So one of these men does admirable things, and the other, the one being disciplined, has admirable things done to him.

P: Yes.

S: If they're admirable, then, aren't they good? For they're either pleasant or beneficial.

P: Necessarily so.

S: Hence, the one paying what is due has good things being done to him?

P: Evidently.

S: Hence, he's being benefited?

P: Yes.

S: Is his benefit the one I take it to be? Does his soul undergo improvement if he's justly disciplined?

P: Yes, that's likely.

S: Hence, one who pays what is due gets rid of evil in his soul?

P: Yes.

S: Now, is the evil he gets rid of the most serious one? Consider it this way: in the matter of a person's financial condition, do you detect any evil other than poverty?

P: No, just poverty.

S: What about that of a person's physical condition? Would you say that evil here consists of weakness, disease, ugliness, and the like?

P: Yes, I would.

S: Do you believe that there's also some corrupt condition of the soul?

P: Of course.

S: And don't you call this condition injustice, ignorance, cowardice, and the like?

P: Yes, certainly.

S: Of these three things, one's finances, one's body, and one's soul, you said there are three states of corruption, namely poverty, disease, and injustice?

P: Yes.

S: Which of these states of corruption is the most shameful? Isn't it injustice, and corruption of one's soul in general?

P: Very much so.

S: And if it's the most shameful, it's also the most evil?

P: What do you mean, Socrates?

S: I mean this: What we agreed on earlier implies that what's most shameful is so always because it's the source either of the greatest pain, or of harm, or of both.

P: Very much so.

S: And now we've agreed that injustice, and corruption of soul as a whole, is the most shameful thing.

P: So we have.

S: So either it's most painful and is most shameful because it surpasses the others in pain, or else in harm, or in both?

P: Necessarily so.

S: Now is being unjust, undisciplined, cowardly, and ignorant more painful than being poor or sick?

P: No, I don't think so, Socrates, given what we've said, anyhow.

S: So the reason that corruption of one's soul is the most shameful of them all is that it surpasses the others by some monstrously great harm and astounding evil, since it doesn't surpass them in pain, according to your reasoning.

P: So it appears.

S: But what is surpassing in greatest harm would, I take it, certainly be the greatest evil there is.

P: Yes.

S: Injustice, then, lack of discipline and all other forms of corruption of soul are the greatest evil there is.

P: Apparently so.

S: Now, what is the craft that gets rid of poverty? Isn't it that of financial management?

P: Yes.

S: What's the one that gets rid of disease? Isn't it that of medicine?

P: Necessarily.

S: What's the one that gets rid of corruption and injustice? If you're stuck, look at it this way: where and to whom do we take people who are physically sick?

P: To doctors, Socrates.

S: Where do we take people who behave unjustly and without discipline?

P: To judges, you mean?

S: Isn't it so they'll pay what's due?

P: Yes, I agree.

S: Now don't those who administer discipline correctly employ a kind of justice in doing so?

P: That's clear.

S: It's financial management, then, that gets rid of poverty, medicine that gets rid of disease, and justice that gets rid of injustice and indiscipline.

P: Apparently.

S: Which of these, now, is the most admirable?

P: Of which, do you mean?

S: Of financial management, medicine, and justice.

P: Justice is by far, Socrates.

S: Doesn't it in that case provide either the most pleasure, or benefit, or both, if it really is the most admirable?

P: Yes.

S: Now, is getting medical treatment something pleasant? Do people who get it enjoy getting it?

P: No, I don't think so.

S: But it *is* beneficial, isn't it?

P: Yes.

S: Because they're getting rid of a great evil, so that it's worth their while to endure the pain and so get well.

P: Of course.

S: Now, would a man be happiest, as far as his body goes, if he's under treatment, or if he weren't even sick to begin with?

P: If he weren't even sick, obviously.

S: Because happiness evidently isn't a matter of getting rid of evil; it's rather a matter of not even contracting it to begin with.

P: That's so.

S: Very well. Of two people, each of whom has an evil in either body or soul, which is the more miserable one, the one who is treated and gets rid of the evil, or the one who doesn't but keeps it?

P: The one who isn't treated, it seems to me.

S: Now, wasn't paying what's due getting rid of the greatest evil, corruption?

P: It was.

S: Yes, because such justice makes people self-controlled, I take it, and more just. It proves to be a treatment against corruption.

P: Yes.

S: The happiest man, then, is the one who doesn't have evil in his soul, now that this has been shown to be the most serious kind of evil.

P: That's clear.

S: And second, I suppose, is the man who gets rid of it.

P: Evidently.

S: This is the man who gets lectured and lashed, the one who pays what is due.

P: Yes.

S: The man who keeps it, then, and who doesn't get rid of it, is the one whose life is the worst.

P: Apparently.

S: Isn't this actually the man who, although he commits the most serious crimes and uses methods that are most unjust, succeeds in avoiding being lectured and disciplined and paying his due, as Archelaus according to you, and the other tyrants, orators, and potentates have put themselves in a position to do?

P: Evidently.

S: Yes, my good man, I take it that these people have managed to accomplish pretty much the same thing as a person who has contracted very serious illnesses, but, by avoiding treatment manages to avoid paying what's due to the doctors for his bodily faults, fearing, as would a child, cauterization or surgery because they're painful. Don't you think so, too?

P: Yes, I do.

S: It's because he evidently doesn't know what health and bodily excellence are like. For on the basis of what we're now agreed on, it looks as though those who avoid paying what is due also do the same sort of thing, Polus. They focus on its painfulness, but are blind to its benefit and are ignorant of how much more miserable it is to live with an unhealthy soul than with an unhealthy body, a soul that's rotten with injustice and impiety. This is also the reason they go to any length to avoid paying what is due and getting rid of the greatest evil. They find themselves funds and friends, and ways to speak as persuasively as possible. Now if what we're agreed on is true, Polus, are you aware of what things follow from our argument? Or would you like us to set them out?

P: Yes, if you think we should anyhow.

S: Does it follow that injustice, and doing what is unjust, is the greatest evil?

P: Yes, apparently.

S: And it has indeed been shown that paying what is due is what gets rid of this evil?

P: So it seems.

S: And that if it isn't paid, the evil is retained?

P: Yes.

S: So, doing what's unjust is the second most serious evil. Not paying what's due when one has done what's unjust is by its nature the most serious and foremost evil of all.

P: Evidently.

S: Now wasn't this the point in dispute between us, my friend? You considered Archelaus happy, a man who committed the gravest crimes without paying what was due, whereas I took the opposite view, that whoever avoids paying his due for his wrong-doing, whether he's Archelaus or any other man, deserves to be miserable beyond all other men, and that one who does what's unjust is always more miserable than the one who suffers it, and the one who avoids paying what's due always more miserable than the one who does pay it. Weren't these the things I said?

P: Yes.

S: Hasn't it been proved that what was said is true?

P: Apparently.

S: Fair enough. If these things are true then, Polus, what is the great use of oratory? For on the basis of what we're agreed on now, what a man should guard himself against most of all is doing what's unjust, knowing that he will have trouble enough if he does. Isn't that so?

P: Yes, that's right.

S: And if he or anyone else he cares about acts unjustly, he should voluntarily go to the place where he'll pay his due as soon as possible; he should go to the judge as though he were going to a doctor, anxious that the disease of injustice shouldn't be pro-tracted and cause his soul to fester incurably. What else can we say, Polus, if our previous agreements really stand? Aren't these statements necessarily consistent with our earlier ones in only this way?

P: Well yes, Socrates. What else are we to say?

S: So, if oratory is used to defend injustice, Polus, one's own or that of one's relatives, companions, or children, or that of one's country when it acts unjustly, it is of no use to us at all, unless one takes it to be useful for the opposite purpose: that he should accuse himself first and foremost, and then too his family and anyone else dear to him who happens to behave unjustly at any time; and that he should not keep his wrongdoing hidden but bring it out into the open, so that he may pay his due and get well; and compel himself and the others not to play the coward, but to grit his teeth and present himself with grace and cour-age as to a doctor for cauterization and surgery, pursuing what's good and admirable without taking any account of the pain. And if his unjust behavior merits flogging, he should present

himself to be whipped; if it merits imprisonment, to be imprisoned; if a fine, to pay it; if exile, to be exiled; and if execution,
to be executed. He should be his own chief accuser, and the
accuser of other members of his family, and use his oratory for
the purpose of getting rid of the greatest evil, injustice, as the
unjust acts are being exposed. Are we to affirm or deny this,
Polus?

P: I think these statements are absurd, Socrates, though no
doubt you think they agree with those expressed earlier.

S: Then either we should abandon those, or else these necessarily follow?

P: Yes, that's how it is.

S: And, on the other hand, to reverse the case, suppose a man
had to harm someone, an enemy or anybody at all, provided
that he didn't suffer anything unjust from this enemy himself—for this is something to be on guard against—if the
enemy did something unjust against another person, then our
man should see to it in every way, both in what he does and
what he says, that his enemy does not go to the judge and pay
his due. And if he does go, he should scheme to get his enemy
off without paying what's due. If he's stolen a lot of gold, he
should scheme to get him not to return it but to keep it and
spend it in an unjust and godless way both on himself and his
people. And if his crimes merit the death penalty, he should
scheme to keep him from being executed, preferably never to
die at all but to live forever in corruption, but failing that, to
have him live as long as possible in that condition. Yes, this
is the sort of thing I think oratory is useful for, Polus, since
for the person who has no intention of behaving unjustly it
doesn't seem to me to have much use—if in fact it has any use
at all—since its usefulness hasn't in any way become apparent
so far.

Plato, *Phaedrus*, 258e–279c

(Reprinted from Plato, Phaedrus, *translated by Alexander Nehamas and Paul
Woodruff, Hackett Publishing Company, 1995.)*

Phaedrus: You ask if we need to? why else should one live, I say,
if not for pleasures of this sort? Certainly not for those you cannot feel unless you are first in pain, like most of the pleasures

of the body, and which for this reason we call the pleasures of slaves.

Socrates: It seems we clearly have the time. Besides, I think that the cicadas, who are singing and carrying on conversations with one another in the heat of the day above our heads, are also watching us. And if they saw the two of us avoiding conversation at midday like most people, diverted by their song and, sluggish of mind, nodding off, they would have every right to laugh at us, convinced that a pair of slaves had come to their resting place to sleep like sheep gathering around the spring in the afternoon. But if they see us in conversation, steadfastly navigating around them as if they were the Sirens, they will be very pleased and immediately give us the gift from the gods they are able to give to mortals.

Ph: What is this gift? I don't think I have heard of it.

So: Everyone who loves the Muses should have heard of this. The story goes that the cicadas used to be human beings who lived before the birth of the Muses. When the Muses were born and song was created for the first time, some of the people of that time were so overwhelmed with the pleasure of singing that they forgot to eat or drink; so they died without even realizing it. It is from them that the race of the cicadas came into being; and, as a gift from the Muses, they have no need of nourishment once they are born. Instead, they immediately burst into song, without food or drink, until it is time for them to die. After they die, they go to the Muses and tell each one of them which mortals have honored her. To Terpsichore they report those who have honored her by their devotion to the dance and thus make them dearer to her. To Erato, they report those who honored her by dedicating themselves to the affairs of love, and so too with the other Muses, according to the activity that honors each. And to Calliope, the oldest among them, and Urania, the next after her, who preside over the heavens and all discourse, human and divine, and sing with the sweetest voice, they report those who honor their special kind of music by leading a philosophical life.

There are many reasons, then, why we should talk and not waste our afternoon in sleep.

Ph: By all means, let's talk.

So: Well, then, we ought to examine the topic we proposed just now: When is a speech well written and delivered, and when is it not?

Ph: Plainly.

So: Won't someone who is to speak well and nobly have to have in mind the truth about the subject he is going to discuss?

Ph: What I have actually heard about this, Socrates, my friend, is that it is not necessary for the intending orator to learn what is really just, but only what will seem just to the crowd who will act as judges. Nor again what is really good or noble, but only what will seem so. For that is what persuasion proceeds from, not truth.

So: Anything that wise men say, Phaedrus, "is not lightly to be cast aside"; we must consider whether it might be right. And what you just said, in particular, must not be dismissed.

Ph: You're right.

So: Let's look at it this way, then.

Ph: How?

So: Suppose I were trying to convince you that you should fight your enemies on horseback, and neither one of us knew what a horse is, but I happened to know this much about you, that Phaedrus believes a horse is the tame animal with the longest ears—

Ph: But that would be ridiculous, Socrates.

So: Not quite yet, actually. But if I were seriously trying to convince you, having composed a speech in praise of the donkey in which I called it a horse and claimed that having such an animal is of immense value both at home and in military service, that it is good for fighting and for carrying your baggage and that it is useful for much else besides—

Ph: Well, that would be totally ridiculous.

So: Well, which is better? To be ridiculous and a friend? Or clever and an enemy?

Ph: The former.

So: And so, when a rhetorician who does not know good from bad addresses a city which knows no better and attempts to sway it, not praising a miserable donkey as if it were a horse, but bad as if it were good, and, having studied what the people believe, persuades them to do something bad instead of good— with that as its seed, what sort of crop do you think rhetoric can harvest?

Ph: A crop of really poor quality.

So: But could it be, my friend, that we have mocked the art of speaking more rudely than it deserves? For it might perhaps reply, "What bizarre nonsense! Look, I am not forcing anyone to learn how to make speeches without knowing the truth; on the contrary, my advice, for what it is worth, is to take me up only after mastering the truth. But I do make this boast: even someone who knows the truth couldn't produce conviction on the basis of a systematic art without me."

Ph: Well, is that a fair reply?

So: Yes, it is—if, that is, the arguments now advancing upon rhetoric testify that it is an art. For it seems to me as if I hear certain arguments approaching and protesting that that is a lie and that rhetoric is not an art but an artless practice. As the Spartan said, there is no genuine art of speaking without a grasp of truth, and there never will be.

Ph: We need to hear these arguments, Socrates. Come, produce them, and examine them: What is their point? How do they make it?

So: Come to us, then, noble creatures; convince Phaedrus, him of the beautiful offspring, that unless he pursues philosophy properly he will never be able to make a proper speech on any subject either. And let Phaedrus be the one to answer.

Ph: Let them put their questions.

So: Well, then, isn't the rhetorical art, taken as a whole, a way of directing the soul by means of speech, not only in the lawcourts and on other public occasions but also in private? Isn't it one and the same art whether its subject is great or small, and no more to be held in esteem—if it is followed correctly—when its questions are serious than when they are trivial? Or what have you heard about all this?

Ph: Well, certainly not what *you* have! Artful speaking and writing is found mainly in the lawcourts; also perhaps in the Assembly. That's all I've heard.

So: Well, have you only heard of the rhetorical treatises of Nestor and Odysseus—those they wrote in their spare time in Troy? Haven't you also heard of the works of Palamedes?

Ph: No, by Zeus, I haven't even heard of Nestor's—unless by Nestor you mean Gorgias, and by Odysseus, Thrasymachus or Theodorus.

So: Perhaps. But let's leave these people aside. Answer this question yourself: What do adversaries do in the lawcourts? Don't they speak on opposite sides? What else can we call what they do?

Ph: That's it, exactly.

So: About what is just and what is unjust?

Ph: Yes.

So: And won't whoever does this artfully make the same thing appear to the same people sometimes just and sometimes, when he prefers, unjust?

Ph: Of course.

So: And when he addresses the Assembly, he will make the city approve a policy at one time as a good one, and reject it—the very same policy—as just the opposite at another.

Ph: Right.

So: Now, don't we know that the Eleatic Palamedes is such an artful speaker that his listeners will perceive the same things to be both similar and dissimilar, both one and many, both at rest and also in motion?

Ph: Most certainly.

So: We can therefore find the practice of speaking on opposite sides not only in the lawcourts and in the Assembly. Rather, it seems that one single art—if, of course, it is an art in the first place—governs all speaking. By means of it one can make out as similar anything that can be so assimilated, to everything to which it can be made similar, and expose anyone who tries to hide the fact that that is what he is doing.

Ph: What do you mean by that?

So: I think it will become clear if we look at it this way. Where is deception most likely to occur—regarding things that differ much or things that differ little from one another?

Ph: Regarding those that differ little.

So: At any rate, you are more likely to escape detection, as you shift from one thing to its opposite, if you proceed in small steps rather than in large ones.

Ph: Without a doubt.

So: Therefore, if you are to deceive someone else and to avoid deception yourself, you must know precisely the respects in which things are similar and dissimilar to one another.

Ph: Yes, you must.

So: And is it really possible for someone who doesn't know what each thing truly is to detect a similarity—whether large or small—between something he doesn't know and anything else?

Ph: That is impossible.

So: Clearly, therefore, the state of being deceived and holding beliefs contrary to what is the case comes upon people by reason of certain similarities.

Ph: That is how it happens.

So: Could someone, then, who doesn't know what each thing is ever have the art to lead others little by little through similarities away from what is the case on each occasion to its opposite? Or could he escape this being done to himself?

Ph: Never.

So: Therefore, my friend, the art of a speaker who doesn't know the truth and chases opinions instead is likely to be a ridiculous thing—not an art at all!

Ph: So it seems.

So: So, shall we look for instances of what we called the artful and the artless in the speech of Lysias you carried here and in our own speeches?

Ph: That's the best thing to do—because, as it is, we are talking quite abstractly, without enough examples.

So: In fact, by some chance the two speeches do, as it seems, contain an example of the way in which someone who knows the truth can toy with his audience and mislead them. For my part, Phaedrus, I hold the local gods responsible for this—also, perhaps, the messengers of the Muses who are singing over our heads may have inspired me with this gift: certainly *I* don't possess any art of speaking.

Ph: Fine, fine. But explain what you mean.

So: Come, then—read me the beginning of Lysias' speech.

Ph: "You understand my situation: I've told you how good it would be for us, in my opinion, if we could work this out. In any case, I don't think I should lose the chance to get what I am asking for, merely because I don't happen to be in love with you. A man in love will wish he had not done you any favors—"

So: Stop. Our task is to say how he fails and writes artlessly. Right?

Ph: Yes.

So: Now isn't this much absolutely clear: We are in accord with one another about some of the things we discourse about and in discord about others?

Ph: I think I understand what you are saying; but, please, can you make it a little clearer?

So: When someone utters the word "iron" or "silver," don't we all think of the same thing?

Ph: Certainly.

So: But what happens when we say "just" or "good"? Doesn't each one of us go in a different direction? Don't we differ with one another and even with ourselves?

Ph: We certainly do.

So: Therefore, we agree about the former and disagree about the latter.

Ph: Right.

So: Now in which of these two cases are we more easily deceived? And when does rhetoric have greater power?

Ph: Clearly, when we wander in different directions.

So: It follows that whoever wants to acquire the art of rhetoric must first make a systematic division and grasp the particular character of each of these two kinds of thing, both the kind where most people wander in different directions and the kind where they do not.

Ph: What a splendid thing, Socrates, he will have understood if he grasps *that*!

So: Second, I think, he must not be mistaken about his subject; he must have a sharp eye for the class to which whatever he is about to discuss belongs.

Ph: Of course.

So: Well, now, what shall we say about love? Does it belong to the class where people differ or to that where they don't?

Ph: Oh, surely the class where they differ. Otherwise, do you think you could have spoken of it as you did a few minutes ago, first saying that it is harmful both to lover and beloved and then immediately afterward that it is the greatest good?

So: Very well put. But now tell me this—I can't remember at all because I was completely possessed by the gods: Did I define love at the beginning of my speech?

Ph: Oh, absolutely, by Zeus, you most certainly did.

So: Alas, how much more artful with speeches the Nymphs, daughters of Achelous, and Pan, son of Hermes, are, according to what you say, than Lysias, son of Cephalus! Or am I wrong? Did Lysias too, at the start of his love-speech, compel us to assume that love is the single thing that he himself wanted it to be? Did he then complete his speech by arranging everything in relation to that? Will you read its opening once again?

Ph: If you like. But what you are looking for is not there.

So: Read it, so that I can hear it in his own words.

Ph: "You understand my situation: I've told you how good it would be for us, in my opinion, if we could work this out. In any case, I don't think I should lose the chance to get what I am asking for, merely because I don't happen to be in love with you. A man in love will wish he had not done you any favors, once his desire dies down—"

So: He certainly seems a long way from doing what we wanted. He doesn't even start from the beginning but from the end, making his speech swim upstream on its back. His first words are what a lover would say to his boy as he was concluding his speech. Am I wrong, Phaedrus, dear heart?

Ph: Well, Socrates, that was the end for which he gave the speech!

So: And what about the rest? Don't the parts of the speech appear to have been thrown together at random? Is it evident that the second point had to be made second for some compelling reason? Is that so for any of the parts? I at least—of course I know nothing about such matters—thought the author said just whatever came to mind next, though not without a certain noble willfulness. But you, do you know any principle of speech-composition compelling him to place these things one after another in this order?

Ph: It's very generous of you to think that I can understand his reasons so clearly.

So: But surely you will admit at least this much: Every speech must be put together like a living creature, with a body of its own; it must be neither without head nor without legs; and it must have a middle and extremities that are fitting both to one another and to the whole work.

Ph: How could it be otherwise?

So: But look at your friend's speech: Is it like that or is it otherwise? Actually, you'll find that it's just like the epigram people say is inscribed on the tomb of Midas the Phrygian.

Ph: What epigram is that? And what's the matter with it?

So: It goes like this:

> A maid of bronze am I, on Midas' tomb I lie
> As long as water flows, and trees grow tall
> Shielding the grave where many come to cry
> That Midas rests here I say to one and all.

I'm sure you notice that it makes no difference at all which of its verses comes first, and which last.

Ph: You are making fun of our speech, Socrates.

So: Well, then, if that upsets you, let's leave that speech aside—even though I think it has plenty of very useful examples, provided one tries to emulate them as little as possible—and turn to the others. I think it is important for students of speechmaking to pay attention to one of their features.

Ph: What do you mean?

So: They were in a way opposite to one another. One claimed that one should give one's favors to the lover; the other, to the non-lover.

Ph: Most manfully, too.

So: I thought you were going to say "madly," which would have been the truth, and is also just what I was looking for: We did say, didn't we, that love is a kind of madness?

Ph: Yes.

So: And that there are two kinds of madness, one produced by
human illness, the other by a divinely inspired release from nor-
mally accepted behavior?

Ph: Certainly.

So: We also distinguished four parts within the divine kind and
connected them to four gods. Having attributed the inspiration
of the prophet to Apollo, of the mystic to Dionysus, of the poet
to the Muses, and the fourth part of madness to Aphrodite and
to Love, we said that the madness of love is the best. We used a
certain sort of image to describe love's passion; perhaps it had
a measure of truth in it, though it may also have led us astray.
And having whipped up a not altogether implausible speech, we
sang playfully, but also appropriately and respectfully, a storylike
hymn to my master and yours, Phaedrus—to Love, who watches
over beautiful boys.

Ph: And I listened to it with the greatest pleasure.

So: Let's take up this point about it right away: How was the
speech able to proceed from censure to praise?

Ph: What exactly do you mean by that?

So: Well, everything else in it really does appear to me to have
been spoken in play. But part of it was given with Fortune's
guidance, and there were in it two kinds of things the nature of
which it would be quite wonderful to grasp by means of a systematic art.

Ph: Which things?

So: The first consists in seeing together things that are scattered about everywhere and collecting them into one kind, so
that by defining each thing we can make clear the subject of any
instruction we wish to give. Just so with our discussion of love:
Whether its definition was or was not correct, at least it allowed
the speech to proceed clearly and consistently with itself.

Ph: And what is the other thing you are talking about, Socrates?

So: This, in turn, is to be able to cut up each kind according
to its species along its natural joints, and to try not to splinter
any part, as a bad butcher might do. In just this way, our two
speeches placed all mental derangements into one common
kind. Then, just as each single body has parts that naturally

come in pairs of the same name (one of them being called the right-hand and the other the left-hand one), so the speeches, having considered unsoundness of mind to be by nature one single kind within us, proceeded to cut it up—the first speech cut its left-hand part, and continued to cut until it discovered among these parts a sort of love that can be called "left-handed," which it correctly denounced; the second speech, in turn, led us to the right-hand part of madness; discovered a love that shares its name with the other but is actually divine; set it out before us, and praised it as the cause of our greatest goods.

Ph: You are absolutely right.

So: Well, Phaedrus, I am myself a lover of these divisions and collections, so that I may be able to think and to speak; and if I believe that someone else is capable of discerning a single thing that is also by nature capable of encompassing many, I follow "straight behind, in his tracks, as if he were a god." God knows whether this is the right name for those who can do this correctly or not, but so far I have always called them "dialecticians." But tell me what I must call them now that we have learned all this from Lysias and you. Or is it just that art of speaking that Thrasymachus and the rest of them use, which has made them masters of speechmaking and capable of producing others like them—anyhow those who are willing to bring them gifts and to treat them as if they were kings?

Ph: They may behave like kings, but they certainly lack the knowledge you're talking about. No, it seems to me that you are right in calling the sort of thing you mentioned dialectic; but, it seems to me, rhetoric still eludes us.

So: What are you saying? Could there be anything valuable which is independent of the methods I mentioned and is still grasped by art? If there is, you and I must certainly honor it, and we must say what part of rhetoric it is that has been left out.

Ph: Well, there's quite a lot, Socrates: everything, at any rate, written up in the books on the art of speaking.

So: You were quite right to remind me. First, I believe, there is the Preamble with which a speech must begin. This is what you mean, isn't it—the fine points of the art?

Ph: Yes.

So: Second come the Statement of Facts and the Evidence of Witnesses concerning it; third, Indirect Evidence; fourth,

Claims to Plausibility. And I believe at least that excellent Byzantine word-wizard adds Confirmation and Supplementary Confirmation.

Ph: You mean the worthy Theodorus?

So: Quite. And he also adds Refutation and Supplementary Refutation, to be used both in prosecution and in defense. Nor must we forget the most excellent Evenus of Paros, who was the first to discover Covert Implication and Indirect Praise and who—some say—has even arranged Indirect Censures in verse as an aid to memory: a wise man indeed! And Tisias and Gorgias? How can we leave them out when it is they who realized that what is likely must be held in higher honor than what is true; they who, by the power of their language, make small things appear great and great things small; they who express modern ideas in ancient garb, and ancient ones in modern dress; they who have discovered how to argue both concisely and at infinite length about any subject? Actually, when I told Prodicus this last, he laughed and said that only he had discovered the art of proper speeches: What we need are speeches that are neither long nor short but of the right length.

Ph: Brilliantly done, Prodicus!

So: And what about Hippias? How can we omit him? I am sure our friend from Elis would cast his vote with Prodicus.

Ph: Certainly.

So: And what shall we say of the whole gallery of terms Polus set up—speaking with Reduplication, Speaking in Maxims, Speaking in Images—and of the terms Licymnius gave him as a present to help him explain Good Diction?

Ph: But didn't Protagoras actually use similar terms?

So: Yes, Correct Diction, my boy, and other wonderful things. As to the art of making speeches bewailing the evils of poverty and old age, the prize, in my judgment, goes to the mighty Chalcedonian. He it is also who knows best how to inflame a crowd and, once they are inflamed, how to hush them again with his words' magic spell, as he says himself. And let's not forget that he is as good at producing slander as he is at refuting it, whatever its source may be.

As to the way of ending a speech, everyone seems to be in agreement, though some call it Recapitulation and others by some other name.

Ph: You mean, summarizing everything at the end and reminding the audience of what they've heard?

So: That's what I mean. And if you have anything else to add about the art of speaking—

Ph: Only minor points, not worth making.

So: Well, let's leave minor points aside. Let's hold what we do have closer to the light so that we can see precisely the power of the art these things produce.

Ph: A very great power, Socrates, especially in front of a crowd.

So: Quite right. But now, my friend, look closely: Do you think, as I do, that its fabric is a little threadbare?

Ph: Can you show me?

So: All right, tell me this. Suppose someone came to your friend Eryximachus or his father Acumenus and said: "I know treatments to raise or lower (whichever I prefer) the temperature of people's bodies; if I decide to, I can make them vomit or make their bowels move, and all sorts of things. On the basis of this knowledge, I claim to be a physician; and I claim to be able to make others physicians as well by imparting it to them." What do you think they would say when they heard that?

Ph: What could they say? They would ask him if he also knew to whom he should apply such treatments, when, and to what extent.

So: What if he replied, "I have no idea. My claim is that whoever learns from me will manage to do what you ask on his own"?

Ph: I think they'd say the man's mad if he thinks he's a doctor just because he read a book or happened to come across a few potions; he knows nothing of the art.

So: And suppose someone approached Sophocles and Euripides and claimed to know how to compose the longest passages on trivial topics and the briefest ones on topics of great importance, that he could make them pitiful if he wanted, or again, by contrast, terrifying and menacing, and so on. Suppose further that he believed that by teaching this he was imparting the knowledge of composing tragedies—

Ph: Oh, I am sure they too would laugh at anyone who thought a tragedy was anything other than the proper arrangement of these things: They have to fit with one another and with the whole work.

So: But I am sure they wouldn't reproach him rudely. They would react more like a musician confronted by a man who thought he had mastered harmony because he was able to produce the highest and lowest notes on his strings. The musician would not say fiercely, "You stupid man, you are out of your mind!" As befits his calling, he would speak more gently: "My friend, though that too is necessary for understanding harmony, someone who has gotten as far as you have may still know absolutely nothing about the subject. What you know is what it's necessary to learn before you study harmony, but not harmony itself."

Ph: That's certainly right.

So: So Sophocles would also tell the man who was showing off to them that he knew the preliminaries of tragedy, but not the art of tragedy itself. And Acumenus would say his man knew the preliminaries of medicine, but not medicine itself.

Ph: Absolutely.

So: And what if the "honey-tongued Adrastus" (or perhaps Pericles) were to hear of all the marvelous techniques we just discussed—Speaking Concisely and Speaking in Images and all the rest we listed and proposed to examine under the light? Would he be angry or rude, as you and I were, with those who write of those techniques and teach them as if they are rhetoric itself, and say something coarse to them? Wouldn't he—being wiser than we are—reproach us as well and say, "Phaedrus and Socrates, you should not be angry with these people—you should be sorry for them. The reason they cannot define rhetoric is that they are ignorant of dialectic. It is their ignorance that makes them think they have discovered what rhetoric is when they have mastered only what it is necessary to learn as preliminaries. So they teach these preliminaries and imagine their pupils have received a full course in rhetoric, thinking the task of using each of them persuasively and putting them together into a whole speech is a minor matter, to be worked out by the pupils from their own resources"?

Ph: Really, Socrates, the art these men present as rhetoric in their courses and handbooks is no more than what you say. In my judgment, at least, your point is well taken. But how, from what source, could one acquire the art of the true rhetorician, the really persuasive speaker?

So: Well, Phaedrus, becoming good enough to be an accomplished competitor is probably—perhaps necessarily—like everything else. If you have a natural ability for rhetoric, you will become a famous rhetorician, provided you supplement your ability with knowledge and practice. To the extent that you lack any one of them, to that extent you will be less than perfect. But, insofar as there is an art of rhetoric, I don't believe the right method for acquiring it is to be found in the direction Lysias and Thrasymachus have followed.

Ph: Where can we find it then?

So: My dear friend, maybe we can see now why Pericles was in all likelihood the greatest rhetorician of all.

Ph: How is that?

So: All the great arts require endless talk and ethereal speculation about nature: This seems to be what gives them their lofty point of view and universal applicability. That's just what Pericles mastered—besides having natural ability. He came across Anaxagoras, who was just that sort of man, got his full dose of ethereal speculation, and understood the nature of mind and mindlessness—just the subject on which Anaxagoras had the most to say. From this, I think, he drew for the art of rhetoric what was useful to it.

Ph: What do you mean by that?

So: Well, isn't the method of medicine in a way the same as the method of rhetoric?

Ph: How so?

So: In both cases we need to determine the nature of something—of the body in medicine, of the soul in rhetoric. Otherwise, all we'll have will be an empirical and artless practice. We won't be able to supply, on the basis of an art, a body with the medicines and diet that will make it healthy and strong, or a soul with the reasons and customary rules for conduct that will impart to it the convictions and virtues we want.

Ph: That is most likely, Socrates.

So: Do you think, then, that it is possible to reach a serious understanding of the nature of the soul without understanding the nature of the world as a whole?

Ph: Well, if we're to listen to Hippocrates, Asclepius' descendant, we won't even understand the body if we don't follow that method.

So: He speaks well, my friend. Still, Hippocrates aside, we must consider whether argument supports that view.

Ph: I agree.

So: Consider, then, what both Hippocrates and true argument say about nature. Isn't this the way to think systematically about the nature of anything? First, we must consider whether the object regarding which we intend to become experts and capable of transmitting our expertise is simple or complex. Then, if it is simple, we must investigate its power: What things does it have what natural power of acting upon? By what things does it have what natural disposition to be acted upon? If, on the other hand, it takes many forms, we must enumerate them all and, as we did in the simple case, investigate how each is naturally able to act upon what and how it has a natural disposition to be acted upon by what.

Ph: It seems so, Socrates.

So: Proceeding by any other method would be like walking with the blind. Conversely, whoever studies anything on the basis of an art must never be compared to the blind or the deaf. On the contrary, it is clear that someone who teaches another to make speeches as an art will demonstrate precisely the essential nature of that to which speeches are to be applied. And that, surely, is the soul.

Ph: Of course.

So: This is therefore the object toward which the speaker's whole effort is directed, since it is in the soul that he attempts to produce conviction. Isn't that so?

Ph: Yes.

So: Clearly, therefore, Thrasymachus and anyone else who teaches the art of rhetoric seriously will, first, describe the soul with absolute precision and enable us to understand what it is: whether it is one and homogeneous by nature or takes many forms, like the shape of bodies, since, as we said, that's what it is to demonstrate the nature of something.

Ph: Absolutely.

So: Second, he will explain how, in virtue of its nature, it acts and is acted upon by certain things.

Ph: Of course.

So: Third, he will classify the kinds of speech and of soul there are, as well as the various ways in which they are affected, and explain what causes each. He will then coordinate each kind of soul with the kind of speech appropriate to it. And he will give instructions concerning the reasons why one kind of soul is necessarily convinced by one kind of speech while another necessarily remains unconvinced.

Ph: This, I think, would certainly be the best way.

So: In fact, my friend, no speech will ever be a product of art, whether it is a model or one actually given, if it is delivered or written in any other way—on this or on any other subject. But those who now write *Arts of Rhetoric*—we were just discussing them—are cunning people: they hide the fact that they know very well everything about the soul. Well, then, until they begin to speak and write in this way, we mustn't allow ourselves to be convinced that they write on the basis of the art.

Ph: What way is that?

So: It's very difficult to speak the actual words, but as to how one should write in order to be as artful as possible—that I am willing to tell you.

Ph: Please do.

So: Since the nature of speech is in fact to direct the soul, whoever intends to be a rhetorician must know how many kinds of soul there are. Their number is so-and-so many; each is of such-and-such a sort; hence some people have such-and-such a character and others have such-and-such. Those distinctions established, there are, in turn, so-and-so many kinds of speech, each of such-and-such a sort. People of such-and-such a character are easy to persuade by speeches of such-and-such a sort in connection with such-and-such an issue for this particular reason, while people of such-and-such another sort are difficult to persuade for those particular reasons.

The orator must learn all this well, then put his theory into practice and develop the ability to discern each kind clearly as it occurs in the actions of real life. Otherwise he won't be any better off than he was when he was still listening to those discussions in school. He will now not only be able to say what kind of person is convinced by what kind of speech; on meeting someone he will be able to discern what he is like and make clear to himself that the person actually standing in front of him is of just this particular sort of character he had learned about in school—to that he must now apply speeches of such-and-such a kind in this particular way in order to secure conviction about such-and-such an issue. When he has learned all this—when, in addition, he has grasped the right occasions for speaking and for holding back; and when he has also understood when the time is right for Speaking Concisely or Appealing to Pity or Exaggeration or for any other of the kinds of speech he has learned and when it is not—then, and only then, will he have finally mastered the art well and completely. But if his speaking, his teaching, or his writing lacks any one of these elements and he still claims to be speaking with art, you'll be better off if you don't believe him.

"Well, Socrates and Phaedrus," the author of this discourse might say, "do you agree? Could we accept an art of speaking presented in any other terms?"

Ph: That would be impossible, Socrates. Still, it's evidently rather a major undertaking.

So: You're right. And that's why we must turn all our arguments every which way and try to find some easier and shorter route to the art: we don't want to follow a long rough path for no good reason when we can choose a short smooth one instead.

Now, try to remember if you've heard anything helpful from Lysias or anybody else. Speak up.

Ph: It's not for lack of trying, but nothing comes to mind right now.

So: Well, then, shall I tell you something I've heard people say who care about this topic?

Ph: Of course.

So: We do claim, after all, Phaedrus, that it is fair to give the wolf's side of the story as well.

Ph: That's just what you should do.

So: Well, these people say that there is no need to be so solemn about all this and stretch it out to such lengths. For the fact is, as we said ourselves at the beginning of this discussion, that one who intends to be an able rhetorician has no need to know the truth about the things that are just or good or yet about the people who are such either by nature or upbringing. No one in a lawcourt, you see, cares at all about the truth of such matters. They only care about what is convincing. This is called "the likely," and that is what a man who intends to speak according to art should concentrate on. Sometimes, in fact, whether you are prosecuting or defending a case, you must not even say what actually happened, if it was not likely to have happened—you must say something that is likely instead. Whatever you say, you should pursue what is likely and leave the truth aside: the whole art consists in cleaving to that throughout your speech.

Ph: That's an excellent presentation of what people say who profess to be expert in speeches, Socrates. I recall that we raised this issue briefly earlier on, but it seems to be their single most important point.

So: No doubt you've churned through Tisias' book quite carefully. Then let Tisias tell us this also: By "the likely" does he mean anything but what is thought to be so by the crowd?

Ph: What else?

So: And it's likely it was when he discovered this clever and artful technique that Tisias wrote that if a weak but spunky man is taken to court because he beat up a strong but cowardly one and stole his cloak or something else, neither one should tell the truth. The coward must say that the spunky man didn't beat him up all by himself, while the latter must rebut this by saying that only the two of them were there, and fall back on that well-worn plea, "How could a man like me attack a man like him?" The strong man, naturally, will not admit his cowardice, but will try to invent some other lie, and may thus give his opponent the chance to refute him. And in other cases, speaking as the art dictates will take similar forms. Isn't that so, Phaedrus?

Ph: Of course.

So: Phew! Tisias—or whoever else it was and whatever name he pleases to use for himself—seems to have discovered an art which he has disguised very well! But now, my friend, shall we or shall we not say to him—

Ph: What?

So: This: "Tisias, some time ago, before you came into the picture, we were saying that people get the idea of what is likely through its similarity to the truth. And we just explained that in every case the person who knows the truth knows best how to determine similarities. So, if you have something new to say about the art of speaking, we shall listen. But if you don't, we shall remain convinced by the explanations we gave just before: No one will ever possess the art of speaking, to the extent that any human being can, unless he acquires the ability to enumerate the sorts of characters to be found in any audience, to divide everything according to its kinds, and to grasp each single thing firmly by means of one form. And no one can acquire these abilities without great effort—a laborious effort a sensible man will make not in order to speak and act among human beings, but so as to be able to speak and act in a way that pleases the gods as much as possible. Wiser people than ourselves, Tisias, say that a reasonable man must put his mind to being pleasant not to his fellow slaves (though this may happen as a side effect) but to his masters, who are wholly good. So, if the way round is long, don't be astonished: we must make this detour for the sake of things that are very important, not for what you have in mind. Still, as our argument asserts, if that is what you want, you'll get it best as a result of pursuing our own goal."

Ph: What you've said is wonderful, Socrates—if only it could be done!

So: Yet surely whatever one must go through on the way to an honorable goal is itself honorable.

Ph: Certainly.

So: Well, then, that's enough about artfulness and artlessness in connection with speaking.

Ph: Quite.

So: What's left, then, is aptness and ineptness in connection with writing: What feature makes writing good, and what inept? Right?

Ph: Yes.

So: Well, do you know how best to please god when you either use words or discuss them in general?

Ph: Not at all. Do you?

So: I can tell you what I've heard the ancients said, though they alone know the truth. However, if we could discover that ourselves, would we still care about the speculations of other people?

Ph: That's a silly question. Still, tell me what you say you've heard.

So: Well, this is what I've heard. Among the ancient gods of Naucratis in Egypt there was one to whom the bird called the ibis is sacred. The name of that divinity was Theuth, and it was he who first discovered number and calculation, geometry and astronomy, as well as the games of draughts and dice, and, above all else, writing.

Now the king of all Egypt at that time was Thamus, who lived in the great city in the upper region that the Greeks call Egyptian Thebes; Thamus they call Ammon. Theuth came to exhibit his arts to him and urged him to disseminate them to all the Egyptians. Thamus asked him about the usefulness of each art, and while Theuth was explaining it, Thamus praised him for whatever he thought was right in his explanations and criticized him for whatever he thought was wrong.

The story goes that Thamus said much to Theuth, both for and against each art, which it would take too long to repeat. But when they came to writing, Theuth said: "O King, here is something that, once learned, will make the Egyptians wiser and will improve their memory; I have discovered a potion for memory and for wisdom." Thamus, however, replied: "O most expert Theuth, one man can give birth to the elements of an art, but only another can judge how they can benefit or harm those who will use them. And now, since you are the father of writing, your affection for it has made you describe its effects as the opposite of what they really are. In fact, it will introduce forgetfulness into the soul of those who learn it: they will not practice using their memory because they will put their trust in writing, which is external and depends on signs that belong to others, instead of trying to remember from the inside, completely on their own. You have not discovered a potion for remembering, but for reminding; you provide your students with the appearance of wisdom, not with its reality. Your invention will enable them to hear many things without being properly taught, and they will imagine that they have come to know much while for the most part they will know nothing. And they will be difficult to get along with, since they will merely appear to be wise instead of really being so."

Ph: Socrates, you're very good at making up stories from Egypt or wherever else you want!

So: But, my friend, the priests of the temple of Zeus at Dodona say that the first prophecies were the words of an oak. Everyone who lived at that time, not being as wise as you young ones are today, found it rewarding enough in their simplicity to listen to an oak or even a stone, so long as it was telling the truth, while it seems to make a difference to you, Phaedrus, who is speaking and where he comes from. Why, though, don't you just consider whether what he says is right or wrong?

Ph: I deserved that, Socrates. And I agree that the Theban king was correct about writing.

So: Well, then, those who think they can leave written instructions for an art, as well as those who accept them, thinking that writing can yield results that are clear or certain, must be quite naive and truly ignorant of Ammon's prophetic judgment: otherwise, how could they possibly think that words that have been written down can do more than remind those who already know what the writing is about?

Ph: Quite right.

So: You know, Phaedrus, writing shares a strange feature with painting. The offsprings of painting stand there as if they are alive, but if anyone asks them anything, they remain most solemnly silent. The same is true of written words. You'd think they were speaking as if they had some understanding, but if you question anything that has been said because you want to learn more, it continues to signify just that very same thing forever. When it has once been written down, every discourse roams about everywhere, reaching indiscriminately those with understanding no less than those who have no business with it, and it doesn't know to whom it should speak and to whom it should not. And when it is faulted and attacked unfairly, it always needs its father's support; alone, it can neither defend itself nor come to its own support.

Ph: You are absolutely right about that, too.

So: Now tell me, can we discern another kind of discourse, a legitimate brother of this one? Can we say how it comes about, and how it is by nature better and more capable?

Ph: Which one is that? How do you think it comes about?

So: It is a discourse that is written down, with knowledge, in the soul of the listener; it can defend itself, and it knows for whom it should speak and for whom it should remain silent.

Ph: You mean the living, breathing discourse of the man who knows, of which the written one can be fairly called an image.

So: Absolutely right. And tell me this. Would a sensible farmer, who cared about his seeds and wanted them to yield fruit, plant them in all seriousness in the gardens of Adonis in the middle of the summer and enjoy watching them bear fruit within seven days? Or would he do this as an amusement and in honor of the holiday, if he did it at all? Wouldn't he use his knowledge of farming to plant the seeds he cared for when it was appropriate and be content it they bore fruit seven months later?

Ph: That's how he would handle those he was serious about, Socrates, quite differently from the others, as you say.

So: Now what about the man who knows what is just, noble, and good? Shall we say that he is less sensible with his seeds than the farmer is with his?

Ph: Certainly not.

So: Therefore, he won't be serious about writing them in ink, sowing them, through a pen, with words that are as incapable of speaking in their own defense as they are of teaching the truth adequately.

Ph: That wouldn't be likely.

So: Certainly not. When he writes, it's likely he will sow gardens of letters for the sake of amusing himself, storing up reminders for himself "when he reaches forgetful old age" and for everyone who wants to follow in his footsteps, and will enjoy seeing them sweetly blooming. And when others turn to different amusements, watering themselves with drinking parties and everything else that goes along with them, he will rather spend his time amusing himself with the things I have just described.

Ph: Socrates, you are contrasting a vulgar amusement with the very noblest—with the amusement of a man who can while away his time telling stories of justice and the other matters you mentioned.

So: That's just how it is, Phaedrus. But it is much nobler to be serious about these matters, and use the art of dialectic. The dialectician chooses a proper soul and plants and sows within it discourse accompanied by knowledge—discourse capable of helping itself as well as the man who planted it, which is not barren but produces a seed from which more discourse grows

in the character of others. Such discourse makes the seed forever immortal and renders the man who has it as happy as any
human being can be.

Ph: What you describe is really much nobler still.

So: And now that we have agreed about this, Phaedrus, we are
finally able to decide the issue.

Ph: What issue is that?

So: The issue which brought us to this point in the first place:
We wanted to examine the attack made on Lysias on account
of his writing speeches, and to ask which speeches are written
artfully and which not. Now, I think that we have answered that
question clearly enough.

Ph: So it seemed; but remind me again how we did it.

So: First, you must know the truth concerning everything you
are speaking or writing about; you must learn how to define
each thing in itself; and, having defined it, you must know how
to divide it into kinds until you reach something indivisible.
Second, you must understand the nature of the soul, along the
same lines; you must determine which kind of speech is appropriate to each kind of soul, prepare and arrange your speech
accordingly, and offer a complex and elaborate speech to a complex soul and a simple speech to a simple one. Then, and only
then, will you be able to use speech artfully, to the extent that its
nature allows it to be used that way, either in order to teach or
in order to persuade. This is the whole point of the argument we
have been making.

Ph: Absolutely. That is exactly how it seemed to us.

So: Now how about whether it's noble or shameful to give or
write a speech—when it could be fairly said to be grounds for
reproach, and when not? Didn't what we said just a little while
ago make it clear—

Ph: What was that?

So: That if Lysias or anybody else ever did or ever does
write—privately or for the public, in the course of proposing
some law—a political document which he believes to embody
clear knowledge of lasting importance, then this writer
deserves reproach, whether anyone says so or not. For to be
unaware of the difference between a dream-image and the
reality of what is just and unjust, good and bad, must truly

be grounds for reproach even if the crowd praises it with one voice.

Ph: It certainly must be.

So: On the other hand, take a man who thinks that a written discourse on any subject can only be a great amusement, that no discourse worth serious attention has ever been written in verse or prose, and that those that are recited in public without questioning and explanation, in the manner of the rhapsodes, are given only in order to produce conviction. He believes that at their very best these can only serve as reminders to those who already know. And he also thinks that only what is said for the sake of understanding and learning, what is truly written in the soul concerning what is just, noble, and good can be clear, perfect, and worth serious attention: Such discourses should be called his own legitimate children, first the discourse he may have discovered already within himself and then its sons and brothers who may have grown naturally in other souls insofar as these are worthy; to the rest, he turns his back. Such a man, Phaedrus, would be just what you and I both would pray to become.

Ph: I wish and pray for things to be just as you say.

So: Well, then: our playful amusement regarding discourse is complete. Now you go and tell Lysias that we came to the spring which is sacred to the Nymphs and heard words charging us to deliver a message to Lysias and anyone else who composes speeches, as well as to Homer and anyone else who has composed poetry either spoken or sung, and third, to Solon and anyone else who writes political documents that he calls laws: If any one of you has composed these things with a knowledge of the truth, if you can defend your writing when you are challenged, and if you can yourself make the argument that your writing is of little worth, then you must be called by a name derived not from these writings but rather from those things that you are seriously pursuing.

Ph: What name, then, would you give such a man?

So: To call him wise, Phaedrus, seems to me too much, and proper only for a god. To call him wisdom's lover—a philosopher—or something similar would fit him better and be more seemly.

Ph: That would be quite appropriate.

So: On the other hand, if a man has nothing more valuable than what he has composed or written, spending long hours twisting it around, pasting parts together and taking them apart—wouldn't you be right to call him a poet or a speech writer or an author of laws?

Ph: Of course.

So: Tell that, then, to your friend.

Ph: And what about you? What shall you do? We must surely not forget your own friend.

So: Whom do you mean?

Ph: The beautiful Isocrates. What are you going to tell him, Socrates? What shall we say he is?

So: Isocrates is still young, Phaedrus. But I want to tell you what I foresee for him.

Ph: What is that?

So: It seems to me that by his nature he can outdo anything that Lysias has accomplished in his speeches; and he also has a nobler character. So I wouldn't be at all surprised if, as he gets older and continues writing speeches of the sort he is composing now, he makes everyone who has ever attempted to compose a speech seem like a child in comparison. Even more so if such work no longer satisfies him and a higher, divine impulse leads him to more important things. For nature, my friend, has placed the love of wisdom in his mind.

That is the message I will carry to my beloved, Isocrates, from the gods of this place; and you have your own message for your Lysias.

Ph: So it shall be. But let's be off, since the heat has died down a bit.

So: Shouldn't we offer a prayer to the gods here before we leave?

Ph: Of course.

So: O dear Pan and all the other gods of this place, grant that I may be beautiful inside. Let all my external possessions be in friendly harmony with what is within. May I consider the wise man rich. As for gold, let me have as much as a moderate man could bear and carry with him.

Do we need anything else, Phaedrus? I believe my prayer is enough for me.

Ph: Make it a prayer for me as well. Friends have everything in common.

So: Let's be off.

Aristotle, *Rhetoric*, Book 1, Chapter 2

(Reprinted from Aristotle, Selections, *translated by Terence Irwin and Gail Fine, Hackett Publishing Company, 1995.)*

Let us, then, take rhetoric to be the capacity to observe the available means of persuasion on a given question. For this is the function of no other craft. Each of the other crafts teaches and persuades about its own subject matter (medical science, for instance, about what promotes health or sickness, geometry about the properties coincident to magnitudes, arithmetic about numbers, and so on for the other sciences and crafts), whereas rhetoric seems to be able to observe what is persuasive on any question presented to it, one might say—that is why we say it practices its craft on no special determinate genus.

Among means of conviction, some are external to the craft, others internal. By 'external' I mean those that we do not supply from our own resources but are given in advance—for instance, witnesses, inquisitions, and such like. By 'internal' I mean those that we can establish through the line of inquiry <proper to the craft> and from our own resources. Hence we must use the external means but find the internal means for ourselves.

The convincing arguments supplied through speech are of three species: (1) Some are found in the character of the speaker, (2) some in the condition of the hearer, (3) some in the speech itself, through proving or appearing to prove.

They are secured through character whenever the speech is delivered in such a way as to make the speaker deserve our confidence. For we have more confidence, and come to have it more quickly, in decent people; this is true, speaking without qualification, on all topics, but it is altogether true on topics where there is variation of opinion rather than an exact answer. This also, however, must result from the speech itself, not from the hearer's previous views about the character of the speaker. For we do not follow some writers expounding this craft, who exclude the character of the speaker from the scope of the craft, on the supposition that it contributes nothing to the persuasiveness of the speech. On the contrary, character provides almost, one might say, the most important means of conviction.

Conviction is secured through the hearers whenever the speech arouses some feeling in them. For we do not give the same verdicts when we feel distress and when we feel enjoyment, or when we are friendly and when we are hostile; indeed writers on rhetoric at present, as we say, try to focus their whole treatment on this alone. We will clarify these questions, taking the feelings one at a time, when we come to discuss the feelings.

People are convinced through the speech itself whenever we prove what is true or appears true from whatever is persuasive on each topic.

[THE RELEVANCE OF RHETORIC TO DIALECTIC AND ETHICS]

Since these are the means of conviction, it is evident that the person who will find them must reason deductively and also observe what is true of characters and virtues and, thereby, of feelings—what and of what sort each feeling is, and from what source and in what ways it arises. Hence it follows that rhetoric is a sort of appendage of dialectic and of the study of character, which is rightly called political science.

This is why rhetoric and those who claim to practice it actually masquerade in the guise of political science. In some cases the reason is lack of education, in other cases boastfulness, and in other cases some other human <weaknesses>. For in fact rhetoric is a part of dialectic and a likeness of it, as we also said at the beginning; for neither of them is scientific knowledge of how any definite subject matter is, but both are capacities for finding arguments.

We have said practically enough, then, about the capacity of rhetoric and dialectic, and about how they are related to each other.

[DEDUCTIVE AND INDUCTIVE ARGUMENT IN RHETORIC]

Now we turn to the convincing arguments that result through proving or appearing to prove. In dialectic one type of such arguments is induction, one deduction, and another apparent deduction. The same is true in rhetoric; for illustration is induction, argumentation is deduction, and apparent argumentation is apparent deduction.

By 'argumentation' I mean rhetorical deduction, and by 'illustration' rhetorical induction. Now, everyone produces convincing arguments by presenting either illustrations or argumentations, and in no other way apart from these. Hence, if a proof must proceed either by deduction or by induction (and this is clear to us from the *Analytics*), each of these <rhetorical forms of argument> must be the same as each of those <dialectical forms>.

The difference between illustration and argumentation is evident from the *Topics*, where we have previously discussed deduction and induction. We can see that a proof that something is so by appeal to many similar instances is induction, in the case of dialectic, and illustration, in the case of rhetoric.

A proof that, when certain things are so, something else apart from these follows because of them, by their being so, either necessary or usually, is called a deduction, in the case of dialectic, and an argumentation, in the case of rhetoric.

It is also evident that each type of rhetoric has its advantages; for the same thing is true here as we said in the work on lines of inquiry. For some types of rhetoric rely on illustrations, others on argumentations, and similarly some orators deal in illustrations, others in argumentations. While certainly speeches using illustrations are no less persuasive, those using argumentations win more applause. Later we will state the reason for this and describe the right use of each <procedure>. For the moment let us define the two kinds of argument more clearly.

[THE SUBJECTS OF RHETORICAL ARGUMENT]

What is persuasive is persuasive to someone; and some things are immediately persuasive and convincing, while other things are persuasive and convincing because they seem to be proved through things that are immediately so. Now, no craft examines the particular; medicine, for instance, does not examine what it is that is healthy for Socrates or Callias, but what is healthy for this type or these types of person—for this is the concern of crafts, whereas the particular is unlimited and not an object of scientific knowledge. Nor, therefore, will rhetoric study the particular thing that is believed, for instance, by Socrates or Hippias, but what is believed by these people, just as dialectic does. For neither does dialectic carry out its deductions from just any random beliefs—for some things appear true to madmen; rather, dialectic begins from beliefs that need some argument, while rhetoric begins from the habitual questions for deliberation.

The function of rhetoric is to deal with the sorts of questions we deliberate about, where we have no crafts, before the sorts of audiences who cannot keep many steps in mind at once or keep track of a long argument. And we deliberate about what appears to admit of being one way or the other; for if something does not admit of becoming or being otherwise than it is, no one deliberates about it, if that is what he supposes, since he gains nothing from it.

Suggested Reading

Notes to students and readers

Aristotle. *On Rhetoric: A Theory of Civic Discourse*. 2nd ed. Translated by George Alexander Kennedy. New York: Oxford University Press, 2006.

Aristotle. *Metaphysics*. Loeb Classical Library ed. Translated by H. Tredennick. Cambridge, MA: Harvard University Press, 1933.

Broad, Bob. *What We Really Value: Beyond Rubrics in Teaching and Assessing Writing*. Logan: Utah State University Press, 2003.

Cicero, Marcus Tullius. *De Inventione*. Cicero: *De Inventione; De Optimo Genere Oratorum; Topica*. Loeb Classical Library ed. Translated by H. M. Hubbell. Cambridge, MA: Harvard University Press, 1976. xi–346.

——. *De Optimo Genere Oratorum*. Cicero: *De Inventione; De Optimo Genere Oratorum; Topica*. Loeb Classical Library ed. Edited by H. M. Hubbell. Cambridge, MA: Harvard University Press, 1976. 349–73.

Han, Fei Tzu. "The Difficulties of Persuasion." In *Han Fei Tzu: Basic Writings*, 73–79. Translated by Burton Watson. New York: Columbia University Press, 2003.

Orwell, George. "Politics and the English Language." *Horizon* 13, no. 76 (1946): 252–65.

Plato. *Gorgias*. Translated by Donald J. Zeyl. Indianapolis: Hackett Publishing Company, 1987.

——. *Phaedrus*. Translated by Alexander Nehamas and Paul Woodruff. Indianapolis: Hackett Publishing Company, 1987.

Quintilian. *Institutio Oratoria*. Translated by H. E. Butler. Cambridge, MA: Harvard University Press, 1980.

Introduction

Conley, Thomas M. *Rhetoric in the European Tradition*. New York: Longman, 1990.

Kennedy, George Alexander. *The Art of Rhetoric in the Roman World: 300 B.C.–A.D. 300 (History of Rhetoric)*. Princeton, NJ: Princeton University Press, 1972.

————. *A New History of Classical Rhetoric.* Princeton, NJ: Princeton University Press, 1994.

————. *Progymnasmata: Greek Textbooks of Prose Composition and Rhetoric.* Leiden: Brill, 2003.

Marrou, Henri Irénée. *A History of Education in Antiquity.* New York: Sheed and Ward, 1956.

Vickers, Brian. *In Defense of Rhetoric.* Cambridge, U.K.: Clarendon Press, 1988.

Williams, James D. *An Introduction to Classical Rhetoric: Essential Readings.* Chichester, U.K.; Malden, MA: Wiley-Blackwell, 2009.

Chapter 1

Burke, Kenneth. *Permanence and Change: An Anatomy of Purpose.* 3rd ed. Berkeley: University of California Press, 1984.

Chabris, Christopher, and Daniel Simons. "The Invisible Gorilla." http://www.theinvisiblegorilla.com

Coyle, Daniel. *The Talent Code.* New York: Bantam Dell, 2009.

Cromie, William J. "False Memories." *Harvard University Gazette*, September 19, 1996. http://news.harvard.edu/gazette/1996/09.19/FalseMemories.html.

Danziger, Shai, Jonathan Levav, and Liora Avnaim-Pesso. "Extraneous Factors in Judicial Decisions." *PNAS* 108, no. 17 (2011): 6889–92.

Ericsson, K. Anders, ed. *The Road to Excellence: The Acquisition of Expert Performance in the Arts and Sciences, Sports, and Games.* Mahwah, NJ: Lawrence Erlbaum, 1996.

Thaler, Richard H., and Cass R. Sunstein. *Nudge: Improving Decisions about Health, Wealth, and Happiness.* New Haven, CT: Yale University Press, 2008.

Valdesolo, Piercarlo. "Flattery Will Get You Far." *Scientific America,* January 12, 2010. http://www.scientificamerican.com/article.cfm?id=flattery-will-get-you-far&page=2.

Chapter 2

Cafferty, Jack. *Cafferty File.* CNN, July 19, 2012. http://caffertyfile.blogs.cnn.com/.

Duhigg, Charles. *The Power of Habit: Why We Do What We Do in Life and Business.* New York: Random House, 2012.

Fielding, Nick, and Ian Cobain. "Revealed: US Spy Operation That Manipulates Social Media." *Guardian,* March 17, 2011. http://www.guardian.co.uk/technology/2011/mar/17/us-spy-operation-social-networks.

Fredrickson, Barbara. "What Good Are Positive Emotions." *Review of General Psychology* 2, no. 3 (1998): 300–319.

Gross, Doug. "Are Social Media Making the Resume Obsolete?" *CNN Tech.* CNN, July 11, 2012. http://www.cnn.com/2012/07/11/tech/social-media/facebook-jobs-resume/index.html.

Hock, Ronald F., and Edward N. O'Neil. *The Chreia in Ancient Rhetoric.* Vols. 1–2. Atlanta: Scholars, 1986.

Ong, Walter J. "The Author's Audience is Always Fiction." *PMLA* 90, no. 1 (1975): 9–21.

Walker, Rob. *Buying In: The Secret Dialogue Between What We Buy and Who We Are.* New York: Random House, 2008.

Chapter 3

Invention

Aesop's Fables.

Burke, Kenneth. *A Grammar of Motives.* California ed. Berkley: University of California Press, 1969

Duhigg, Charles. *The Power of Habit: Why We Do What We Do in Life and Business.* New York: Random House, 2012.

Moneyball. Directed by Bennett Miller. Story by Steven Zaillian and Aaron Sorkin. Performances by Brad Pitt, Robin Wright, and Jonah Hill. Columbia Pictures, 2011. DVD.

Plato. *Gorgias.* Translated by Donald J. Zeyl. Indianapolis: Hackett Publishing Company, 1987.

Style

Clark, Peter Roy. *Writing Tools: 50 Essential strategies for Every Writer.* New York: Hachette, 2006.

Fish, Stanley. *How to Write a Sentence.* New York: Harper, 2011.

Hale, Constance. *Sin and Syntax: How to Craft Wickedly Effective Prose.* New York: Broadway Books, 1999.

Johnson, Christopher. *Microstyle: The Art of Writing Little.* New York: Norton, 2011.

Lakoff, George, and Mark Johnson. *Metaphors We Live By.* Chicago: University of Chicago Press, 2003.

Lanham, Richard A. *A Handlist of Rhetorical Terms.* 2nd ed. Berkeley: University of California Press, 1991.

Orwell, George. "Politics and the English Language." *Horizon* 13, no. 76 (1946): 252–65.

Strunk, William, Jr., and E. B. White. *Elements of Style.* 3rd ed. New York: Macmillan, 1979.

Zinsser, William. *On Writing Well.* 30th Anniversary ed. New York: Harper, 2006.

Memory

Carruthers, Mary, and Jan M. Ziolkowski, eds. *The Medieval Craft of Memory: An Anthology of Texts and Pictures.* Philadelphia: University of Pennsylvania Press, 2002.

Cicero, Marcus Tullius. *The Craft of Thought: Meditation, Rhetoric, and the Making of Images, 400–1200.* Cambridge: Cambridge University Press, 1998.

———. *Rhetorica ad Herennium.* Loeb Classical Library ed. Translated by Harry Caplan. Cambridge, MA: Harvard University Press, 1954.

Foer, Joshua. *Moonwalking With Einstein: The Art and Science of Remembering Everything.* New York: Penguin, 2010.

Johnson, George. *In the Palaces of Memory: How We Build the Worlds Inside Our Heads.* New York: Vintage, 1991.

Quintilian. *Institutio Oratoria.* Quintilian Book 11, Chap. 2. Translated by H. E. Butler. Cambridge, MA: Harvard University Press, 1980.

Yates, Frances A. *The Art of Memory.* Chicago: University of Chicago Press, 1966.

Delivery

Austin, Gilbert. *Chironomia: A Treatise on Rhetorical Delivery.* Carbondale: Southern Illinois University Press, 1966.

Bowden, Mark. *Winning Body Language: Control the Conversation, Command Attention, and Convey the Right Message—Without Saying a Word.* New York: McGraw, 2010.

Bulwer, John. *Chirologia or the Natural Language of the Hand.* Edited by James W. Cleary. Carbondale: Southern Illinois UP, 1974.

Cicero, Marcus Tullius. *De Optimo Genere Oratorum. Cicero: De Inventione; De Optimo Genere Oratorum; Topica.* Loeb Classical Library ed. Edited by H. M. Hubbell. Cambridge, MA: Harvard University Press, 1976. 349–73.

———. *On the Ideal Orator.* Translated by James M. May and Jakob Wisse. Cambridge: Oxford University Press, 2001. 3.213.

Graff, Gerald, and Cathy Birkenstein. *They Say, I Say: The Moves That Matter in Academic Writing.* New York: W. W. Norton, 2007.

Kendon, Adam. *Gesture: Visible Action as Utterance.* Cambridge: Cambridge University Press, 2004.

Lieberman, David J. *You Can Read Anyone: Never Be Fooled, Lied to, or Taken Advantage of Again.* Lakewood, NJ: Viter Press, 2007.

Poole, Garry. *The Complete Book of Questions: 1001 Conversation Starters for Any Occasion*. Minocqua, WI: Willow Creek, 2003.

Quintilian. *Institutio Oratoria*. Translated by H. E. Butler. Cambridge, MA: Harvard University Press, 1980. Quintilian, *Institutes of Oratory* 11.3.6–7.

Reynolds, Garr. *Presentation Zen*. Berkeley, CA: New Riders, 2009.

Reynolds, John Frederick, ed. *Rhetorical Memory and Delivery*. Hillsdale, NJ: Lawrence Erlbaum, 1993.

Sheridan, Thomas. *A Course of Lectures on Elocution*. London, 1762.

Siddons, Henry. *Practical Illustrations of Rhetorical Gesture and Action*. London, 1822.

Welch, Kathleen E. *Electric Rhetoric: Classical Rhetoric, Oralism, and a New Literacy*. Cambridge, MA: MIT Press, 1999.

Chapter 4

Babiak, Paul, and Robert D. Hare. *Snakes in Suites: When Psychopaths Go to Work*. New York: HarperCollins, 2007.

Bernays, Edward. *Propaganda*. Brooklyn, New York: Ig Publishing, 2004.

Castiglione, Baldassare. *The Courtier*. Translated by George Bull. London: Penguin, 1967.

Foucault, Michel. *Discipline and Punish: The Birth of the Prison*. Translated by Alan Sheridan. New York: Vintage, 1979.

Greene, Robert. *The 48 Rules of Power*. New York: Penguin, 2000.

Han, Fei Tzu. "The Difficulties of Persuasion." In *Han Fei Tzu: Basic Writings*, 73–79. Translated by Burton Watson. New York: Columbia University Press, 2003.

Harvey, Gordon. *Writing with Sources: A Guide for Students*. 2nd ed. Indianapolis: Hackett Publishing Company, 2008.

Machiavelli, Niccolò. *The Prince*. New York: Bantam, 2003.

Nietzsche, Friedrich. *Thus Spoken Zarathustra: A Book for Everyone and No One*. Translated by R. J. Hollingdale. London: Penguin, 1969.

Siu, Ralph Gun Hoy. *The Craft of Power*. New York: Wiley, 1979.

Stout, Martha. *Sociopath Next Door*. New York: Broadway-Random, 2005.

Tzu, Sun. *The Art of War*. Oxford: Oxford University Press, 1967.

Works Cited

Ancowitz, Nancy. "Public Speaking for Private People." *Psychology Today*. Sussex, October 23, 2009. http://www.psychologytoday.com/blog/self-promotion-introverts/200910/public-speaking-private-people.

Aristotle. *On Rhetoric: A Theory of Civic Discourse*. 2nd ed. Translated by George Alexander Kennedy. New York: Oxford University Press, 2006.

———. *Metaphysics*. Loeb Classical Library ed. Translated by H. Tredennick. Cambridge, MA: Harvard University Press, 1933.

———. "On Sophistical Refutations." In *On Sophistical Refutations: On Coming-to-Be and Passing Away*. Translated by E. S. Forster and David J. Furley. Cambridge, MA: Harvard University Press, 1992.

The Aristocrats. Directed by Paul Provenza. Performances by George Carlin, Don Rickles, and Chris Rock. Lionsgate, 2005.

Augustine. *On Christian Doctrine*. Translated by D. W. Robertson. New York: Macmillan, 1987.

Austin, Gilbert. *Chironomia: A Treatise on Rhetorical Delivery*. Carbondale: Southern Illinois University Press, 1966.

Banks, Iain. *The Crow Road*. San Francisco: McAdam/Cage, 1992.

Barthelme, Frederick, and Steven Barthelme. *Double Down: Reflections on Gambling and Loss*. New York: Houghton, 1999.

Benjamin, L. T., Jr., T. A. Cavell, and W. R. Shallenberger. "Staying with Initial Answers on Objective Tests: Is it a Myth?" *Teaching Psychology* 11 (1984): 133–41.

Blue, Laura. "Obesity Is Contagious, Study Finds." *Time*. July 25, 2007. http://www.time.com/time/health/article/0,8599,1646997,00.html.

Bowden, Mark. *Winning Body Language: Control the Conversation, Command Attention, and Convey the Right Message—Without Saying a Word*. New York: McGraw, 2010.

Broad, Bob. *What We Really Value: Beyond Rubrics in Teaching and Assessing Writing*. Logan: Utah State University Press, 2003.

Bucholz, Chris. "The Best TED Talk Ever Given." *Cracked.com*. Demand Media, July 6, 2012. http://www.cracked.com/blog/the-best-ted-talk-ever-given/.

Bulwer, John. *Chirologia or the Natural Language of the Hand*. Whitefish, MT: Kessinger, 2003.

Burke, Kenneth. *A Grammar of Motives*. California ed. Berkeley: University of California Press, 1969.

———. *Permanence and Change: An Anatomy of Purpose*. 3rd ed. Berkeley: University of California Press, 1984.

Cafferty, Jack. *Cafferty File*. CNN, July 19, 2012. http://caffertyfile.blogs.cnn.com/.

Carruthers, Mary. *The Book of Memory: A Study of Memory in Medieval Culture*. Cambridge: Cambridge University Press, 1990.

————. *The Craft of Thought: Meditation, Rhetoric, and the Making of Images, 400–1200*. Cambridge: Cambridge University Press, 1998.

Carruthers, Mary, and Jan M. Ziolkowski, eds. *The Medieval Craft of Memory: An Anthology of Texts and Pictures*. Philadelphia: University of Pennsylvania Press, 2002.

Castiglione, Baldassare. *The Courtier*. Translated by George Bull. London: Penguin, 1967.

Churchill, Winston. "We Shall Fight on the Beaches." Speech. House of Commons, London. June 4, 1940.

Cicero, Marcus Tullius. *De Inventione. Cicero: De Inventione; De Optimo Genere Oratorum; Topica*. Loeb Classical Library ed. Translated by H. M. Hubbell. Cambridge, MA: Harvard University Press, 1976. xi–346.

————. *On the Orator: Books 1–2*. Loeb Classical Library ed. Translated by E. W. Sutton and H. Rackham. Cambridge, MA: Harvard University Press, 1942.

————. *On the Orator: Book 3. On Fate. Stoic Paradoxes. Divisions of Oratory*. Loeb Classical Library ed. Translated by H. Rackham. Cambridge, MA: Harvard University Press, 1942.

————. *Rhetorica ad Herennium*. Translated by Harry Caplan. Cambridge, MA: Harvard University Press, 1954.

Clark, Peter Roy. *Writing Tools: 50 Essential Strategies for Every Writer*. New York: Hachette, 2006.

Clark, Ruth. *Building Expertise*. San Francisco: Pfeiffer, 2008.

Connolly, Thomas. *Rhetoric in the European Tradition*. Chicago: University Press of Chicago, 1990.

Coulter, Anne. *Guilty: Liberal "Victims" and Their Assault on America*. New York: Crown, 2008.

Coyle, Daniel. *The Talent Code*. New York: Bantam Dell, 2009.

Danziger, Shai, Jonathan Levav, and Liora Avnaim-Pesso. "Extraneous Factors in Judicial Decisions." *PNAS* 108, no. 17 (2011): 6889–92.

Davies, Leonard E. *Anatomy of Cross-Examination: A History and the Techniques of an Ancient Art*. 2nd ed. Bloomington, IN: Xlibris, 2004.

Duhigg, Charles. *The Power of Habit: Why We Do What We Do in Life and Business*. New York: Random House, 2012.

Dutton, Kevin. *Split-Second Persuasion: The Ancient Art and New Science of Changing Minds*. Boston: Houghton Mifflin Harcourt, 2010.

————. *The Wisdom of Psychopaths: What Saints, Spies, and Serial Killers Can Teach Us About Success*. New York: Farrar, Straus, and Giroux, 2012.

Dweck, Carol. *Mindset: The New Psychology of Success*. New York: Ballantine, 2006.

Eliot, T. S., "Philip Massinger." In *The Sacred Wood: Major Early Essays Collection*. Mineola: Dover, 1998.

Erasmus, Desiderius. *The Adages of Erasmus*. Compiled by William Barker. Toronto: University of Toronto Press, 2001.

————. *The Collected Works of Erasmus*. Translated by Margaret Mann Phillips. Compiled by R. A. B. Mynors. Toronto: University of Toronto Press, 1982.

Ericsson, K. Anders, ed. *The Road to Excellence: The Acquisition of Expert Performance in the Arts and Sciences, Sports, and Games*. Mahwah, NJ: Lawrence Erlbaum, 1996.

Ericsson, K. Anders, Ralf Th. Krampe, and Clemens Tesch-Romer. "The Role of Deliberate Practice in Acquisition of Expert Performance." *Psychological Review* 100, no. 3 (1993): 363–406.

Everitt, Anthony. *Cicero: The Life and Times of Rome's Greatest Politician*. New York: Random House, 2001.

Fairhurst, Gail T., and Robert A. Saar. *The Art of Framing: Managing the Language of Leadership*. San Francisco: Jossey-Bass, 1996.

Fielding, Nick, and Ian Cobain. "Revealed: US Spy Operation That Manipulates Social Media." *Guardian*, March 17, 2011. http://www.guardian.co.uk/technology/2011/mar/17/us-spy-operation-social-networks.

Fish, Stanley. *How to Write a Sentence*. New York: Harper, 2011.

Fisher, Roger, and Daniel Shapiro. *Beyond Reason: Using Emotions as You Negotiate*. New York: Penguin, 2005.

Flower, Linda, and John R. Hayes. "A Cognitive Process Theory of Writing." *College Composition and Communication* 32, no. 4 (December 1981): 365–87.

Foer, Joshua. *Moonwalking With Einstein: The Art and Science of Remembering Everything*. New York: Penguin, 2011.

Forer, B. F. "The Fallacy of Personal Validation: A Classroom Demonstration of Gullibility." *Journal of Abnormal and Social Psychology* 44, no. 1 (1949): 118–23.

Foucault, Michel. *Discipline and Punish: The Birth of the Prison*. Translated by Alan Sheridan. New York: Vintage, 1979.

Four Weddings and a Funeral. Directed by Mike Newell. Performances by Hugh Grant and Andie MacDowell. Gramercy Pictures, 1994. Film.

Franklin, Benjamin. *The Autobiography of Benjamin Franklin*. Mineola, NY: Dover, 1996.

Fredrickson, Barbara. "What Good Are Positive Emotions." *Review of General Psychology* 2, no. 3 (1998): 300–319.

Freeman, Kathleen, trans. *Ancilla to the Pre-Socratic Philosophers*. Cambridge, MA: Harvard University Press, 1983.

Gibson, W. Walker. *Tough, Sweet & Stuffy: An Essay on Modern American Prose Styles*. Bloomington: Indiana University Press, 1966.

Gilovich, Thomas, Robert Vallone, and Amos Tversky. "The Hot Hand in Basketball: On the Misperception of Random Sequences." *Cognitive Psychology* 17 (1985): 295–314.

Goffman, Irving. *The Presentation of Everyday Life*. New York: Anchor-Doubleday, 1959.

Goldstein, Noah J., Steve J. Martin, and Robert B. Cialdini. *Yes! 50 Scientifically Proven Ways to Be Persuasive*. New York: Free, 2008.

Graff, Gerald, and Cathy Birkenstein. *They Say, I Say: The Moves That Matter in Academic Writing*. Norton: New York, 2007.

Graves, Frank Pierrepont. *Peter Ramus and the Educational Reformation of the Sixteenth Century*. New York: Macmillan, 1912.

Greene, Robert. *The 48 Laws of Power*. New York: Penguin, 2000.

Gross, Doug. "Are Social Media Making the Resume Obsolete?" *CNN Tech*. CNN, July 11, 2012. http://www.cnn.com/2012/07/11/tech/social-media/facebook-jobs-resume/index.html.

Hale, Constance. *Sin and Syntax: How to Craft Wickedly Effective Prose*. New York: Broadway-Random, 1999.

Hallinan, Joseph T. *Why We Make Mistakes*. New York: Broadway-Random, 2010.

Han, Fei Tzu. "The Difficulties of Persuasion." In *Han Fei Tzu: Basic Writings*, 73–79. Translated by Burton Watson. New York: Columbia University Press, 2003.

Hays, Constance. "What They Know About You." *New York Times*, November 14, 2004. http://query.nytimes.com/gst/abstract.html?res=FB0C14F63D5B0C778DD DA80994DC404482.

Heath, Chip, and Dan Heath. *Made to Stick*. New York: Broadway-Random, 2007.

———. *Switch: How to Change Things When Change Is Hard*. New York: Broadway-Random, 2010.

Hill, Kashmir. "How Target Figured Out a Teen Girl Was Pregnant Before Her Father Did." *Forbes*, February 16, 2012. http://www.forbes.com/sites/kashmirhill/2012/02/16/how-target-figured-out-a-teen-girl-was-pregnant-before-her-father-did/.

Hock, Ronald F., and Edward N. O'Neil. *The Chreia in Ancient Rhetoric*. Vols. 1–2. Atlanta: Scholars, 1986.

Huff, Darrell, and Irving Geis. *How to Lie with Statistics*. New York: W. W. Norton, 1993.

"Ideas That Stick." *Ideas That Stick*. Edited by Lawrence Riddick. n.p.: 2012. http://www.theideasthatstick.com/.

Isocrates. "Antidosis." In *On the Peace. Areopagiticus. Against the Sophists. Antidosis. Panathenaicus*. Edited by George Norlin. Cambridge, MA: Harvard University Press, 1982. 182–365.

Johnson, Christopher. *Microstyle: The Art of Writing Little*. New York: Norton, 2011.

Johnson, George. *In the Palaces of Memory: How We Build the Worlds Inside Our Heads*. New York: Vintage, 1991.

Kahneman, Daniel. *Thinking, Fast and Slow*. New York: Farrar, Straus, and Giroux, 2011.

Kendon, Adam. *Gesture: Visible Action as Utterance*. Cambridge: Cambridge University Press, 2004.

Kennedy, George A. *A New History of Classical Rhetoric*. Princeton, NJ: Princeton University Press, 1994.

Kia. "Black Sheep Kia Hamsters Video." KiaAustralia, 2010. Television Advertisement.

Klein, Gary. *Sources of Power: How People Make Decisions*. Cambridge, MA: MIT Press, 1999.

Lakoff, George, and Mark Johnson. *Metaphors We Live By*. Chicago: University of Chicago Press, 2003.

Landsburg, Steven. *The Armchair Economist*. Revised ed. New York: Free Press, 2012.

Lanham, Richard A. *A Handlist of Rhetorical Terms*. 2nd ed. Berkeley: University of California Press, 1991.

Lee, Dan P. "'I Just Want to Feel Everything': Hiding Out With Fiona Apple, Musical Hermit." *Vulture*. 2012. http://www.vulture.com/2012/06/hiding-out-with-fiona-apple-musical-hermit.html.

Lehrer, Jonah. *How We Decide*. New York: Houghton, 2009.

Levine, Robert. *The Power of Persuasion: How We're Bought and Sold*. New York: Wiley, 2003.

Lieberman, David J. *You Can Read Anyone: Never Be Fooled, Lied to, or Taken Advantage of Again*. Lakewood, NJ: Viter Press, 2007.

Lippmann, Walter. *Public Opinion*. New York: Free Press, 1922.

Machiavelli, Niccolò. *The Prince*. New York: Bantam, 2003.

Maurer, David W. *The Big Con: The Story of the Confidence Man*. Indianapolis: Bobbs-Merill, 1940.

McHaney, Roger. *The New Digital Shoreline: How Web 2.0 and Millennials Are Revolutionizing Higher Education*. Sterling, VA: Stylus, 2011.

Mercer, Rick. "Talking to Americans." YouTube video. Canadian Broadcasting Corporation, November 5, 2006. http://www.youtube.com/watch?v=seYUbVa7L7w.

Michelin. "Because So Much Is Riding on Your Tires." Television advertisement. TWC, 1990.

"Monopolar Expedition." *The Big Bang Theory*. Television episode. Directed by Mark Cendrowski. Performances by Jonny Galecki, Jim Parsons, and Kaley Cuoco. CBS, March 11, 2009.

Morley, John. "Academic Phrasebank." *Academic Phrasebank*. University of Manchester, April 20, 2005. http://www.phrasebank.manchester.ac.uk/.

Murphy, James J. *Quintilian on the Early Education of the Citizen-Orator*. Indianapolis: Bobbs-Merrill, 1965.

Nassim, Taleb. *The Black Swan*. New York: Random House, 2007.

Nietzsche, Friedrich. *Beyond Good and Evil*. Translated by Helen Zimmern. New York: MacMillan, 1907.

———."On Truth and Lie in an Extra-Moral Sense." In *The Portable Nietzsche*. Edited and translated by Walter Kaufmann. New York: Penguin, 1976.

———. *Thus Spoken Zarathustra: A Book for Everyone and No One*. Translated by R. J. Hollingdale. London: Penguin, 1969.

Nixon, Charisse. "Learned Helplessness—Dr. Charisse Nixon." YouTube video. Penn State Erie. January 29, 2008. http://www.youtube.com/watch?v=p6TONVkJ3eI.

Nordquist, Richard. "Model Place Descriptions: Four Descriptive Paragraphs." About: Grammar and Composition. *New York Times*, n.d. http://grammar.about.com/od/developingparagraphs/a/placedesc.htm.

O'Connor, Anahad. "Woman, 41, is Executed in Virginia." *New York Times*, September 23, 2010. http://www.nytimes.com/2010/09/24/us/24execute.html?_r=3&hp.

Ong, Walter J. "The Author's Audience Is Always Fiction." *PMLA* 90, no. 1 (1975): 9–21.

Orwell, George. "Politics and the English Language." *Horizon* 13, no. 76 (1946): 252–65.

Perelmen, Chaim, and Lucie Olbrechts-Tyteca. *The New Rhetoric: A Treatise on Argumentation*. Translated by John Wilkinson and Purcell Weaver. Notre Dame, IN: University of Notre Dame, 1969.

Plato. *Gorgias*. Translated by Donald J. Zeyl. Indianapolis: Hackett Publishing Company, 1987.

———. *Phaedrus*. Translated by Alexander Nehamas and Paul Woodruff. Indianapolis: Hackett Publishing Company, 1987.

———. *The Republic*. Translated by C. D.C. Reeve. Indianapolis: Hackett Publishing, 2004.

Plous, Scott. *Psychology of Judgment and Decision Making*. New York: McGraw, 1993.

Poole, Garry. *The Complete Book of Questions: 1001 Conversation Starters for Any Occasion*. Minocqua, WI: Willow Creek, 2003.

Quackenbos, George Payn. *Advanced Course of Composition and Rhetoric*. New York: D. Appleton, 1861.

Quintilian. *Institutio Oratoria*. Translated by H. E. Butler. Cambridge, MA: Harvard University Press, 1980.

Ratey, John J. *A User's Guide to the Brain: Perception, Attention, and the Four Theaters of the Brain*. New York: Vintage, 2002.

Reynolds, Garr. *Presentation Zen: Simple Ideas on Presentation Design and Delivery*. Berkeley, CA: New Riders, 2009.

Reynolds, John Frederick, ed. *Rhetorical Memory and Delivery: Classical Concepts for Contemporary Composition and Communication*. New York: Routledge, 2009.

Rosencrantz and Guildenstern Are Dead. Directed by Tom Stoppard. Performances by Gary Oldman, Tim Roth, and Richard Dreyfuss. Cinecom, 1991.

Rugg, D. "Experiments in Wording Questions." *Public Opinion Quarterly* 5 (1941): 91–92.

Schiappa, Edward. "Did Plato Coin *Rhetorike*?" *American Journal of Philology* 111, no. 4 (1990): 457–70.

Schopenhauer, Arthur. *Law and Politics*. London: Penguin, 2004.

———. *The Wisdom of Life* and *Counsel and Maxims*. Translated by Bailey Sunders. Stilwell: Digireads.com, 2008.

"Selective Attention Test." *Invisible Gorilla* video. Directed by Daniel Simmons and Christopher Chabris. March 10, 2010. http://www.theinvisiblegorilla com/ gorilla_experiment.html.

Shawshank Redemption. Directed by Frank Darabont. Performances by Tim Robbins and Morgan Freeman. Columbia Pictures, 1994. Film.

Sheridan, Thomas. *A Course of Lectures on Elocution*. London, 1762.

Siddons, Henry. *Practical Illustrations of Rhetorical Gesture and Action*. London, 1822.

Silverman, Craig. "Interview 2.0: There's No Easy Way to Ace This One." *Globe and Mail*, May 17, 2009. http://www.theglobeandmail.com/life/work/interview-20-theres-no-easy-way-to-ace-this-one/article1140885/print/.

Siu, Ralph Gun Hoy. *The Craft of Power*. New York: Wiley, 1979.

Stevens, Betsy. "What Communication Skills Do Employers Want? Silicon Valley Recruiters Respond." *Journal of Employment Counseling* 42, no. 1 (2005): 2–9.

Stout, Martha. *Sociopath Next Door.* New York: Broadway-Random, 2005.

Strunk, William, Jr., and E. B. White. *Elements of Style.* 3rd ed. New York: Macmillan, 1979.

Sussman, Dalia. "New Poll Shows Support for Repeal of 'Don't Ask, Don't Tell.'" *New York Times,* February 11, 2010. http://thecaucus.blogs.nytimes.com/2010/02/11/new-poll-shows-support-for-repeal-of-dont-ask-dont-tell/.

Swales, John M., and Christine B. Feak. *Academic Writing for Graduate Students: Essential Tasks and Skills: A Course for Nonnative Speakers of English (English for Specific Purposes.* Ann Arbor: University of Michigan Press, 1994.

Tannen, Deborah. *That's Not What I Meant.* New York: Ballantine, 1986.

————. *You Just Don't Understand: Women and Men in Conversation.* New York: Ballantine, 1990.

Territory Ahead website. 2011. http://www.territoryahead.com/.

Thaler, Richard H., and Cass R. Sunstein. *Nudge: Improving Decisions about Health, Wealth, and Happiness.* New Haven, CT: Yale University Press, 2008.

Theophrastus. *The Characters of Theophrastus.* Translated and introduction by Charles E. Bennett and William A. Hammond. New York: Longmans, 1902.

Thucydides. *The Peloponnesian War.* Edited by David Grene. Translated by Thomas Hobbes. Chicago: University of Chicago, 1989.

Tigar, Michael E. *Examining Witnesses.* 2nd ed. Chicago: American Bar, 2003.

Toulmin, Stephen E. *The Uses of Argument.* Updated ed. Cambridge: Cambridge University Press, 2003.

Tzu, Sun. *The Art of War.* Oxford: Oxford University Press, 1967.

"Vacation Solution." *The Big Bang Theory.* Television episode. Directed by Mark Cendrowski. Performances by Johnny Galecki, Jim Parsons, and Kaley Cuoco. CBS, February 9, 2012.

Valdesolo, Piercarlo. "Flattery Will Get You Far." *Scientific America,* January 12, 2010. http://www.scientificamerican.com/article.cfm?id=flattery-will-get-you-far&page=2.

Vickers, Brian. *In Defense of Rhetoric.* Cambridge, U.K.: Oxford University Press, 1989.

Vygotsky, Lev S. *Mind in Society: Development of Higher Psychological Processes.* Cambridge, MA: Harvard University Press, 1978.

Walker, Rob. *Buying In: The Secret Dialogue Between What We Buy and Who We Are.* New York: Random House, 2008.

Weaver, Richard M. *The Ethics of Rhetoric.* Davis, CA: Hermagoras, 1985.

Welch, Kathleen E. *Electric Rhetoric: Classical Rhetoric, Oralism, and a New Literacy.* Cambridge, MA: MIT Press, 1999.

Wellman, Francis. *The Art of Cross-Examination.* New York: Touchstone, 1997.

Wiley, Charles Albert. *Elocution and Oratory: Giving a Thorough Treatise on the Art of Reading and Speaking (1869).* Whitefish, MT: Kessinger Publishing. 2010.

Yates, Frances A. *The Art of Memory.* Chicago: University of Chicago Press, 2001.

Zinsser, William. *On Writing Well.* 30th Anniversary ed. New York: Harper, 2006.

Image Credits

Figure 1: (the white-gloved perfectionist) ©iStockphoto.com/Hulton Archive.

Figure 2: (football coach) ©iStockphoto.com/james_boulette.

Figure 3: (George Carlin) Reprinted by permission of the George Carlin Estate.

Figure 5: (hand chart) © iStockphoto.com/Steve_Vanhorn.

Figure 8: (crayon image) Christian Faur, *Experiment 5*, 2008. www.christianfaur .com. Reprinted by permission.

Figure 10: *Rhetorica*, engraved by Cesare Bassano, from Bibliothecae Alexandrinae icones symbolicae P.D. Christofori Giardae cler. reg. S. Pauli elogijs illustratae (1628).

Figures 11, 13, 14, 15: (two hands; hands; postures; finger) John Bulwer, *Chirologia and Chironomia*. London: Thomas Harper, 1644.

Figure 12: (stained glass) Joseph Kranak, *The Cloisters*, 2008. www.creativecommons .org/licenses/by/2.0/deed.en.

Figure 16: (Due tomorrow?) www.troll.me.

Figure 17: (shark) © iStockphoto.com/Peter_Nile.

Figure 18: (goldfish) © iStockphoto.com/Irina Tischenko.

Index

48 Rules of Power, The, 306, 309

Abilene Paradox, 42
absurd sign, 166
academic argumentation, 228
act to intention or purpose,
    154
ad hominem, 17
*Advanced Course of Composition
    and Rhetoric,* 170
advertising, 273, 279
Aesop's Fables, 137
allegory, 299
"Allegory of the Cave," 69
analogy, 26, 120, 141, 147
anchoring, 42
Antidossis, xxiv
Antonius, 140
aphorism, 160–70
apologia, 61
aporetic moment, 112
Apple, Fiona, 127–28
arête, 58, 322
argument ad baculum, 85
argument ad misericordiam,
    85
argument ad populum, 85
argumentation, xx–xxi, 19-23, 85,
    228, 233, 269, 384–85
argumentative
    errors, 233
    heuristics, 119
arguments
    based on eyewitness testimony,
        28–30
    based on sources (authority),
        30–35
    based on survey data, 37–42

from availability, 41. *See also*
    cognitive biases
    semantic, 186
"Aristocrats, The," 286
Armchair Economist, The, 150
arrangement, 108, 111, 172–82, 222, 224
Art of War, The, 334
assertion, 20–24, 228–37
assimilation bias, 42
assumption, 8, 21, 70, 229, 264
asymmetrical schismogenesis, 89
asystasis, 147–48, 172, 333
attentional blindness, 25
audience, 71–85, 319–20
audience analysis, 71–72
Austen, Gilbert, 206
authority, 13, 30–41, 230–31

Babiak, Paul, 307
background (*narratio*), 180
backgrounds (and images), 198–200
Bambi, 47, 266
bandwagon effect, 42
Barnum, P.T., 169
Barnum statements, 302
BATNA (The Best Alternative to a
    Negotiated Agreement), 270,
    272, 319
beg forgiveness/appeal for
    sympathy, 142. *See also* topics
    of last resort.
begging the question, 14
bias, 14. *See also* cognitive bias.
Big Bang Theory, The, 156–57, 287
bios, 61–67
blind eye, 14
body language, 207–8, 240, 247
Britannica, 37

Buffet, Warren, xxv
Bulwer, John, 206,
Burke, Kenneth, 157

Cafferty File, 107
Cafferty, Jack, 78
Callicles, 113–17, 119
canons of rhetoric, chapter 3
    arrangement, 108, 111, 172–82,
        222, 224
    delivery, 108–11, 203–10
    invention, 108, 110, 111–72
    memory, 197–203
    style, 182–86
Carlin, George, 43, 82
Castiglione, Baldassarre, 306
catapygon, 206
celebrity, 14
Chirologia, 206
Chironomia, 206
chreia, 65
Cicero, 108, 140, 178, 204
claim, 22, 24, 235. See also
    proposition.
clairvoyance, 253, 301–5. See also
    cold reading.
CNN, 78–79,
cognitive bias, 41–48, 233, 265–66,
    274, 324,
coherence, 43. See also illusion of
    coherence.
cold reading, 301–5. See also
    clairvoyance.
collection, 119, 123, 127
common practice, 14
commonplace, 157–63
    commonplace book 215–17, 238
composition, (gambler's fallacy),
    43
conclusion
    peroration, 181
    from evidence, 231
    to a paper, 237
    valid and invalid, 10–11

confidence, 260–61
    overconfidence, 261–62
    underconfidence. See learned
        helplessness.
confirmation (conformatio), 180.
    See also confirmation bias.
confirmation bias, 27, 43, 213
connotation, 186–90. See also
    denotation.
contention, 229
convicium facio, 206
Costco, 270
Coulter, Anne, 3, 24, 228
Courtier, The, 306, 314
Coyle, Daniel, 261
Craft of Power, The, 306
CreativeCommons, 81
critical thinking, 24–28, 41,
    68, 249
cross-examination, 240–48, 300

Dame Rhetoric, See Rhetorica.
data, 22, 230, 236
    survey data, 37–41
Davies, Leonard E., 244
decision-making, 249. See also
    deliberation.
deduction, 231
deductive reasoning, 10, 22
definition, 7, 15, 119, 231
deliberation, 249–52, 325
deliberative rhetoric 249–52.
    See also deliberation.
delivery, 108–11, 203–10
demographics, 71–75
denotation, 186. See also
    connotation.
Desiderius Erasmus of Rotterdam,
    169
devil term, 189–90
dialectic, xxi–xxii, 112–15
    dialectical invention, 123–33
    dialectical topics, 119–20
    elenchic dialectic, 112–13

Gorgias and dialectic, 117–19
Platonic dialectic, 115–16
diction, 186–89
Didot, Firmin, 68
Difficulties of Persuasion, The,
    293–96, 306
dilemma, 15. *See also* false
    dilemma.
distraction, 15
division, 119, 123, 180
double standard, 15
Dutton, Kevin, 46, 307

editing, 193–97
ekphrasis, 215
elenchus, 112–13
Eliot, T.S., 239
elocution, 205
emotional intelligence, 88–89, 333
emotional strategies (of
    persuasion), 92–105
empiria, xviii–xix
encomium, 61, 67, 140
endowment effect, 43
enthymeme, 20–21, 180, 232
episteme, xviii–xix
epitaphios, 61
epithet, 15
epithumia, 123
Ericsson, Anders, 108
errors in reasoning, 13–19
ethos, 50–51, 56–57
eugenese, 136
eulogy, 61
evidence, chapter 4
exaggeration, 15
examination, 242–44. *See also*
    cross-examination.
exordium, 179–80
exposition, xx
exposure effect, 43

fallible sign, 164
false dichotomy, 85–87

false dilemma, 44
Fei, Han, 293–96
figures of speech, 191–93
flatterer, the, 159
Forer, Bertrand R., 302
Forer statements (Barnum
    statements), 302
Foucault, Michel, 307
Four Weddings and a Funeral,
    287
frame-breaking strategies, 156
framing, 149–52
Franklin, Benjamin, 101, 169
fundamental attribution error,
    44, 51

Gallup.com, 40
general topics of the preferable,
    138–40
generalization, 16
gesture, 203, 205–6, 208–10
Gibson, Walker, 2
Globe and Mail, xxv–xxvi
God term, 189–90
Gorgias, xxi, 9, 50, 113–15, 117–21
Gottfried, Gilbert, 286
Green, Robert, 306

Hallinan, Joseph T., 261
halo effect, 44–45, 233
Hamlet, 131
Hare, Robert D., 307
Heath, Chip, 236, 261, 304
Heath, Dan, 236, 261, 304
herding instinct (bandwagon
    effect), 42–43
Herodotus, 291
heuristic, xix, 111, 119, 254–56
hindsight bias, 26, 45, 266
Hippocrates, 169
Hobbes, Thomas, 167
House, 254
Huff, Darrell, 268
humor, 285–91

ignorance, 16
illusion of coherence, 26
image map, 200
images, 198–200, 223, 302
improbable sign, 165
incomplete reasoning, 16
indirection, 179, 299, 300
indirect marketing, forms of,
    280–82
inductive reasoning, 11–13
infallible sign, 163
inference, 10, 120–21, 231
ingratiation, 241–42, 296-299
*Institutes of Oratory (Institutio
    Oratoria)*, 204–5, 296
interior (body) paragraph, 236–37
interrogation, 240
intimidation, 241–42
intonation, 203
introduction (exordium), 179–80,
    235
intuition, 249, 253–56
invention, 108, 110, 111–72
"Invisible Gorilla, The," 25
irony, 299
Irving Younger's 10
    Commandments, 244, 245–47
Isocrates, xxiv
issue, 143–47, *See also* asystasis
    (non-issues).

Jake, 10–11, 83
Jaws, 47, 266
justification, 249, 252–53

Kahneman, Daniel, 267, 294
Klein, Gary, 255
koina, 158
Korax, 147

La Rochefoucauld, 169
Landsburg, Steven E., 150
Lanham, Richard, 192
Law and Politics, 169,

Lawrence "Yogi" Berra, 169
lead, 236
learned helplessness, 100, 262–63
Lehrer, Jonah, 86
Lippmann, Walter, 68–69
loci communes, 158
locus, 157
logic, 8–19
love, 123–26

Machiavellian rhetoric, 306–17
Machiavelli, Niccolò, 306
maxim, 134, 167–71
McHaney, Roger, 3
memory, 197–203
Mercer, Rick, 268
metaphor, 229
misleading information, 16
mnemonic, 198
modal, 22,
modality, 231–32
Moniz, Antonio Egas, 33

nag-withdraw, 89
naïve realism, 45, 274
narratio (background), 180
narrative, 231, 282–90
Nassim, Taleb, 167–68
nature, 17
negotiation, 269
neutral language, 184, 191
New Digital Shoreline, The, 3
Newton, Elizabeth, 304
Nietzsche, 169, 292, 306
Nixon, Charisse, 263
non sequitur, 17
novelty, 17

observation, 230
"Omar Testifies Against Bird,"
    248
On Invention (De Inventione), 178,
    204
On Sophistical Refutations, 135

On the Ideal Orator (De Oratore), 203, 389
opinion, 229
order, 17
origin, 17
Orwell, George, 183, 193, 195, 300
Othello, 158

panegyric, 61
Parker, Dorothy, 169
partitio (division), 180
peroration (conclusion), 181
Perot, Ross, 289
persona, 72–75
personal attack (*ad hominem*), 17
Phaedrus, 2, 100, 126, 174, 201
philosophy, xxii, 113–15
Picasso, 239
placebo affect, 113
plagiarism, 237–340
plain style, 183, 296
Plato, xxi–xxii, 3, 9, 69, 112–14, 115–26, 174, 201–3
Platonic dialectic, 115–32
Plous, Scott, 188–89, 267
"Politics and the English Language," 183, 193, 195
Polus, 113, 119
popularity, 17
post hoc, ergo propter hoc, 163
poverty, 18
Power of Persuasion: How We're Bought and Sold, The, 189
practice, 224
prejudicial sign, 165–66
premise, 10–11, 229
presentations, 221–24
price, 269–70
Prince, The, 306, 308
principle of separate gains and losses, 275
probability, 264–68
probable sign, 165
progymnasmata, 161

proof, 230–33
proposition, 229
proverb, 167–71
pseudoaudience, 75–76
psychopath, 307–9
Public Opinion, 68

Quintilian, 161–62, 204–5, 287, 290, 296

rainbow ruse, 303
Ramus, Peter, 205
Ratey, J. J., 86
reading with the grain/against the grain, 1–8, 122, 319
rebuttal, 22, 231
recency effect, 45
reduction, 45–46
refutation (*refutatio*), 181
Republic, The, 69
research, 32–33, 269
retail, 273–76,
revising, 218–20
rhetor, 221, 318–20
rhetoric
    canons of, chapter 3
    deliberative 249–52. *See also* deliberation.
    Machiavellian, 306–17
Rhetorica (Dame Rhetoric), 199–200
Rhetorica ad Herennium, 198, 204
ridicule, 18
Rosencrantz and Guildenstern are Dead, 131–33
rule of reciprocity, 100

Saint Augustine, 238
Schopenhauer, Arthur, 169, 298
search satisfaction, 46
self-deprecation, 289–90
semantic arguments, 186
Shakespeare, 131, 158

"Shawshank Redemption Red
    Released," 259
signs, 163
Simonidesm, 198
Simpsons, The, 103
simultaneity, 18
simultaneity and causation, 46
Siu, Ralph Gun Hoy, 306, 309
slippery slope, 16, 18
Socrates, 50, 112, 115–17, 174, 178, 201
Socratic method, 112
specificity, 47
Split-Second Persuasion, 46
stage fright, 225–27
stasis theory, 112, 142, 143–44, 172
stereotype, 67–71
stock character, 158
Stoppard, Tom, 131
Stout, Martha, 307
straw dog, xxii, 18, 146, 237
style, 182–86. See also plain style.
sunk cost bias, 47
sunk cost fallacy, 275
superstitious sign, 166
syllogism, 21
synecdoche, 193

Tannen, Deborah, 89, 297
taste/value confusion, 48
tautology, 19
Techne, xviii, xix–xx
TED (Technology, Entertainment,
    and Design), 207
tells of deception, 241
Theophrastus, 159
Theuth, 201–2
Thinking Fast and Slow, 39, 151, 255
Thompson, Jennifer, 30

Thus Spoke Zarathustra, 306
Tigar, Michael, 244–47
Tisias, 147
topics, 134–37
    dialectical, 119–20
    of bios, 62–65
    of interpretation, 141
    of last resort, 141–42
    of praise and blame, 140–41
    of the preferable, 138–40
Toulmin model of argumentation,
    19–24, 230
Toulmin, Stephen, 21
tradition, 19
trope, 192–93
Twain, Mark, 169
twenty questions, 248
Tzu, Sun, 306

Uses of Argument, The, 23

virtual audience, 80–85
vituperation, 67, 140
voice, 203–5
volume, 203
Vygotsky, Lev S., 212, 263

warrant, 22
Wason selection task, 43
wealth, 63
Wikipedia, 37
"Wire: Michael & Marlo, The,"
    316
wishful thinking, 19

Zeno, 199
zone of proximal development,
    212, 263